T0326249

HISTORY AND REVOLUTION

HISTORY AND REVOLUTION

Refuting Revisionism

Edited by

Mike Haynes and Jim Wolfreys

VERSO

London • New York

First published by Verso 2007
© in the collection, Verso 2007
© in the individual contributions, the contributors 2007
All rights reserved

1 3 5 7 9 10 8 6 4 2

Verso
UK: 6 Meard Street, London W1F 0EG
USA: 20 Jay Street, Suite 1010, Brooklyn, NY 11201
www.versobooks.com

Verso is the imprint of New Left Books

ISBN-13: 978-1-84467-151-9 (pbk)
ISBN-13: 978-184467-150-2 (hbk)

British Library Cataloguing in Publication Data
A catalogue record for this book is available from the British Library

Library of Congress Cataloging-in-Publication Data
A catalog record for this book is available from the Library of Congress

Typeset in Bembo by Hewer Text UK Ltd, Edinburgh
Printed in the USA by Courier Stoughton Inc.

Contents

Introduction   Mike Haynes and Jim Wolfreys   1

1. Radicalism and Revisionism in the English Revolution   25
   Geoff Kennedy
2. Twilight Revolution: François Furet and the Manufacturing
   of Consensus   50
   Jim Wolfreys
3. The French Revolution: Revolution of the Rights of Man
   and the Citizen   71
   Florence Gauthier
4. Liberals, Jacobins and Grey Masses in 1917   93
   Mike Haynes
5. 'Our Position is in the Highest Degree Tragic':
   Bolshevik 'Euphoria' in 1920   118
   Lars T. Lih
6. The New Anti-Communism: Rereading the Twentieth Century   138
   Enzo Traverso
7. Communism, Nazism, Colonialism: What Value has the Analogy? 156
   Marc Ferro
8. What Produces Democracy? Revolutionary Crises, Popular
   Politics and Democratic Gains in Twentieth-Century Europe 172
   Geoff Eley
9. Revolutions: Great and Still and Silent   202
   Daniel Bensaïd

Notes   217
Index   257

Introduction

History and Revolution

Mike Haynes and Jim Wolfreys

Revolutions happen. *The Guinness Book of Records* once recorded the interesting fact that Bolivia had had more of them than any other country. But in this instance the almanac, a source of useful information unduly neglected by historians as well as other social scientists, was wrong. True revolutions are shattering events; they help to turn the world upside down, if only for a moment. The many 'revolutions' that Bolivia had recorded were often merely changes at the top with little or no wider impact. Had they been true revolutions society could not have survived there. There is a large literature on what constitutes such revolutions. There are also a large number of cases that might be considered, from the American War of Independence in the eighteenth century, which gave rise to what is today the world's most powerful state, to the Chinese Revolution of 1949 which began to build a new order in the world's most populous state. But our focus here is different. Important though such revolutions were in the history of those states, they do not claim the same attention as greater revolutions whose story and impact has reached out beyond the immediate events and the states in which they occurred to set markers for historical change not only in the West but the world over. And just because these revolutions and the arguments surrounding them are so prominent in our sense of development so they have also raised the biggest debates and become the battlegrounds of ideas about the process of social and political change itself.

The first of these revolutions occurred in Britain in the mid-seventeenth century. Feudalism was giving way to capitalism in many parts of Western Europe but the process was uneven and tensions were widespread. States were ill-formed, monarchs were trying to assert their authority against the old power of the landed class and the Church, and increased trade, manufacturing and urban life were slowly giving rise to new social groups with new demands. Britain, or rather England and Wales with Scotland and Ireland still only partially integrated, saw two decades of turmoil to which contemporaries could not give the name 'revolution' because the word had not yet been invented in its modern sense. Yet the events of these years constitute the first of the great revolutions, at the dawn of the development of what would eventually become a global capitalist system.

In 1640 Charles I was forced to summon Parliament to deal with his tax problems, themselves caused by war, after London merchants had refused to give him more help. A 'court' party of large titled landowners formed against a 'country' party of lesser gentry who widened the debate in order to gain support. This quickly involved a mass of people who had hitherto been on the margins of political life. This process changed alliances and allegiances. It polarized argument and between 1642 and 1643 civil war broke out. In 1649 bridges were finally burned with the execution of Charles I. This led to the Commonwealth or republic between 1649 and 1653 before politics was stabilized in a Protectorate under Oliver Cromwell between 1653 and 1658. After Cromwell's death the process of change eventually led to a restoration of the monarchy under Charles II in 1660.

For contemporaries these events were traumatic. The physical destruction was considerable. These years saw the undermining of old structures and ways of doing things. Yet they were also constructive periods. Revolutions concentrate change, they open new possibilities, some of which – perhaps many of which – will not be taken but which nevertheless become markers for the future. And this happened in England not just because of conflicts at the top of society but because politics became the concern of a much wider proportion of the population than had hitherto been imaginable.

In 1789 an even more spectacular revolution began in France, the contemporary and future resonance of which was much greater than that of the English Revolution before it. In the intervening years the uneven development of capitalism had continued, to be seen less in a growth of output than in social change. And with this change came new waves of tension. Some even see the French Revolution as part of a wider Atlantic revolution stretching from the American colonies in their own revolutionary War of Independence to Switzerland. But the revolution that began in France in 1789 with the storming of the Bastille and which saw the French monarch lose his head in 1793 stood higher than any of them. France at this point was probably the most powerful state in the world. In the West it was the centre of ideas, culture and even fashion. Its language was the language of respectable society. All this intensified the resonance of the French events. But the revolution produced something else that made it stand out as a self-conscious appeal to the world. The Declaration of the Rights of Man embodied part of this wider claim. It was, said Mirabeau, 'applicable to all times, all places and all climes'.

Such claims were extraordinary. They stretched across the known world and beyond it. They stretched into the past and they stretched into the future. They were not sincere. They did not apply to women, they did not apply to slaves and they were meant to apply only with qualifications to the poor of France. But great revolutions unleash the genie from the bottle and, as in seventeenth-century England, in late eighteenth-century France we see the emergence of pressure from below, people becoming more conscious, making claims of their own, widening arguments and going beyond the narrow confines of the language of political rights to look critically at the social and economic basis of power.

It is not surprising then that the powers of Europe tried to crush the revolution in France, not surprising either that they turned on their own radicals to repress them lest the infection spread. By the late 1790s the French Revolution had exhausted much of its power, allowing Napoleon to seize part of the legacy even as he ditched another part. But in the wider sense the French Revolution remained unconfined. Its spectre hovered over the minds of conservatives and radicals alike in the nineteenth century. It was only dethroned as a reference point, and then not completely, by the Russian Revolution of 1917.

Russia in 1917 was Europe's most populous state, its armies played a central role in the war effort of the Entente led by Britain and France against Germany and Austro-Hungary and their allies in the First World War. This revolution made an even greater appeal to present and future, holding out the prospect of going beyond a capitalist system that had failed to resolve so many human problems and which had also brought the world to global war. But Russia itself was a weaker part of that global system; many of the elements of the old order survived so that its revolution looked two ways, as Lenin and Trotsky, its two most prominent leaders, said. In the countryside the mass of peasants wanted to gain land and achieve what French peasants had more than a century before. In the towns the workers looked forward to a new age of which socialists the world over had only dreamed.

Like France after 1789, Russia in 1917 presented a huge challenge, a challenge made greater because the Bolsheviks and the Left Socialist Revolutionaries, who led the Russian Revolution through its most radical phase in 1917–18, believed that it could only survive if it became international. The Western powers again combined to support a bloody civil war, with catastrophic economic, social and ultimately political consequences. When the First World War ended, revolutionary crises emerged in several countries but they did not lead to success and revolutionary Russia remained isolated. This encouraged a process of degeneration that led to the emergence of Stalin's bloody regime, which stood the hopes and aspirations of 1917 on their head.

Why do these revolutions still lay claim on us? The answer is simple. They changed the world and in so doing helped to make our world and to point beyond it. This makes them profoundly uncomfortable events for those who believe that, for better or worse, we live in the best of all possible worlds where there exists only a limited space for some tinkering to bring improvement. Such views are not the monopoly of conservatives. Liberalism emerged out of the English and French Revolutions as a radical doctrine but became less radical over time, and more complacent liberals made their peace with the established order. As they did so they became less inclined to speak positively of the past actions that had helped them up on their way. Sometimes, at particular times, the generalization of conservative self-satisfaction and a fear of radical change became overwhelming. The great historian Trevelyan once said that a historian who wished to understand a period should read, read and read until he hears the voices of the age talking to him. If future historians succeed in understanding the record of the recent past through this process then the dominant voices from the last two decades of the twentieth century will be those symbolized by the claim of Francis Fukuyama that 'history had ended'. There were no longer great alternatives to be fought for, only events to come. And, irony of ironies, instead of historians simply following where others have led, as they so often do, they will also hear the loud voices of historians themselves diminishing the revolutions of the past in order to enhance the negativities of the present. But if history has a way of falsifying the optimistic hopes of generations of revolutionaries so it has no less regularly falsified the hopes of those satisfied with the status quo. At the turn of the twenty-first century the yearning sense that beneath the complacency at the top of society there was something fundamentally wrong with the world, fundamental inequalities to be addressed, tasks still to be achieved, was given new voice by mass protests across the globe. Suddenly 'the lords of humankind' who had once met quietly at sessions of the G7, the International Monetary Fund, the World Bank and the newly formed World Trade Organization found themselves not only exposed to the light but the subject of bitter criticism. And the debates about history that were pronounced over only a few years before now began to be seen in a new light because they not only informed the present but were informed by it, as they have always been.

The essays in this book reflect these concerns, but not with the intention of producing a polemical new history to serve the immediate needs of a new generation. Instead they confront the arguments that have been so dominant in the last two decades, and confront them as historians sensitive to the idea that history is not only not over but that this argument can be made with a confidence missing in recent years.

If in the last decades of the twentieth century new and more conservative trends emerged in historical inquiry several historians writing about the great revolutions captured this new spirit more than others: Conrad Russell and John Morrill writing on the English Revolution; François Furet and Simon Schama writing on the French Revolution; and Orlando Figes and a cluster of others writing on the Russian Revolution. Moreover if these authors echoed themes of a much earlier conservative historiography they came from less traditional backgrounds and dressed their arguments up in the more fashionable garb of the day. The political thrust of this new history was clear. It echoed a philosophical distrust with 'grand narratives' – with ideas of human emancipation. It reflected the failure of projects that claimed to be alternatives to Western capitalism, such as those in the old Soviet bloc or the Third World. And it was tied together with a suspicion of the dangers of mass action and the argument that such action could, and probably would, lead to the worst kind of tyranny and brutality. It was now argued that 'socialism' as the most important radical alternative had failed and history had to be rewritten to accommodate what was effectively the triumph of 'liberal democracy' and the 'market'. The sociologist Anthony Giddens, writing in 1994, said, 'long accustomed to thinking of itself as the avant-garde, socialism has suddenly become archaic, consigned to the past it once despised'.[1] Radical politics was to be reduced to the vacuities of the 'third way'. Others concurred; Donald Sassoon ended his discussion of the history of socialism by arguing that liberal democratic politics 'are the only Left that is left' – socialist goals had now to be explicitly reduced to managing capitalism with no special role attached to class as structure, source of conflict and movement.[2]

There is a paradox in this renewed 'liberal' dominance that a number of commentators have pointed to. As liberalism has declined as an organized political force it has become an almost universal set of ideas through which politics is said to operate and, as a particular view of 'democracy' and the 'market', it is the major means though which capitalism is legitimized today. 'From the New Right conservatives to democratic socialists, it seems we are all liberals now', said Richard Bellamy in 1992.[3] Fukuyama's argument that there is 'a universal human evolution in the direction of free societies' deriving from 'the empirically undeniable correlation between advancing industrialisation and liberal democracy' was but an extreme expression of this view of the necessary and beneficent dominance of the 'liberal order'.[4] In these terms revolution no longer has a future but it must also be given an attenuated past. Revolutions that sought and seek to go beyond the liberal capitalist agenda are clearly disqualified. Other revolutions are of value only insofar as they contributed to the realization of that agenda.

Put bluntly, this view emasculates both the more radical and the darker sides of liberalism in favour of an image of liberalism as the politics of the benign and safe middle, a view captured in Ralf Dahrendorf's comment that, 'the liberal rarely needs to be ashamed of the realities created in his name as the socialist has to be much of the time'.[5] But this view also fails to address the extent to which the effective emasculation of liberalism as a doctrine of emancipation reflected not merely an accommodation to the world but an accommodation to a world whose path of development has systematically undermined the conditions for the realization of the original project. Liberalism as a political force became a more pragmatic politics of power and accommodation. The result has been that liberalism as a set of ideas has been bent and reduced – what threatened to be a lion lives today as a mouse. What passes for 'liberalism' today denies people the capacity to influence large parts of their lives, reducing 'democratic politics' to the narrow vision that Schumpeter gave it. Democracy is an 'institutional arrangement for arriving at political decisions in which individuals acquire the power to decide by means of a competitive struggle for the people's vote'. 'Democracy is the rule of the politicians', or as Alastair Macintyre once put it, 'the role of the ordinary citizen is to provide others with power'. 'In the modern world, the distinctive function of the political system is to arrange compromises amongst a plurality of often competing views, rather than to achieve a rational consensus upon a non-existent common good', writes Bellamy in precisely these terms.[6]

It was not always so. Liberalism had its major roots in the eighteenth-century Enlightenment and before that the English Revolution. But liberalism needed what Thomas Paine first called 'the age of revolutions' to help crystallize key aspects of it as a set of ideas and to help realize many of the political and social demands associated with it. While Enlightenment philosophers gradually elevated the role of reason as part of the politics by which humanity could be emancipated, they had only a limited sense of the practical agency by which society might be changed. They shared a distaste for the mass of the propertyless even if they did not express it quite as crudely as Voltaire in 1768 when he said, 'as regards the people, they will always be stupid and barbarous. They are oxen which require the yoke, a goad, and some hay'. But they equally had a limited confidence at that time in the capacity of the propertied middle classes to whom their writings often appealed. This pushed them towards enlightened monarchy as the agent of change, but enlightened monarchs too failed to live up to their expectations and the idea of a top-down enlightened absolutism creating a transformation in society was badly running out of credibility by the 1780s. It was revolution, first in the North American colonies and then in Europe – centring on France between 1789 and 1794 – that helped break the blockage.

It is not unusual today to separate out the American and French Revolutions in Burkean terms – praising the former for its limited (and by implication more democratic) character and condemning the latter for its unlimited and more 'totalitarian' character. But classical liberalism did not divide itself so neatly and Burke is a peculiar hero for latter-day liberalism. The importance of the French Revolution in this respect was less that it was 'a classic bourgeois revolution', in the sense of a model to be repeated, than the way it unblocked change in the heart of Europe, concentrating and intensifying it and creating a political agenda that is still with us today. The revolution helped to produce classical liberalism but it also helped to produce much more. Revolution is a tangled process, the more so the more intense the revolution is. 'In every great revolution involving large masses of people, there is always more than one projected alternative, more than one insurgent group, more than one revolutionary programme. In the course of the upheaval one or another of them may be dominant for a time', wrote Heinz Lubasz in the 1960s.[7] How the French Revolution as a whole was and is read, and the reading of the place of these alternatives within it, has always been a political act and a socially conditioned one at that. For example, at one level a positive image of the French Revolution encouraged nineteenth-century liberalism, at another level the negative image of terror, civil war, the 'mob' and the Napoleonic resolution discouraged it. Where reform came more easily the story of revolution as 'excess' better fitted the spirit of liberal politics. Where reform was more difficult and where the forces of change were weaker and those of reaction more strongly entrenched, the image of the revolution as a bold leap served the needs of both liberals and radicals better.

But classical liberalism was in its time a revolutionary doctrine, sometimes in spite of liberals themselves. Its universal claims were and are important, but so too is the way that it was constantly compromised by the narrower sectional interests of the groups on which it rested. This creates a tension for modern historians. One solution is to try to go beyond liberalism as a theory and to unpick the weaknesses of its practice both in its own terms and those of a broader critique. But if this is ruled out then commentators must necessarily reduce the theory to the practice and write history accordingly.

The problem here is that liberalism was essentially a negative doctrine that aimed to undermine the restrictive and partial institutions of the old regime. But, as its critics have argued, liberalism could not offer an alternative end, nor could it offer a way of evaluating policies and politics that could command assent even among liberals themselves. This helps to explain the very wide range of day-to-day positions that have been argued to be compatible with liberalism as 'high theory'. Indeed in the first instance liberals could not even agree that liberalism should be based on the universalization of narrower political rights. Liberalism was 'liberal' before it was democratic even in the nominal sense. By the late nineteenth century a disillusioned Pareto, now shifting to the right, could lament that liberalism could not properly come into play in the rest of Europe in the same sense that it had in Britain because the individual and ethical qualities that the bourgeoisie needed were taking second place to crude self-interested individualism and self-interested factions. This led to the corruption of politics as the playground of interest groups and in this context the baton of change was being passed to 'socialism'. Thus he wrote in 1899:

> Not only in Italy, but in all Europe, one observes the strange phenomenon of the socialists, who, in the battle for liberty, take the place deserted by the liberals . . . Let us put theory to one side, in practice . . . the socialists more or less alone put up an effective resistance to the oppression of governments and fight against . . . militarism.[8]

This lack of positive content to liberalism helps us to understand how, once sufficient debris of the old order had been removed, liberalism and liberals succumbed so easily to pressures to accommodate to the existing order. The individualism of liberalism did not preclude radicalism but it gave to that radicalism an air of what Macintyre called 'moral exhibitionism'. Liberals could be swept up and inspired by the power of great events and the role of the people in them. Consider, for example, the inspiration that Berlioz took from Paris in 1830. Ironically, given the way that some historians have reinvented a conservative concern with the mob, it was for Berlioz the 'holy rabble' that engaged him as he walked the streets, 'pistol in hand':

> I shall never forget how Paris looked during those famous days: the frantic bravery of the guttersnipes, the enthusiasms of the men, the wild excitement of the whores, the grim resignation of the Swiss and Royal Guards, the strange pride of the working class in being, as they said, masters of Paris and taking nothing; the young men bragging of fantastic exploits which were based on feats of genuine courage but became so thickly embellished in the

telling as to sound preposterous. It was not enough to have stormed the cavalry barracks in the rue de Babylone with quite heavy losses; they had to announce with a gravity worthy of Alexander's veterans, 'We were at the capture of Babylon.' . . . Parisians! Charlatans – charlatans of genius, if you like, but charlatans! And the music that there was then, the songs, the harsh voices resounding through the streets – nobody who did not hear it can have any idea what it was like![9]

But once the honeymoon period that seems to characterize all great events disappeared liberals lacked a means of navigating between alternatives. In particular, not seeing the extent to which choices were socially constructed rather than a product of individual autonomy, they were often quick to abandon the popular movement and to condemn the real people whose fictional name they invoked to justify their policies.

Classical liberalism entered a period of crisis from the middle of the nineteenth century as many of the conditions which gave rise to it disappeared and as challenges emerged from the left and the right. This caused liberalism to fracture both politically and doctrinally, but what really did for what remained of the classical liberal tradition was the impact of the First World War and the Russian Revolution. However, it would be the degeneration of the Russian Revolution into Stalinist dictatorship that would help re-open a wider space for an attenuated form of liberalism.

1917 consolidated a new political polarization that left liberalism hanging in most advanced societies. The dilemma that Bentley detects in British liberalism was apparent much more widely: 'A new framework imposed itself at once in the nature of political language . . . one that would prove deeply unfavorable to the promulgation of a Liberal message that did not sound like a diluted version of Conservatism or a dangerous dalliance with Communism.'[10] For a brief period Bolshevism as an expression of revolutionary socialism saw itself as an international project for a socialist revolution that would help to realize and go beyond the dream of human emancipation that liberalism had failed to deliver. Why this was not how it developed is widely discussed elsewhere, including by some of the authors in this book; what is important for us here is that the degeneration of the revolution from its high ideals led to the identification of a global challenge to capitalism with the fortunes of Russia as a modernizing great power with a state-controlled economy and a blatantly undemocratic (however defined) political system. This degeneration pulled much of the international left with it. Those who held to a different conception (Trotsky was the most notable) were marginalized.

The condescension of the present now rests heavily on the shoulders of those who from the 1930s fellow-travelled the Russian road. Initially what attracted many of them was precisely the appearance of ordered progress, and the suppression of the politics and individuals associated with the libertarian phases of the revolution. The shift in the position of Sidney and Beatrice Webb from opponents of 'Bolshevism' to believers in Stalin's 'New Civilization' is but the best-known example of this. The attraction of 'Russia' as an alternative depended, of course, on more than the myths that Stalin's propagandists cultivated. There was also an element of repulsion created by conditions in the West in the 1930s, not least the economic crisis, the paralysis of the middle ground and the shift to the right and far right. This helped forge not only a communist left that identified uncritically with Stalin's Russia but also a broader left milieu that expressed the same tendencies. The result was that arguments about past and present became inevitably bound up with the twists and turns of ideas and practice in Russia.

After 1945 the space for a more positive view of revolution widened. Fascism had been defeated but Stalin's Russia had survived and incorporated large parts of Eastern Europe as satellites. Beyond Europe new models developed in China and Cuba. Decolonization also seemed to be a revolutionary process as did, at a deeper social level, claims for economic growth as a process of modernization. Historians also began to be attracted to social science models and theory and debates over the nature of change. Thus, writing in 1955, Perez Zagorin could begin his discussion of 'The English Revolution' by openly linking the past history of revolution to the present:

> . . . it is no exaggeration to call revolution the master theme in the history of the present age. A will to social transformation self-conscious, planned and guided by doctrine, has come to dominate human affairs. At work for an interval in the revolution of the seventeenth century in England, and pressing forward without intermission since the revolution at the close of the eighteenth century in France, its scope is now world wide. Illusions it has bred in plenty, and tragic miscarriages mark its course. Yet its potency has but intensified as fresh groups and classes have come forth to infuse it with their interests and ideals. In the socialist and colonial revolutions of our day, the movement of which it is the driving force has turned white hot. It is in a single continuous process, however, that these latter have succeeded the middle class revolutions of the preceding period.[11]

Such lyrical assessments of revolution as 'a single continuous process' had their critics, and especially in the 1960s one thrust of social science theorizing (and also of historical engagement) came from commentators linked to the foreign policy establishment in the US who were concerned to understand revolution in order to prevent it. But even many of these shared the assumptions wrapped up in Zagorin's peroration. Then in the late 1960s the turmoil of US involvement in Vietnam and the radicalization of 1968–72, especially 1968 itself in Paris and Prague, helped to reinforce the claims of revolution and the attack on the idea that 'liberal democracy' had some transcendent claim on the human future.

What none of this did, however, was to undermine the linkage that most continued to make between a possible future and the fate of particular states like Russia, China or other 'models' that were taken up. In an early critique of the 'new left' *from the left*, Peter Sedgwick disparaged the way that so many commentators, despite their evocation of mass action, actually looked 'not down to the grassroots, but upwards' towards states said to embody 'the alternative'. They were not always uncritical of what they found but they believed that inadequacies could be overcome, especially as these societies developed. Isaac Deutscher embodied this perspective in his analysis of Russia – following many of Trotsky's criticisms but arguing that economic development would undo bureaucratization. In his case the view 'upwards' proved so compelling that he even criticized workers' revolts when they did occur in the Russian bloc in the 1950s. But the equivocations produced by this type of thinking went much wider. C.B. Macpherson, for example, marked out a distinguished career as a perceptive critic of liberal democracy, but in his most widely read work, instead of using his critique of liberal democracy to generate a more general critique of the world and in this sense returning to the critical spirit of Marx, he argued that democracy could take and was taking different forms and if these were more imperfect than those in the West they would prove less so over time. There were he suggested, 'three worlds of democracy' – one was the contradictory liberal democracy of the West, one was in the Soviet bloc and the other in the Third World. These latter worlds were beginning to demonstrate their economic viability, were catching up and would possibly overtake the then advanced world. Today the argument is embarrassing:

> The Soviet Union is no longer considered unviable; its achievements during the war and its subsequent technological advances have made this clear. Most of Eastern Europe has been brought into the Soviet orbit, and is no longer regarded as likely to move into the liberal-democratic pattern. China has moved entirely outside the Western orbit. And on top of this, most of the underdeveloped areas of Africa and South and East Asia have achieved independence in circumstances which led them to become one party states. With few exceptions they have not moved into the Soviet camp . . . but they have pretty decisively rejected both the ethos and the actual institutions of our individualist liberal . . . democracy. And all these countries consider

themselves to be democratic . . . Liberal democracies can no longer expect
to run the world, nor can they expect that the world will run to them.[12]

It is true that, especially after 1968, the basis for criticisms of these societies
widened on the left and anxiety grew about their deficiencies even in the
formerly loyal Communist parties but few wanted to cast them aside
completely. Perhaps no area of historical writing expressed these contradictions more sharply than discussion of the Russian Revolution. A new
generation of largely Anglo-American scholars developed the 'social history'
of the revolution seeking to show that October 1917 had been a genuine
mass revolution and to trace the engagement of ordinary workers, soldiers
and peasants in the process. One might have thought that this would pose
even more sharply the issue of what came later; if 1917 had been a genuine
revolution was there a process of degeneration and how far did it go? But
most historians engaged in the discussion of the revolution drew back from
discussing this. Sometimes this appeared to happen by default, many
historians saw themselves as historians of 1917 and its *antecedents*, but this
choice can hardly have been coincidental. Others who did look forward dealt
with the problem by partial criticism of Stalinism. One of the most widely
read was Stephen Cohen who insisted that Stalinism was based on 'discontinuity', but then also implied that some kind of socialism still existed in
Russia so that the discontinuity appeared rather less radical than he claimed.
It was not difficult therefore for a growing chorus of conservative historians
and thinkers, encouraged sometimes by their own disillusioned flight from
the left, to charge this historiography with hypocrisy and naivety, of lending
support to 'the totalitarian nightmare', even if they were unable to refute the
detail of the argument about 1917 itself.

It is easy to see how this type of approach set up much of the left for the
fall. With the coming of Gorbachev and another ostensible reform 'upwards'
many fell for what looks with hindsight like a sucker punch. Now they
believed Gorbachev would deliver the process of a humane socialism only for
this programme to fail too. As the Soviet bloc faltered and as Third World
models failed the types of argument that we have identified invited the
Fukuyama response just as they invited the disparagement of the whole
process of radical change. Liberal democracies could expect to run the world
and by the 1990s they appeared to be the only game in town.

Except, of course, that none of the problems that had created earlier
doubts about the liberal model had disappeared. To the contrary they had
intensified, which accounts for the peculiar 'liberalism' of modern day liberal
democracy. Writing in the 1960s Alastair Macintyre said: 'What is interesting
is that no other single theme has so engaged western political theory as the

attempt to show that this [liberal] ideal is never realised, that people cannot rule themselves, that ruling in politics and management in industry are necessarily the specialised function of minority elites, and that inequality is a political and social necessity.'[13] The next decades would amply confirm this judgment. Therefore when the Berlin wall came crashing down in 1989, and with it the identification of the Russian bloc with any potential and variable future, there was a peculiar hollowness to the moment of 'liberal' triumph. Here was no optimistic vision of the future but simply an endorsement of the present. It was perhaps this hollowness that accounted for the fact that in the writing of history the balance was increasingly being tipped towards explaining both the dangers of revolution itself and those of political engagement.

REVOLUTION REDUCED

Bliss may well have been a sensation beyond the emotional range of François Furet, champion of sober moderation, but to have been nearing retirement age in 1989 must have been very satisfying for him. Since the 1960s he had fought a determined, often acrimonious struggle against the idea of revolution.[14] Having left the French Communist Party and embarked on a critique of his former comrades' interpretation of the French Revolution he had taken a long view, choosing his targets and his weapons carefully. Two decades later, he, along with a number of very able English and American collaborators, was widely credited with the demolition of what had hitherto been the prevailing academic orthodoxy over the nature and origins of the Revolution. Readings of the event as a cataclysmic social upheaval or a watershed in economic terms were replaced by a narrowly political interpretation of 1789 as marking the birth of modern democracy. Furet was a man for his times. In late 1980s France his Revolution without revolution went hand in glove with President Mitterrand's socialism without socialism and Prime Minister Michel Rocard's reformism without reform. Indeed, one of the defining moments of the period leading up to the 1989 bicentenary was a remark made by Rocard as a guest on a radio programme hosted by Furet: 'Among the multiple consequences of the great Revolution,' he declared, 'there is one which is important. It's to have convinced many people that Revolution is dangerous and that, if it's possible to get by without it, that's no bad thing.'[15]

In many ways, Furet's proclamation that the French Revolution was over was a necessary prelude to Fukuyama's assertion of the end of history. After his year as 'king of the bicentenary' Furet lost no time in finding other targets to attack; with the period of ideological conflict opened up by the French

Revolution considered closed, revolutionary culture itself could be pronounced all but dead. In *The Passing of an Illusion* Furet raised the stakes still further, announcing that communism's vision of an alternative society had the same anti-bourgeois roots as fascism. Each shared with the popular movement which had thrown the 1789 Revolution off course a desire to subordinate the individual to the collective and produced similar results: extremism and violence. As the icing on the cake, Furet was even able to invoke one of the most derided aspects of Marxist-influenced historiography, the *'sens de l'histoire'* (meaning or direction of history), to support his worldview:

> The famous *'sens de l'histoire'* is inverting itself before our eyes. Communism has ceased to be the future of democracy; democracy has become the future of communism. Because what events in Prague, Berlin, Bucharest, after Warsaw and Budapest, are bringing to us are nothing other than the ideas of 1789, or even those of the American Revolution: the rights of man, popular sovereignty, free elections, the market . . . Day is dawning over twentieth century Europe for the second time. After 1945, 1989.[16]

Revisionism generally shares a view of revolutions as, to paraphrase George Taylor, political acts with social consequences rather than social acts with political consequences. The lasting achievement of revisionist historiography of the French Revolution has been to discredit the idea that the event brought about a change in France's social order. Against the 'determinism' of social explanations of historical change, which focus on class antagonisms, revisionists emphasize the primacy of the political. Their tendency to see revolutions as narrow political events rather than broader social transformations means that extraordinary circumstances – war, famine, counter-revolution – figure little in explanations of why protagonists sometimes act in ways which would otherwise be considered extreme or intolerable. The focus on elite activity and the attempt to establish a causal link between ideas and events leaves little room for the active role played by groups who do not form part of the elite. Popular insurgencies, violence and insurrection are no longer integral to revolutionary change but an unnecessary distraction, or worse, a reactionary brake on modernization and peaceful reform. In the case of the French Revolution, the intervention of the rural and urban poor has been held responsible for throwing the revolution off course. The event is no longer perceived as a bloc and the 'democratic' phase of the revolution between 1792 and 1794 is sometimes seen, by Furet for example, as a parenthesis or diversion, tarnishing the achievements of 1789. According to this reading, events were thrown off course by an 'ideological dynamic' which careered out of control, culminating in Robespierre's voluntaristic attempt to solve everything through politics. The fatal flaw of the revolutionaries of 1789 was to generate unreasonable expectations of what was possible through their appeal to universal values, and to generate a dangerous notion of man's capacity to control events by sheer political will. It is here, in the attempt 'to create a new man', that the French Revolution's link to totalitarianism is located.[17]

The absence of any meaningful social conflict in these histories makes it harder to explain the tensions between the revolutionary government and either the monarchy or France's rural and urban poor. The revolutionary sans-culottes, a 'red herring' as far as Alfred Cobban was concerned, play only a symbolic role, their obsession with betrayal and retribution part of 'the revolutionary staging of political action'. The Terror is therefore explained not in terms of the circumstances of war and counter-revolution, but with reference to the symbolic re-establishment of the power of the people through the punishment of 'villains' and 'plotters'. With popular mobilization understood as theatre, all that remained was to find someone to stage the Revolution. Up stepped Simon Schama, who in the late 1980s took time out from an acclaimed career as an academic historian to embark on a 'chronicle' of the event. If, as Laurence Stone has argued, the abandonment of coherent, scientific explanations of historical change and their replacement with narrative leaves only individuals and their ideological motivations, then this trend finds its highest expression in Schama's prose. In his hands the event becomes a frenzy of gratuitous violence generated by 'the chaotic people'. The Revolution itself becomes inexplicable.

Such negative interpretations of the French Revolution chimed with prevailing hostile attitudes towards the Russian Revolution in the post-1989 order. But who would write a suitably reproving account of that experience? Orlando Figes' *A People's Tragedy* provided an environment in which more traditional, conservative historians than Figes, like Richard Pipes, could prosper. History, as told by Furet, Schama, Figes and company, appears to be no more than a random succession of chance events. But revisionist accounts are by no means free of their own reductionism. In the case of the French Revolution, as Florence Gauthier has argued, the identification of 1789 with the birth of democracy obscures the antagonism between different conceptions of liberalism, one based on the political freedoms associated with the universal rights of the individual and the other associated with economic liberalism, the latter by no means dependent on the former. Indeed, the consolidation of bourgeois rule in France accompanied the suppression of democratic institutions – the constitution of 1795 did away with the democratic institutions established between 1792 and 1794 and violated the Declaration of the Rights of Man by tying the right to vote to wealth rather than the individual.[18] More generally, but in the same vein, Geoff Eley has presented a convincing argument against the assumption either that liberalism is necessarily the automatic political outlook of the bourgeoisie, or that liberalism is necessarily synonymous with democracy. How otherwise to account for the identification of nineteenth-century liberals with forms of suffrage based on property rights, or the bourgeoisie's frequent opposition to democratic reform? Historians who reduce liberalism to the status of an abstract set of universal rights are unable to discern either its specific development as an autonomous political current, or the very different national patterns which shaped the rhythms of democratic reform. For Eley, the bourgeoisie displays not so much a unitary liberal democratic conscious-ness as an outlook shaped by the 'fragmented, individualistic pursuit of other less political virtues' such as competition, merit, secularism, law and order.[19] If the French Revolution still emerges as a bloc it is not, in Bensaïd's evocative image, one that is 'compact and homogenous': 'It is flawed, articulated, crossed by intimate fractures and internal convulsions. A sort of round fruit, which the worm has got into. A bag into which has slipped the rotten apple which will spoil the others. The worm of the particular. The rottenness of private egotism.'[20]

Showered with praise and prizes, Furet was undoubtedly the centre of attention in 1989. But he began to let success go to his head; in 1994, he chose to invite a troublesome and potentially embarrassing uncle to the party. The German philosopher-historian Ernst Nolte had won many admirers in the 1960s for his book, *The Three Faces of Fascism*. He went on to lose many of them two decades later for his part in the Historians' Debate when he portrayed the Nazi camps as a 'logical' response to the Communist gulag. Furet's decision to salute Nolte's work as among the 'most profound' of the post-war period simply confirmed what had been implicit in Furet's own work all along: that despite the *bric-à-brac* of influences and approaches that informed his writing, Furet was not a historian of the French Revolution at all. Instead, in the manner of Nolte, he was a historian of ideas. Like André Glucksmann, leading light of France's *nouveaux philosophes* who took intellectual circles by storm in the late 1970s, Furet's belated discovery of the horrors of the gulag offered him a compelling interpretative framework. The pop-philosopher Bernard-Henri Lévy, who played a supporting role in the *nouvelle philosophie* episode, conveys the gist of this framework very well:

> Philosophy has in fact held power at least twice in the West: in 1793 first, in the Committee of Public Safety, which held the Encyclopaedia in one hand

and the guillotine in the other; then in 1917, in the Marxist brains which, claiming to give birth to the good society, brought death to the world. The dream was not born yesterday, then, but it is established that it always turns into a blood bath.[21]

When the Revolution does appear in Furet's work it does so through the prism of the Soviet Union. The Terror, he wrote in *Interpreting the French Revolution*, would have to be reconsidered in the light of its similarity with the gulag. The ideological motivation behind his work became clearer in *The Passing of an Illusion*, which argued that anti-fascism had allowed communism to mask its crimes. It fell to a follower of Furet's, Stéphane Courtois, to draw further conclusions from this analysis. In the preface to *The Black Book of Communism*, which the late Furet had been due to write himself, Courtois argued that the Holocaust had obscured other twentieth-century crimes, first among them being the gulag. There followed a fairly unseemly row that involved the book's contributors squabbling over the accuracy of Courtois' figure of a hundred million victims of communism. Some of the participants subsequently disowned the project. Perhaps Furet would have done the same, since his acknowledgement of the specificity of the Holocaust had, to his credit, always limited the extent to which he was prepared to engage in relativist arguments about it. But when the cream of France's history profession found themselves in a room with the awkward duo, Nolte and Courtois, listening in stony silence to Nolte rattling on about the 'rational kernel' of Nazi anti-Semitism and the way in which the Nazi vision was 'supported in reality', were some of them left wondering where Furet's revisionism was leading them?[22]

All in all, it did Furet's image no good to associate himself with Nolte, a man who had emerged with little credit from the Historians' Debate, who not only saw Nazism and the Holocaust as responses to Stalinism and the gulag, but who claimed that Holocaust victims bore some responsibility for their fate. Furet's courting of Nolte in 1994 – when fears of a resurgence of neo-Nazi activity across Europe, especially in France, Italy and Germany, were very real – meant that, although careful to distance himself from the most outrageous of Nolte's utterances, Furet began to look like a man out of time.[23]

Confirmation that this was so came the following year when France was brought to a standstill by three weeks of strikes and demonstrations against the Gaullist Juppé government's plans to reform the social security system. For the first time Furet and his collaborators at the *Fondation Saint-Simon*, a think tank devoted to the forging of links between academics, politicians and entrepreneurs based on a mutual identification with neo-liberalism, lost some of their chutzpah. The *Fondation*, in many ways defined by Furet's reinterpretation of the French Revolution and its implicit worldview which saw elites as the bearers of modernity and change, rejected mass mobilization from below as generally reactionary and destructive and aspired to consensus forged by the institutions of representative democracy. December 1995 exposed a polarization at the heart of French society, confirmed the increasing irrelevance of these institutions, and gave voice to a powerful backlash against the technocratic neo-liberalism espoused by Furet *et al.*

The *Fondation* eventually folded in 1999, claiming that its work was complete. But Furet himself, in his last article before he died in 1997, gave the lie to this claim. In a jaded piece of barely contained frustration, published a decade after his announcement that France's exceptional status as a divided country no longer applied, Furet surveyed with dismay the state of a nation which had just elected a Socialist prime minister on the most radical platform of any government since 1981. He saw a country still 'obsessed with its particularity', which identified with public service and social security, and which refused to abide by the laws of a '*fin de siècle* world'. More worrying, though, was the kind of world that had emerged following the 'new dawn' of 1989: 'Contrary to what one might have believed, the collapse of Soviet communism has been accompanied by a shift to the left in West European public opinion. Capitalism is victorious, has become humanity's only horizon. But the more it is triumphant, the more it is hated.'[24] How galling for Furet to find that the 'illusion' of the communist ideal, after the collapse of all the regimes which appropriated its name, was still on its feet. As the German business journal *Wirtschaftswoche* put it in the dying days of the Kohl government:

> Eggs crack on pavements, and fireworks explode. Thousands of miners besiege the government quarter in Bonn in defence of state subsidies for their industry . . . Germany 1997, a new whiff of class struggle . . . No political commentator in recent years has got it as wrong as Francis Fukuyama, who, after the collapse of really existing socialism in Eastern Europe, declared the 'End of History', claiming that capitalism had finally and decisively beaten all 'competing ideologies'. Socialism might have failed economically, but as a political ideal it is turning out to be extremely hard to kill.[25]

Furet may have welcomed the revolutions of 1989 as the crowning glory of his own personal heyday and as the vindication of a wider worldview which he espoused, but subsequent events have made the fall of the Eastern bloc regimes look just as much like the beginning of a new era as the end of an old one. The look of uncomprehending horror on Ceausescu's face as first one, then two, then hundreds and thousands of people found the courage to boo his last public speech, was soon to appear on the faces of other leaders. By the mid-1990s the progress to modernization envisaged by Thatcher, Berlusconi, Juppé and Kohl had been thrown off course by popular mobilizations. By the turn of the century, from the Zapatistas of Chiapas to the anti-capitalist protests of Seattle, Prague, Nice, Genoa and Barcelona, powerful currents of resistance had emerged to challenge the neo-liberal order which had seemed so comfortably consensual a decade or so earlier. With no anti-communism to shield it from criticism, *fin de siècle* Western capitalism began to look exposed. Firstly, the economic dream began to collapse: the Asian tiger economies crashed in 1997, the following year Russia's financial markets went into meltdown, early in the new century the Argentinean economy, crippled by debts, fell apart. In some instances crisis brought people onto the streets. Revolution hit Indonesia. In December 2001, protests in Argentina brought down a government and united the population against the IMF. 'When I saw columns coming from all the neighbourhoods of the city after the president announced the state of siege', remarked one of the protesters, 'I thought, "This is like the fall of the wall. This is the fall of the neo-liberal wall".'[26]

Furet's Revolution was often described as a 'lukewarm' revolution for lukewarm times. During the bicentenary one of his colleagues was even moved to ask whether such lukewarm observers would ever be able to understand such an 'ultra-hot' period of history.[27] In an intellectual climate conditioned by the Cold War, Furet's lack of understanding of popular movements and revolts did not matter much, obscured as it was by the sheer *élan* of his attack on social history. But in the post-1989 world, in which polarization threatens consensus and governments are increasingly forced to listen to the street, the reading of history developed by Furet and his acolytes is now looking inadequate. This book sets out to explore some of these inadequacies, some of the silences and omissions and errors, and, it is hoped, to open up avenues leading to alternative readings.

REFUTING REVISIONISM

What follows is divided into two sections. The opening chapters deal with the English, French and Russian Revolutions and their treatment by revisionist historiography. The second half of the book examines some of the debates and themes arising from attempts to revise downwards the significance of revolution's role in history. The rebuttal of these readings is

based on a reassertion of the importance of revolution in human development and a recasting of the role of the political, rejecting the revisionist
conception of ideology as an autonomous and irreducible sphere imposed
by demagogues on society from without. Politics emerges as a realm of
choices and uncertainties resolved through struggle, neither the mere
product of economic development, nor completely detached from social
conflict. Such an understanding means moving beyond the narrow and
prescriptive conception of bourgeois revolution which sometimes surfaces
in the work of traditional social historians, and which takes on a caricatural
role in revisionist denigrations of social history. This involves grasping the
course of economic and social progress as uneven, with remnants of
previous forms of development co-existing with new forms of social
organization. This in turn, as Geoff Kennedy argues in his examination
of radicalism in the English Revolution, requires seeing the transition from
feudalism to capitalism as something other than a linear, teleological
process. Politics interacts with this broader framework not simply by
postulating some abstract utopian future, but develops in response to a
shifting and unpredictable present. Attempts to conceive of ideology as
nothing more than the rationalization of material grievances is therefore
rejected as akin to the reductionism denounced so loudly and often by the
revisionists themselves. More importantly revisionism is shown to be
unable to explain why millions are moved to act in defence of political
causes, or why specific political currents emerge.

The role played by revolution with regard to economic transition is taken
up by Jim Wolfreys in an assessment of the gap between intentions and
actions in the French Revolution. The tumultuous leaps in consciousness
experienced by those caught up in revolution are viewed not so much as
instances of hubris, of revolutionary arrogance, but as evidence of the
profoundly conservative attachment to existing institutions and values which
characterizes periods of comparative stability. Such leaps, in other words, are
a feature of the jagged course of historical development. Tensions ripple
beneath the apparently calm surface of society before rending it apart.
Revisionism, by contrast, may be seen as a form of quietism, disparaging
the revolutionary quest for equality as a demagogic refusal to respect the
limits imposed by liberal democracy in the pursuit of social stability. These
limits however, as Florence Gauthier demonstrates, could only be imposed
by breaking with the liberalism of reciprocal rights that flourished during the
French Revolution, and which conceived a far more extensive set of political
and social freedoms than those which survived it. In addressing this question
Gauthier focuses on one of several major blind spots in the revisionist case –
the issue of slavery. Its abolition may have been one of the greatest

achievements of the revolutionary period, but it merits not even a passing reference in Simon Schama's *Citizens*. Neither do the protagonists of slave liberation, such as Toussaint l'Ouverture, find places in Furet and Ozouf's hefty *Dictionary of the Revolution*. Yet the abolition of slavery, Gauthier argues, was a cornerstone of the humanist political freedoms wiped out by Thermidorian reaction in 1795. This liberal humanist tradition has since slipped from memory, its legacy misappropriated or distorted by crude Stalinist conceptions of bourgeois revolution that dismiss the rights of man as bourgeois window-dressing, or by naive liberal readings which celebrate the declaration of rights but fail to acknowledge that those without property were denied them.

As a consequence history tends to be reduced to the question of economic power, while politics, as we have seen, is confined to a separate sphere. The point that politics is linked to the broader sweep of social development by choices made in response to changing circumstances is made by Mike Haynes in his chapter on the Russian Revolution. Haynes argues that the important choices are not just those made by the victors, and illustrates this process through an examination of the response of other parties to the Bolshevik revolution. The Bolsheviks' emphatic rejection of historical development as a rigid succession of discrete social orders, their grasp of its combined and uneven unfolding, undercuts the charge of adventurism made against their leap into the revolutionary crisis of 1917. But what of the decisions taken by others? What of the liberals, revived by the crowds who took to the streets in February but fearful of them too? What of the Mensheviks and Social Revolutionaries, who condemned themselves to defending a failing bourgeois revolution against their own supporters before turning their backs on the soviets and the socialist revolution? Historians hostile to Bolshevism rarely ask such questions, largely because the generally accepted narrative of the Revolution portrays Lenin's party as the only active political element around, manipulating and plotting their way to power.

While Haynes questions widespread assumptions about the internal democracy of the Bolshevik party and about their rivals' attitude towards ordinary Russians, Lars Lih's examination of war communism takes issue with one of the key pillars of the revisionist case: the prevailing view of the Bolshevik outlook during this period as one of overweening optimistic voluntarism. His analysis of Trotsky's writings of 1920 evaluates what was really meant by terms like 'the militarization of labour', what role repression played in their efforts to maintain control of the economy, and what the grandiose delusions of the Bolsheviks, as viewed through the prism of mainstream historiography, actually constituted. The dreams that emerge from Lih's analysis revolve less around fantasies of creating new men than sober exhortations to pay attention to detail. If a new world was in the making it was one which would allow Moscow workers to admire a single new apartment block with hot water running through the bathroom taps, a fledgling socialist state in which there was still a place for illicit home-brewing.

According to Lih, the fact that our partial and distorted understanding of Trotsky and war communism has remained largely unchallenged is partly the fault of the Trotskyists themselves and of the picture that those like Isaac Deutscher chose to paint of him. As Enzo Traverso argues however, attempts to understand the history of communism by making distinctions between the respective roles of Trotsky and Stalin or even between other communist figures and, for example, Pol Pot, are lost on the new breed of revisionists. Traverso demonstrates in his critique of anti-communist readings of the twentieth century that the preferred tools of 'anti-totalitarian' writers like Stéphane Courtois are not those of critical analysis and evaluation but the much blunter instruments of ideologically-driven assertion and denuncia-tion. Courtois sets to work on the history of communism with a bludgeon, flattening out the contours of context and contradiction until he is able to hold up something that looks like Nazism. Courtois' casual relativism draws on the more sophisticated work of Furet and also owes a considerable debt to Nolte, whose concerted and flawed efforts to present Nazism and Stalinism as two sides of the same coin relied, as Traverso argues, on obscuring the links which bound Nazi repression and expansionism to the campaigns of colonial conquest and extermination waged by Western liberal powers during the nineteenth century.

Marc Ferro reminds us that these links were an explicit and important part of Hannah Arendt's study of totalitarianism, something that those who employ her analysis most vociferously to bolster their own efforts to assimilate Nazism with communism choose to ignore. And for good reason, since once Nazi anti-Semitism is set free from its roots in the racism of previous eras it becomes much easier to portray Nazi atrocities as a response to the horrors of Stalinist rule, as Nolte does, rather than an intensification of tendencies already present in the process of building imperialist nations. Such a portrayal is made easier by the 'forgetting' of the history of colonial repression and torture on the one hand, and by the tendency to assess the record of the regimes concerned either in relation to the role of their leaders or in purely conceptual terms on the other. A predilection for the history of ideas is a common thread running through revisionist historiography. As Ferro shows, while the use of concepts such as democracy, totalitarianism or colonialism may offer insights into the presumed 'nature' of a particular regime, its relationship to society at large tends to be obscured.

This applies equally to the question of how the rest of society parti-
cipates in supposedly totalitarian regimes as to the relationship between
popular participation and democracy. And it applies, as Geoff Eley argues
here, not just to historians but to political scientists, politicians, media
commentators and all those who have helped make common currency of
the notion that in post-1989 Europe 'democracy' is the product not of the
active engagement of real people whose struggles forge and shape it, but of
market forces. The result is an impoverished understanding not just of the
dynamics of popular participation, but of democracy itself. Eley's examination of the democratic gains made during the course of the twentieth
century turns the revisionist conception of democracy on its head. In
contrast to those who seek to restrict the scope for legitimate political
action within the narrow confines of a rigid institutional framework bound
in by the rule of law, Eley argues that genuine democratic gains tend to
occur only when this framework breaks down. Democracy, in other
words, flourishes not when consumed in moderation but when taken
to excess. It is the achievement of ordinary people prepared to break the
limits imposed on them by their social order.

Until recently such thinking may have appeared radically at odds with
world events. During the 1980s the constraints of liberal democracy had been
imposed with even greater rigidity, summed up in France by what became
known as the '*pensée unique*' and in Britain by the Thatcherite slogan, TINA:
'There is no alternative'. By the end of the following decade the American
social critic Russell Jacoby was reflecting that this outlook now defined the
age, one of 'political exhaustion and retreat' in which 'the idea that history
contains possibilities of freedom and pleasure hardly tapped' had been killed
stone dead.[28] In the pages of *New Left Review* Perry Anderson greeted the
new century with the depressing observation that not since the Reformation
had there been so total an absence of alternative worldviews to the status quo.
Yet barely two years later many hundreds of thousands had demonstrated
internationally around the slogan 'another world is possible'. In 2003 anti-
war protests worldwide were of a size and scale that dwarfed those of the
1960s. What was going on? The old mole of revolution, evoked by Daniel
Bensaïd in this book's final chapter, had been at work again, silently
burrowing away beneath the surface of events.

If, as Bensaïd argues, the crisis-ridden twentieth century has changed
forever the mythical function of revolution as an indeterminate promise of
progress, an engagement is nevertheless underway with revolution as 'the
algebraic formula for social and political change in contemporary societies'.
In different ways, possibilities of untapped freedom and pleasure are beginning, albeit cautiously, to be evoked again. How can power be contested?

How might alternative forms of democracy work? What might society look like after capitalism? In their search for answers activists and intellectuals are returning to familiar figures – Gerrard Winstanley, Thomas Paine, Marx, Lenin, Guevara – and interrogating them.[29] Revolutions happen. This book sheds some light on why and how.

1

Radicalism and Revisionism in the English Revolution

Geoff Kennedy

In the early 1970s, the historian Lawrence Stone emphasized that despite the often ferocious nature of the debates concerning the cause of the English Civil War and Revolution, most of the participants of the debate agreed that the politics of the Civil War were related, in some way, to the ongoing social transformation of early modern English society.[1] Shortly after Stone had uttered those words, a revisionist trend in English historiography emerged that not only confronted the empirical problems that had plagued the traditional social interpretation of the Civil War and Revolution, but also attacked the very methodological basis upon which that interpretation rested. Attacking what they claimed to be the social reductionism, teleology and anachronism of the traditional social interpretation, revisionist historians busied themselves with presenting their own interpretations of the events of that period. The result of this collective effort was a substantial body of work that cast the revolutionary politics and the radical political thought of the period in a considerably more conservative light.

While revisionist historians have made some significant critiques of the traditional social interpretation of the English Revolution, their alternative approaches to radicalism and revolution are problematic. In their attempts to treat politics as an irreducible phenomenon, revisionists have divorced political activity from its larger social context and characterized radical political ideologies merely as *ad hoc* rationalizations for material grievances. However, these revisionist approaches tell us little about how the specific nature of radical politics related to the social context of early modern England. Revisionists either reproduce the problems of reductionism that they seek to redress, or they merely re-examine the historical record and reject the previous conclusions of Marxists and Whigs by simply denying the presence of radicalism *as it is defined by Whigs and Marxists*. Radicalism, in these cases, is not conceptualized in a different way – it is merely denied. Most revisionists, therefore, have not provided us with new insights into radicalism *per se*; they have merely reproduced traditional Marxist and Whig conceptions of radicalism in order to deny their existence. Rather than allowing us to understand the different ways in which historical actors undergo a process of radicalization, we get a static traditionalism in its place.

It is not enough, however, to confront the revisionists by merely reasserting the conventional interpretations of the Revolution and the traditional readings of radical political thought. It is not enough for Marxists to merely redefine and reassert the bourgeois nature of the Revolution and use that as their framework for understanding the radical political ideas that were articulated during the Revolution. New insights into the broader social context of the Revolution – the transition from feudalism to agrarian capitalism – can provide the starting point for a new social interpretation of the Revolution as well as a renewed social history of the radical political ideas of the period. An understanding of the development of agrarian capitalism and the Revolution that eschews the problems of the bourgeois revolution paradigm of the traditional social interpretation can give us a better sense of the significance that class politics played in the Revolution, as well as the class nature of the radical ideas that were produced at the time.

THE DEBATE ON THE ENGLISH REVOLUTION AND THE REVISIONIST CHALLENGE

The purpose of the social interpretation of the English Revolution was to account for a particular political conflict by relating it to longer-term developments in English society. In this sense, the traditional social interpretation was meant to provide a more rigorous *explanation* of the course of historical events than the nineteenth-century political historiography that preceded it.[2] The most notable articulations of the traditional social interpretation were put forward by R.H. Tawney, Christopher Hill and Lawrence Stone.[3] Building on work done in the fields of social and economic history, as well as historical sociology, this traditional social interpretation of the Revolution sought to embed the political conflict of the Civil War in the social transition from feudalism to capitalism. Christopher Hill's Marxist interpretation of the English Revolution was designed to provide an alternative to the 'bourgeois' history of the likes of Gardiner by depicting the Civil War as a class war and the Revolution as an event similar in kind to the French Revolution that followed over a century later. Firmly ensconced in the traditional Marxist framework of the 'bourgeois revolution', Hill argued that, unlike the French case, the English Revolution was led by the progressive sections of the gentry – who represented a 'rural' bourgeoisie – in alliance with the urban bourgeoisie, intent on sweeping away the old feudal order.[4] For Tawney, the outbreak of the Revolution needed to be explained in relationship to what he referred to as the rise of the gentry.[5] The century prior to the Revolution, according to Tawney, was a period of decline for the old, conservative landed aristocracy. In its place a revolutionary, capitalistic gentry emerged which sought to supplant the old feudal nobility by radically transforming the state.

In general then, the Marxist version of the social interpretation viewed the Civil War as the result of a rising bourgeois class – either the gentry, or the progressive gentry in alliance with the bourgeoisie – overthrowing a feudal nobility who, in the midst of a transition to capitalism, responded by fettering the development of the productive forces of capitalist production through the maintenance of monopolies in trade and industry and the passage of unparliamentary taxation on industry.[6] Thus, it was in the material interest of this rural bourgeoisie to rise up and overthrow the feudal nobility. The English Revolution was, according to this interpretation, the first of the great bourgeois revolutions that would eventually transform the European political landscape.[7]

Lawrence Stone, in his 1948 article entitled 'The Anatomy of the Elizabethan Aristocracy', sought to support Tawney's thesis of the rise of the gentry by providing statistical evidence of the decline of the aristocracy due to over-expenditure and conspicuous consumption.[8] However, the stinging criticism that this piece received at the hands of H.R. Trevor-Roper forced Stone to modify his thesis.[9] The debate that ensued hinged on the contention of the alleged 'rise' of the gentry. In opposition to this 'rise of the gentry' thesis, Trevor-Roper argued that the cause of the English Revolution was not a rising gentry opposing a declining aristocracy but, rather, was the result of the *decline* of the 'mere gentry' – the middle sort of men whose main source of wealth stemmed mainly from land. In the face of declining agricultural revenues due to inflationary prices, numbers of the 'mere gentry' who relied largely on agricultural incomes were declining. This 'mere gentry' formed the social basis of support for the country 'party' which sought to decentralize the English state by deposing the established court party of aristocrats who had managed to maintain a monopoly over court-based incomes. The rising class in this period was not the gentry but, rather, the yeomanry.[10]

So what we have so far are two competing conceptions of a social interpretation of the English Civil War and Revolution; one that defined the conflict in terms of a rising capitalist gentry supplanting a declining feudal aristocracy, and the other in terms of a declining gentry supplanting a monopolistic feudal aristocracy. Either way, the class lines of political conflict were clearly drawn. At the core of the traditional social interpretation lay the notion that revolutionary political change was related to revolutionary social transitions. In this sense, there existed a social basis to politics and political conflict in which the latter could only be understood in relationship to the former. Revolutionary politics were seen as a political manifestation or a political response to social developments that were geared toward fostering their progress.

Hand in hand with the debates surrounding the cause of the Civil War, scholarship emerged which debated the character of the political ideas of the era. Revolutionary contexts breed revolutionary ideas, and such progressive political thought was found in the works of the Levellers, Agitators and Diggers on the left of the spectrum and, to a lesser extent, in the works of some of the more moderate figures associated with the parliamentary cause. The Levellers were said to be the political representatives of the petit-bourgeois class of artisans, yeomen and unincorporated merchants. For C.B. Macpherson, the Levellers' belief in 'self-propriety' reflected this petit-bourgeois class position and represented a form of possessive individualism that put them in a similar position as Locke, Hobbes and Harrington.[11] While not as radical as some scholars had previously thought,[12] the Levellers still represented the political expression of new social forces in England at the time, characterized by bourgeois conceptions of right as opposed to feudal conceptions of tradition and continuity. In a sense, they anticipated the modern bourgeois society that England was to become. For others, the Levellers were true democrats who advocated something close to full manhood suffrage – a remarkably radical proposal for the time, which was defeated by the more conservative elements of the Revolution.[13] Despite the differences scholars may have had on the extent of Leveller radicalism, the general consensus was that the Levellers represented a break from a mainstream politics that relied upon conservative arguments of tradition and historical continuity as opposed to abstract principles of right and justice. Eventually becoming allies with the Levellers, the New Model Army was said to be significant for the development of radical politics due to the democratic form of organization that spontaneously emerged within the army alongside the official hierarchical chain of command. Electing Agitators – which meant Agent, or Adjutator – the rank-and-file, with the significant help of a radical core of junior officers, sought to establish an alternative democratic structure within its ranks in order to pursue its goal of democratizing the English state. Thus, the New Model Army Agitators shared with the Levellers a concern for basing the English constitution upon 'principles of justice and common right'.[14]

For Marxists and other socialist historians, the Diggers represent the first communist movement that espoused a proletarian ideology.[15] Advocating an anti-capitalist ideology and a communal form of organization, the Diggers were committed to a radical project of social and economic reform that would see the earth restored to its original condition as a 'common treasury' of communal property, albeit in a progressive and non-traditional way.[16] The Digger movement was seen as either part of a larger movement towards Reformation, such as that which had occurred on the continent in the previous century, or as a part of a tradition of lower-class radicalism that spanned all the way back to the Lollards.[17] For others, it was either Gerrard Winstanley's movement from an unconventional Christian agitator to a rationalist and secular communist, or his eventual adherence to a kind of utopian socialism, that became the significant aspect of Digger radicalism.[18]

In the early 1970s, however, emerging trends in historiography were leading to new criticisms of the social interpretation of the Civil War and Revolution that did not merely lead back to revamped expositions of the older Whig interpretations.[19] This new 'revisionist' trend rejected both the Whig political interpretations that emphasized the parliamentary cause as well as the Marxist-inspired social interpretations of the 1940s, 1950s and 1960s. While this new historical revisionism has its roots in G.R. Elton's criticism of the 'high road to civil war', and Herbert Butterfield's criticism of the Whig interpretation of history, it was Conrad Russell who did the most to initially push forward the debate on the social interpretation.[20] His criticism was twofold. First, he rejected what he considered to be the teleology of the social interpretation, that is, the notion that historians sought to explain the causes of the Civil War with the outcome already in mind. As the Whigs explained the cause of the Civil War in terms of the outcome of parliamentary supremacy, so the proponents of the social interpretation explained the causes in terms of the outcome of the rise of the gentry. In this sense, the Civil War seemed to be inevitable from at least the beginning of the Stuart period.[21]

Secondly, Russell criticized what were becoming recognized as the serious empirical shortcomings of the social interpretation.[22] Building on the problems that had been highlighted by earlier critics, Russell pointed out that neither the gentry nor the bourgeoisie seemed to be acting as a class; in fact, both the gentry and the merchant community were split down the middle by the events of the Civil War. On top of this, Russell pointed out that it was not clear how the rise of the yeomanry would lead to the splitting of the gentry. In the absence of any significant correlations between class position and political affiliation, class analysis was said to be useless in understanding the Civil War. Secondly, Russell pointed to an absence of revolutionary intention. The alleged bourgeois revolutionaries did not seem to intend to create a revolution that would overthrow the feudal vestiges of English society – quite the contrary, in fact. Russell would consistently make the case that the intention of political actors was not revolutionary conflict but, rather, consensus and conciliation. Given all of these facts, the social interpretation increasingly appeared to be built on a shaky empirical foundation.

Given the failures of the traditional social interpretation, revisionists would move away from attempts at explaining the Civil War and Revolution in social terms, and either seek to explain it in purely political terms, or abandon explanation altogether and focus instead on providing a descriptive narrative of events. If neither the social conflict between antagonistic classes nor the constitutional conflict between Crown and Parliament could account for the Civil War, then its causes needed to be found elsewhere. Those revisionists who still believed that the examination of causes was a worthy endeavour began to focus their attention on the incompetence of Charles I and the dissolution caused by the Scottish and Irish Rebellions. Thus, the dynamic of the Revolution was either invested in the actions of individuals, or in the causal effect of exogenous forces such as war. As such, the search for long-term causes of the Civil War and Revolution has been abandoned for shorter-term contingent events that led to the outbreak of war.

REVISIONISM, REVOLUTION AND RADICALISM

Given the revisionist interpretations of the Civil War, it also becomes necessary to re-evaluate the allegedly radical political and social thought that was produced at the time. The old approaches to radicalism are characterized as 'anachronistic' in the sense that they project contemporary meaning on to ideas of the past; and they are guilty of treating ideas as mere reflections of an underlying social reality that is deemed to be more significant than the realm of thought. One form of anachronism is the insistence on the existence of conflicting political ideologies and oppositional forms of politics. Whereas Whigs and Marxists emphasize the existence of conflicts between Crown and Parliament, or between the various social classes that existed in early modern England, revisionists make the case that such conflict was the unintentional result of mismanagement and incompetence by political leaders. Consensus, not conflict, was the nature of early modern English politics and political thought.[23]

Instead, revisionists argue that the period leading up to the Civil War was one of ideological and political 'consensus' between parliamentarians and royalists.[24] Russell has re-examined the Whig assumption that ideological divisions regarding fundamental constitutional issues existed between a 'government' side allied with the Crown and the 'oppositional' politics of Parliament from the outset of the seventeenth century.[25] In his critique of the 'high road to civil war', Russell argues that Parliament was in fact engaged in a politics of conciliation with the Crown due to the fact that it was not nearly as powerful as previous historians had believed.[26] In the absence of any organized opposition in the modern sense of the term, Parliament was dependent upon a politics of persuasion as opposed to a politics of coercion.[27] For example, Russell argues that the Parliament of 1621 was characterized by a desire to restore good relations with the king and an attack on corrupt royal servants and monopolists – not the Crown as an institution.[28] Similarly, in 1626, the failure of the king to obtain tonnage and poundage lay not with resistance by Parliament but by the actions of corrupt privy councillors.

In support of this consensus-based approach to politics, Mark Kishlansky has sought to downplay the significance of radical politics during the Civil War and Revolution.[29] Revolutionary ideologies and adversarial politics are relegated to *ad hoc* rationalizations of personal grievances amongst parliamentarians – both radical and moderate. English politics prior to 1646, argues Kishlansky, was based upon consensus, not conflict. The consensus politics that defined Parliament broke down with the exile of the king; parliamentary government witnessed the transformation of individual grievances into adversarial politics, which were represented by the formation of political parties. The existence of adversarial politics provoked the military intervention that transformed the Civil War into a Revolution. So the whole series of events that culminated in a Revolution is characterized as a series of breakdowns amidst the normal functioning of English politics.

In a similar vein, John Morrill has argued that the area of contention amongst parliamentarians did not concern constitutional issues, but rather, issues of religion.[30] In terms of legal-constitutionalism, Morrill argues that there was, in 1640, no desire to alter, but rather desires to *conserve* the ancient constitution. In Morrill's words, there was 'no will to new model the constitution, to reform it root and branch, let alone to create parliamentary sovereignty'. What drove the legal-constitutionalist critique of royal government was therefore not the ideal of parliamentary sovereignty, but the dislike of royal mismanagement by Charles I, who they considered to be an inept monarch. Reform of the Church proved to be the policy area that upset the consensual nature of parliamentary government and drove a wedge between members of Parliament who were united in their desire to conserve the ancient constitution of King, Lords and Commons.[31]

Parliamentary politics, in this period, were therefore characterized by consensus, not conflict. Political conflict eventually did erupt, not due to a clash of constitutional ideologies, and most certainly not due to a clash of socio-economic interests, but rather due either to religious difference, individual grievance or royal mismanagement. If the dynamic of the political conflict can be found in Parliament at all, it therefore lies in the conflict arising from religious differences, or from competing individuals eager to reap the rewards of patronage.

However, parliamentary politics is not the only area that has undergone a revision. Extra-parliamentary politics have also been reinterpreted in ways that downplay the significance of what used to be considered the radical nature of the politics of particular extra-parliamentary groups such as the Levellers, New Model Army Agitators and the Diggers. Against the conventional view that Leveller ideas penetrated the New Model Army and fostered its political radicalization, Kishlansky has sought to drive a wedge between the New Model Army and the Levellers, arguing that although the two organizations met at Putney, they travelled there on two separate 'paths'. Instead, Kishlansky emphasizes the material grievances of the army. Thus, it was not so much political principle that was the driving force behind the radicalism of the army (if we can even say the army was radical) but, rather, a narrow self-interest concerning the payment of arrears. John Morrill also downplays the radicalism of the New Model Army by calling into question its relationship with the Levellers and its commitment to Leveller ideas.[32] Citing the material divisions between the army's interest in securing its own bread-and-butter issues of arrears and indemnity and the Levellers' desire for a decentralized democratic state (or lack of state, as Morrill claims), Morrill argues that the army's commitment to Leveller principles of popular sovereignty were merely 'ideological jam' for its more basic bread-and-butter interests. Once Parliament began to address the army's concerns, Morrill argues, the rank-and-file fell in line with their leadership. The Putney debates, therefore, represent the ideas of a clique of officers who were fundamentally out of touch with the army rank-and-file, whose real interests were represented in the *Humble Representation* to Parliament on 8 December 1647.

Going even further in downplaying the radicalism of the era are the revisionist historians of political thought. If revisionist historians like Russell, Morrill and Kishlansky can be said to reinterpret radical politics and political ideas as the rationalizations of the material interests being pursued by self-seeking individuals, the revisionist historians of political thought can be said to have turned radicalism on its head – radicalism has become reaction. J.C. Davis has sought to re-evaluate the radical political thought of the period by rejecting approaches to radicalism that seek to assess radical politics in terms of their 'realism'.[33] This 'radicalism as realism' approach – put forth by

Christopher Hill – seeks to relate the nature of radicalism to the concrete possibilities of a given social context. Davis argues that this approach is problematic because it assumes an identifiable linkage between social reality and social thought (in which the latter is explained in terms of the former). The problem with this, argues Davis, is that it 'assumes that there is an entity called reality and that we might describe radicals (as others) in terms of their adherence (or otherwise) to it; in terms of their realism and its spectrum; from realists to cranks; from the practical to the utopian'.[34] Realism, therefore, is too subjective a category to be of use in an evaluation of radical political thought. Davis thus accuses 'realists' such as Hill of reducing radical thought 'to an epiphenomenon of something which is itself an intellectual construction (our perception of reality) – a fact which is not often appreciated by the practitioners of this craft'.[35] But even if we could establish a clear link between social reality and social thought the realism approach, argues Davis, assumes that early modern English society was undergoing a transition. If such a transition is absent, as Davis claims it is, then radicalism is impossible.[36]

In place of this realistic approach Davis presents his own, allegedly objective, textual approach to determining radicalism. What Davis proposes is simple; in order to be considered radical, the work of a political thinker must de-legitimize the existing order, legitimize a new order that will supersede the old, and provide a 'transfer' mechanism by which this new and legitimate social order can be established. Radicalism, therefore, is not a matter of social commentary or the articulation of realistic alternatives to the existing social order. Rather, it is a process of constructing a set of objective, textual criteria by which we may measure the degree of radicalism attained by a particular thinker. In more specific terms, radicalism is a process of de-legitimization, legitimization and transfer. In evaluating the potential radicalism of a thinker's work, 'We should begin by looking at them as radicals in performance of the necessary and minimal functions of radicalism, rather than at their success as social commentators or as paradigmatic thinkers.'[37]

Some revisionists go so far as to reject the term 'radical' altogether. Conal Condren makes a case for the inherent anachronism of the term, arguing that it belongs to a post-French Revolution context of political discourse.[38] The problem is that this discourse has taken its terms for granted and that scholars often take their own linguistic devices as given when attempting to understand the pre-Revolutionary world. A consequence of this neglect is the anachronistic imposition of contemporary meanings on to the past. As products of the post-Revolutionary discursive era, terms such as radicalism have come to attain a number of meanings – extreme, an abrupt departure from the norm, and/or a disposition towards innovation. But Condren has a problem with these meanings because they contain within them what he calls an 'ambiguous notion of pseudo-explanatory status'. If we can 'abstract from such figures a shared radicalism, we have identified an independent force for progress, which in its manifestations can then be designated as the structural process of radicalism'.[39] In other words, radicalism has become a reified concept that is read into the political ideas of the past imbued with its own progressive agency, and attempts to translate what was initially believed to be radicalism into our own terms merely assume that the 'later configuration of abstract nouns, itself part of an extensive reformulation of the political domain, does simply clarify less adequate or formalised locutions, rather than enable us to impose our world on the half-silences of the past'.[40] So Condren is denying even the existence of conceptual equivalents across time, for somewhere down the line, our translation of metaphors into a set of 'dispositional labels' led to the realignment of the meaning of those meta-phors themselves.[41] So our translations are worse than they need be because such a translation inevitably results in a realignment of meaning. In the case of term 'radical' what Condren does is reduce the term to its Latin root *radix* – meaning, ironically enough, root – and compares it to its nineteenth-century dispositional label. Equivalency between the metaphor and the dispositional label is lost; in fact, they seem to mean entirely opposite things.

As a result, radicalism is not as prevalent in seventeenth-century England as was once believed. This does not necessarily mean, however, that there was no space for oppositional politics in early modern English. What it means, rather, is that early modern English politics is characterized in terms of 'alternative claimants of a mantle of authentic tradition and its necessary conservation'.[42] This 'shared culture of common assumptions'[43] has become an increasingly popular weapon in the revisionist arsenal as it also finds its way into the feminist revisionism of the period. For Mulligan and Richards, political discourse is not only solely understood in relation to discursive structures, political discourse is *determined* by these very structures.[44] Existing concepts determine the way in which we understand our experiences. As such, it is impossible for historical actors to escape from the concepts that give meaning to their own society. In other words, political thinkers are 'caged' by their own context.[45] At the base of these conceptual structures are a series of common beliefs or 'shared assumptions' within which agents construct their discourses. The conclusion that is reached – somewhat anti-climacti-cally – is that criticism of existing structures occurs *within* those very conceptual structures, rather than outside of them. This in itself is not controversial; radical thinkers do not critique their own social mores from some Archimedean point external to their society. Rather, they engage in critique from within, and with concepts specific to, that society. However, it is the way in which Mulligan and Richards use this conclusion that is problematic. Radicalism is determined by the ability to 'radically' break from the shared assumptions that form the base of the conceptual structures that in turn provide us with meaning in our own societies. Radicalism therefore becomes a virtual improbability – if not an impossibility.

The result of this revisionist approach to early modern English political theory is that movements and ideas that were once thought radical, due to specific aspects of their oppositional nature, are now deemed to be reactionary. For Davis, what is significant about the work of Gerrard Winstanley and the Diggers, for example, is not their radical social activism and social thought as put forward by Marxist scholars, nor their development of a rationalist critique of English society but, rather, Winstanley's arrival at a kind of totalitarian utopianism.[46] For Mulligan and Richards, it is the existence of a specific set of shared assumptions that undermine the alleged radicalism of Gerrard Winstanley. Although they recognize that Winstanley sought to undermine most of the existing social and political institutions that buttressed the dominance of the landed classes over the poor – private property, the common law, monarchy, the clergy and the Church – he maintained his support for the patriarchal family. This is enough to undercut any radical potential, for the authors argue – without any evidence I may add – that women would be worse off in Winstanley's utopia than they would be in the status quo of early modern England.[47] Seaberg makes the argument that because the Levellers did not reject the common law in itself, they merely rejected the current administration of the law as opposed to the continuity of English politics from the time prior to the Norman Conquest.[48] From this basis, the Levellers could be said to have adhered to an argument of historical continuity – that the Norman Conquest did not represent a break in the English legal tradition. This would put them in a much more conservative camp politically and theoretically.[49]

Ultimately, there is a tension that lies at the heart of historical revisionism. One of the main purposes of the revisionist trend in history and political thought is to avoid the problems of reducing ideas and historical events to offshoots of economic developments. While such a goal may prove to be admirable in principle, some revisionist practitioners have gone too far in conflating narrow economism with broader issues of social context. Thus, Glenn Burgess remarks that the problem with the historical work of the 1950s, 1960s and early 1970s was that it attempted to 'graft onto a basically Whig political history some sort of social dimension' despite an apparent absence of empirical evidence.[50] The problem for revisionists is that they do not believe that any significant or meaningful link exists between society and politics or social reality and political thought.[51] As an alternative to this 'social reductionism', revisionists seek to approach the study of politics and political thought as if the 'political' is an irreducible sphere of activity, that is, that politics can only be understood in isolation from a broader social context.

Initially, however, revisionist historians characterized ideology as an intellectual rationalization for material grievances – a characterization that the most vulgar of Marxists could easily agree with.[52] Conceptions of parliamentary sovereignty are cloaks for the petty self-interest of parliamentarians, Leveller ideology is merely a rationalization of army grievances.[53] As soon as those grievances were met, the ideology was cast aside. Thus, historical actors are concerned primarily with their own material interests and they act in accordance with pursuing and satisfying those interests. At a very trivial level this is true, but it fails to tell us much about the qualitative distinctions between different kinds of interests. In other words, the *social constitution* of those material interests – and the relations of power that constitute those interests – is absent from the revisionist approach because it is believed that attempting to explain something in social terms is tantamount to social reductionism. Revisionists were therefore guilty of economic reductionism, but it was a reductionism that was even more problematic than the kinds of reductionism that they themselves criticized because it did not have an adequate analysis of the interests that ideologies were meant to reflect.

Eventually, revisionist historians found it difficult to maintain the position that ideologies merely served as *ad hoc* rationalizations for material grievances. If ideology is merely a form of intellectual rationalization after the fact, how could it come to assume such a significant force in mobilizing groups of people around a particular cause? In light of these difficulties, some revisionists have turned in the opposite direction to insist that the dynamic force behind the Civil War and Revolution was not material interest but, rather, religious difference.[54] While some revisionists see this as a blow against caricatures of revisionism that over-emphasize its focus on factionalism instead of principle, it could be said that this merely represents a move away from the stated purposes of revisionism – the autonomy of the political sphere.[55] One then wonders what is specifically 'political' about the narratives of a revisionism that now claims that religion cannot be reduced to politics? If politics and religion are treated as fundamentally intertwined phenomena, then how is this revisionist insight any different from early approaches to the study of the period?

REVOLUTION AND SOCIAL TRANSFORMATION

The revisionist 're-evaluation' of radicalism and the rejection of the social interpretation of the Revolution rest upon either a downplaying of the significance of social change in early modern England, or upon the outright rejection of the argument that early modern England was a society undergoing a profound transition. It rests its case upon the empirical failings of various incarnations of the traditional social interpretation of the Revolution. But revisionist historians have been too quick to abandon the principles of the social interpretation of the Civil War and Revolution in light of its empirical problems regarding the identification of specific social classes in early modern England. They have thus been too quick to claim that the transition from feudalism to capitalism had nothing to do with the Revolution or the development of radical politics and radical political thought. The problem with the traditional social interpretation, however, is not the principle of relating political events to underlying social developments but, rather, the way in which historians have conceived of the transition to capitalism, and the way in which they relate political actors to this context of social transition. Proponents of the social interpretation of the Revolution have often depicted the transition to capitalism in terms of the antagonism between a feudal landed class and a capitalist merchant bourgeoisie. In light of the revisionist challenge to the traditional social interpretation, many Marxists have sought to re-articulate the meaning of the concept of 'bourgeois revolution'.[56] But such attempts serve only to illuminate the inadequacy of the term itself. What is needed is a new social interpretation that moves beyond the conceptual fetters of the bourgeois revolution paradigm.

There are three ways in which the transition from feudalism to capitalism is significant for an understanding of the English Revolution and the development of radical politics in early modern England. In terms of the nature and distribution of forms of social power the development of capitalism leads to the development of new social classes as well as new relations of power between existing classes, which forms the basis of new modes of radical political action and radical political thought. Secondly, the development of agrarian capitalism has an impact on the nature of the English state, thereby forming the context for new kinds of struggle around the form and the role of the state. Lastly, in terms of the political dynamic of the Revolution, the rise of capitalism forms the social context within which new political alliances based upon these changes in the class relations of England are formed and drive the revolutionary process. In the case of the Revolution it is the alliance between the extra-parliamentary 'new merchant interlopers' and the parliamentary group of 'improving' aristocratic landlords who form the political dynamic behind the revolutionary process. All three of these developments are intrinsically intertwined. The process of class formation – the changing nature of the aristocracy and the monarchy, the differentiation of the peasantry and the assault on the customary rights of the latter – cannot be separated from the process of state formation. Similarly, the process of state formation forms the context within which we can understand the political dynamics of the Revolution itself, both in terms of the political alliances formed and the nature of the conflict itself.

The rise of capitalism had significant implications for the relations between lords and the peasantry as well as between the aristocracy and the Crown.[57] Agrarian capitalism essentially emerged out of the 'shell' of landed property and the specific nature of feudal lordship in England. English lordship, as opposed to its continental counterparts, was not characterized by the territorial powers of jurisdiction that were characteristic of politically constituted forms of property under feudalism.[58] The Norman Conquest virtually eliminated the pre-existing Saxon nobility and subjugated the whole of the English peasantry as a single, territorial unit. As a result, the Norman aristocracy underwent a peculiar process of class formation – one that would distinguish it from its continental counterparts. English lords never managed to complement their undoubted powers as landowners and lords of tenants with corresponding jurisdictional and political powers. The kind of appropriation of public power that occurred in France during the collapse of the Carolingian Empire did not occur the same way in England. Institutions of public authority survived in England and were transformed and consolidated by the Normans after the Conquest. The Norman invaders excluded individual landlords – the magnates – from developing the kind of extra-economic powers that French nobles had acquired. *Haute Justice* was dealt through royal jurisdiction. Thus, Rodney Hilton points out that, 'instead of this being an appropriation of public power by the private lord, the private lord had been appropriated as an agent by the public power'.[59]

English lords therefore owed the possession of their estates to relations of fealty to the king and his descendants, rather than to possession of the seigneurial ban. English lords, therefore, had arbitrary power only over their immediate dependants – those peasants holding villein tenure on the manor. Thus lordship was domestic, rather than political, which meant that English lords remained subject to the royal jurisdiction of the king, and the power of the king rested upon the co-operation of the nobility. The English aristocracy had, therefore, ceased to rely for their own survival on the exercise of extra-economic forms of surplus extraction, such as the direct use of force over the peasantry. In response to the crisis of lordly incomes, English lords needed to find new ways of increasing their incomes that did not entail the extension of their extra-economic forms of surplus extraction.[60] Since their powers of lordship were limited to dependants upon their own manors, as opposed to the territorial powers available to French *seigneuries*, English lords were unable to 'squeeze' the peasantry through a process of re-enserfment – particularly after the peasant revolt of 1381.[61] The absence of extra-economic forms of surplus extraction compelled the landed classes to assimilate customary tenures to their demesne, thereby transforming it into a form of leasehold that would be subjected to competitive economic rents.[62]

The process by which the customary tenures were transformed into leasehold and thereby subjected to the imperatives of the market in land took the form of the enclosure movement. The significance of the enclosure movement is that it resulted in the differentiation (and subsequent elimination) of the peasantry through a prolonged and systematic elimination of custom and its supersession by the common law.[63] Prior to the enclosure movement, agrarian production had been subjected to a system of community regulation, finding its expression in common use-rights and falling under the rubric of 'custom'.[64] Although common rights of usage were never encoded, where peasant organization remained somewhat strong these rights assumed the force of law. This system of custom, however, existed in direct antagonism with the common law established by William the Bastard after the Norman Conquest of 1066. Whereas custom was based upon communal rights of usage, the common law was based upon the individual rights of freehold tenure. The significant aspect of the enclosure movement is to be found in the fact that 'the normative community regulation of production, and all common rights and obligations, were dissolved even where the customary tenancies remained'.[65] The fundamental impact of the enclosure movement had to do with the elimination of land regulation based on custom; the enclosure movement marked the supremacy of individual rights of tenure, rights that trumped the customary use-rights of the peasantry. The elimination of customary use-rights and their supersession by the development of exclusive and absolute rights of private property signalled a 'wholesale transformation of agrarian practices, in which rights are assigned away from users and in which ancient feudal title is richly compensated in its translation into capitalist property-right'.[66] The conflict over enclosure can therefore best be regarded as a 'struggle between rival models of the human relationship to the land – between a rights-based model that gave the direct producers some measure of immediate access to the agrarian means of production, and a model of absolute property that gave them such access only through the mediation of the capitalist wage form'.[67] Thus, the battle to retain customary use-rights *to* common land as against the encroachment of absolute and exclusive rights *in* land represented an arena of class conflict.[68]

However, the development of capitalism in the English countryside represented more than merely an 'improvement' of the land and an increase in labour productivity. It also represented a new form of coercion. Far from being a new source of opportunity, the emergence of a capitalist market represented, for the bulk of the English people, a new form of dependence.[69] Whereas in feudal times peasants were subjected to the extra-economic forms of surplus extraction wielded by both king and lord, the 'freeing' up of labour under capitalism entailed a substantive separation between the peasant and their non-market access to the means of their own social reproduction. The market becomes a 'major axis of class division between exploiters and exploited, between buyers and sellers of labour power, and a new coercive instrument for capital, the ultimate discipline in its control of labour'.[70] This new form of compulsive dependence, in contrast to the more direct forms of feudal coercion, assumes a seemingly invisible form. Separated from their non-market means of social reproduction, workers must sell their ability to labour or perish. Instead of possessing the power to directly procure their own subsistence goods, they now must secure themselves a wage – i.e., money – in order to purchase these same subsistence goods.

However, while much has been said about the separation of the rural producers from their means of social reproduction and how formal relations of dependence and servitude were replaced by dependence upon the market for labour, it also needs to be said that the landed classes themselves were also dependent upon the market for their own social reproduction. This relation of market dependence has two aspects: first, between capitalist farmers, landlords and wage-labourers, and second, between capitalist farmers and landlords themselves – the ability of the landed classes to reproduce themselves *as they were* relied, indirectly, upon the creation of wage-labour itself. This form of market dependency leaves the capitalist farmer and improving landlord vulnerable – under very specific conditions – to labour withdrawals. This has important implications for our understanding of the social dynamic of capitalist relations of production for it helps us understand how the social power of the emerging capitalist class can be challenged – particularly in a context where these new social relations are still only in ascendancy.

The social dynamic of capitalist relations of production and power lies in the specific way in which capitalists attain and reproduce themselves as individuals and as a class. Here, we need to discuss two things. First, as I have argued above, the social basis of class power under capitalism assumes the form of a purely economic means of appropriating the surplus labour of the direct producers. It is upon this social form of appropriation that the social power of capitalists is attained and reproduced. But at the same time, capitalist farmers exist in a relation of competition with each other over the very inputs that they need to reproduce themselves as individuals and as a class. This competitive dynamic is the result of the specific relationship that exists between capitalist tenant farmers and their landlords. The rent-profit relationship between the two classes creates a competitive pressure towards labour productivity. Given the 'free' nature of labour, the only way to appropriate more surplus is to intensify labour productivity and increase the concentration of estates. As Ellen Wood points out:

> This unique system of market dependence entails specific systemic requirements and compulsions shared by no other mode of production: the imperatives of competition, accumulation, and profit maximisation. And these imperatives, in turn, mean that capitalism can and must constantly expand in ways and degrees unlike any other social form. It can and must constantly accumulate, constantly search out new markets, constantly impose its imperatives on new territories and new spheres of life, on all human beings and the natural environment.[71]

It is this specific form of market dependence that creates the competitive dynamic of capitalist production relations. The need to constantly 'improve'[72] the land resulted in a host of transformations in the English countryside; changes that led to the expropriation of the small peasantry, transformations in the organization of agrarian labour and the enclosing and engrossment of estates.

The development of agrarian capitalism has significant implications for the formation of the English state, which become crucial in understanding the nature of the Civil War and Revolution. Under capitalist social relations, a 'separation' of the economic and political spheres occurs in a manner that transforms the social basis of power of the propertied classes. These new relations of power do not assume the form of privileged juridical status or the capacity to utilize armed force as assumed under feudal social relations. Rather, the ability to appropriate the surplus produce of the labouring classes assumes a purely 'economic' form. This power is predicated upon the ability to separate the rural producer from the direct access to his or her means of subsistence by mediating it through the market. Thus, the social basis of the power of the English landed classes – both landlord and tenant farmers – takes on a specific form that distinguishes it from older feudal forms of social power. Equally important, however, is the changed relationship between the aristocracy and the Crown. In effect, the relationship of feudal dependence between the landed aristocracy and the Crown thus becomes severed. The English aristocracy ceased to rely for its survival on the exercise of extra-economic forms of surplus extraction, such as the direct use of force over the peasantry (as in France),[73] and ceded these powers to an increasingly unified English state in return for the protection of a system of property relations in which landlords relied upon rents accrued from market-dependent commercial tenants. In effect, the reliance on economic forms of income (competitive rents) severed the dependent relationship between the landed classes and the Crown. No longer did the landed classes need to rely on the distribution of political offices and privileges at the hands of the Crown for their source of income. Thus, the English landed classes did not compete with each other for state offices – a 'piece' of the state in terms of politically constituted property.[74] Rather than a state that would give them *access* to private property, what the landed classes needed was a state that *protected* existing private property rights. By the sixteenth century, the aristocracy *as a whole* was not in decline. Rather, those factions of the aristocracy who had engaged in capitalist forms of agriculture in fact benefited, in the long run, from the rise of capitalism.[75] In relation to its European counterparts the English state, therefore, 'represented the most unified and solidified institutional system in Western Europe at this date'.[76]

The severing of this dependent relationship between the landed classes and the Crown also had a significant impact on the ability of the Crown to reproduce itself in traditional ways, for the basis of its social power rested in the creation of a patrimonial following – that is, a group of nobles and courtiers dependent upon the king for political privileges essential for *their* survival.[77] The movement towards landlord dependence on competitive rents rather than politically constituted property (in the form of the coercive extraction of customary and fixed rents) deprived the Crown of its traditional social basis of political power. The changing nature of the relationship between the aristocracy and the Crown would have its impact on conflicts over the nature of the state itself. Thus, the potential for conflict between the landed classes and the Crown over issues of property would assume the political form of constitutional disputes over prerogative and the nature of the 'ancient constitution'. On the one hand, therefore, we have a landed aristocracy that is now dependent upon economically competitive rents, as opposed to access to politically constituted forms of private property, for its economic survival. On the other hand, we have an English monarchy that is head of an increasingly centralized state, characterized by a universal legal jurisdiction and a monopoly on the legitimate use of force yet, at the same time, is losing its access to independent forms of wealth for its economic survival. What exists, therefore, is a relationship of interdependence: the landed aristocracy is dependent upon the powers of the Crown to maintain the sanctity of private property from those who would challenge it; and the Crown is dependent upon the landed aristocracies' consent – through Parliament – to forms of taxation that would enable it to survive.

The transition from feudalism to capitalism also had a significant impact on the bourgeois classes.[78] Basing its wealth on the mere transportation of goods, the merchant elite made its wealth on the basis of buying cheap and selling dear, as opposed to finding cheaper sources of labour to reduce the costs of production. This form of mercantile trade is a typical pre-capitalist form of commercial activity. Like their capitalist successors, pre-capitalist merchants were vulnerable to fluctuations in the supply and demand of their goods; but because their profit was dependent upon buying cheap and selling dear, pre-capitalist merchants attempted to offset their dependence on the market in historically specific ways. The most rational course of action was to restrict access to their trade either by controlling trade routes or levying extensive entry fines on those who wished to partake in their trade. The purpose of merchant exclusion, therefore, was to ensure that an adequate demand for their goods existed. The established merchant oligarchy was politically dependent upon the Crown for the privileges that it enjoyed, in the form of patents and monopolies, in order to retain the exclusiveness of its trade. In return for the granting of these trading privileges, the Crown would have access to customs duties and other forms of import tariffs in order to offset its own fiscal crisis.

In response to this mercantile exclusiveness, upwardly mobile artisans and tradesmen who sought access to the riches that could be earned through trade had to find new ways into the trading business. Excluded from entry into the merchant oligarchies by excessive entry fines, and prevented from entering into established trade routes by the monopoly powers of the merchant companies, the 'merchant-interlopers' sought to ally themselves with the class of capitalist landlords. A convergence of interests between the improving landlords and the merchant-interlopers formed the basis of a political alliance that was to transcend Parliament and locate the dynamic of the Civil War and Revolution within the extra-parliamentary politics of London radicalism which was constituted by broad sections of the 'middle sort of people'.[79]

So what we have is a new social interpretation of the Civil War and Revolution that situates it within the context of the transition from feudalism to capitalism in which agrarian capitalism emerges out of the shell of landed property and feudal lordship as opposed to the rise of an urban or rural bourgeoisie at the expense of a feudal nobility. The rise of capitalism results in a change in the nature of power relations at the level of English society; commercial landlords and capitalist tenants employ impersonal forms of coercion in the form of competitive economic rents over a peasantry that is being polarized between those who succeed in the land market, and those who do not. The latter thus become separated from their non-market access to the means of their own subsistence and social reproduction in a way that compels them to sell their ability to labour in return for a wage. Rather than two easily identifiable classes facing off against each other in intentional forms of class struggle, we see that the transition from feudalism to capitalism splits the existing classes of England down the middle – landed aristocracy becomes divided between improving landlords and 'idle', neo-feudal lords; alongside the established feudal merchant oligarchy emerges an class of interlopers engaging in new forms of capitalist trade; and out of the differentiation of the peasantry emerges a class of capitalist tenant-farmers on the one side and a rural proletariat on the other.

LEVELLERS, AGITATORS AND DIGGERS

All of this provides us with the appropriate context within which to evaluate the radicalism of the English Civil War and Revolution. The changing relationships of power that stem from the development of agrarian capitalism establish the particular dynamic that characterizes the development of English state formation, so it is within this context that we must interpret alleged radicals such as the Levellers, Agitators and Diggers.

The Levellers never put forth a coherent and consistent programme for communal property, and nor should we be surprised by this fact. Representing the class of small producers, both urban and rural, the Levellers opposed practices that would jeopardize the existence of small property. Nonetheless, they were not strictly 'backward-looking' or reactionary in the sense of opposing change in a politically and socially conservative sense. Indeed, the Levellers put forth some significantly radical political ideas that, if implemented, would have seriously challenged the rule of the dominant propertied class. Most specifically, the conception of sovereignty put forward by the Levellers was one of *popular* sovereignty in which the basis of legitimate political authority was vested, not in Parliament, but in the people themselves. The rights of freeborn Englishmen were to be vested in the individual, not in any mediating corporate political bodies such as in France.[80] The way in which the Levellers defined popular sovereignty, however, opened the possibility of social levelling – hence the epithet, Leveller. While many Levellers shrank away from such charges, others were more intent on pursuing the logic of their own argument to its conclusion – a conclusion that would lead to radical political consequences. A fundamental aspect of this form of sovereignty was the way in which some Levellers dealt with the issue of private property, obligation and consent.[81]

At the army debates at Putney Church, in which army Agitators, Levellers and army grandees debated the points put forth in the Levellers' *Agreement of the People*, the nature of the relationship between private property and state power was exposed and debated. In discussing the issue of electoral reform, fundamental questions of property, consent and obligation to authority were raised. Colonel Rainsborough, a representative of the New Model Agitators and ally of the Levellers, made the case that when it comes to consent, even the 'poorest he that is in England has a life to live as the greatest he . . . that every man that is to live under a government ought first by his own consent to put himself under that government'. Sovereignty, therefore, is of the popular variety. But even more significantly, it is to be granted to each man equally, regardless of class position. Rainsborough's position contains another radical element – the right of resistance being granted to the poor. In the same statement, Rainsborough argues that 'the poorest man in England is not at all bound in a strict sense to that government that he has not had a voice to put himself under'.[82] So not only is consent linked to the franchise in the sense of being the essence of consent, consent is also the prerequisite for the obligation to obey authority. The flip side of this is that, since the poorest of England have not consented to the existing government, they have a right to resist it.

Understandably, such a position caused quite a stir both among army grandees and more moderate Levellers. Ireton responded by telling Rainsborough that such a position would need to be justified by recourse to natural right. But political power is a civil, not a natural right. Natural right, or what the English liked to call the birthright of an Englishman, accords only to the freedom to live – peacefully, one would presume – in England. The right to exercise political power, namely the right to choose one's representatives, was a civil right that was predicated upon one having a permanent interest in the kingdom – in other words, property. We can only really understand the significance of this debate if we read it in the context of the rise of agrarian capitalism. Since private property under capitalism is separated from its 'extra-economic embellishments', it is no longer considered to be a politically constituted form of private property. This changes the relationship between property and political power. In England, membership in the political community is not predicated upon noble birth or membership of a guild, or representation by a feudal corporation; rather, it is based upon 'free birth' or 'birthright' of the individual. This expansion of the political community presents problems for a ruling class that seeks to maintain its control over the state. Consent is now bestowed upon legally free individuals, not their legally superior representatives, and implies the right to vote. This argument represents a radical innovation on traditional conceptions of consent in which no logical connection exists between consent and voting.[83] As such, political discussions regarding consent and obligation to authority now assume a different form – a propertied franchise. The Levellers are proposing a significant extension of the existing franchise that would have significant consequences on the distribution of power and property in England. Realizing this, Ireton makes the distinction between tacit and express consent – a distinction that would be articulated more fully by John Locke at the close of the century – which attempts to overcome the radical conclusions of the Leveller position.[84]

Similarly, the ideas and activity of Gerrard Winstanley and the Diggers must be understood within the context of agrarian capitalism and the Revolution. Winstanley has a unique insight into the specific relationship between political and economic power in early modern English society, both at the level of the state and at the level of social class. At the level of social class, he understands that the ability to buy the labour power of another is a form of power in itself. Thus Winstanley conceives of wage labour as a form of bondage: the ability of one social class to compel the other to work for wages therefore 'forces one part of the creation, man, to be a slave to another'.[85] By doing so, landlords and the men of property are able to lift themselves up to be 'rulers and lawmakers over them that lifted them up',[86] effectively becoming the ruling class in society. But Winstanley goes further in presenting a multifaceted notion of class exploitation. Along with the notion that the institution of wage-labour leads to the lifting up of the tyrants over the poor, we have an understanding of the compulsions of capitalist competition at the level of buying and selling. Due to the elimination of the communal regulation of production, the provision of basic needs is now mediated through the market. But this mediation is not equal. Those who have more will now be able to have greater access to goods. Through the inequalities of capitalism, Winstanley notes that the rich have 'outreached the plain-hearted in buying and selling',[87] leading to the further enrichment of the former and the impoverishment of the latter. What is interesting here is that these two notions of oppression have been neglected by most commentators as being forms of oppression. Rather, most contemporaries referred to 'free' labour and the 'freedom' to buy and sell or to dispose of one's property. Without an understanding of the changing social relations of early modern England – particularly the emergence of agrarian capitalism – these facets of class oppression make little or no sense.

But Winstanley adds another dimension to this notion of oppression: the abuse of public authority by which public figures use the civil power to pursue their private interests. This latter aspect of Winstanley's notion of oppression concerns the relationship between public authority and the constitution of private interests in early modern English society; more specifically, the way in which the private ownership of land becomes the basis of public power and, conversely, how that same public power is utilized to serve the interests of the landed classes. In order to understand what this entails we need to analyse Winstanley's contempt for the laws of England. As argued above, the significance of the enclosure movement is to be found in the systematic elimination of communal regulations of agrarian production. The means by which the landed classes eliminated the customary rights of the peasantry was through the common law. But the common law was also a weapon used by the landed classes to prevent the poor from attempting to regain their non-market access to land and resources. Winstanley's contempt for these laws is unambiguous even at the worst of times, for it is through these laws that the landed classes govern as if 'the earth were made peculiarly for them'.[88] Thus far his critique of the common law corresponds with Thompson's assertion that the law was a weapon utilized by the landed classes to pursue their own private interests.

What we have then, in the work of Winstanley, is the beginning of an understanding of the relationship between state power and private property in an early modern England characterized by the emergence of agrarian capitalism. The acquisition of land is a political act that takes the form of theft, 'bloody and subtle thievery', which allows those who acquire land to become justices, rulers and state governors. But he also presents us with an understanding that wage-labour is a relationship of power and that the market itself is a coercive social relationship, for it compels the poor to compete, without communal regulations, against the wealthy and the powerful, leading to the increasing impoverishment of the former. The alternative to this state of affairs, according to Winstanley, is to make the earth a common treasury for all.[89]

In a context of profound social change – one in which the peasantry was being split into landless labourers on the one side and wealthier freeholders on the other – rearticulating customary rights in this way poses a threat to those freeholders trying to reproduce themselves in an increasingly competitive agrarian market. This appeal to custom becomes radical – as opposed to 'backward looking' or 'traditional' – once it is understood that the customary use of the land is in fact an *obstacle* to the further pursuance of the interests of the landed classes, both landlords and freehold tenant farmers. Resistance to enclosure could take many forms, many of them destructive or negative forms of resistance: arson, riot, fence-breaking, destruction of records, mobbing of surveyors. Other forms of resistance such as lobbying, petitioning and letter writing, were less destructive and perhaps less effective.[90] What sets the Diggers apart from other anti-enclosure movements is the fact that they represented an articulate, *positive* response to the assault on customary use-rights to the land; they actively reasserted what they considered to be their time hallowed birthright against the interests of 'improving' landlords.

So although Winstanley's programme is not one of violent expropriation of enclosure estates but, rather, a peaceful programme of labour withdrawal, a threat is still being posed to the landed classes. As Dow has pointed out, since Winstanley has a proper understanding of the social basis of the political power of the ruling landed classes, he also realizes that a programme of collective labour withdrawal would eliminate the social relations of emerging agrarian capitalism – wage-labour.[91] To argue this is not to read Marxian categories into Winstanley's thought, nor is it to claim that somehow he is a precocious Marxist. It merely serves to highlight the social and political consequences of Winstanley's own analysis – that the working poor, 'by their labours they have lifted up tyrants and tyranny; and by denying to labour for hire they shall pull them down again'.[92] Given the relationship between private property and state power outlined by Winstanley, the withdrawing of labour would have disastrous affects on the ability of the landed classes to maintain their position of political dominance. To claim, therefore, that the Diggers accepted the legal validity of existing enclosures solely because they did not lay claim to those that already existed is to engage in a kind of semantic reductionism – one that conceives of enclosures as merely a quantitative change in tenure, and that misunderstands the complexity and class nature of the antagonism between customary use-rights and capitalist forms of private property. And to claim that Winstanley's radicalism is nullified due to his acceptance of the patriarchal family is a claim that needs to be substantiated if we are to take it seriously.

CONCLUSION

Given the empirical problems that plagued the traditional social interpretation, revisionists have approached the Civil War and Revolution in a way that treats politics as an irreducible phenomenon. The purpose of this is to attain a greater historical understanding of radical politics and political ideologies by avoiding the twin perils of anachronism and teleology which, revisionists argue, are the result of the social reductive approaches of both Marxist and Whig historians. The politics and ideology of the period, therefore, is open to revision and reinterpretation. Consensus becomes the substitute for conflict and, as a result, oppositional politics and the radical ideologies that were once believed to be constitutive of them, are now either downplayed or else transformed into their opposite by being characterized as *ad hoc* rationalizations of individual grievances and interests.

The real problem of the revisionist approach to history, however, is the way in which it abstracts political activity and political ideologies from their larger social context. In an attempt to avoid the problems of 'social reductionism', revisionists have neglected to examine the ways in which 'interests' are socially constituted by social relations of power. As a result, interests, and the social relations of power within which they are embedded, are merely treated as given, and we thus have no way of distinguishing between the interests of different historical actors and how those interests form the basis of a collective politics. For revisionists, interests are individualized and, as a result, merely express themselves in the form of patronage and ambition. Politics, therefore, is merely regarded as the ambitious pursuit of self-interest amongst men of power, which often assumes a reactionary or conservative form.

If, however, we are to have a truly historical understanding of events of the past, we need to relate political activity and political ideologies to their social context in a way that avoids the crude reductionisms of past approaches. Historical context requires more than merely situating political actors and political thinkers within the context of 'episodic' political 'crises' that form the background of political debate. Historical contexts – despite some very significant contingencies – are characterized by 'continuity in the form of a residue of the past in the present, of persistent social structures, institutions, arrangements, and patterns of human conduct'.[93] By situating the events and ideas of the Civil War and Revolution within the more recent characterizations of the transition from feudalism to capitalism, we can avoid the problems of the traditional social interpretation and explain the significance that the nature of the transition had on the political conflicts and political ideas of the period. Firstly, we have a better understanding of the ways in which the transition from feudalism to capitalism changes the nature of social power within early modern English society and forms the basis for political action by providing the context for new forms of political activity and alliance. Secondly, we have a more complex picture of how class matters in the early modern period. If the transition from feudalism to capitalism resulted in the polarization of existing classes *as well as* the creation of new ones, then the empirical problems resulting from the class analysis of the traditional social interpretation can be overcome. Most importantly, we can see the events of the period as being related to the process by which historical actors attempt to reproduce themselves as they already exist, within a context that is changing the nature of their interests and the nature of their power. In the process, new forms of political action and new forms of political ideology are developed, not in anticipation of the future but, rather, as a response to an ever-changing present.

2

Twilight Revolution: François Furet and the Manufacturing of Consensus

Jim Wolfreys

There is a moment in Tolstoy's *Anna Karenina* when Vronsky, Anna's lover, looks uncomprehendingly at his watch, unable to take in what time is being shown. Such is his emotional distraction that Vronsky's mind cannot make the link between the shape made by the hands and the images associated with the hour that give it meaning (children coming home from school, tea in the afternoon, etc.). For Eisenstein the task of the revolutionary filmmaker was to link these images to form an understanding of events. For Walter Benjamin, who was to evoke a similar quest for the 'true historical image', writing history was the art of 'giving dates their physiognomy'.[1] Cornelius Castoriadis later noted another kind of dissonance between time and event in his reflections on May 1968. At the very moment when a new mood of defiance was developing, when people were beginning to find new attitudes and values, nobody seemed able to find new political forms to house the burgeoning new content of the May events. Intellectuals chose to emphasize structures, evacuating 'living history' from their outlook in the process, and the movement dissipated into dissertations on desire, or power or Maoism.[2]

One group of intellectuals, whose star rose on the back of the failed hopes of 1968, was to take this rejection of living history one step further. The new philosophers interpreted history by uncoupling revolutionary moments – 1789, 1917 – from the circumstances and actions that constituted them. Cataclysmic upheavals were explained in terms of the ideas that apparently lay behind them. Any meaning that could subsequently be gleaned from history lay in the work of Solzhenitsyn or Foucault: humanity as victim, subjugated for all time by successive forms of domination. Solzhenitsyn, having opened their eyes to atrocities committed in the name of Soviet Russia, to which they had hitherto seemed oblivious, became their Shakespeare, their Dante.[3] What he enabled them to see was the common thread which ran through and linked the Jacobin Terror, the Soviet gulag and the Nazi concentration camps – the ideological justification of crimes carried out in the name of the state.[4] The conclusion? 'He who says total power . . . says total knowledge',[5] or, better still, 'there is no world, only discourse'.[6] To a disoriented left coming to terms with the aftermath of 1968 and the belated realization that 'really existing socialism' was a sham, the new philosophers appeared, as Dominique Lecourt has observed, like characters from a Dostoevsky novel: 'On the brink of the Apocalypse . . . presenting themselves as the sorrowful heirs to human history in its entirety – its tragedies, its deaths by the million, its hopes, but also – and above all – its disillusions'.[7]

Against the tyranny of Hegel's universal history, which set revolution on the path to totalitarianism, they counterposed an ersatz spirit of rebellion shot through with fey catastrophism: 'Socialism or capitalism? The question no longer means very much when the worst is possible.'[8] This theatrical pessimism brought with it a downgrading of the role of intellectuals, their time as 'oracle' was up[9] and Bernard-Henri Lévy was on hand to offer his services as apologist or watch-dog for the status quo: 'We will never again remake the world, but at least we can stay on guard to see that it is not unmade.'[10] For some within their circle, like Maurice Clavel, this meant that Marxism, already on the defensive, had to be finished off for good. 'If these two imbecilities, Marxism as a tool of analysis and as a tool of criticism, are allowed to survive for another two years,' he announced in 1977, 'people will end up thinking: the only way to free ourselves of the gulag is through Marx! And the whole thing will start again! Hellish vicious circles. These circles must be smashed.'[11]

The onslaught against those 'totalizing theories' that saw meaning, let alone structure, in history had far reaching effects. Paris, in Perry Anderson's memorable phrase, became the 'capital of European intellectual reaction'.[12] Various anti-Marxist tracts won a significant audience and a new orthodoxy began to emerge around the values of consensus, 'modernization' and the free market.[13] As far as social criticism was concerned, the erosion, during the 1980s and 1990s, of analyses which sought to grasp society as a totality meant that the concept of exploitation was superseded by the more flexible notion of exclusion. Poverty was henceforth lamented but not necessarily fought, since 'exclusion' denoted a state of affairs that required remedy but did not identify its source or indicate solutions. The corollary of this shift was the perception that those without homes or jobs or status were victims who needed to become the object of humanitarian campaigns if their suffering was to be relieved.[14] Morality therefore began to fill the gap left by the vision of an alternative society that had risen and fallen with the revolutionary movements of the 1960s. World events – from Yugoslavia to Rwanda and Zimbabwe – were increasingly interpreted as struggles between Good and Evil, viewed through an ethical framework which conceived man 'in a negative and victimary way'.[15] This subordination of politics to ethics, which chimed with the displacement of the collective by the private sphere as the repository of meaning and purpose in life,[16] meant that such conflicts came to be understood, as Alain Badiou puts it, from a single perspective: 'the sympathetic and indignant judgement of the spectator of the circumstances'.[17]

THE END OF THE FRENCH REVOLUTION

An important element in the forging of this consensus was the concerted effort to diminish the importance of the most enduring symbol of France's insurrectionary tradition, the French Revolution. The attack on the social history of the Revolution involved much more than the conflict between rival Parisian academic networks which pitted revisionists like François Furet at the École des Hautes Études en Sciences Sociales against left-wing historians like Albert Soboul and Michel Vovelle at the Sorbonne. Although this was an important aspect of the debate, it was staged in the much broader context of the Revolution's historic legacy. Michael Löwy has summarized its principal aspects: its role in establishing the oppressed as actors in their own liberation; the spawning of movements, often written out of official histories, belonging to a tradition of the oppressed (women, Daniel Guérin's 'bras nus', the Enragés); the unfulfilled dream of a new world articulated by figures like Gracchus Babeuf and Théroigne de Méricourt; and the 'utopian surplus' contained in the promise of liberty, equality, fraternity, whose realization would entail the abolition of bourgeois rule. Small wonder, then, that so much time, and blood, had been spent in trying to end the Revolution.[18]

This was the task taken up by François Furet. Although French public opinion would even today class him as one of the leading historians of the Revolution, Furet was never, strictly speaking, a historian of the event itself so much as a historiographer. He did not shed new light on aspects of the Revolution in the manner of Albert Soboul's sans culottes, or Georges Lefebvre's peasantry. Nor did he provide the kind of empirical evidence that buttressed other revisionist accounts, like those of George V. Taylor or Guy Chaussinand-Nogaret.[19] The basic thrust of Furet's interpretation was to downgrade the significance of the revolutionary period opened up in 1789 and to minimize the extent to which it marked a historic break. He tried to replace the view of the Revolution as a sweeping social upheaval that transformed France with a narrowly political interpretation of the event that saw the birth of modern democracy as its sole notable legacy. His attack on social historians was twofold. First, he offered a re-reading of the Revolution that sought to understand the event independently of broader social and economic questions in order that its specifically political significance might be drawn out. His second target was Marxism, or at least the narrow doctrinal determinism popularized via the Communist Party.

Furet's revisions developed in three stages.[20] In 1965, he and Denis Richet produced a critique of the prevailing emphasis on social explanations of the Revolution's origins; 1789 was less a conflict between aristocrats and bourgeois than an accident, the effect of which was to complete a process of liberalization begun under the *ancien régime*. The period of constitutional reform opened up in 1789 was, they argued, thrown off course following the King's flight to Varennes in the summer of 1791. The intervention of the peasantry and *sans culottes*, forces which opposed progress and modernization, saw the Revolution taken over by a new and foreign dynamic, propelled by plot theories and the thirst for revenge. Only after Thermidor was the Revolution put back on track. The reworking of classic conservative and liberal analyses of the Revolution undertaken by Furet revived a long-standing distinction between the years 1789 and 1791, viewed in a positive light, and the 1792–94 period, considered a disaster.[21]

By 1978, when the influence of the new philosophers was reaching its peak, Furet had modified his interpretation and sharpened his attack on social history. Emboldened by the positive reception accorded both to the new philosophers and to Solzhenitsyn, he declared that the idea of revolution could no longer be dispensed from criticism.[22] In the case of 1789, social history had shifted the focus of debate away from the political by taking the myth of the revolutionary break with the past and applying it to the transition from feudalism to capitalism. The Revolution thus became part of the inevitable advance of capitalism. The Marxists had found justification for their linear conception of human progress by taking the revolutionary bourgeoisie's own view of its heroic role at face value. Furet offered a series of objections to the notion of bourgeois revolution. To start with, the content of the revolution must be separated from its modality. Drawing heavily on the work of the conservative historian Augustin Cochin, Furet portrayed the entire Revolution as a deviation or a 'permanent skidding out of control', driven by an autonomous politico–ideological dynamic.[23] It was, Furet claimed, a feature of all revolutions that their triumph over the previous decaying and isolated order led to the recasting of the revolution's history in epic terms. This meant that the old regime's power and its continuing threat were exaggerated. In the case of 1789, the Revolution's providential nature was portrayed in three ways: economically, its liberation of productive forces marked the birth of capitalism; socially, it sealed the victory of the bourgeois over the aristocrat; and politically, bourgeois power represented the victory of Enlightenment ideas over privilege. This myth went under the name of bourgeois revolution. Furet sought to destroy it.

By the end of the 1980s, a less polemical vision of the Revolution was being expressed in works like Furet's *Revolutionary France 1770–1880* and Keith Baker's *The French Revolution and the Creation of Modern Political Culture*, to which Furet contributed. This so-called 'post-revisionist' consensus was based on a methodological assumption that 'thinking' the Revolution required a focus on discourse and political culture rather than social and economic issues. If the Revolution could not be understood in terms of its causes, what kind of event emerged from Furet's reading? It was a phenomenon with its own logic, engendering its own consequences, that was neither the product of otherwise irreconcilable social conflicts, nor conditioned by circumstances: 'there are no revolutionary circumstances, there is a Revolution which feeds off circumstances'. Events did not propel the Revolution forward, or change its course, but were imbued with meaning by revolutionaries, obsessed with conspiracy theories, who had already anticipated these events. The flight to Varennes, therefore, offered the opportunity for a 'national consecration of the aristocratic plot',[24] but presumably could equally have been interpreted as an innocent outing by moonlight, only for the revolutionaries to declare it evidence that the monarchy could not be trusted.

In some ways Furet's desire to make light of the role of circumstances in shaping the Revolution is understandable, since his attack on Marxist-influenced accounts was based on the contention that they negate the unpredictability of events by inserting them into a rigid cause-and-effect chain of historical necessity. But Furet turns circumstances into little more than an alibi. It is Revolutionary ideology that produces the Terror, by overemphasizing 'the meaning of circumstances that it gives rise to itself'.[25] With nobody in control of events, Jacobin ideology becomes the site upon which conflicts are resolved and the means whereby unity is achieved. The Revolution therefore attributes meaning to itself – the smashing of a state that was already broken. The import of their actions hidden from them by the veil of ideology, the revolutionaries cannot see that their achievement is the same as the that of *ancien régime*: the formation of a centralized democratic state. This, for Tocqueville, is where the gap between actions and perceptions lies – in renaming the state the revolutionaries think they have invented it. To the question of how the Revolution can represent continuity but be experienced as a break, Furet thus responds, 'the French Revolution is not a transition, it is a beginning, and the fantasy of a beginning'.[26]

Social historiography perpetuates these myths of the revolutionary bourgeoisie. The heroic role attributed to it skews understanding of the transition from a feudal to a capitalist order, portraying it not as an objective process but as simply the glorious achievement of the bourgeoisie.[27] The events of 1789 and the development of capitalism are therefore inscribed as necessary stages on the path to 1917 and the establishment of a socialist society. Politically, this allowed Lenin to present the Bolshevik revolution as part of a legitimate culture of Western civilization, linked through class struggle to the overthrow of successive social orders.[28] For historians the result was determinism, the role of chance and contingency overshadowed by that of a conscious class subject fulfilling the revolutionary role which history had allotted it. As we have seen, Furet saw the Revolution's political and social effects as part of a much longer process of change. As for its economic consequences, he was dismissive: 'Capitalism takes a long time to start up, if it's the Revolution which initiated it.'[29] There was no difference, he argued, between nineteenth-century society under Louis-Philippe and the France of Louis XIV. If capitalism was brought to France through revolution, he asks, why then was it able to take over major European nations in the nineteenth century without revolution?[30]

This argument is one of the mainstays of the revisionist case. 'How many social historians', asks Bill Edmonds, 'still see the French Revolution (or any other) as a model of bourgeois revolution?'[31] Various indicators of France's comparative backwardness in economic terms have been cited to back up Cobban's argument that 'the substitution of a capitalist-bourgeois order for feudalism is a myth',[32] that this was not a 'capitalist revolution'.[33] These include the persistence of small-scale agricultural and artisanal production, the high proportion of those still working on the land and the unchanging nature of rural life – static, according to some accounts, since the thirteenth century.[34] Many historians have concluded that the Revolution itself was either unable to alter the predominantly feudal nature of French society or acted as a barrier to the emergence of a modern economy as a result of the disruption and isolation caused by the revolutionary upheavals. France between 1789 and 1870 was therefore famously characterized by Cobban as a society of 'stagnation without stability'.[35] The Revolution itself was no longer a cataclysm 'in which one economic order came to an end and a new one dawned', but merely the last great crisis of the feudal order which was nevertheless able to remain in place before eventually fading away 'in a puff of railway smoke, half a century later'.[36]

By the end of the 1990s a leading British historian of the Revolution could declare that 'the dead orthodoxies . . . have at last been left to rest in peace', while acknowledging that no rival interpretation had emerged to fill the space they had left.[37] The post-revisionist picture of the Revolution has three basic characteristics. First, explanations of revolutionary motivations based on 'interests' are replaced by an emphasis on 'passions'.[38] Second, the interpretation of circumstances as arbitrary and the primacy given to ideology entails an exaggeration of the autonomy of the political sphere, which, paradoxically, frequently involves taking the Jacobins' voluntaristic illusions at face value. Finally, revisionist readings of the Revolution invariably minimize the extent to which it marked a break in social and economic terms. What this means, in terms of how the concept of 'bourgeois revolution' is understood, is the subject of the rest of this chapter. Below we examine the role of the bourgeoisie and its relationship to the rest of society, before looking at the Revolution's influence on the transition from feudalism to capitalism. We end with an assessment of the revolutionary dynamic and of the role of revolution in history.

A 'BOURGEOIS REVOLUTION'?

'The bourgeoisie of the theory', according to Cobban, 'are a class of capitalists, industrial entrepreneurs and financiers of big business; those of the French Revolution were landowners, *rentiers* and officials'.[39] Cobban picked an easy target. What is being demolished here is a vulgar stages theory of revolution, a caricature of social history according to which the bourgeoisie consciously made the revolution in order to establish a capitalist mode of production. While Soboul and Lefebvre may have underplayed the extent to which there was collusion between bourgeois and nobles, neither argued that the commercial bourgeoisie had spearheaded the Revolution. Furet's claim that the notion of bourgeois revolution has been empirically discredited, 'notably by the late Alfred Cobban', is therefore wide of the mark.[40] What Cobban shows is that only a small proportion of National Assembly deputies in 1789 could be considered part of the commercial bourgeoisie.[41] A number of studies have subsequently demonstrated that an accurate reflection of the social basis of organized militancy is not to be found in the composition of delegations to the National Assembly, simply because these delegations, for obvious reasons, tended to contain a disproportionate number of lawyers, better versed in the rules of public debate than other professions.[42] One fairly open-eyed assessment of the debate argues that although there may be 'no shred left of the Marxist argument that capitalism was the main force in the remaking of France', the empirical grounds for showing that capitalist elements played only a peripheral role in 1789 are thin.[43]

But widespread acceptance of revisionist claims appears to have obscured the rather fragile basis on which they rest. Even some anti-revisionists have accepted their arguments. George Comninel, in *Rethinking the French Revolution*, an ostensibly Marxist analysis of the debate, contends that 'the long-standing claims to historical validity of the Marxist interpretation of the French Revolution have been exploded'.[44] William Doyle sums up the crude view of Marxism held by many revisionists, labelling it 'a theory of history which assigns a central role to the bourgeoisie as the representatives and beneficiaries of capitalism'.[45] Whatever claims may have been made in the name of 'Marxism's' alleged theory of history, neither Lefebvre nor Soboul themselves portray bourgeois revolution as the achievement of a class-conscious commercial bourgeoisie. While the Revolution, for Lefebvre, 'opened the way for capitalism', he was always at pains to stress that it was not made 'for the sole advantage of the bourgeoisie'.[46] Rather than the 'conscious triumph of a class subject', bourgeois revolution is better understood as providing a legal and political framework within which industrial capitalism may develop.[47] It is a political revolution that facilitates the development of capitalism, but is not a revolution which can be reduced to the question of economic transition.

Moreover, while the conflicts and tensions created by economic modernization open up a space for the pursuit of democratic reform, democracy is neither an obligatory stage on the path to capitalism, nor the inevitable outcome of bourgeois revolution. It is only really in this way that the active involvement of the 'mob' in such upheavals can be explained. As Geoff Eley has argued, 'insurgent people pursue revolution against the very class bourgeois revolution is supposed to promote'.[48] The bourgeoisie needs the peasants and the urban poor in order to win and defend its power. But it must also contain their revolt if the revolution is to be controlled. In other words, as Régis Debray reminded Furet, 'To think the French Revolution is not to reduce what took place to what was thought . . . it is to ponder the hiatus between what is thought and what takes place.'[49] What emerges from bourgeois revolution is the political rule of a minority class and the development of capitalism. Yet, its rule is won by collective action. This is where the gap between the intentions of the actors in revolutionary struggles and the consequences of their struggles can be measured. It is a gap predicated on a contradiction pithily summed up as early as 1793 by two members of the Convention, Elie Lacoste and Jeanbon Saint-André: 'It's absolutely essential to keep the poor alive if you want them to help you win the revolution.'[50]

For those at the bottom of society the Declaration of the Rights of Man was initially little more than symbolic, since equality of rights, in Lefebvre's words, remained 'an illusion to those lacking means to use it'.[51] The supposedly autonomous revolutionary upheavals which took place after the August 1789 Declaration unfolded in part because its proclamation of the end of the feudal order was seen as meaningless if the seigneurial dues imposed on the peasantry's land remained in place and if the changes achieved were not to be defended once the counter-revolution was underway. Furet does acknowledge the 'essential role' of the popular classes in the abolition of orders and feudalism, the replacement of contractual law for divine right, the birth of *homo democraticus* and representation, freedom of work and free enterprise, but fails to explain their motivations. The issue of equality, for example, exists not as a practical question but as a purely ideological one. In this sense, Albert Soboul's identification of hunger as the common experience binding artisans, shopkeepers and workers together during the Revolution,[52] is, quite apart from what it says about the events themselves, simply a far more convincing explanation of what hunger is and what it does, than Furet's view of socio-economic realities as mere pretexts for ideological blueprints. As Gwynne Lewis rightly points out, 'property is a word which unlocks the major mysteries of the revolution', something not lost on Edward Burke, for whom the principal contradiction of the Revolution centred on the incompatibility of universal or 'metaphysical' truths and the very particular, individual property rights of the ruling elite.[53]

If the originality of the French Revolution derives from the bourgeoisie's emphasis on equality of rights,[54] its unfolding is shot through with the tensions and conflicts arising from different perceptions of what this equality might mean. Having attacked the property rights of the aristocracy and the Church, the bourgeoisie was to become aware that it had in the process undermined the sanctity of private property *tout court*. The millions who threw themselves into the Revolution were not therefore simply fighting the bourgeoisie's battle unawares. They did not, as Daniel Guérin puts it, 'take the offensive with the intention of making a "bourgeois" revolution'.[55] They were making their own revolution and their enemy was privilege and oppression, whether clerical, noble or bourgeois in form. Unable to close down the Revolution, the bourgeoisie continued to pursue its goal of transforming feudal into bourgeois property rights, but in the process was driven by popular pressure to demolish the feudal order.[56]

As the power of the parliamentary assembly was challenged by organs of people's democracy, the struggle over different perceptions of how universal rights might be translated into everyday relations opened up a further conflict over the question of popular sovereignty. The popular movement's starting point was not an abstract conception of what form democracy should take. 'The people', as Guérin remarks, 'weren't philosophers'. Their practical engagement in revolutionary struggle led them to take hold of existing, centuries-old democratic forms like the commune and to extend and transform them. In the process, 'the unsophisticated logic of the people made short work of the ruses that were meant to distract them from their path. They made their own deduction, despite all the attempts to forbid it.'[57] Efforts to sideline such questions by portraying the Revolution as an 'intra-class' conflict,[58] or as 'civil war within the ruling class over essential issues of power and surplus extraction'[59] leave us with a shrunken image of the Revolution from which living history is absent. Understanding revolution requires both an understanding of elite concerns and an awareness of, as Claude Langlois puts it, 'a history that begins from far back or below, the history of constraints, the weight of men, the condition of roads, the yield of grain'.[60] That the Revolution involved a struggle between elites does not require that its significance be reduced to this single element.[61] Neither, however, can it be understood merely in terms of the transition from a feudal to a capitalist order.

In the debate over how and when France modernized, reality has often been overlooked in pursuit of a caricature of one sort or another. Exaggerating France's 'backwardness' became a stock-in-trade for anyone seeking to play down the impact of the Revolution; pointing to the feudal nature of nineteenth-century French society implied that the Revolution had changed little. Numerous studies have cited residual attachment to pre-Revolutionary values and attitudes to explain industry's orientation towards the luxury goods first developed under the *ancien régime* rather than mass production, while the obduracy of backward-looking artisans, whose family and craft-based ties formed networks of resistance to change, have been seen as a barrier to the introduction of new technology in industry.

Understanding of French development has been further hampered by the interpretation of the British path to modernization as some kind of norm. In fact, when compared to other European nations, France appears far less 'retarded', and while the Revolution itself may not have transformed the economy overnight, it did create the environment in which change was possible, eventually allowing France to become a major industrial power.[62] Older forms of production, moreover, rather than simply representing a backward-looking obstacle to development before being swept away by the factory system, were themselves subject to internal changes. This process of 'proto-industrialization' entailed the subordination of artisans to capitalist entrepreneurs and an increased division of labour within the workshop.

Assumptions about the survival of 'pre-industrial' household and work-shop forms of production long into the nineteenth century are therefore misplaced. Although the outward form of production remained, significant internal changes had taken place, which represented an important stage in the development of a capitalist economy. The struggles that were played out in craft-based industries cannot be characterized simply as a battle between modern and antiquated forms of production. At their heart was the question of control. New machinery, like variations in piece rates, was one of the means available to merchants of extending control over the production process; the fact that it made the process more efficient was not the only reason for its introduction. The resistance of those who spun cloth or made shirts to factory conditions and new technology was motivated by similar concerns:

> French labourers continued, like the weavers of eighteenth-century guilds, to desire freedom from the need to finely calculate the value in monetary terms of every move of the finger, every break for a little drink and talk, every decision to take an extra moment fixing up a piece of work to look the way it ought to. One did not have to be dedicated to a trade and full of its *esprit de corps* to want such things. One only had to be alive and to be working.[63]

Liu's study of the textile industry in the Choletais region of France shows how small producers were able to deploy a variety of strategies to wrest the advantage from the merchants, working longer hours or limiting consumption in order to undercut merchant prices or simply reducing prices where open access to markets was available. Both weavers and merchants were forced to adapt in response to the other's ruses, making the path of development unpredictable. In the Choletais, the successful defence of collectively negotiated uniform piece rates by weavers in the 1840s challenged the merchants' ability to insure themselves against the vagaries of the cloth market by reducing rates and passing the consequences of price fluctuations on to weavers. The weavers were aided and abetted by small merchants who imported cheap yarn from England rather than investing in their own mills and who were able to offer higher rates, attracting labour away from the more established industrial mills and undermining the mill owners, whose higher fixed costs made them more vulnerable to increases in piece rates.

The mill owners, having failed to prevent further rises in the face of continuing collective protests by the weavers, were faced with the choice of investing in powerlooms or withdrawing from cloth production in the area. Since the move to factory production would involve the proletarianization of weaving and the heightening of social tensions that were already running high – protests in 1849 had seen crowds marching through the streets of Cholet shouting 'The tariff or death!'[64] – local industrialists pulled out of cloth production and limited themselves to spinning and finishing. Proto-industrialization, then, was not a linear process, as the existence of a long-standing handicraft tradition could act not only as a bridge, but also as a barrier to capitalist development.[65] 'If the private costs exceed the private benefits,' argue North and Thomas, 'individuals ordinarily will not be willing to undertake the activity even if it is socially profitable.'[66] Only when cotton shortages provoked by the American Civil War forced prices up and drove thousands of weavers out of work did the balance of forces shift in the region. Small producers who had spearheaded resistance to mechanization in the 1840s were the hardest hit by rising costs, and now found themselves unable to prevent the centralization of production and the introduction of power-looms.[67]

McPhee attempts to place such questions at the heart of his analysis of the peasantry, explaining the slow pace of French agriculture's modernization not by the peasantry's stubborn clinging to little parcels of land, but in terms of the failure to eradicate landed property, denying peasants access to bigger parcels of land.[68] The survival of rented property long after the Revolution – in 1892 it made up 47 per cent of agricultural land – is identified as a major factor in the imposition of inefficient practices on rural France. But the Revolution nevertheless paved the way for the replacement of polyculture by removing the burden of seigneurial tithes on peasant farmers who could then afford to risk greater specialization. Similarly, the creation of a uniform legal framework and currency, a system of weights and measures, and the removal of feudal obstacles to internal free trade facilitated the development of a national market. As Rosenthal reminds us, in the absence of radical upheavals, it is by no means certain that these changes would have inevitably occurred piecemeal over time: 'marshes and irrigation canals were not important enough to create the condition of systemic social change. Hence, reform would be possible only as part of a more general process of change whose causes lay outside of agriculture – a revolution.'[69]

The fact that change took place slowly and unevenly in the century that followed should not obscure the fact that change took place. As in the industrial sector, the key measure of agricultural society was to be found not in the size of farms, but in the nature of production – while some regions remained subsistence-based and autarkic throughout the century, many areas had moved to commodity production by the mid-nineteenth century, with increased specialization taking place. Mechanization was nevertheless limited by farm size, and in many areas improved productivity was due to the replacement of fallow with sown pastures, more intense cultivation or better irrigation, rather than new technology. Yet, although France was divided between more advanced northern and eastern areas and the less developed south and west, it is misleading to pinpoint the transformation of rural France in an 'illusory watershed'[70] between tradition and modernity under the Third Republic. Such a view tends not only to obscure the pockets of development that existed within otherwise slowly developing areas, but also to conflate the slow development of certain regions with rural development nationally. When attention is focused on French agriculture as a whole, rather than the most backward areas, the image of a subsistence-based sector with only parochial horizons fades. The convergence of grain prices by the end of the eighteenth century, the fiscal demands on peasants, which forced them to sell crops for cash, and the close link between rents and agricultural prices all point to the existence of a national market long before the 1870s.[71]

Under the Third Republic, the 'revolutionary dramatising'[72] by Republicans of the need to destroy the *ancien régime* and any last vestiges of feudalism led to frequent characterizations of the peasantry as a feudal brake on development, and public stigmatizing of the banks as a 'financial aristocracy' and of the major railway companies as parasitic remnants of the old order.[73] The polemical nature of the modernization debate has constantly blunted understanding of transition in France. The notion that economic development is dependent on the outcome of political struggles runs the risk of reducing the whole complex process to a battle of wills. Conflict between peasants and landlords, or between merchants and capitalists, obviously influenced the way in which development took place, but it cannot be singled out as a separate, determining feature. Liu's weavers may have forced industrialists to pull out of the Choletais in the 1850s, but they were powerless to stave off the effects of the blockade of the American South in the 1860s. France's development was characterized by the resilience of old forms of production, certainly, and by the accommodation of new forms with old, as well as by the triumph of new over old, but the clashes and compromises which took place were part of a wider web of relations which linked local and national actors to the world market.

Modernization, then, should not be seen as a pre-determined inevitability but as a complex process where development takes place, but at different times and in different ways. That the Revolution provided a framework for the development of capitalism should not obscure the fact that it also affected the course of this development, sometimes – it is true – stunting or distorting it. To understand the Revolution in this way means going beyond the impoverished conceptual matrix offered either by crude stages theories of modernization or by the rather more polished vulgarity of revisionism. The concept of bourgeois revolution is a very blunt instrument if understood simply as a class struggle between the bourgeoisie and nobility whose conscious goal and immediate outcome is a change of mode of production from feudalism to capitalism. But neither, as we shall see below, can the

Revolution be understood in terms of the autonomy of the political sphere. Bourgeois revolutions are affected by the anonymous historic process of economic development and transition, but they are also made by real people engaged in conflicts who try to make sense of specific, immediate circumstances. 'Initiatives and intentions' therefore tend to follow paths 'not inscribed in the global context'.[74]

THE REVOLUTIONARY DYNAMIC

That 'neo-Jacobin adventism' – as Edmonds puts it – 'the idea of Revolution as the sudden substitution of one social order for another', has been discredited, should be welcomed.[75] For the most part, however, the dismantling of crude notions of bourgeois revolution has not added to understanding either of the process of transition or of its relationship to political change. The two are generally viewed as completely separate phenomena. Transition has therefore become a matter for economic historians, while politics, or the study of the Event, has opened up an apparently endless seam of research for all manner of historians, chroniclers and cultural commentators. If part of the impact of revisionist historiography derives from its demolition of vulgar Marxism, its success has also been due to the focus on an area given less prominence by social historians – the role of culture and identity in shaping consciousness and the role of 'discourse' in shaping politics. But if human identity and action are, as Keith Baker has argued, 'discursively constituted',[76] what does this tell us about the role of politics in society? If, as Furet argues, it is necessary when dealing with an event that is greater than its causes or conditions to forget these causes and conditions 'in order to think the event',[77] what are the ties, if any, that link political to social and economic developments? Does a discursively constituted political sphere, in other words, generate its own autonomous reality?

Revisionism, as we have seen, follows traditional conservative readings of 1789 in seeking to explain the event above all in terms of its own dynamic. For Furet, social interpretations of political conflicts during the Revolution normalize what must be explained by rationalizing the political dynamic of the event. The Revolution itself places this (social) symbolism at the centre of political action and it is around this – not class interests – that struggles for power turn.[78] The Jacobins' 'imaginary discourse of power . . . becomes an absolute power over society'.[79] Clearly the powerful role played by the unfolding of the revolutionary process, its fears and hopes and furies, is a crucial element in understanding what happened. One only has to read Georges Lefebvre to be reminded of the Revolution's 'mythical character' as a 'complex of ideas generating energy and initiative'.[80] In the hands of the revisionists, however, this mythical element tends to squeeze out reality until the political becomes a principle of autonomous explanation.[81] William Doyle, for example, describes the Revolution as a process whereby the 'collective imaginings of society' become 'the very fabric of its own history'.[82] Furet, as we have seen, goes further, seeing actual history being outbid, 'on behalf of an idea', by revolutionary consciousness 'as if its function was to reconstruct through the imagination the whole social edifice which had fallen to pieces'.[83]

William Sewell has shown how it is in the interplay between everyday reality and ideas that the events of the Revolution begin to make sense. He shows how bourgeois reactions to the storming of the Bastille were initially hostile, the minutes of discussion in the National Assembly on the evening of 14 July referring to the 'disastrous news'. The following day one of the members of the Assembly warned that the storming of the Bastille would carry the people 'to an excess of fury that is very difficult to stop', but on the afternoon of 15 July, a delegation went from the Assembly to Paris. There they found not a seething and violent mob but the 'capital bathed in the glow of a joyous and generous patriotism'. Representatives from the Assembly were greeted as heroes and began to rethink their assumptions. On 16 and 17 July, it became clear that the fall of the Bastille had strengthened the Assembly against the king. On the 17 July, Louis, in what was widely perceived as an act of capitulation, appeared on the balcony of the city hall wearing a revolutionary red, white and blue rosette. By 20 July, the National Assembly had recognized the storming of the Bastille as an act of necessary violence against despotism, a legitimate popular revolution. The modern meaning of revolution was therefore established and accepted not just by radicals but also by conservatives, who hoped that by conferring legitimacy on specific, symbolic acts of popular violence they could stop it spreading. And so the struggle over the meaning and the limits of revolution began.[84]

Furet's claim that 'Revolutionary consciousness outbid real history on behalf of an idea' may chime with his attempt to set an earlier date for the point at which the limits of the Revolution (and the counter-revolution, considered over by 1790)[85] were reached, but we cannot understand history in this way. To attack teleological interpretations of history is one thing, but to insist on the predominance of ideas merely invites another kind of determinism. Once events are separated from their circumstances they become random. As Georges Lefebvre remarks, 'Events have their immediate roots not in their antecedents but in the men who intervene by interpreting those events.'[86] Sewell's account of how 14 July became the symbolic act of the Revolution bears this out. Various Marxist accounts of the revolutionary process have attempted to come to terms with such issues.

Marx's own analysis of Jacobinism, his frequent references to the way in which the Jacobins succumb to the 'Roman illusion', carrying out their revolution in the garb and language of antiquity, confusing modern representative democracy with the Roman Republic, offer evidence of the importance accorded not just to the autonomy of the political under the Terror but to the role played by myth and illusion in its realization.[87] Marx's stress on the Terror's function as a plebeian means of accomplishing the bourgeoisie's revolution sets great store by the hypertrophy of the political sphere during the Terror, as the state achieves political autonomy from the society which it strives to hold in check.

Löwy finds Marx's emphasis on the Roman illusion excessive, and suggests that Marx fails to locate Jacobin ideology within a class analysis of the Jacobins' role in the Revolution.[88] But this stress on the desire to delve into the past is only partly about ideology, however, reflecting Marx's awareness of the myth-making that is common to all victorious revolutions on the one hand, and more immediate anxieties concerning the revolutions made with one eye on the past in his own lifetime on the other. He believed that the Jacobins' Roman illusion derived from the contradiction between their unheroic achievement – the establishment of a mundane bourgeois order – and the heroic means required to bring it into being. The Revolution therefore drew on the past in order to 'drug' itself against its own content. The Jacobins found the 'self-deceptions' they needed in the imagery of Roman antiquity which allowed them to express themselves on the 'high plane of the great historical tragedy'.[89]

'The tradition of all the dead generations', as Marx famously put it, 'weighs like a nightmare on the brain of the living.'[90] Political revolutions are accomplished comparatively swiftly, but transition from one mode of production to another, as we have seen, is a related but distinct process that takes place at different speeds in different places and during which elements of previous modes of production can co-exist with the new for many decades. Likewise, the ideas which people carry around in their heads can outlive the economic and social conditions that gave rise to them in the first place. In the same vein, Trotsky argued that social change does not take place smoothly, in the way a mechanic changes his instruments, as the need arises. Existing institutions are taken as permanent fixtures of people's lives. So the sudden changes in mood and outlook during mass upheavals are the consequence not of 'revolutionary consciousness outbidding real history on behalf of an idea', but of the opposite – deep conservatism:

The chronic lag of ideas and relations behind new objective conditions, right up to the moment when the latter crash over people in the form of a catastrophe, is what creates in a period of revolution that leaping movement of ideas and passions which seems to the police mind a mere result of the activities of 'demagogues'.[91]

Did the revolutionaries of 1793 and 1848 evoke the past out of hesitancy and fear, or was this part of the process of learning a language, which involves constantly translating the new one back into the mother tongue until it has been fully assimilated?[92] Undoubtedly both, and more besides. Marx distinguishes between the two dates, however, arguing that the Jacobins' invocation of the past was not about nostalgia, reviving the ghost of revolution, but about rediscovering its spirit, 'of magnifying the given task in the imagination, not of fleeing from its solution in reality'. Socialist revolution, by contrast, would not be able to draw 'its poetry from the past, but only from the future', and would have to rid itself of 'all superstition with regard to the past'. 'In order to arrive at its own content, the revolution of the 19th century must let the dead bury their dead. Then the words went beyond the content; now the content goes beyond the words.'[93]

Trotsky saw the Russian Revolution as a 'master-builder of symbols', presenting the entire phenomenon in concentrated form. But its symbolism was too grandiose, fitting awkwardly with the creativity of the individual in revolutionary times.[94] Lives lived through revolution become too dynamic to get used to anything. On the high tide of momentous events, public thinking becomes audacious, 'It grasps facts on the wing, and on the wing links them with the thread of generalisation.'[95] Sewell, in an interesting qualification to Marx's comments on the Roman illusion, notes that classical masks were largely absent from the language that carried through reform between 1789 and 1791. It was only once the situation grew more desperate, when the revolutionaries had to deal with war, regicide and revolt from below, that they found the language of Enlightenment rationalism wanting and turned to the heroic register of classical antiquity. This imagery was not imposed on the Jacobins by the *sans culottes*, but reflected instead their classical bourgeois education and indeed outlived the Republic itself, Napoleon inaugurating the Empire in 1804 and becoming a modern Caesar.[96] Once the tide of events turns, moreover, consciousness begins to recoil, identification with the ideas and actors most associated with the revolution weakens, and the capacity for generalization shrinks.[97] In this changed context, symbols loom larger and public consciousness takes refuge in the cult of the Supreme Being, or of Napoleon, or of Lenin. In this sense, the institutionalization of revolutionary iconography represents not the victory of revolutionary consciousness over real history but its opposite – the revenge of real history, of 'the prejudices and confusion which humanity is dragging in its wagon-train behind it'.[98]

Such an understanding is only really possible if Baker's one-sided conception of the discursive constitution of social realities is rejected. As Sewell has noted, by forgetting the corollary, that discursive realities are socially constituted, Baker effectively transmogrifies the social into the symbolic and 'erases the social dimension of human action' from his analysis. Thus, while Baker correctly notes that 'meanings are always implicitly at risk',[99] these shifting meanings are only comprehensible in the context of 'the inherent contradictions of motivated social action'[100] – the intervention of individuals whose behaviour is shaped by and rooted in the course of society's development. What, then, is the relationship between this intervention and the broader sweep of human development? We have already seen how the struggles of French weavers in the nineteenth century were able to alter but not stem the course of industrial production. Does this mean, as one conventional Marxist view has it, that 'influential individuals can change the individual features of events and some of their particular consequences but they cannot change their general trend which is determined by other forces'?[101] Paul Ginsborg suggests a more nuanced approach, in this case with regard specifically to bourgeois revolution, which stresses the interplay between process and moment. In the case of France, although the moment of Revolution made a decisive contribution to the general development of French society, creating an institutional framework within which capitalism could flourish, there is no discernible chronological link between the event and the process of industrial growth.[102] Human activity, as Lukács argues, is best understood as neither subject to 'formal, transhistorical laws', nor simply at the mercy of chance and contingency.[103] During the course of history, moments are thrown up in which the essential tendencies of its development are crystallized. Such moments – wars, revolutions, insurrections – demand action, the outcome of which will affect in turn the subsequent unfolding of the process. In this way, circumstances can be seen to be constituted in part by subjective action. History, then,

. . . is no longer an enigmatic flux to which men and things are subjected. It is no longer a thing to be explained by the intervention of transcendental powers or made meaningful by reference to transcendental values. History is, on the one hand, the product (albeit the unconscious one) of man's own activity, on the other hand it is the succession of those processes in which the forms taken by this activity and the relations of man to himself (to nature, to other men) are overthrown.[104]

REVOLUTION IN HISTORY

Crude Marxist determinism crushes the relationship between history and human personality. Living societies cannot be reduced to their economic relations since each thread of the productive process – material, military, legal, artistic, and so on – 'has its own rhythm and its own temporality'. These 'heterogeneous temporalities' of history mean that its development cannot be conceived in linear terms.[105] Politics must therefore be identified neither as an entirely autonomous sphere, nor as a component of some inflexible mechanism, but as a product of the inharmonious development of living societies, a thing not of ordained epochal successions but of 'zigzags, ebbs and flows',[106] located at 'the point at which these discordant times intersect'.[107] In Françoise Proust's words, 'modern time does not flow cumulatively and peacefully, but is made up of thunderbolts which wound and break out with crazy speed'.[108]

What remains to be said about the alternative proposed by Furet *et al*? For all its emphasis on the role of chance and indeterminacy, revisionist historiography frequently makes do with a narrow empiricism. Cobban's discovery that the commercial bourgeoisie was absent from the National Assembly, which instead was full of lawyers; the endless studies devoted to 'proving' the feudal character of nineteenth-century France, with their painstaking enumeration of the relative numbers of workers and peasants, farms and factories; the revelation that elites in society, whether noble or bourgeois, shared some of the same values: despite the truths contained within it, the revisionist case, built upon these cornerstones, is nevertheless undermined by an enduring lack of imagination.

How, then, to discern the sense of individual acts amidst the flood of meaning brought along by cataclysmic upheavals? Schama's solution is straightforward. Flurries of individual acts hurtle across the page, suffocating meaning until only a general impression of catastrophe is left. Furet offers a less frantic version of the same thing. His methodology, he informs readers of *The Passing of an Illusion*, follows the classic path of the historian: 'the inventory of ideas, wills and circumstances'.[109] Furet's rejection of necessity as a form of determinism means, as we have seen, that the politics that emerge in his writing are curiously mutilated. 'An understanding of our era is only possible if we free ourselves from the illusion of necessity: the century is only explicable, to the extent that it is at all, if we accord it its unforeseen character.'[110] But his necessity is a one-dimensional thing. Most people could live without the necessity whose corollary is a history that is pre-determined or inevitable, but what about irreducible necessity, the bare necessities of life: the elements, food, clothing, shelter?

As far as Furet is concerned, necessity and contingence are not linked but diametrically opposed to each other.[111] The kind of unbounded, unrestricted possibility to which he alludes is an abstract, capricious possibility, unforeseen but also unreal and infinite. Set against the weight of the actual course of events such ephemeral alternatives appear whimsical, as, by extension, do the actions of those pursuing alternative goals to those achieved. In striving to make sense of individual acts by viewing them in isolation, Furet conceives of political autonomy in a vacuum, stripping the notion of meaning. With the political sphere cut loose from society, the historian is then free to people it with personalities driven by passions rather than interests and needs. Liberated from dealing with historically conditioned circumstances, he is no longer obliged to show the imprint of social conflicts on behaviour, the 'individual scratches made by a higher law of development'.[112] The irony of Furet's interpretation now becomes clear. The history he writes, far from possessing a physiognomy, is as devoid of real possibilities as the vulgar determinism he seeks to discredit. Both, moreover, produce the same result: quietism.[113]

In his history of the 'bras nus', Daniel Guérin tells the story of the trial of Sébastian de Lacroix and 'other extremists' who, following their insurrectionary activities in May 1793, are accused the following year of almost going 'beyond the limit at which the revolution stopped'.[114] All revolutions are partly about the discordance between the hopes of the participants and the social reality within which their aspirations are forged and develop. Yet Furet interprets these aspirations as a refusal to accept reality – they are unreasonable. The 'uncontrollable and interminable character' of the French Revolution derives from the 'passion for equality, itself by definition unsatisfied'. Behind the flag of equality 'is hidden an escalation without limits, inscribed in the principle of democracy'.[115] Whereas Marx, argues Furet, reduces democracy to a myth or an illusion, Tocqueville understands that 'in the illusion of democracy lies precisely its truth'.[116] The exercise of democracy therefore involves the imposition of limits. Furet is keen to see them respected more rigorously. Having pared the Revolution's achievements down to the bare minimum, he then attempts to fence in what he considers the Revolution's only legacy, the establishment of democracy, labelling any attempt to extend its boundaries an unrealizable aspiration. Left to cope with this impoverished legacy stands the bourgeois, master of the economy but aware that his dreams of democracy can never be realized:[117]

These abstract promises (liberty, equality) create an insurmountable space between people's expectations and what society can offer them. They thus render any debate or agreement about the limits of democracy obsolete.

They even invalidate the concept, which would imply a closed future and satisfied partners.[118]

CONCLUSION

Bourgeois revolutions, wrote Marx, quickly achieve their goals, but in order to come to terms with the turmoil of its revolutionary upheavals and achievements, bourgeois society 'has to undergo a long period of regret' so that its legacy may be assimilated in sober fashion.[119] Furet was well fitted for this prosaic task and, as others have remarked, distinguished himself as a historian of ends – the end of the French Revolution, the end of communism, the end of French exceptionalism.[120] His story, intended as an epilogue to the history of the Revolution, unfolded in what Furet took to be a gathering gloom and told of the 'twilight of the religious war opened up in the years of the French Revolution', the 'twilight battle of Gaullism', the 'twilight of the historic exceptional election', 'the twilight of the revolutionary spirit'.[121] 'It's getting dark', as Bob Dylan might have said, 'too dark to see'. In common with the new philosophers, Furet's work warns against the 'master thinkers', the ideologues whose desire to build new men leads to the Terror, the gulag and the concentration camp. His place lies alongside Bernard-Henri Lévy, guarding the world so that it will not be unmade. 'Here we are,' he wrote shortly before he died, 'condemned to live in the world that we are living in.'[122] While it is easy, after the experience of Hitler and Stalin, to understand this outlook, what if Walter Benjamin was right and catastrophe was not something that recedes behind us, but is instead stretched out on the road before us? What if, in other words, catastrophe also means that 'things "go on like this" '?[123] As we survey the wreckage of Iraq and contemplate the next stage of the war on terror, such ideas do not seem so fanciful. One thing is clear, however: if we are to grasp and make sense of the historical images that light up this road, more sophisticated instruments than those fashioned by Furet and company will be needed.

The French Revolution: Revolution of the Rights of Man and the Citizen

Florence Gauthier

SLAVERY OR FREEDOM?

The French Revolution, revolution of the rights of man and the citizen, abolished the feudal regime and slavery in the colonies without any compensation for the lords and masters. The red cap of freedom expressed the link between these two great gains of civil and political liberty on a world scale. It also pointed to their common origin in slavery, whether the heritage of ancient slavery in the forms of serfdom and in the transformations of feudal relations over the centuries, or modern slavery as invented by Europeans in the American colonies.

Moreover, relations of a capitalist type were developing in what we call the modern era. It was possible to observe in France progress in the concentration of landed property through the expropriation of a growing section of the peasantry from its inheritable tenures, but also the advance in the concentration of agriculture in the hands of a small layer of cultivating tenant-farmers who practised the 'merging of farms', by gathering together the various markets in rented land, and also the establishment of a private market in food, supplies. Here, economic power transformed the social need to eat into a food weapon or corn war, which killed, as we know, in the form of 'contrived shortages'.[1]

The French Revolution was the expression of popular resistance to such capitalist forms accurately described as 'tyrannical political economy' to which the response was the demand for and the working out of a 'people's political economy'. This opened up a crucial debate, which is still continuing. In the American colonies, sugar plantations, with their labour force imported according to the needs of the planter – a division of labour which was purely manual for work in the fields and highly mechanized with regard to the processing of sugar – produced for export and made attractive profits possible. By the eighteenth century, it enabled people to make a real fortune. This sugar cultivation was the product of a slave-owning capitalism, which drew the admiration of the economic philosophers known in France by the name of Physiocrats. It also gave rise to criticism of this form of economic domination which, after having destroyed and depopulated the West Indies, repopulated them with African captives who were enslaved so that sugared coffee with rum in it could be served on European tables.

The French Revolution was also an experiment in inventing democracy which proclaimed the rights of man and the citizen – an experiment characterized by the immense task of building popular sovereignty, enlarging a democratic public space, the construction of a supreme legislative authority and a citizenry which played an effective part in the formulation of the laws.

In fact the revolutionary theory of the rights of man and the citizen conceived of civil and political liberty in opposition to slavery. Assuming the unity of the human race, whose members were born free and had natural rights, freedom was conceived in two forms:

- personal freedom, the precious fruit of the massacres of the wars of religion which revealed the practical means of protecting freedom of thought and conscience by a right envisaged as being based on reciprocity: I am free on condition that I am not subordinated to the power of any other man and on condition that I do not subordinate any other man to my power;
- freedom in society, or citizenship, a practical means of maintaining the right of personal freedom: we are free in society when we obey, not men, but laws in the formulation of which we have taken part and to which we have given our consent.

This political theory, which centres on the assumption that man is made to live freely, has been asserted throughout the modern period, as a *liberalism of reciprocal rights* or, alternatively, as the equality of rights. Here a problem emerges: the fact that this *liberalism of reciprocal rights* could be a revolutionary theory from the sixteenth to the eighteenth century has scarcely left any trace in our own day. This theory of freedom was subsequently misappropriated and diverted from its meaning and goals, as we shall see.

THE PROLEGOMENA OF LIBERTY: 1789

The Estates General which met at Versailles on 5 May 1789 transformed itself into a Constituent National Assembly on 17 June, then, by the Tennis Court Oath on 20 June, swore not to disperse until it had given France a constitution.

Revolution: Act I

The whole process of convening the Estates General; the electoral system which gave the right to vote to heads of families (of either sex) established in a locality; the drawing up of the registers of grievances; the election of deputies mandated by their electors; the replacement of the Estates General, which was an extended King's Council, by a Constituent National Assembly – all this makes up the revolutionary social contract and was experienced as such by contemporaries. These ideas – of national sovereignty, of social contract, of constitution, of citizenship, of supreme legislative authority – were not abstract ideas, nor were they remote from the people; quite the contrary, they were ideas which had been widely popularized and had become established reality. The Constituent Assembly had put an end to the Estates General *on its own initiative*, and had installed a new authority, deriving from elections, which had just overthrown the monarchy established by divine right in France and transferred the king's sovereignty to the people. This was Act I of the Revolution.

Revolution: Act II

The second act of the Revolution was played out in the countryside. The vast peasant rising of July 1789, known as the Great Fear, spread as fast as the sound of an alarm bell. If we take into account the fact that it followed on from the peasant revolts of the previous spring, it was the whole French countryside rising up against the feudal regime. The peasant revolts combined food riots with armed insurrections which were anti-monarchical, in opposition to the administrators, tax-collection and the legal system, anti-ecclesiastical in the refusal to pay tithes, and above all anti-feudal. In this respect the village communities directly attacked the landlords' property titles – whether they were nobles, commoners or clergy – either to burn them, or to force the landlord to sign a declaration that he would waive his rights in future. They also reappropriated common property that had been taken over by the landlords, and used it immediately by sending their cattle to graze there, and by re-establishing customary rights.

It was therefore the destruction of seigneurialism that was aimed at by these actions, which attacked the seigneurial institutions, but not individual persons, with extraordinary violence. Georges Lefebvre, the historian of the Great Fear,[2] has stressed a very remarkable fact: during the Great Fear several hundred seigneurial dwellings were visited, the property titles were burnt, some castles were demolished and sometimes set fire to, but there was no violence against the landlords or their servants. At the same time the great institution of the monarchy found itself paralysed, with administrators abandoning their posts and preferring to hide or flee.

It was the peasantry that made an offer of a social contract to the landlords. In order to understand it correctly let us rapidly recall the structure of seigneurialism at this time. In 1789, seigneurialism was formed of two parts, the seigneurial portion and the territory subject to annual dues. The seigneurial portion consisted of the landlord's residence, the land which was cultivated for the upkeep of his household, land considered to be useful such as forests where he exercised the noble sport of hunting, and lands which the landlord rented out for tenant-farming or share-cropping. The territory subject to dues involved a complex property form since the rights were shared between the landlord and peasant dues-payers. The dues upheld the seigneurial system, but also the rights of the dues-payer, and in the first place his right of inheritable tenure. The landlord could not expropriate the tenant-farmer, and the latter had to pay rent and submit to the landlord's justice.

It should be remembered that in 1789 about half the cultivated lands of the kingdom belonged to the territory subject to annual dues, and the other half to the seigneurial portion (land let for tenant-farming or share-cropping). The offer of a social contract, which the peasantry made to the landlords, was to divide the seigneurial property: the territory subject to annual dues to the dues-payers and the seigneurial portion to the landlords. Moreover, as far as common property was concerned, the peasantry refused any division and demanded, on the one hand, the recognition of this form of property to the village communities, and on the other hand the restoration of all common land taken over since 1669 – the date of a compromise royal edict which permitted, in certain circumstances, the appropriation of a third of this property by the landlords, with the other two thirds being left to the village community.

Finally, as far as lands let out for tenant-farming or share-cropping were concerned, the peasantry proposed legislation for the renewal of leases which, essentially, abolished their revocable status and reduced the total sum of rent to be paid. The spirit of this last proposal aimed to keep access to land – the peasant's essential requirement for work – as free as possible. Let us stress that on this point the peasantry was divided, since the wishes of small cultivators were different from the interests of large tenant-farmers cultivating land. In the areas close to towns these large tenant-farmers were after the profitable market of supplies for the town and made agreements among themselves to reserve the land to be rented and to exclude the small cultivators.

To return to the offer of a social contract formulated by the peasantry: in the first place it expressed a conception of association which asserted the *right to life and the means of preserving it for everybody*, including the landlords as individuals, and rejected the exclusion of some of its members. The peasantry did not say to the landlords, 'We want to take everything and then we shall kill you', but, 'You want to take everything. We are telling you to share.' Here the peasant formulation attacked the seigneurial monopoly of land in order to prevent it progressing further. In fact, the landlords still hoped to appropriate the territory subject to dues, in order to get rid of the dues which amounted to much less than rents in the form of tenancies or share-cropping.

The peasantry's offer was based on the right of inheritance in the perspective of a total abolition of rent. Lands of this type had existed in the Middle Ages, under the name *allodium*, free land that was not subject to any feudal-seigneurial right. It should be made clear that the concept of seigneurial property referred to a form of exclusive land ownership, of a Roman type. But that of the peasantry corresponded to a *generalization of allodium* which would replace the paying of dues; the burning of the landlord's property titles expressed in the clearest possible fashion this desire to *transform dues-paying into allodium by fire*.

All too often historical writing has tried to see a mysterious instinct for property attributed to a no less mysterious peasant mentality which, far from illuminating the peasant concept of right, obscures the centuries-old struggle of the peasants against different forms of rent. It should be clearly understood that *allodium* is not an exclusive form of property, but combines individual and collective rights, well-known to historians and even better to the peasants themselves![3]

Secondly, the peasant offer of a social contract allows us to see clearly that the village communities were taking control of their own affairs at the level of the economic and social management of agriculture, and asserting that they were fully aware of the purely unearned and parasitic character of seigneurial property – with some very rare exceptions. Thus they presented themselves as the inheritors of the landlords at the level of the economic management of the countryside, which is what they in fact became with the Revolution.

To this offer of a social contract, the landlords responded, partially, with refusal, thus provoking civil war in France. But the seigneurial resistance was eventually beaten, and the offer of the peasantry was achieved in the shape of agrarian reform and the adoption by revolutionary legislation of the peasant concept of right.

THE 1791 CONSTITUTION AGAINST THE DECLARATION
OF THE RIGHTS OF MAN AND THE CITIZEN

The great peasant rising did not achieve the favourable response it expected. It had frightened the seigneurial landowners, whether noble or commoner and, on the night of 4 August 1789, the Constituent Assembly tried to cheat by giving a contradictory reply to the peasant request. In fact, the Assembly decreed with one hand what it took back with the other. It enunciated a principle of a constituent nature by decreeing that: 'The National Assembly entirely abolishes the feudal regime', and here responded to the peasant expectation, but it deprived it of all content by retaining the redemption of feudal rights. To free themselves of rents weighing on the dues-payers, the peasants had to compensate the landlord. By its refusal to decide clearly, the Assembly was leaving the job of doing so to the relations of forces – four years of civil war and two revolutions followed before legislation gave the peasants a favourable response.

Moreover, the Assembly promised, on the same night of 4 August, to give a declaration of rights as a constitutional foundation. On 26 August the Declaration of the Rights of Man and the Citizen was adopted. This text proclaimed the natural rights of man and the citizen with reference to the modern philosophy of natural right and its principles of sovereignty as the common property of a people, and of reciprocal rights. At this point, the division between *left* and *right* acquired its political meaning. The left wanted to apply the principles of the Declaration of the Rights of Man and the Citizen, and the right sought to evade them and, if possible, get rid of this text, regarded as burdensome, which condensed the theory of this *revolution of the rights of man and the citizen*.

Six peasant risings from 1789 to 1792

Thus the Constituent Assembly responded to the peasant demand with the redemption of feudal rights. The decree of 15 March 1790 even made redemption impossible by obliging well-off and poor peasants to redeem together, which was unfeasible. It revealed the determination of the landlords, nobles or commoners, to do everything possible to maintain the seigneurial rents intact. It also prepared to use force by decreeing martial law on 23 February 1790. We can see that the seigneurial counter-revolution believed that the popular movement was only a straw fire that it could easily extinguish.

Never did legislation unleash such great indignation. The peasants understood the Assembly was betraying them. Five further peasant risings followed that of July 1789 in the period up to the revolution of 12 August 1792:

- second peasant rising of winter 1789–90, in Brittany, the Massif Central and South West
- third peasant rising of winter 1790–91, from Brittany to Gascony
- fourth peasant rising of summer 1791, from Maine to Périgord, from the Massif Central to the Languedoc
- fifth peasant rising of spring 1792, in the Paris basin, the Massif Central, the South West and the Languedoc
- sixth peasant rising of summer–autumn 1792, throughout the country

These armed peasant movements combined disturbances about food with the refusal to pay taxes, tithes and seigneurial rents, and pursued the burning of the landlords' property titles and the recovery of common land which had been expropriated.

Resumption of the Corn War

The Constituent Assembly had also attempted a new experiment with unlimited free trade in grain. The Corn War resumed on an ever-vaster scale. Disturbances about food took on unprecedented forms. The public markets were depleted, so people went to the producers to get grain or stopped corn convoys travelling by road or canal in order to establish popular granaries.

Aristocracy of the rich or democracy?

The social fear on the part of property owners had led the Assembly to establish suffrage based on property qualification, reserving citizenship for property owners – what became known as an *aristocracy of the rich*. The response of the democratic movement was, on the one hand, to create popular societies which increased in numbers, opening a public space for information, discussion of contemporary problems and proposals in the form of petitions, and, on the other, to vest authority in primary assemblies, meeting places created for the election of deputies to the Estates General in 1788–89.

The property qualification amounted to dividing citizens into two groups: *active citizens*, who enjoyed all civil and political rights, and *passive citizens* who were deprived of the exercise of political rights and excluded from political society. The democratic movement attempted wherever it could to prevent the exclusion of passive citizens from these primary assemblies, which had become, since the reorganization of municipalities, assemblies of the electoral divisions of communes. We should note that in the countryside the general assemblies of village communities normally involved inhabitants of both sexes, just like the assemblies of electoral divisions in lower-class areas of the towns, thus it was the exclusion of women and passive citizens which characterized the meetings of active citizens.

We should also stress that the system of property qualification even excluded adult sons who had not yet inherited from their parents from the exercise of political rights. It should be noted that the conception of a personal right was defended by the advocates of natural reciprocal rights – rights attached to the person and to all persons, and not to wealth. Thus there were many divergent conceptions of right and of social and political behaviour which separated the aristocracy of the rich from the democratic movement.

Martial law

In a major martial law of 26 July 1791 which recapitulated previous partial decrees, the Constituent Assembly criminalized as *seditious assembly* all the forms the popular movement had adopted since the start of the Revolution: refusal to pay feudal rents, tithes or taxes, disturbances about food opposed to the so-called freedom in trade of grain, and strikes by rural or urban wage-earners. It should be noted that the Le Chapelier law, which aimed at repressing strikes by agricultural workers – the most frequent at the time – and by urban artisans, was an integral part of the martial law and was contained within the great recapitulative law of 26 July 1791. These seditious gatherings were suppressed by the martial law. It was in common use in the countryside and was applied once, in a particularly brutal fashion, in Paris under the name of the 'massacre of the Champ de Mars', on 17 July 1791.

The Constitutionalization of slavery in the colonies

In the American slave colonies, the system of the slave market based in Africa began to go into crisis in the second half of the eighteenth century, for it was ever more difficult to acquire captives, and prices rose. One grouping among economists, including the Physiocrats and their successors around Turgot, proposed various solutions that entailed transforming the system of reproducing the labour force. In part these solutions were tried out in the eighteenth century. They involved replacing the African slave market by reorganizing labour on the plantations through the breeding of slaves locally in the colonies. The system known as the *coolie trade* also had its origins at this time. The idea of colonizing Africa itself by creating plantations there was first mooted and colonial companies engaged in negotiations and prospecting to this end.

In France, the banker Clavière entrusted to his secretary Brissot the job of founding a Society of Friends of the Blacks in 1788, on the model of societies of the same name established in London and Manchester. Clavière and Brissot addressed the planters and traders, their plan being to solve the crisis of slave labour by preparing settlers and governments to replace the trade in captured African slaves by the breeding of slaves on the spot. Later, Condorcet, a member of the Society of the Friends of the Blacks, envisaged, after the breeding of slaves had been gradually introduced over several generations, a change of status which would enable the slave to redeem himself, by compensating the owner, and thus to become a so-called free wage-worker.[4]

On the other hand, a grouping defending the common rights of humanity called into question the policy of force and conquest pursued by the monarchy, and the economic rule that had been established in the American colonies. A Society of Citizens of Colour was formed in 1789. One of its leaders, Julien Raimond, met Cournand and Grégoire and helped to enlighten the left about the situation in the American colonies and about the activities of the colonial party, assembled in the Massiac Club, which influenced the policy of the Constituent Assembly through Barnave and his friends the Lameths who owned sugar refineries in St Domingue.

To understand the situation in St Domingue, it is necessary to make clear that the colonists licensed by the king in the sixteenth century had married African women and thus formed a new mulatto humanity who became their heirs. The second generation of planters were largely mulattos as were the following, until the appearance of competition between Creole settlers (born in the colony) and new settlers who had come to make their fortunes. The latter thought it would be possible for them to expropriate the settlers of colour and to take away their property. *Colour prejudice* appeared and developed in the second half of the eighteenth century. It consisted of establishing *segregation within the class of masters*, in order to exclude from it those members discriminated against on grounds of colour.

Segregationist settlers succeeded in taking power as a result of the events of 1789 and attempted to purge the ruling class of its mulatto members. In 1789 and 1790, the colonial assemblies of St Domingue were formed exclusively of white settlers, while violent attacks were made on free men of colour and the whites who supported them, paving the way for a 'St Bartholomew's Day massacre of free people of colour'. An unprecedented crisis opened up, dividing and weakening the class of masters in St Domingue. The free people of colour had to take arms to protect themselves and created safe havens.

They also deserted the local militias, which maintained the slave system in existence. Caught between the threat of extermination by the segregationist settlers and the preservation of the slave order, they were rapidly obliged to ally with the slaves. A revolutionary process began in St Domingue.

Julien Raimond, a rich mulatto settler who was in France, therefore informed some of the revolutionaries of the explosive situation in the colonies and helped them to understand the policy of the settlers and their influence in French society and in the Constituent Assembly. Raimond helped the left to work out its position on the colonial question and the same left helped him to formulate a revolutionary project in a colonial society where liberty and equality, as conceived in opposition to civil and political slavery, were totally unknown. A remarkable exchange was established here, a project of a 'cosmo-politics' of freedom, an experiment which, although valuable, has scarcely been noticed except by a few – all too few – historians.[5]

The right speaks out against the Declaration of Rights

The Declaration of the Rights of Man and the Citizen had scarcely been voted for when the colonial party expressed its refusal of the principles in the Declaration in a remarkable form. In effect they presented the Declaration of Rights as a reign of terror directed against the settlers:

> We felt first of all that this new order of things should encourage the greatest circumspection on our part. This circumspection has grown . . . it has become a sort of terror which we saw the Declaration of the Rights of Man posit, as the basis of the constitution, absolute equality, identical rights for all and the freedom of all individuals.[6]

This claim that the Declaration of Rights is equivalent to terror directed against the settlers, which is extraordinary for a twenty-first century reader, expresses in a particularly disturbing form the paradox which is contained in the word 'terror'. Jean-Pierre Faye has stressed that the historical resonance of the word 'terror' dates from the French Revolution.[7] Here the colonial party sheds a harsh light on its unexpected origin. And it was the whole of the right, not just the colonial party, which took up and developed this theme to its final consequences, as we shall see.

It was from the end of 1790 that the democratic movement began to formulate clearly, with respect to the overall policy of the Constituent Assembly, criticisms which drew out the contradictions between its collected decrees and the principles of the Declaration of the Rights of Man and the Citizen. Let us take a few examples.

The maintenance of slavery and the recognition of segregationism in the colonies[8] violated the first article of the Declaration of Rights: 'Men are born and remain free and equal in rights.'

The system of property qualification which excluded passive citizens violated the universal concept of natural right as proclaimed in the Declaration, and in particular articles three and six: 'The source of all sovereignty resides essentially in the nation . . . The law is the expression of the general will. All citizens have the right to concur personally, or through their representatives, in its formation.'

The martial law violated these same principles and also article two which recognized the right of resistance to oppression: 'The aim of every political association is the preservation of the natural and inalienable rights of man. These rights are freedom, property, security and resistance to oppression.'

Robespierre synthesized this criticism in one of the founding texts of the democratic movement, by illuminating fully how the decrees of the Constituent Assembly had imposed a new form of civil and political slavery on the excluded, and introduced a definition of freedom which contradicted the one used in the Declaration of Rights:

> Finally, is the nation sovereign when the majority of individuals who make it up are stripped of the political rights which constitute sovereignty? No, yet you have just seen that these very decrees deprive the great majority of French people of them. So what would your Declaration of Rights be if these decrees were allowed to survive? An empty formula. What would the nation be? A slave nation, for liberty consists in obeying the laws we have given ourselves and servitude consists in being obliged to submit to a foreign will. What would your constitution be? A pure aristocracy. For aristocracy is a state where one group of citizens are sovereign and the rest are subjects. And what sort of aristocracy? The most unbearable of all, that of the Rich.[9]

The Constitution of 1789 was scarcely complete when the slave rising in St Domingue made its colonial, pro-slavery and segregationist policy obsolete. On the night of 22 August 1791, the slaves on the plain of Le Cap discovered their own strength. They had grasped the unexpected opportunity offered to them by the war of skin colour which, for the first time, was weakening the domination of the class of masters, whether white or of colour. Less than two years later, it was once again the Le Cap region that initiated the abolition of slavery.

The Legislative Assembly, which in France followed the Constituent Assembly, responded by recognizing the civil and political rights of people of colour and created, from the name of its decree, the 'citizens of 4 April 1792'.

The measure came too late since the slave rising had put freedom for all on the agenda, but it introduced something of the principle of legal equality in law into a disintegrating colonial society.

In France the pro-war project of Brissot's supporters aimed to divert the Revolution into a war of conquest in Europe which would enable France to enrich itself, to find allies and to deflect the popular democratic movement from its political and economic objectives. Now the king and queen were able to use Brissot's project to their own advantage, by declaring war and allowing the Austro-Prussian armies to repress the democratic movement and restore royal power. The Legislative Assembly declared war on 20 April 1792 and the king, as head of the executive, encouraged his general staff to lose it.[10] These betrayals provoked the Revolution of 10 August 1792.

THE REVOLUTION OF 10 AUGUST 1792
PREPARES A NEW CONSTITUTION

This Revolution, situated between the last two peasant risings, responded immediately to the peasant movement, even before the Convention was elected, with the agrarian legislation of 20–28 August 1792. This recognized that the communes had ownership of common land and abolished, of course without redemption, all the seigneurial rights over the dues-payers. The common lands taken over by right of partition since 1669 were restored to the communes. As can be seen, this legislation expropriated the landlords of a large part of their property.

The Convention was elected by universal suffrage. In the countryside and in the lower-class electoral divisions in the towns, women frequently took part in voting which, moreover, was traditional in the villages. On 21 September, the date of its first meeting, the Convention unanimously voted for the abolition of the monarchy in France.

Brissot's supporters, known as Girondins since their break with the Jacobin Club, had become the rallying point for opponents of the Revolution of 10 August and of democracy. If they had been part of the left under the Legislative Assembly, they formed the right wing of the Convention. Although they had only a minority of elected deputies, the Girondins won the majority of votes in the first months of the Convention.

Openly opposed to the popular movement, the Girondin government refused to apply the agrarian legislation of 20–28 August 1792. The continuation of the Corn War allowed the opening of a remarkable debate in the Convention from September to December 1792, and made it possible to define the programmes in greater detail. But on 8 December 1792, the Convention approved the Girondin proposals, which consisted of extending the policy of the Constituent Assembly in favour of unlimited freedom of the grain trade and of the current means of enforcing it, namely martial law.

However, the Girondin refusal to listen to the people did not succeed in preventing the democratic movement from taking one aspect of economic policy into its hands. In fact, during the autumn and winter of 1792–93, the communal democracy that was evolving in France took control of policy with regard to supplies, the fixing of prices of essential goods, supplies to markets and assistance to paupers. Thus the ministry of the interior headed by the Girondin Roland was gradually stripped of its powers in favour of the communes. It should be stressed that this was how the separation of powers was established in France at this time, and this was how a true communal democracy was built in practice, where citizens' meetings in village general assemblies or urban commune electoral divisions elected their municipal councils, police officials and justices of the peace. These same general assemblies controlled their elected representatives who had the responsibility of applying the laws, but also food policy as well as social assistance. It should be made clear that there was no such thing as what is described as administrative centralization, with state apparatuses separated from society.[11]

The programme of *popular political economy* was defended by the Mountain. The term Mountain did not indicate an organized party of the sort we understand today, but rather a general project, a set of principles laid out in the Declaration of the Rights of Man and the Citizen, which acted as a compass to guide thought and action. Chaumette, who was chief magistrate of the Paris Commune, gave a definition that deserves to be recalled: 'The Mountain, this rock of the rights of man.'

There existed a large number of parties in the form of clubs, popular societies and electoral division societies. Some joined together by similarity, by affinity, in order to organize a campaign, launch a petition, send a delegation to another electoral division or region or to the Convention in order to present a demand or draft law. This was how a very strong awareness of the sovereignty of the people, linked to the effective exercise of citizenship as participation in the formulation of the laws, was formed at this time. In the festivals of 1792–94, the sovereign people was symbolized by Hercules, certainly an image of strength and unity, but also one which recalled his arduous labours, for the construction of civil and political liberty was not easy. Hercules accomplished his feats while climbing the Mountain that led to liberty, to its reciprocal, namely equality, and to fraternity.

To try and put a brake on the progress of Hercules, the Girondins, who could see clearly that within France the reality of power was slipping away from them, tried to oppose the Revolution of 10 August 1792 by insulting the people and the Mountain.

They tried to prevent the king's trial, then the sentence, but failed. They tried to steer the Revolution off course by provoking a war of conquest in Europe. But the war they presented in the innocent guise of the liberation of peoples turned into annexation pure and simple with the decree of 15 December 1792. The annexed peoples did not like 'armed missionaries'[12] and resisted the occupation. On the political level, the Girondin war of conquest was a crushing defeat which divided the peoples of Europe, helped to turn their sympathies away from the Revolution, and strengthened their princes as soon as they resisted the occupying French armies. The tragedy of the Republic of Mainz, the failure of which forced its supporters to take refuge in France, illustrates the disastrous consequences of this war of conquest.

The Mountain, which on this question was represented by Robespierre, Marat and Baillaud-Varenne, had denounced the errors and dangers involved in such a policy from the very first time it was advocated in 1791. The Mountain was opposed to any war of conquest, in the name of the right of peoples to self-determination, and this was a breaking-point with the Girondins and the supporters of Brissot. Robespierre and Grégoire in particular made a contribution to renewing the principles of a law of nations which respected national rights and was opposed to all forms of conquest, whether military or commercial, and they thus laid the bases of a 'cosmo-politics' of freedom in the hope of putting an end to the policies of conquest of the European powers.

As far as the slave colonies were concerned, in particular St Domingue, the Girondin government did not favour the revolution that was developing there. From late 1791 onwards, many settlers emigrated to London and sought the support of Prime Minister Pitt. The leaders of the colonial counter-revolution – Malouet, Cougnacq-Myon, Venault de Charmilly, Montalembert – negotiated the British occupation of the French colonies in order to preserve slavery there, and promised to supply French officers and men to the British navy. In spring 1793 the British navy in Jamaica was reinforced, while Montalembert and La Rochjacquelin prepared to land in St Domingue.

It was in this context that in February 1793 the Girondin government appointed a governor for St Domingue, Galbaud, who arrived on the island in May. Galbaud took the side of the slave-owning settlers and tried to remove from office the Civil Commissioners Polverel and Sonthonax who were preparing to abolish slavery. The battle of Le Cap was going Galbaud's way when the intervention of the insurgent slaves transformed the whole situation. Galbaud was defeated and fled, followed by ten thousand settlers: it was the end of white rule in St Domingue.

Polverel and Sonthonax had been rescued by the insurgent slaves and undertook to give their full personal support to the revolution of universal freedom and the equality of skin colour. On 24 August 1793 the inhabitants of the Le Cap region presented a petition demanding universal freedom. On 29 August Sonthonax took the initiative of establishing universal freedom throughout the island and for the first time proclaimed in St Domingue the Declaration of the Rights of Man and the Citizen. He then proposed to organize the election by the new citizens of a delegation from St Domingue, which would carry the news to the Convention and would ask, with maximum publicity, for the French Revolution to give its support. The election took place at Le Cap on 23 September. Six deputies were elected according to the principles of the equality of skin colour: two blacks, two whites and two mulattos. A few days later the deputies Belley, Dufaÿ and Mills, a living flag expressing the equality of skin colour, set out for France via the United States of America. The colonial lobby did not want the delegation to get to Paris alive, and in fact it took four months to reach France, suffering attacks throughout its journey, but succeeding in escaping its enemies.

In St Domingue the British navy had landed in September 1793 at two points on the island in an attempt to block the revolution of universal freedom which was beginning on the American continent.

To return to France in spring 1793 – the failure of the Girondin policy was obvious; in April the war of conquest became a military debacle and France was no longer an occupying power but was itself threatened; the Austrian army was occupying the Nord *département* and was, in particular, reimposing tithes and seigneurial rights.

Since the election of the Convention, a new Constituent Assembly, discussion on the constitution had been held back because the Girondin government wanted to weaken the democratic movement. A final man-oeuvre revealed the fears of the Girondins. On 29 May, in the absence of a large number of deputies from the Mountain who had been sent on missions to the frontiers to organize national defence, the Convention voted without debate for a version of the Declaration of Rights that replaced the notion of *natural right* with that of the *rights of man in society*. This was a new political theory, which abandoned the reference to the modern philosophy of natural right, which underlay the Declaration of 1789. The aim of society was no longer to establish the natural rights of man by imposing respect for these rights on the public authorities but, on the contrary, the public authorities were to allocate rights without reference to a shared and agreed ethic. The theory of the Revolution was overturned in favour of a new political theory in the interests of the possessing classes. These accumulated factors produced the Revolution of 31 May to 2 June 1793.

THE REVOLUTION OF 31 MAY TO 2 JUNE 1793
RE-ESTABLISHES THE DECLARATION OF NATURAL RIGHTS

This new insurrection organized in Paris with the assistance of soldiers who had come from the provinces to ensure the defence of the French frontiers did not overthrow the Convention, but demanded the recall of the twenty-two Girondin deputies who were considered to be 'disloyal to the people'. Put under house arrest but not imprisoned, several of the twenty-two fled and decided to join up with the royalist counter–revolution which was combining civil war with the war on the frontiers.

From 31 May to 2 June 1793 onwards it was the political proposals of the Mountain which were supported by the majority of the Convention until 9 Thermidor Year II (27 July 1794).

The first initiative taken by the Mountain was to give, at last, a favourable response to the peasant movement by immediately applying the abolition without redemption of the rights weighing on the dues-payers as a result of the law of 17 July 1793. Common land was made over to the communes by the law of 10 June 1793 and common lands taken over by the landlords over the previous forty years were restored to the communes, together with all partitions carried out since 1669. The sale in small portions of national property (property of the Church and of *émigrés*) was made easier by the law of 3 June and some of this property was distributed free of charge to paupers by the law of 13 September. The destruction of fortified castles and the burning of the property titles of the landlords over the dues-payers were legalized by the law of 6 August. Finally, the equal division of inheritances between heirs of either sex, including illegitimate children who had been recognized, was instituted by the law of 26 October 1793.

No subsequent government, however much it claimed to be restoring the *ancien régime*, dared to touch the law of 17 July or the reappropriation of the common land. More than half the cultivated land was thus made into *allodium* in favour of the peasants, and the collective nature of communal property was legally recognized in France.

The second initiative of the Montagnard Convention was to settle down immediately to work on the Constitution. On 23 and 24 June, the Declaration of the Rights of Man and the Citizen re-established natural rights in continuity with that of 1789, and the Constitution installed a social and democratic republic. It should be made clear that the martial law was formally abolished on 23 June, with all its component parts, including the Le Chapelier law.

Universal male suffrage was open to all men aged over twenty-one born in France or who had been living in the republic's territory for at least a year.

Citizenship was attached to the fact of *living there*, and represented an interesting experiment in citizenship attached to the person and not to what we nowadays call nationality. It should be noted that this open definition of citizenship derived from common law, especially the Parisian, which granted rights of citizenship to anyone who had lived in Paris for a year.

In recent years the Revolution has been much criticized for having failed, indeed refused, to give rights of citizenship to women. It should be noted that this important question of political rights was still not resolved in our own period, even in a country such as France which, we should remember, only gave women the right to vote in 1946. But as far as the Revolution is concerned, we know that the question was posed as early as 1789, for example, in the Fraternal Society of Both Sexes, and later in the women's societies like that of the Revolutionary Republican Women. That the question should have been posed is remarkable. As far as the practices of citizenship are concerned, we must distinguish between the right to vote and the right to be elected to positions of responsibility. We have already seen that women took part and voted in the primary assemblies and general assemblies of the village communes and of urban assemblies made up of the common people. For it is well established that what was decisive here was which class one belonged to; women of the common people took part in the primary assemblies, but not women of the upper classes. Is this a class distinction? Did the domestication of women go along with this distinction on the basis of class? That is what popular traditions seem to point to.

The exclusion of women took place on the level of the right to be elected to positions of responsibility. The question to be examined here is that of the consciousness of women themselves, for we have no example of a woman elected to a post of responsibility, even as chair of a session in the general assembly of an electoral division. Only women's societies tried out such functions among themselves. But it is important to note that the Revolutionary Republican Women did not demand the right of women to be elected to functions of responsibility, but first of all demanded *the right of women to bear arms* like citizens, as a first expression of their participation in the sovereignty of the people, and they took part in military training exercises.

The third problem the Montagnard Convention had to resolve was that of provisions. A programme known as the Maximum for prices of essential foodstuffs was organized during the summer of 1793 and complemented the agrarian legislation which, as we have seen, facilitated access to the land and distributed plots of land to poor peasants in order to increase the direct production of food. In September 1793 the list of essential foodstuffs was drawn up, prices and commercial profits were fixed in relation to urban and rural wages which were increased, and markets were controlled by the creation of public granaries in each commune. The producers had to declare to the communes the total amount of their production and markets were supplied by requisition. Thus the unrestricted freedom of the grain trade was abolished, as was the means of applying it – martial law. It was this rich experience of economic, social and political democracy that inspired the project which Babeuf and the Equals put forward in 1795–96.[13] For as long as the Maximum was applied – that is, until autumn 1794 – the population was supplied with urgently needed products (food and the basic raw materials required by artisans).

The abolition of slavery supported by the Montagnard Convention was undoubtedly one of the most remarkable advances in the rights of humanity. It will be recalled that the deputation from St Domingue arrived in France in January 1794, despite all the efforts to prevent it by the colonial party. On 16 Pluviôse Year II (4 February 1794) the deputation based on equality of skin colour presented to the Convention the mandate it had received from the revolution in St Domingue. It proposed an alliance between the two revolutions, a common policy against the French settlers and their Spanish and British allies involved on both sides of the Atlantic. The Convention accepted this offer and extended universal freedom to all the French colonies. In April 1794 it sent an expedition of seven ships to the Caribbean with arms for St Domingue and troops to back up the decree abolishing slavery in the other French colonies. Slavery was abolished in Guyana and Guadeloupe in June 1794. In Saint Lucia abolition was carried through, but the British reconquest re-established slavery in 1796.

A common policy calling into question the whole colonial, slave-owning and segregationist system, and a process of decolonization, was then embarked upon.[14]

The revolutionary government, a name given by Saint-Just from 10 October 1793 onwards to a specific form of government, became in the twentieth century the object of the most absurd interpretations.

On 9 Thermidor, the Thermidorians accused Robespierre, isolating him as a scapegoat, of aspiring to dictatorship and spread the extraordinary slander that he wanted to marry Louis XVI's daughter and re-establish the monarchy! But it was in the late nineteenth and early twentieth centuries that 'aspiring to dictatorship' changed, in historical writing, into a 'fully established dictatorship'. In this same period political theories originated which favoured the establishment of dictatorships of left or of right. Then the label 'dictatorship' was stuck on to the 'revolutionary government', with Leninist, then Stalinist and Trotskyist Marxisms all evaluating it positively. In the period 1950–60 non-Marxist historians kept the term 'dictatorship' and evaluated it negatively. In the 1970s, there were even philosophers – or those who claimed to be – who asserted that the French Revolution had been the womb of the totalitarianisms (in the plural) of the twentieth century! They needed a genocide, so they invented one: the Vendée, a regional civil war between revolution and counter-revolution, became a Franco-French genocide! Confusion had reached its high point . . .

However, it is possible to get back to the facts. From 10 August 1792 to 1795, the legislative body in France was effectively the supreme authority, according to the objectives of the theory of the Revolution as set out in the two Declarations of the Rights of Man and the Citizen from 1789 and 1793. The Constitution of 1793 established a legislative centrality according to which the legislative body, formed of a single chamber, made universally applicable laws. Executive power was decentralized, the application of the laws being carried out on the level of the commune by an elected municipal council. Moreover, the communal authorities exercised real local autonomy, as we have already seen.

On 10 October, having heard Saint-Just's report, the Convention voted for the establishment of the revolutionary government until peace was restored. What was at stake? The legislative body still made the laws. This revolution within government consisted of imposing a heavy responsibility on the elected agents of the executive, which remained decentralized, by obliging them to give accounts of their administration every ten days to the superior authority (commune, canton, *département*) which communicated these to the ministry by correspondence. Agents of the executive who did not make the laws public, or who obstructed their implementation, were removed from office and replaced by new elected representatives. It should be added that the Committee of Public Safety, created on 6 April 1793, was formed of deputies elected every month by the Convention and was responsible to it. The role of this Committee was to propose measures of public safety to the Convention, which alone made the decisions, and to exercise the right of inspection by the legislative over the ministries.

Thus the 1793 Constitution was properly applied under the Montagnard Convention as far as the organization of legislative authority was concerned. On the other hand, the revolutionary government modified the constitutional organization of the executive power that provided for the election of ministers. We can now make it clear that, contrary to the accepted view, the Constitution of 1793 was mainly put into practice except as regards this one matter of the election of ministers to the head of the executive.[15]

There was violence and repression, but for all that there was no dictatorship. Constraint was in fact considered as necessary in order to establish right and justice and to combat counter-revolution. There too, if we keep a sense of proportion, legal repression was moderate. The Revolutionary Tribunal created on 10 March 1793 and abolished on 31 May 1795,[16] passed judgement on 5215 cases, pronounced 2791 death sentences and 2424 acquittals.[17] Such moderation does not imply justification, but it should be recognized that bloodbaths were not a reality of the period.

It is however important to try to understand what path this Revolution attempted to pursue, amidst the greatest dangers: the advance of the rights of man and the citizen in the very real functioning of civil institutions where legislative power was effectively the supreme power and the agents of the executive were held responsible. The advance of the rights of man through the questioning – endlessly attempted and considered – of repression and the death penalty, as Saint-Just proposed in the Ventôse decrees by abolishing the death penalty. The central question has been posed by Jean-Pierre Faye: 'How is it possible that the time of the Terror, a repressive period if ever there was one, was at the same time, and *contradictorily*, the foundation of the anti-repressive freedoms of the West?'[18] It is this path which it is urgent to take anew.

CONCLUSION: DEFEAT OF THE RIGHTS OF MAN AND THE CITIZEN

On 26 June 1794 the military victory confirmed that of the Montagnard Convention and brought peace within reach. The opponents of the democracy of the rights of man and the citizen put an end to the experiment by organizing the plot of 9 Thermidor Year II (27 July 1794). A simple vote by the Convention enabled the arrest of those whom the Thermidorians called the *Robespierrists*, a vote followed by their immediate execution without trial.

The Thermidorian Convention transformed Fleurus' victory into a new war of conquest; five months later, in December 1794, the Rhineland and Holland were occupied. Inside France, democratic institutions were dismantled, the Commune of Paris abolished and the democratic representatives were purged. The policy of the Maximum was rescinded, the unlimited freedom of trade was re-established and the food weapon again became lethal. Martial law was re-established on 21 March 1795. Finally, the Constitution of 1793 was replaced by that of 1795. Boissy d'Anglas, who drafted it, expressed the spirit of the new political theory which was a revival of the aristocracy of the rich: 'We must be governed by the best, the best are the most educated, and you will only find such men among those who own property, are attached to the country which contains it and to the laws which protect it' (23 June 1795).

The new Constitution replaced the natural rights of man and the citizen with the rights of man in society which the Girondins had tried to impose on

29 May 1793 and for the same reasons – the new political theory of the possessing classes diverged from the humanist ethic, which we have seen operating in the Declarations of Rights of 1789 and 1793.

The war of conquest in Europe was combined with the colonial project. Boissy d'Anglas justified a form of inequality between human societies by a theory that deserves to be remembered. Against the idea of the freedom of the human being as a natural universal right he asserted that only the northern climate, which moreover he restricted to Europe and the United States, was suitable for political liberty, and that the rest of the world was condemned to suffer the domination of these countries! He thus invented an extraordinary theory of the *rights of northern men to dominate the world*.

The crude nature of such a way of thinking is evident, as is the regression it entails on the intellectual level, in comparison with the Enlightenment. The defeat of the Revolution of the rights of man and the citizen was accompanied by the defeat of the Enlightenment.

In 1802 Bonaparte finished off the defeat of the rights of man by re-establishing slavery in the colonies. The measure provoked a new revolution in St Domingue which led to the independence of the Republic of Haiti on 1 January 1804. However, slavery was re-established in Guadeloupe, despite a bitter resistance to such an abomination, and in Guyana.

No, 1795 and its consequences do not reconnect with the principles of natural right declared in 1789, and then in 1793, but illustrate the failure of the rights of man and the citizen and the triumph of the specific interest of the possessing classes, of the politics of money, of the despotism of economic power. No, Napoleon Bonaparte was not an heir of the Enlightenment, nor of the revolution of the rights of man. Let us be clear, the possessing classes, conquerors in Europe and colonialists outside Europe, carried through a counter-revolution. The revolution of the rights of man and the citizen was not a *bourgeois* revolution, but a revolution of natural humanist right which attempted to liberate humanity from the doctrinal despotism of the churches, from the despotism of the state separate from society, from the despotism of conquering economic power which was colonialist and segregationist, from the despotism of sexual difference erected into a means of domination of one sex over the other. This experiment, even if it failed, demonstrates the presence at this time of a democratic movement able to construct an economic, social and political theory based on equal exchange and the reciprocity of rights, in both domestic and foreign policy. This experiment was able to describe itself as 'popular political economy' in the framework of a 'cosmo-politics' of freedom, for it already knew that the political is necessarily global, 'cosmo-political', for empire existed since the 'discovery' of America. It was also possible for this experiment to be put into practice in 1792–94, as a genuine alternative to the feudal, capitalist and slave systems.

The Thermidorian reaction and its aftermath were the moment of a victory of the possessing classes, which opened up a process of counter-revolution against the revolution of the rights of man and the citizen. We should stress a remarkable fact, which is too often neglected – from 1795 onwards the break with the political theory of the Revolution took the form of the disappearance of a declaration of the natural rights of man and the citizen in the constitutions of France. It is true that the revolutions of 1830, 1848 and 1871 proposed to re-establish a declaration of the rights of man and the citizen, but none of them had the time to do so. The long eclipse of the declarations of natural rights lasted until . . . 1946. So it was only after the victory against Nazism that the Declaration of Rights of 1789 reappeared in French constitutional law.

The Stalinist – or the right-wing Marxist – version saw in the theory of the rights of man and the citizen merely bourgeois phraseology and divorced itself from the very concrete history of the revolutions of liberty which affirmed that the right to vote and the rights of freedom of conscience and expression were very real freedoms. For its part, the current liberal inter-pretation took part in the same concealment by limiting freedom purely to the rights of the possessing classes.

Thus history has been reduced to that of economic power by ignoring, forgetting and despising all the history of this humanist political freedom, or liberalism of reciprocal rights, which postulated that human beings were made to live freely, conceived of a civil and political liberty in opposition to slavery and theorized the practical forms of freedom in society with the aim – still relevant today – of overcoming the dangers inherent in the exercise of political powers or, more precisely, 'cosmo-political' powers. Slavery or freedom for the whole of humanity.

Liberals, Jacobins and Grey Masses in 1917

Mike Haynes

HISTORY SHIFTS

On 13 December 1917, Morgan Philips Price, the *Guardian* correspondent in Russia, wrote from Petrograd that the Bolsheviks were 'incapable of constructive work. They are destructive Jacobins who believe that by flaming decrees, passionate speeches, terrorism and the guillotine that they can create a worldly paradise.' Yet two weeks later he wrote to his sister that, despite rapidly worsening physical conditions, 'physically starving, I was mentally fed with the joyful news that Russia, Red, Revolutionary triumphant Russia had overthrown her capitalist tyrants, burst her chains and had set out on the road to peace'.[1] Price was possibly the best-informed Western correspondent in Russia during the Revolution. He had lived there for several years, his Russian was fluent and he had travelled widely to report on the progress of the Revolution. His uncertain attempts to understand what was going on around him show how difficult it was at the time to make sense of the Russian Revolution and its wider significance. He had no sense that two decades later the twentieth anniversary of the Revolution would be celebrated in a country in the grip of Stalin's dictatorship with several hundred thousand executed in that year and millions imprisoned. In 1917–18, the Revolution seemed to Price to be an attempt to end a bloody world war that he opposed, to halt the slide into chaos within Russia and to unblock the stalemate that appeared to exist in the wider world. But Price was also torn by the way that the struggle for power – even in a revolution based on mass participation – also involved an element of realpolitik and force.

In mainstream historiography, this has always been seen to lend the Revolution an element of illegitimacy and to point forward to Stalinism. The Stalinist regime itself claimed to derive directly from 1917 even as it murdered many of those on the left who had taken part in the events of that year. In this sense Soviet and Cold War Western writing tended to have a mirror image quality – while the former proclaimed 'continuity, good', the latter said 'continuity, bad'. The so-called 'social history school' of Western historians in the 1970s and 1980s offered a partial challenge to this, presenting a view of the Revolution as a mass popular uprising in which the Bolsheviks were as much pushed as pushing. But it was only a partial challenge, for when it came to the issue of how deep a break Stalinism was few were prepared to declare it complete.[2] Hence, when Soviet society collapsed in 1991 the past equivocations came home. It was not so much that these historians dis-covered a truth that they had hitherto not known. It was hardly the case that they were ignorant of the brutality of Stalinism. Rather, they lost a handhold for their ambiguity in the power of an existing state. They were sent spinning in their analysis, sometimes ending with conclusions that were almost the opposite of what they had argued earlier.[3]

The most important reversal, if only in terms of readership, came from Orlando Figes in his *A People's Tragedy: The Russian Revolution 1891–1924*, a work which attempted to do for the Russian Revolution what Simon Schama's *Citizens* had attempted for the French Revolution nearly a decade before. For Figes, author of a major study of the peasantry in war and revolution, 'the ghosts of 1917 have still not been laid to rest'. His book was intended to help this by showing how the tragedy of the Revolution flowed from over-ambition and violence. If 'liberal-democratic triumphalism' had been overdone in the wake of 1991, liberal democracy itself was now the only way forward. This was not least the case in Russia where what was then called the 'Red-Brown' alliance of fascists and ex-Stalinists, in 'their violent rhetoric, . . . class for discipline and order . . . [and] angry condemnation of the inequalities produced by the growth of capitalism, and . . . xenophobic rejection of the West' reflected conceptions which they had 'adapted from the Bolshevik tradition'.[4]

Yet this revisionism of the revisionists is a return to a much older agenda, albeit dressed up in the fashionable language of the day. The Revolution was, in its own terms, 'premature'. Despite Engels' warning in 1895 that 'the time has passed for revolutions accomplished through the sudden seizure of power by small conscious minorities at the head of unconscious masses', the October Revolution was exactly such an insurrectionary Jacobin coup.[5] And what-ever the degree of class consciousness attained by some workers, this was more than compromised by the way the popular movement also spawned violence of a more brutal kind from the darker, greyer side of the lower classes stimulated by and incorporated into Bolshevism.[6] Thus the Revolu-tion necessarily unravelled towards Stalinism because of its internal contradictions. There was no betrayal of the revolution by Stalin – only a more or less logical development from it.

The effect of this shift has been profoundly conservative. In Russian terms it helped to legitimize by default the choices not made in 1917. But it also helped to legitimize the new regime of the 1990s by ruling out the idea of more radical change from below. Not only was there no alternative to the substantial social continuity at the top of society in Russia and other parts of the former USSR, but it was apparently now sufficient for the old/new leaders to declare their abandonment of past totalitarian views and their mistaken faith in Lenin and Marx in order to secure their place in the present. But the effect extended beyond Russia. 1917 was the most sustained mass revolutionary episode in world history since 1789 and if it necessarily ended badly then what does that say about the possibility of radical change in the future?

Yet there is a puzzle in this argument. Despite well-known views to the contrary, most Western specialists have been sceptical of the idea that tsarist Russia could have developed into a prosperous constitutional democracy.[7] Since the collapse of the Soviet Union this view has not fundamentally changed. Historians in Russia, freed of the need to toe a party line, have written more positively on tsarism but, East and West, once we discount the nostalgia and the fairly blatant attempts to use history to legitimate the post-1991 transition, what is remarkable is how limited the revisionism has been.[8] This creates a paradox in much of the writing on 1917 – it is more a critique of the choices that were made by Lenin and the Bolsheviks than a direct attempt to vindicate the choices that were *not* made and the possibilities that did *not* occur. The Bolsheviks are damned for what they did, implicitly absolving others for the responsibility for what they did or did not do. How tenable is this view?

LIBERAL DILEMMAS AND COMPROMISES

In 1856 in London Alexander Herzen published the programme of Russia's first group publicly aspiring to emulate Western European-style liberalism: 'Liberalism! This is the slogan of every educated and sensible person in Russia. This is the banner which can unite around it people of all spheres, all classes, all tendencies . . . In liberalism lies the whole future of Russia.'[9] Why did this prove false?

An obvious answer is provided by the famous argument penned by Peter Struve in his early days as a Marxist that, 'the further east one goes in Europe, the meaner, more cowardly and politically weak the bourgeoisie becomes, and the greater are the cultural and political tasks that fall to the proletariat'.[10]

When Struve wrote these words he believed that the limited development of capitalism in Russia also limited the possibility of liberalism. But in the following years he abandoned his 'Marxism', eventually emerging as Russia's leading 'liberal conservative' in the first half of the twentieth century. His subsequent belief that progress was possible through mutual accommodation reflected an idealist approach. Liberalism did not have to be anchored in capitalism or a strong middle class. It could derive as much from ideological and cultural commitment. But if this is the case why was this commitment not made? The answer for those who accept Struve's starting point is both ideological and tactical. For historians like Schapiro and Pipes, liberalism in Russia, both as an ideology and a party political force, was compromised and undermined because many of those who should have been liberal mixed their ideas and politics with elements of *populism* and *radicalism*.[11] Beyond this was then the issue of tactics, especially after 1905, with some blaming tsarism for refusing an accommodation with Russian 'liberalism' and others blaming Russian 'liberalism' for rejecting the hand of tsarism. It is not our intention here to discount such issues, but to the extent that they played a role then, contrary to Struve's later argument, they need to be set in the context of the pattern of social and economic development. The irony of Struve's vision is that the political insight of the younger man perhaps holds the best key to the failure of the political project of the older man.

Why should bourgeois liberalism be 'meaner, more cowardly and politically weak' in a country like Russia? It was Trotsky who laid out the most satisfactory social analysis of this in his writings on Russian development before and after 1905.[12] His analysis of Russia's early development drew on liberal accounts, notably those of Miliukov, in seeing tsarism as a political form that dominated the social estates. This domination partly reflected the backwardness of Russia, though he rejected the view that Russia was so backward that it was the state which created the estates. But autocratic domination also arose from the way that the Russian state had to carve a geopolitical space for itself against hostile neighbours, especially in the west. This forced it to privilege military needs and to exploit the peasants to pay for them – a process which then helped to perpetuate the backwardness that became increasingly evident in the nineteenth century. Had Russia been left to its own devices then over the very long run it might have developed more independent estates and an autonomous middle class. But capitalism developed as an international system and did not allow this space. Global development began to pull Russia into the world economy. This led to what Trotsky called a pattern of 'uneven and combined development' where the larger elements of backwardness existed alongside the smaller elements of modernity, interacting with and reinforcing one another. So far as liberalism was concerned the consequence was the speedy development of a small and more modern bourgeoisie whose role derived less from a 'natural' internal development than the inflow of foreign funds and state sponsored industrialization. Although consumer goods production was the major part of industrial output before 1914 (and even more so if smaller scale industry is included) the more dynamic element in economic growth came from the state through state-sponsored industry and protection. This helped to create a greater gap between big and small capital in Russia than was found in the West and a greater dependency of big capital on tsarism. But the relationship was not entirely one-sided. In trying to control the social and political consequences of uneven development, the tsarist autocracy might not have been at one on a whole range of issues with the wider business class but, if only in its own interests, it had to recognize and respond to their economic role.[13] This (inter)dependency made the Russian bourgeoisie ill-placed socially and economically to challenge tsarism politically. Worse, this process also created a small but concentrated working class and did nothing to solve the problems of the mass of the peasants so that, unlike in Western Europe, it was harder to develop them as a bastion of small propertied support in defence of 'order'. Thus the bourgeoisie had also had reason on its left to fear provoking too radical a confrontation with the authorities.

Indeed, Trotsky argued, this created a situation where the Constitutional Democrats or Cadets, the main liberal party, drew heavily on sections of the gentry and the intelligentsia and professions for the mainstay of its support. This social base, at a tangent to Russian industry, trade and commerce as a social force, allowed Russian liberalism to dally with radical programmes. But insofar as liberals sought to find a base and reflect the interests of these more authentically bourgeois groups they had to develop a more conservative politics in practice. This dilemma ripened between 1905 and February 1917.

The high point of reform in Russia came in the midst of the 1905 revolution with the tsar's October Manifesto. Even in liberal circles there was sharp disagreement about the extent of the concessions this involved. But what can be less doubted is that in constitutional terms every step that followed involved a retreat from any serious form of constitutional democracy. This forced liberals into a defensive holding operation, which was never completely secure (evidenced both by the plots of ministers against the third and fourth Dumas and their alienation of much of the Octobrist support that had existed in 1905–7). The Stolypin *coup d'état* of 3 June 1907 further narrowed what Miliukov called the 'pseudo-constitution' that emerged from 1905, by violating the fundamental laws and disbanding the second Duma and then changing the electoral laws to make them even more restricted. But the political substance of what followed, as reflected in the elections to the third Duma, was easily summarized by Miliukov for an American audience in early 1908:

> About thirty thousand large proprietors received the right to elect the majority of the third Duma. Practically no more than nineteen thousand came to the polls, and they chose for the electoral colleges more than half of the electors for the whole of Russia, 2,618 out of 5,160. The remaining 2,542 might belong entirely to the opposition; the majority was in advance assured to the large land-owners. Thus there is no exaggeration in saying that the majority of the present Duma is elected by 19,000 proprietors of the larger landed estates. They control 300 and odd members, while only 100 to 150 members represent large democratic masses and belong to the opposition. Some of them as, for instance, the St. Petersburg delegates are chosen by a larger vote (20,000 each) than all three hundred members of the majority.[14]

This attempt to narrow the political space created in 1905 did not arise simply from a wilful defence of autocracy. Rather it arose from a recognition that genuine democratization would open up the question of wider social reform. Miliukov argued that the consequence of 1905 had been to draw the autocracy and nobility closer together in the face of peasant disturbance. He spoke, only partly ironically, of the fears that now beset the gentry.

> It is now common to hear of country houses transformed into veritable castles, manned with armed forces hired from Caucasian warrior tribes, to protect the noble homes. On some estates searchlights are actually used at night to disclose the invisible foes who come to burn the house or even blow up its inhabitants.[15]

Indeed the Stolypin reforms were not, as so often presented by Western historians, a step towards a more adequate capitalism, but an attempt by the nobility to set the peasant community against itself and so avoid losing their own lands either to some compensated scheme of state land purchase or even more radical rural change.[16]

The existence of this 'pseudo-constitutional' regime, which seemingly became more 'pseudo' over time, did indeed pose tactical issues for liberal forces, whether the more conservative Octobrists, the Progressives or the Cadets themselves. Political stances on constitutional issues and relations with tsarism did not always coincide with wider political programmes. The Cadets, for example, despite their often sharp attacks, were more co-operative than they had been in the first and second Dumas. Indeed, they were sometimes politically to the right of the smaller group of Progressives who were otherwise to the right of the Cadets in terms of their social programme. But none of these groups wanted a return to the confrontation that had occurred in 1905 and the reason for this was more than tactical.[17]

Despite its unevenness Russian capitalism was strengthening. The years 1908–14 saw a second industrial surge and a period of relative prosperity, which gave greater confidence to the business community and some of its Young Turks like Paul Riabushinskii and Alexander Konovalov. In 1912 Riabushinskii had declared that 'the merchant is coming', and one business paper wrote that

> Our New Year's toast is raised in honour of the bourgeoisie, the Third Estate of contemporary Russia; to this force which is gaining strength and is growing mightily, which thanks to the spiritual and material riches inhering in it has already left far behind the degenerating *dvorianstvo* [landed aristocracy] and the bureaucracy which controls the country's destinies . . .[18]

But this growth also had its effects on the workers and was reflected in the recovery of the labour movement after 1910–11 from the repression and downturn that followed 1905. That year had shown that liberal hopes might be put at risk by actions on the street and in the factories. The elections to the second Duma (also based on an indirect but wider franchise than the third and fourth), in which the parties of the left had stood and done well, also showed that beyond political reform might come social reforms leading in an undesired direction. While Miliukov and other leading figures had few qualms about attacking the nobility and gentry, they were less enthusiastic about arguments that threatened the power of the lords of industry and trade. In this sense the classic liberal dilemma of having to steer a path between right and left heightened in these years and all the more so because the restrictions on wider political activity by the authorities deprived politics in the Duma of the wider base that parliamentary politics was developing elsewhere in Europe.[19]

But there was another element to this ambiguity and ambivalence. After the military humiliation in the Russo-Japanese War and diplomatic humiliation in the 1908–9 Bosnian crisis, tsarism sought to recover its status through the so-called 'Great Programme', which, especially through the expansion of the navy, was intended to underpin a major step forward in military power. This was attractive not only to conservative forces. Struve articulated a vision of Russian liberal imperialism. In 1908 he talked of 'Great Russia', echoing Stolypin. Struve's nationalism led him to articulate a mystique of the Russian state alongside a more pragmatic concern with economic interests. He saw 'liberal imperialism' as a way of re-enforcing the national ideal: 'the touchstone and yardstick of all so-called domestic politics of government as well as [political] parties ought to lie in the answer to the question; in what measure does the policy further the so-called external power of the state?' 'Russian liberalism will always doom itself to impotence until such a time as it acknowledges itself to be Russian and national.'[20] But there was a contradiction here. Struve's arguments, said Pokrovsky from the left, meant demanding 'from one and the same plant that it blooms with roses and tasty pears . . . You can only have one and naturally, the practical bosses of Mr Struve have always preferred pears to roses. First you must have enough to eat – and the various pleasant things in life can wait.'[21] Struve's national and imperial call was not immediately embraced by all liberals but, because liberalism was cast within a national great-power framework, the pull to these poles, if necessary at the expense of other reforms, was evident in Russia no less than elsewhere in Europe.

Moreover the drive to improve Russia's position as a great power also had direct socio-economic effects leading to military expenditure with an emphasis on munitions and shipbuilding which, Gatrell showed some time ago, explains the pre-war boom as much as more autonomous consumer expansion does. In the extreme case of the Putilov works the output of railway equipment fell from 53.3 per cent to 29.6 per cent of total production between 1900 and 1912 while defence products rose from 14.6 per cent to 45.8 per cent in the same period.[22] Thus whatever the tensions with tsarism politically, the economic tie was still very real.

War resolved these tensions by bringing liberalism in all its forms into the *union sacrée* to fight what was portrayed as a defensive war, albeit one that provided the opportunity to achieve expansionist war aims. Of course, the patriotic wave swept up part of the socialist movement too, but in Russia it was the liberals' final compromise with tsarism that was the most important immediate effect of the war. Much to the embarrassment of the right of the Cadet Party, the newspaper *Rech* was initially closed for a day by the censor who feared its previous opposition to war in the build-up of the crisis. But when the Duma met for one day on July 26 it was Miliukov who overcame resistance in the Cadet Party from those who accepted the war but still wanted to extract an internal price for support. 'We are united in this struggle; we set no conditions and we demand nothing.' There was, said Miliukov later, 'only one condition for our collaboration with the government – victory'. The Cadets had effectively adopted the earlier arguments of Struve even if he now moved further to the right as they did so.[23] The Cadet statement to the Duma spoke of 'our first duty [being] to preserve [Russia's] position as a world power' and in support of the defence of this, 'let us postpone our domestic disputes, let us not give our adversary even the slightest excuse for relying on the differences which divided us'.[24] It was Miliukov's strong support for using the war to increase Russian power especially in the South that led to him being called 'Miliukov-Dardanelsky'. In his memoirs he implies that he saw this epithet as a partial compliment. Anxious to show how this support fitted in with the needs of a modernizing Russian capitalism, he quoted approvingly a contemporary who wrote that his position was 'based not on the old Slavophile mystic ideology but in the tremendous fact of the rapid economic development of the Russian South which can no longer remain without free access to the sea'.[25] But it is difficult also to avoid the argument that no less than for government itself, indeed perhaps more so, war offered the liberals the chance to overcome tensions in their position by seeking a resolution or path to a more civil redemption through war. In spring 1916 Morgan Philips Price wrote to C.P. Trevelyan in England that

> the intellectuals and bourgeois, merchants and capitalists, who constitute the Cadet and kindred parties . . . are the most keen for carrying on the war to the end, and the most bitter haters of everything German in the country . . . These Progressives, or Russian liberals . . . are . . . on all foreign questions [the] most chauvinist of any party in Russia, and are great believers in war to the last gasp as a means of saving Russia internally.[26]

' "Literary chauvinism" considerably outweighed the actual mood even of pretty bourgeois circles', Alexander Shlyapnikov later wrote.[27] It is characteristic of the inversion of values that patriotic war enthusiasm produced in liberal circles that Miliukov could unselfconsciously condemn 'international socialism' for fanning 'into blazing flame the social hostility of the people' to such an extent that they carried away 'the elements of truly healthy internationalism not beneath but above – in the cultural strata, in ideas, and institutions' – strata, in reality, most enthusiastic about national war.[28]

The government was more than happy to exploit this gift to its own advantage. Rodzianko, as the Octobrist leader of the Duma, and Miliukov, as Cadet leader, were both anxious to keep politics within the Duma. Miliukov had to go further and also try to hold the line against more radical tendencies within the Cadet Party. Cadet policy was symbolized by his comment on 14 February 1917, the day of the opening of the last ever session of the Duma, that 'our only deeds are our words'. The maximum demand that the Duma moderates would support was 'a minority enjoying national confidence', not 'a ministry responsible to the Duma' – hoping, said one *Okhrana* report, 'to effect a peaceful revolution? or evolution?, clandestinely, with the sanction of the government itself'.[29]

The equivocations that this produced in the Duma were well discussed in English by Raymond Pearson and subsequent research has largely filled out his account.[30] The result was that liberals had also to share the responsibility for the war and its effects. Of course they would have preferred a 'clean' and efficient war on their own side, the better to carry out the killing of the other side. National war was legitimate and necessary. The illegitimate thing was to try to stop the war short of final victory, which is what happened in 1917.[31] But the responsibility for the scale of the blood that was spilled did not lie, said Chkeidze in the Duma in July 1915, at the door of the government alone:

> The Fourth Imperial Duma was, on the whole, at one with the Government. Not only the Reactionaries but even our Imperialists from the Capitalist classes and a considerable portion of the Radical Russian Intelligentsia have considered union with the Government a source of new strength. The Fourth Duma has undertaken . . . co-operation with the Government, and within the limits of the present regime . . .[32]

It is worth pausing for a moment on the dimensions of the bloodshed that followed not simply because of the light it throws on liberal predilections for certain types of violence but because, while the general link between war and revolution is well understood, the very direct ways in which the pain and violence of war might have contributed to the anger and violence of revolution is less commented on.

We know that before April 1917 mobilization added 13.7 million to the peacetime army of 1.4 million and several hundred thousand after.[33] We only know the number of Russian dead within huge margins of error. A recent authoritative demographic count prefers to give upper and lower bounds, which range from 1.7 million to 3.37 million.[34] These are all aggregate statistics. Measuring what they meant to people is more difficult. It seems likely that many hundreds of thousands of deaths were never even reported to families at home. Parents, wives (a sample study showed that 65.6 per cent of troops killed, wounded and missing were married) and children therefore waited in vain for sons, husbands and fathers who would never return.[35] If tsarism could not keep track, perhaps some hoped the post-February regime could: 'in the months that separated the two revolutions,' writes Catherine Merridale, 'the Petrograd Soviet was bombarded with letters testifying to this disorientation, loss and pain. Tens of thousands wanted help in finding their missing relatives – "at least tell me they are dead, so that I can pray for them" – while others pleaded for their sons and husbands to come home. "They have taken them all," one woman wrote, now hoping that a democratic government would make amends.'[36]

For those who did come back there were physical and mental scars of war. Again the figures are imprecise. 5.148 million were hospitalized in the rear according to one set of statistics, 2.8 million from wounds and 2.3 million from illness but this includes some double counting. On the other hand it excludes large numbers treated at the front. A significant minority of all of these would carry some disability for life.[37] Psychological scarring was also widespread. S.A. Preobrazhenskii, who became a shell-shock expert, suggested that psychological casualties were four times as numerous as physical ones. An estimated 1.5 million veterans were too ill to return to work or normal family lives.[38]

War also led directly to the creation of a huge refugee population. By January 1917 some 4.9 million refugees had been registered and there were perhaps another half a million unregistered refugees.[39] Refugees fled partly to escape the fighting, especially in the retreats of 1915. The demographer Volkov gave a figure of over 300,000 members of the civil population killed in the fighting on the Eastern Fronts. But others were forced to move by the Russian military because they were considered suspect Poles, Germans and, above all, Jews. Official policy, opposed it is true by the liberals though not always to the limit, helped to legitimize a pogrom atmosphere. In turn, in some areas dispossessed, displaced and diseased refugees themselves took to looting and violence as they sought security.[40]

Neither the physical nor the psychological impact of the violence that war brought with it could be contained at the front. 'The war', said Alexander Blok, 'was when humanity really turned brutal and the Russian patriots in particular'.[41] Gorky, often quoted as a critic of 'irrational mob violence' in 1917, also made this point.[42] 'Human life has become cheap, very cheap, too cheap. For a fourth year human blood is being spilled, for a fourth year mankind gives up to the Moloch of war its finest achievement – its priceless gift – its life . . . Man has lost the best aspects of this nature, love and compassion.'[43] The February Revolution would do nothing to stop this. On 25 March Kamenev wrote that Russia 'had asked for peace, and they [the previous regime] gave her a river of blood, bitterness and corpses' but soon the accusation would be made no less about the Provisional Government.[44]

The February Revolution occurred in spite of, rather than because of, anything that Russian liberals did. Indeed they were desperate to avoid it. In the short term Miliukov rose to the occasion but neither he nor any other political or social leader could overcome the legacy of the past and the way that February intensified the dilemmas of liberalism by the huge shift to the left in the popular mood. The first Provisional Government would give way to three coalitions in the short time before it fell in October.

After February the Cadets became the authentic focus of bourgeois support drawing to them business figures and groups that had hitherto kept a varying distance. Kerensky said that they now 'organised all the political and social forces of the country representing the interests of the propertied classes, the high command, the remains of the old bureaucracy, and even fragments of the aristocracy'; Rosenberg describes them as 'the political core of bourgeois Russia'.[45] But with the radicalization that occurred they had no hope of establishing a mass base that could compete with the parties of the left. Their membership probably arose to around 100,000 but their electoral fortunes, though varying, were weak. Even in Petrograd and Moscow, wrote Rosenberg, 'Russia's first elections of the revolutionary period show the Cadets with a staggering loss of city influence and prestige in the two strongest areas of past support'. This weakness, evident in the next months in other elections, was confirmed with the vote for the Constituent Assembly, which gave them only 6–7 per cent of the national total. Thus 'with their own limited natural constituency, the Cadets themselves could never claim to rule on the basis of representative principles', argued Rosenberg.[46]

How then were they to achieve their ends of continuing the war to maintain and extend Russia's position as a great power and to stabilize it internally? One way was ideological, through constant insistence that the Revolution had clear limits that should not be transgressed – a view which they tried to impress not only on the wider public debate but especially on leaders to the left of them.[47] Beyond this, it was necessary to try to manipulate the political process through internal and external pressures on the Provisional Government. Indeed, politics at the top between February and October came to have an element of chicken about it. Speaking at the First Congress of Soviets Tsereteli said that, 'the Right says, let the Left run the Government, and we and the country will draw our conclusions; and the Left says, let the Right take hold, and we and the country will draw our conclusions . . . Each side hopes that the other will make such a failure, that the country will turn to it for leadership.'[48] Yet it is surely striking that in this contest each major crisis of the Provisional Government involved the liberal-bourgeois elements either abandoning it completely or abandoning it temporarily to bring pressure on it. When the Cadets left the Provisional Government (over possible Ukrainian separation) Kerensky denounced them: 'On the front, thousands are giving up their lives – and you here, you desert your posts and smash the government.'[49]

It was the inability to make this pressure work to stabilize the situation that increasingly disposed key figures and social groups to look beyond 'politics' towards a military saviour. In this sense, the intricacies of who did what in the run-up to the failed Kornilov coup are neither here nor there. Indeed given some of the indecisiveness in the past and the current stakes it is not surprising that figures like Miliukov may have hoped for rather than actively encouraged Kornilov's plans. The significant point is that a coup of some sort increasingly seemed to be the only way out. And when the half-hearted one attempted by Kornilov failed, the same imperatives remained. Unless the crisis was resolved in some other way it was only a matter of time before another attempt was made. Indeed if we follow Richard Pipes in seeing Peter Struve as the liberal who had the courage to see earlier and more clearly than other liberals what was necessary, then it is significant that he was not disheartened by the collapse of Kornilov's venture, thinking that another time would come.[50]

JACOBINISM AND REVOLUTION

This failure of bourgeois liberalism to imprint itself on Russia had been anticipated by the left. The solution, as the left saw it, was therefore for revolutionary democracy to help clear the path to a capitalist, bourgeois, democratic regime. This view was shared by almost all the left before 1914 including Lenin, save for some left Socialist Revolutionaries (SRs) and Trotsky who, as we have seen, had begun to develop the basis of an alternative argument. The strength of the commitment to the idea of 'bourgeois democratic revolution' derived from the belief that capitalism had to and would develop nationally before socialism became possible. What the left had to do, therefore, was assist in this development by encouraging the most radical democratization while defending the interests of the workers and peasants.

Trotsky's theory of permanent revolution broke with these limits. Capitalism was an international system creating contradictions in a country like Russia that prevented it travelling the road that Western Europe had travelled. The war also pushed Lenin, Bukharin and others to a similar position, especially in the context of the way that capitalism had moved into an imperialist phase where national and international contradictions and war become more closely meshed together.[51]

But to their critics on the left, then and since, this was seen to lead only to an adventurist attempt to overstep the bounds of the possible. However, the rejection of the argument rests less on a rejection of its analysis of the contradictory pattern of development – as I have tried to show, the experience of Russia confirms it – than on its consequences.

We can take as an example Baruch Knei-Paz's sympathetic but critical account of Trotsky's argument. For Knei-Paz the problem is not Trotsky's analysis of the contradictions of backwardness but the political consequences of this argument in the idea of 'permanent revolution'. Trotsky argued the working class would be forced to the front, could take power and inaugurate a wider European revolution which would then help the weak reactionary state break out of its backwardness. But, argues Knei-Paz, the very back-wardness which pushed the working class forward also had its 'vengeance' in making this working class too weak to take and sustain power itself. This is a good example of the approach to the revolution that sees it as deriving from a problem with no solution – a view that Knei-Paz, like most other historians, does not state explicitly but the sense of which permeates his account. Seeking to impose a solution to this contradiction led Trotsky and the Bolsheviks more widely to 'over-estimate . . . the workers and mass con-sciousness'. From this it followed that Trotsky, no less than Lenin, had to support the substitution of party for the weak class, adopting a Jacobin model which Trotsky had once attacked Lenin for holding. As Knei-Paz puts it, the theory of permanent revolution 'could not be put into practice without Lenin and the Bolsheviks' and this Jacobin model was not only the secret of the success of the Bolsheviks in 1917 but also their subsequent downfall.[52]

This deployment of the concept of Jacobinism has a long history but, as we suggested earlier, the critique of 'Bolshevik-Jacobinism' and what Trotsky once called 'Maximilian Lenin' has gained new force. It is important therefore to make some distinctions. Firstly, there is the real Jacobinism of the French Revolution, which is discussed elsewhere in this volume. Secondly, there is the rhetorical evocation of the French Revolution and its imagined categories in the course of subsequent revolutions. The power of the image of revolutionary France has been so strong that a sense of it has suffused debate for two centuries, and in Russia in 1917 it was everywhere from the use of the term 'citizen' to the singing of the 'Marseillaise' to the use of its terminology as a crutch for contemporary political debate.[53] However, the sense of Jacobinism as it is currently deployed is more specific than this. It is an argument about substitutionism – the substitution of a minority in the name of the majority through a party-led insurrectionary coup – and it is in these terms that it is wielded against Lenin, Trotsky and the Bolsheviks in 1917.

But what those who use this argument have failed to notice is that October can just as easily be seen as a democratic attempt to resolve a Jacobin dilemma that much of the rest of the left created for itself and which had led *it* into a cul-de-sac. What these less radical sections objected to was not 'substitution-ism' *per se* but what they saw as substitutionism for 'socialism'. What they defended and practiced, and what was ultimately their downfall, was their own 'substitutionism' for a failed bourgeoisie – ironically, in terms of the normal argument, a more authentic form of Jacobinism.

The left initially resisted the idea of participation in the Provisional Government precisely on the grounds that it was a bourgeois government with bourgeois tasks. Only Kerensky broke with this position. With the three coalition governments, both the SRs and the Mensheviks effectively began to play the role of substitutionism believing that they now had to assist in carrying out the bourgeois revolution when the bourgeoisie would not. They were trapped into this role because, as Neil Harding once said, 'they bucked the argument' of reconsidering what was happening in the Russian Revolution. The mainstream of the SR party and the Mensheviks remained

> rooted in the synthesis of 1905 (economic analysis – comparatively low development of capitalism, derivative political practice – the realisation of the democratic revolution). In 1917 they bitterly criticised Lenin's proposals for an advance to socialist practice but made little or no attempt to confront the theoretical basis for which this was derived.[54]

The dilemmas that arose from this were most obvious in the divisions among the Mensheviks over what to do. For Potresov it was necessary at all costs to 'secure the responsible participation of progressive elements of the bourgeoisie', though it is striking that such formulations implied that the onus in maintaining the role of the bourgeoisie did not so much lie on the shoulders of the bourgeoisie itself as on the left. With the withdrawal of the Cadets from the first coalition in July this dilemma grew. The main Menshevik leadership seemed to say that any bourgeois ally would now do, in order to give credibility to the bourgeois revolution in which the bourgeoisie was actually playing a tiny role.

> The Soviets are supported only by a minority of the population, and we must strive by all means to have those bourgeois elements, which are still able and willing to defend with us the conquests of the revolution, take over with us . . . the enormous responsibility for the fate of the revolution.

But who were these remaining bourgeois elements? If they existed at all they appeared to be quite marginal, certainly they did not include the Cadets:

> The conduct of the Cadet Party must be regarded as treacherous and criminal. It refused to submit to the demands of democracy and deserted the Government, so as to leave the still inadequately organised and struggling revolutionary democracy, but especially the proletariat, alone to fight against

the chaos and the growing counter-revolution. Equally treacherous and criminal is the conduct of the industrialists who are secretly contributing to the disorganisation of economic life, so as to force the helpless working class to accept their own terms . . .[55]

At this point Trotsky was chiding those who held such views as being calves to the tigers of the real Jacobins.[56]

Further to the left, Martov seemed to want to be such a 'tiger'. With the temporary withdrawal of the Cadets from the Provisional Government in early July he argued that 'the last organised group of the Russian bourgeoisie had turned its back on the Revolution' and was going over 'to the attack against the peasants' and workers' democracy'. It was therefore necessary to respond 'by taking over state power'; 'there is only one proper decision for us at present: history demands that we take power into our own hands. The Revolutionary Parliament [the Congress of Soviets] is bound to take account of this. . .' But still, it seemed, only with the aim of carrying out the most radical democratization and reform without ultimately compromising capitalism in Russia in order to be able to hand power back (in what way?) at some later stage to the bourgeoisie. The Kornilov coup magnified these contradictions even more because much of the left now drew the conclusion that no coalition was possible with the bourgeoisie or its political representatives. Postresov, faithful to the logic of bourgeois revolution, denounced the refusal of a coalition as 'worse than Bolshevism. This is absurdity', but the idea that 'revolutionary democracy' could substitute for the bourgeoisie was implicit in the arguments that the non-Bolsheviks (and now left SRs) remained committed to.[57]

In the immediate aftermath of October Martov went back to Marx and Engels to find grounds for attacking 'Bolshevik Jacobinism', but his discussion (only partially unwittingly?) caught the pre-October dilemma just as well. While Marx and Engels had emancipated themselves from earlier Jacobin conceptions, suggested Martov, they had also recognized the possibility of a 'premature' conquest (Marx), 'a fortuitous conquest' (Martov) of power by the people or their leaders before the stage of maturity for socialism was reached. This, however could only be a 'momentary' political domination over the bourgeoisie on the basis not of 'conscious masses' but 'masses which are simply in revolt' (Martov). Whoever allowed this would then have to play the Jacobin role of making the bourgeois revolution for the bourgeoisie – but was this more a description of the Bolsheviks or of the socialists who were supporting the Provisional Government?

In making this argument, the aim is to do more than stand the normal approach on its head for its own sake. The fact that the SR and Menshevik leaderships tried to carry out this role of *limiting* one revolution, if necessary against the opposition of the groups they claimed to represent, whilst *carrying out* another in the interests of the groups that they opposed, created enormous contradictions for them. If they were to play the role of Jacobins to the bourgeoisie they had also to play the role of Jacobins against their own supporters and, to some extent their own desires. This was put clearly by A.V. Peshekhonov, who had been the Popular Socialist Minister of Food from May to August, in a passage quoted by Lenin in his pamphlet 'Can the Bolsheviks Retain State Power?'

> In essence these demands are just. But this programme which we fought for before the revolution, for the sake of which we made the revolution, and which we would all unanimously support under other circumstances constitutes a very grave danger under present conditions . . . when it is impossible for the state to comply with [these demands]. We must first defend the whole – the state, to save it from doom, and there is only one way to do that; not the satisfaction of demands, however just and cogent they may be, but, on the contrary, restriction and sacrifice, which must be contributed from all quarters.[58]

This contradiction eventually exacted a fatal political price for the Mensheviks and SRs. First, it had an impact on the level of active support for both the Revolution and these parties. In the autumn of 1917, two tendencies are evident as popular frustration grew with what had been achieved – there is evidence of both a shift to a more passive position in some quarters and a shift to greater radicalism in others. In one sense, this is characteristic of the peak that occurs in any genuinely revolutionary situation since such a situation cannot be sustained indefinitely. Seizing the moment is then the centre of the crisis. Allowing it to pass does not mean that the crisis will fall back to some lower level of compromise – it is more likely, and certainly was more likely in Russia in 1917, to open up the possibility of another attempted coup from the right. The radicalization, however, provided the opportunity for the party that benefited from it to take more decisive action. Thus in late August and September 1917 we see SR and Menshevik support in both local elections and the elections to the Soviets shifting significantly to the Bolsheviks, giving them a number of spectacular victories.

The crisis was no less evident in the haemorrhaging of the membership from the Mensheviks and what Melancon calls a 'stampede' from the SRs towards the Bolsheviks. Fragmentation grew within these parties as their base was pulled to the left. Among the Mensheviks we know that by their August conference only some 5 per cent of the delegates supported Postresov and the right, 55 per cent the centre's 'revolutionary defencism' associated with Liber and Dan, and the remainder different left platforms – support for which sees to have grown in the period that followed. But the most spectacular tension arose within the SRs, where a left SR faction that eventually became the Left SR Party crystallized, and took with it at least half the party and possibly the majority of members.

These tendencies forced the leaderships of these parties to rise even more above their members. The internal political separation of the leadership grew further, weakening claims to legitimacy. This was most notably the case in the SRs. As early as their May congress the left SRs had got only one seat on the Central Committee despite having the support of some 20 per cent of delegates and on some motions 40 per cent. By August and September many more sections of the party had swung to the left, causing the Central Committee to expel the Petrograd, Voronezh and Tashkent organizations for being too left wing. As electoral lists were drawn up for the Constituent Assembly, they were weighted in favour of the centre and at the expense of the left. The decision to join the last coalition caused a huge row in which the Central Committee rode down opposition. It opposed calling both the party congress and second All-Russian Congress of Soviets, it then discouraged delegates from attending until it thought this might backfire. The main leaders then walked out with the Mensheviks and expelled the left SRs who remained behind, seizing the party's assets so the left was forced to establish a new party. Thus, while it may be that up to 60 per cent of the delegates at the Constituent Assembly were SR in one form or another, the claim that this entitled the centre-right SRs to form a government over the Bolsheviks and the Left SRs ignores the way the group at the top had effectively stolen the party from its members and the left, who were allowed a mere 40 representatives at the Assembly.[59]

This points to an interesting conclusion that few historians have been prepared to confront – Bolshevik successes in 1917 reflected the fact that they were a substantially more democratic organization than their competitors. Their membership grew throughout the period, the party welcomed groups like the Inter-District Group, it was able to incorporate new figures into its leadership, there was not the same social differentiation that was apparent in the other parties and there was not the same differentiation in political perspectives because there was a serious and lively debate about what was happening that mattered not only in an intellectual sense but also in a political sense. But were the workers, as Martov said, not 'conscious masses' but 'masses which are simply in revolt'?

GREY MASSES

This disparagement fits ill with the analysis of developing class consciousness, especially in the towns, but it is easy to find many contemporaries stressing exactly this. They did so, however, more as a corollary of their political arguments than as a result of a genuine attempt to come to terms with either what was going on below or the character of the revolutionary crisis. It was a commonplace in early twentieth-century Russia to talk of the 'dark' masses, the 'grey' masses and the like to describe not only the peasants but also less skilled sections of the working class. Even workers themselves could use this language of one another. But in intellectual circles its use intensified after 1905 and in 1917 itself. Yet, for all the well-known doubts about the quality of education and literacy, there had been a considerable expansion before 1917. In this sense, the 'grey' masses were rather less 'grey' than they had been at any time before; however, the discourse of 'grey' and 'dark' was not intended as a sociological but more a political designation.

A sense of distance from, and fear of, the lower classes was a commonplace of conservative thought in tsarist Russia no less than elsewhere in Europe before 1914.[60] Although liberals and more radical groups had traditionally expressed a sense of 'love of the common people', the 'common people' – first as peasants, then as workers – were easier to love in the abstract than as individuals with all their faults. Moreover they were easier to love as a 'suffering class' on whose behalf one fought than as peasants or workers who fought for themselves. So long as the peasantry was capable of little more than a succession of local challenges, and so long as the working class was ill-formed, this contradiction mattered little. Indeed frustration with what Alexander Blok called, in his 1908 essay on the 'People and the Intelligentsia', the 'dreadful laziness and dreadful torpor' of the people, might spur the *intelligent* to greater heights. It was when the 'laziness' and 'torpor' appeared to give way to a more serious challenge from below that problems arose, and this is what happened increasingly after 1900 and in 1905. A sense now emerged, said Blok, of 'the slow awakening of a giant . . . a giant waking with a singular smile on his lips'. 'Writers and public figures, officials and revolutionaries' might meet with 'workmen, sectarians, tramps and peasants' but there was now a greater sense of a gap and foreboding about its consequences. 'No *intelligent* smiles like [the awakening giant]', wrote Blok; 'we would think we knew all the ways of laughing there are, but in the face of the muzhik's [peasant's] smile . . . all our laughing instantly dies; we are troubled and afraid'.[61]

It was the revolution of 1905 that helped bring a gnawing sense of how great the gap was between the cultured sections of Russian society and the mass of the people, and also to widen the gap between liberals and the left. For liberals, the most inspiring element of 1905 was its least radical phase and the most threatening its most radical time. The first phase involved significant popular action that forced the tsar's October Manifesto, but until this point the liberals felt in control of the popular movement and so they also felt at one with it. Even Struve was briefly affected by this spirit; two days before Bloody Sunday he had written in exile that 'there are no revolutionary people in Russia yet', but when he returned to Russia in October 1905 he briefly regretted his 'terrible sin' of lack of faith in the people.[62] However, it was just at this point that control began to slip away and in November and December the revolution entered a second phase, with workers – encouraged by the left – organizing themselves more independently to demand social reform as well as political change. Those who sympathized with the abstract people might well now find themselves at risk from the real people. It was rather as if, said Vasilii Rozanov (in an image he would use of 1917 itself), the performance of the Divine Comedy was over; 'the public gets up. "Its time to put on our overcoats and go home". They look round. But there are neither overcoats to put on, nor houses to go to.'[63]

At the same time the government also encouraged wider patriotic disorders and pogroms, which led to some 10,000 people being hurt and 3,000 deaths (the figures are Miliukov's).[64] Thus if the strikes of November and December and the Moscow uprising showed the danger of revolution, the pogroms showed the danger of sections of 'the people' mobilized from the right. A third sense of unreliability emerged in the Spring of 1906, when the First Duma was disbanded and the Cadets appeal for passive resistance evoked only a limited response. The people, it seemed, would not come when they were called but when they did come they were a dangerous, unpredictable and possibly uncontrollable force.

This sense found several expressions in the years between 1906 and 1914. The most substantial in an intellectual sense was the series of essays under the title *Vekhi* (Landmarks) in which, led by Peter Struve, former Marxists and radicals re-evaluated their position. The *Vekhi* authors attacked the previous pretensions of the intelligentsia and emphasized that political freedom was dependent on prior moral and cultural change and the recognition of the importance of a legal order – not least by the intelligentsia itself. Beyond this, the authors also attacked illusions about 'the people'. It was the essay by Mikhail Gershenzon that put this latter argument most bluntly and which created the greatest furore. Gershenzon argued that there was deep-seated popular hatred for intellectuals (and the upper classes) in Russia that was qualitatively different from that in the West. There, hatred on both sides remained within a rational discourse and could be politically directed and resolved. In Russia it had an emotional quality that went beyond this. Here the people

> See our human and specifically Russian face but do not sense in us a human soul; thus they hate us passionately, probably with an unconscious mystical horror. They hate us even more profoundly because we are their own. This is the way we are; not only can we not dream of fusing with the people, but we must fear them worse than any punishment by the government, and we are condemned to bless that authority which alone with its bayonets and prisons manages to protect us from popular fury.[65]

The subsequent *Vekhi* debate saw the authors attacked not only from the left but also by moderate and radical liberals including the mainstream of the Cadet Party, which obviously could hardly endorse such a blatant argument for a retreat from serious political engagement in the present.[66] But, as is so often the case, the *Vekhi* group captured a moment in respect to the wider trajectory of liberalism and the intelligentsia and posed a question in relation to the popular movement, where concern was also evident more widely in Russian society in a degree of moral panic over issues like hooliganism, morality and sexuality.[67]

During the war these concerns seemed to grow. Indeed, in his memoirs Miliukov even records that at this point he read Taine on the French Revolution.[68] It is easy to understand, therefore, his sense of foreboding that politics might again become the preserve of the ignorant people. Miliukov, said Chernov, 'never spoke the language of the people. For him it was a tremendous alien force.'[69] Speaking at the Council of Ministers in August 1915, Sazonov seized on the conservatism of Miliukov and the Cadets with an evaluation no less brutal that the one on the left: 'If one manages this nicely and gives them a little way out, the Cadets will be the first to come to an agreement. Miliukov is the greatest bourgeois, and he fears the social revolution more than anything else. And, in general, the majority of the Cadets are trembling for their fortunes.'[70] Indeed a significant part of the Cadet leadership was even nervous about the party's own membership. One provincial member characterized the leadership's view of the members: 'You are not needed, we here in Petrograd watch all for you and never make mistakes. . .' The leaders were the party and the party was the leaders. 'We ourselves are the democratic masses', said Rodichev, rejecting the view that the people were being ignored.[71]

Another part of the irony of February 1917, therefore, is that while it was mass action on the streets that briefly restored some credibility to liberalism as a progressive force it was also a sense of the 'grey' and 'dark' forces within this mass action that panicked them.[72] *Svobodnyi naroda* wrote, 'the larger part of the dark masses of people simply are not able to understand the present meaning of freedom'.[73] Thus it became necessary to hold the line against the 'dark', 'grey' forces below. Tyrkóva-Williams – on the right of the Cadets – argued that 'human dignity consists not so much in receiving life's bounties as giving one's best to life', a philosophy which, as a woman of means (and married to an English gentleman), she no doubt found comforting. But below her were 'workmen [who] unaccustomed to intelligent discipline and lacking strong moral and professional traditions destroyed all industry with childish behaviour'. Here was a revolution of 'licentious appetites', a 'bacchanalia' of demands and one in which the focus on material gains was seemingly inversely proportional to the intellectual level of the participants. But some of the idealization of the past still survived for her: 'One may boldly assert, despite all the crimes committed by the mob, [that] the masses were more innocent, and better than their leaders'.[74] This was not a view shared by Pitrim Sorokin, or so it appears from his pseudo diary of 1917. From the very first moments of February, he suggested, he had felt that 'the mob mind was beginning to show itself and that not only the beast but the fool in man was striving to get the upper hand'. The reality of the Revolution appeared to be symbolized not only by mob violence but effeminacy and sexual promiscuousness, which ranged from couples in the street, to the activities of the prostitutes; from Kollontai's voracious sexual appetite (sic), to Zinoviev's 'womanish voice' and 'his fat figure . . . hideous and obscene, an extraordinary moral and mental degenerate'.[75] The venom of such portraits (Lenin's face, said Sorokin, reminded him 'of those congenital criminals in the albums of Lombroso') reminds us that, to the extent that a sense of class and class conflict was constructed through discourse, this was a double-sided process.

In the original *Vekhi* collection Bulgakov had remarked that:

> The intelligentsia oscillates continually and unavoidably between two extremes, uncritical worship of the people and spiritual aristocratism. The need to show this uncritical reverence in one form or another (in the form of old fashioned populism, originating with Herzen and based on a belief in the essentially socialist character of the Russian people, or in the more recent Marxist form, in which only one section of the people, the proletariat, rather than the nation as a whole, is reckoned as having this character) arises from the very foundations of the intelligentsia's creed. But a contrary principle also arises necessarily from these same foundations – an attitude of arrogance towards the people as the object upon which salvific influence is to be

exerted, as children who need a nanny to educate them in 'awareness', who are unenlightened in the intelligentsia's sense of the word.[76]

Immediately after October, Bulgakov penned a series of dialogues in which different individuals try to make sense of the Revolution (interestingly, without there being a Bolshevik present). In one exchange he returns to this theme – an 'author' remarks of 'the shared looks of the soldiers and sailors; they are now bestial, hideous, especially the latter, and the whole lot of "comrades" seem devoid of souls and dominated by instincts only by a kind of Darwinian ape – *homo socialisticus*'. But the 'author' is answered by the 'diplomat', an amoral character who had done his service to his country without being taken in by any of the rhetoric:

> quite lately you were ready to kneel before a soldier's grey cloak! What an aristocratic, undignified way of regarding the people: crusaders today and brutes tomorrow! While they are really mere ignorant men, who have been forcibly led to the slaughter, stood it at first, were recorded with full marks, and afterwards lost their temper, 'self-determined themselves' and showed their innate ruthlessness. Crusaders indeed! You can't get over the official lie, which is as fulsome as the flattery strewn nowadays by official scribes before proletarian potentates.[77]

In the hands of those who thought about the popular movement in more systematic terms, this idea of the backward masses came to have a more precise meaning. So, far from class consciousness being associated with radicalism and backwardness with moderation, the relationship was inverted. Thus on the right of the Mensheviks, for the Defencist group, Potresov argued that it was necessary to 'rally . . . the broad masses of the proletariat aiding it in every way to improve its class organisation and to combat the rebellious and predatory tendencies of an enlightened section of the working class which is disturbing the regular and democratic advancement of its cause'.[78] The centre Mensheviks talked of the danger to freedom posed by 'the union of all the dark forces, of the secret and open counter-revolutionists. Counter-revolution can derive its strength only from mass support. . .' What was needed was 'incessant educational and organisational activity' to pull workers to the Mensheviks and to understand why they were 'refusing to seize all power'. Thus, far from class consciousness coming to mean a situation in which, in a famous phrase, 'men, as a result of common experience (inherited or shared), feel and articulate the identity of their interests as between themselves, and as against other men whose interests are different from (and usually opposed to) theirs', for more moderate theorists

and politicians on the left it represented 'darkness'.[79] True class consciousness, true enlightenment over darkness, was that which understood the need
for a degree of restraint and co-operation with the bourgeoisie!

However, it was possible to be both class conscious and constructive, and
to the extent that the writings of 'social historians' in the 1970s and 1980s
elaborated this their work will remain a major contribution. Indeed, perhaps
the fact that Russia held together in the way that it did had something to do
with the self-organization from below that developed with the radicalization? Philips Price certainly felt this:

> I can confidently say that after my recent journey in the interior of Russia in
> the last two months, that if it were not for the revolutionary councils in the
> towns, villages and among the soldiers of the garrisons, the anarchy would be
> fifty times worse . . . Of course it is plain that the ruling classes in England
> and their allies, the bourgeoisie here, must in order to save their class
> privileges discredit all movements like those which inspire the Russian
> revolution . . .[80]

Doomed to take place, doomed to fail, might be a good summary of the
conclusions of much current historical writing on the Russian Revolution;
but, as we have tried to show, if choices existed in 1917 then they existed on
both sides. Making the Bolsheviks appear as the only dynamic force is not
only one-sided, it also provides an alibi for those who made other choices.
But the choices that they made were important and conditioned what
happened. Remaining trapped within a rigid theoretical framework, they
finally abandoned the Revolution at a crucial moment in walking out of the
Soviets. We should perhaps leave the last word to Sukhanov who, opposing
the takeover of power, nevertheless drew a crucial distinction when the
Mensheviks and Right SRs abandoned the Soviet:

> I was thunderstruck . . . First of all, no one contested the legality of the
> Congress. Secondly, it represented the most authentic worker-peasant
> democracy . . . thirdly, the question was: Where would the Right Men-
> sheviks and the SRs leave the Congress for? Where would they go from the
> Soviet? The Soviet, after all was the revolution itself . . . So where could one
> go from the Soviet? It meant a formal break with the masses and the
> revolution. And why? Because the Congress had proclaimed a Soviet regime
> in which the minute Menshevik-SR minority would not be given a place! I
> myself considered this fatal for the revolution, but why link this with
> abandoning the supreme representative organ of the workers, soldiers and

peasants? . . . The old bloc could not swallow its defeat and the Bolshevik dictatorship. With the bourgeoisie and with the Kornilovites – yes; but with the workers and peasants whom they had thrown into the arms of Lenin with their own hands – impossible.[81]

5

'Our Position is in the Highest Degree Tragic': Bolshevik 'Euphoria' in 1920

Lars T. Lih

'Russia – looted, weakened, exhausted, falling apart.' Thus reads the first sentence in the volume of Lev Trotsky's writings containing his speeches on economic issues during 1920 – a sentence that appropriately sounds the keynote of the sombre rhetoric of that grim year.[1] The world war and then the civil war had drained Russia's resources and ripped apart the interdependent pre-war economic organism, and yet a large military establishment still had to be supported. The transport system was on the verge of utter collapse. Industry had no goods to give the peasants for their grain. The peasants were understandably reluctant to part with their grain for nothing and indeed had less and less for themselves. Inflation had destroyed the financial system. Disease, hunger and cold stalked the land. The lives of the workers had gotten worse, not better – the promises of the Revolution were more distant than ever. No wonder Trotsky angrily asked how the newspapers dared to publish optimistic articles. Didn't they see that 'our position is in the highest degree tragic'?[2]

The Bolsheviks would hardly have been sane if they had not realized how grim the situation was. But wait – the most eminent scholars in the field, on both the left and the right, assure us that the Bolsheviks were in fact far from fully sane in 1920. The devastation caused by the war did not bother them, indeed, 'the mood of 1920 remained on the whole one of complacency'.[3] 'Complacency' is too mild a word for many historians, who prefer 'euphoria'.[4] Russia in 1920 was 'a theatre of the absurd' in which the depressing reality was presented 'as if it were what it was supposed to be, as imagined by the Communist leaders'.[5] And what did the Communist leaders imagine reality to be? 'In a veritable ideological delirium, the most colossal economic collapse of the century was transmogrified into really-existing Communism, the radiant future *hic et nunc*.'[6]

No wonder Sheila Fitzpatrick finds that 'the Bolsheviks' perception of the real world had become almost comically distorted in many respects by 1920'.[7] Indeed, it is rather comical that most Bolsheviks believed that 'the war economy measures applied during this period offered the shortcut to socialism that had been dubbed a childish "leftist" dream a short while before'.[8] And no doubt when we read that grain requisitioning by force was 'regarded by the Party, from Lenin down, as not merely socialism, but even communism' – or that the entire party thought for a brief period at the end of 1920 that the Soviet countryside was already fully socialized – it is hard to suppress a smile.[9] Ultimately, though, it is not very funny, when we consider 'the millions of victims who had paid with their lives for the leaders' brief moment of frenzy'.[10]

If what the academic experts say is true, then the real question about the Bolsheviks in 1920 is not 'what were they thinking?', but 'what were they smoking?' According to the standard view, 'war communism' – the name given *ex post facto* to the policies and the outlook that reached its apogee in 1920 – was essentially a *hallucination*. There is no milder word for it. One of the main supports for this academic consensus is none other than Trotsky, whose rather un-euphoric words we have already cited. Trotsky's speeches, appeals, directives and pamphlets from 1920 make up one of the most extensive and easily available sources of evidence for the Bolshevik world-view during 'war communism'. He wrote so much during this one year that one wonders how he found time to do anything else. We shall test the 'euphoria' consensus by looking at this body of material and establishing the connections Trotsky made between the national economic crisis, Bolshevik policies, and the socialist transformation of society.

One of the key issues in the centuries-long discussion of the French Revolution is the relation between the original aims of the Revolution in 1789 and its radical outcome in 1793. Was the Terror a perversion of revolutionary aims, a natural outgrowth, or just a transitory necessity? 'War communism' has the same sort of implication for our understanding of the aims of the Revolution in 1917. There is thus a parallel between the issues explored here and the issues in other essays in this volume. Yet there is also a striking contrast. The amount of documentation and sophisticated argument about the relations between 1789 and 1793 is staggering, because historians have always understood the importance of these links. The debate is at a correspondingly high level, whatever we may think of current trends. But this is not true in the case of the Russian Revolution. As will become evident, the most elementary facts about the Bolshevik outlook in 1920 have *not* been established. 'Theatre of the absurd' is in reality a good description of debates about war communism, since all sides attribute views to Trotsky and other Bolshevik leaders that are the exact opposite of what they were trying to pound home to their audiences in speech after speech.

The theme of the present collection of essays – 'refuting revisionism' – also hardly fits the present essay, since the hallucinatory view of war communism is for all practical purposes an unchallenged consensus. The portrayal of war communism as nothing but a set of destructive fantasies plays a key role in discrediting the Russian Revolution, if only because it provides a direct bridge between 1917 and the Stalin era. Yet, as we shall see, it was not originally created by those hostile to the Revolution – it was created and is still defended today by the left, and particularly by Trotsky loyalists. This essay will show that Trotsky in 1920 is too important a subject to be left to the Trotskyists.

MILITARIZATSIIA: 'A NATURAL, SAVING FEAR'

'Russia's industry lay in ruins, there was barely any transport, and the one pressing problem was how to save the towns from imminent starvation, not how to bring about a Communist millennium.'[11] Leszek Kolakowski thus expresses the views of historians who have castigated the Bolshevik leaders for neglecting the national emergency of 1920 in favour of their ideological hobbyhorses. Central to this charge is the set of policies adopted in early 1920 under the general label of 'militarization of labour'. These policies were predicated on the assumption that military hostilities were coming to an end and that economic reconstruction was the order of the day – and so (historians conclude) these policies cannot be dismissed as simply a response to the civil-war emergency. No, militarization is how the Bolshevik leaders now conceived of socialism or in any event Soviet Russia's long-term future. As the principal architect and defender of these policies, Trotsky is Exhibit A of this accusation – especially since his eloquent defence of labour militarization, contained in the grimly titled *Terrorism and Communism*, is easily available in English.

All this is very odd. 'Militarization' is a label for a rather disparate set of policies whose connecting link was that they were all meant as responses to an economic crisis caused or greatly exacerbated by the civil war. 'Militarization' *means* national emergency. And no one was more insistent about this than Trotsky.

'Why do we speak of militarization? Of course, this is only an analogy, but one that is very rich in content.'[12] The core of this analogy for Trotsky was not any particular organizational feature of the army. It was rather that the army represented the supremacy of the whole over the part when a nation was faced with a life-or-death battle for survival. In speech after speech throughout the year, Trotsky tried to impress upon his audiences that this was exactly how they should perceive the economic situation – as literally a life-or-death crisis. The key word in his understanding of militarization is 'ruin' (*gibel'*). 'We must tell the masses that breakdown and ruin threaten all of Soviet Russia.'[13] This situation of mortal danger is the basis of the analogy with the army:

> What is an army? The army is the one organisation in the world in which a person is obligated to give his life unconditionally and fully. An army demands bloody sacrifices. It is not concerned with the sacred interests of the individual and demands sacrifices in the name of the interests of the whole. Our economic position is like the military position of a country surrounded by an enemy that is two or three times stronger than it. An habitual, normal regime – an habitual, normal method of work – will not save us now. We need an exceptional wave of labour enthusiasm, an unprecedented readiness of each one of us to sacrifice himself for the revolution, and we need an exceptionally authoritative economic apparatus that says to each particular person: it's tough for you, you're sick, I know it, but despite the fact that I know it's tough for you, I give you orders, I put you to work in the name of the interests of the whole. This is militarization of labour.[14]

What was needed was 'an internal militarization, based on complete understanding and dictated by a situation of fear – a natural, saving fear when faced with the ruin of the country'.[15]

There were two other qualities of army life that Trotsky consistently put forward as a model. One was 'exactness' (*tochnost'*), a word that pops up frequently in his speeches along with an entourage of hard-to-translate terms: *akkuratnost', ispolnitel'nost', formlennost', iasnost'*. This bundle of qualities evokes a combination of the reliability of the ideal German with the get-up-and-go of the ideal American – in other words, the ideal organization man. Trotsky, like many Marxists of his generation, saw the modern world as a clash of large-scale organizations, which meant that these individual qualities were life-and-death matters for whole societies. The transition to the New Economic Policy (NEP) made no difference to Trotsky's views. In a *Pravda* article of December 1921 entitled 'Man, we could really use some exactness!', he insisted 'Exactness and accuracy [are] among the most necessary traits of an aware, independent, cultured human being.'[16]

Another common theme in Trotsky's speeches of this era is the claim that the Red Army was in many ways a mirror of Soviet Russia as a whole. Trotsky was certainly not saying that Soviet Russia in 1920 or socialist society in general was or should be a compulsory hierarchical organization. He was talking about the basic *class relations* of Soviet Russia. *All* armies (according to Trotsky) reflected the basic class relations of the larger society around them, and the Red Army was just an example of this. For Trotsky, the essential fact about the Red Army was that it represented a winning combination of the peasantry, the military *spetsy* and the 'advanced workers'. In contrast, the White armies reflected the class hostility between peasant and officer and correspondingly fell apart. The Bolsheviks won the civil war because 'the soviet regime created an army in its own likeness, and this army learned how to win'.[17] Thus Trotsky used the Red Army as a model of *class partnership*. (Of course, Trotsky was at pains to emphasize that this partnership could only work because of the monopoly position of a disciplined party.)

So much for metaphors – what actual policies lay behind them? The labour militarization policies can be summarized as follows. First, locate and mobilize scattered skilled workers. Second, organize in the most coordinated and expedient way possible the onerous 'labour duties' already widely imposed on the peasantry. Third, put vitally important 'shock' enterprises on a 'war footing' in which food rations were more solidly guaranteed but also in which workers were officially tied down to the enterprise. Fourth, create 'labour armies' out of military units caught between full combat readiness and full demobilization. Fifth, 'shake up' the trade union leadership in the crucial transport sector. Sixth, and most generally, install a regime of the strictest possible labour discipline.

We leave to one side questions about whether these policies were well thought out, whether they were implemented in a competent way or even whether they actually ended up improving the economic situation. Our concern here is what these policies tell us about how the Bolsheviks, and Trotsky in particular, viewed socialism in 1920. We note first of all that they do not give the impression of a leap into the unknown of a socialist utopia – rather, they seem to be responses to specific and very real problems. We note further that although the policies were defended under the rubric of 'universal labour duty', they are in fact constructed on the 'shock' principle of diverting resources into the most urgent sectors.

This 'shock' logic comes out particularly in the policy of putting crucial factories on a war footing. Some historians write as if the Bolsheviks wanted to militarize all factories, but this would have contradicted the entire logic of the policy.

> The most important factor of success [in these crucial factories] is the increased ration, but this ration is given out along with a war footing status. Obviously, it would be senseless to put industry as a whole on a war footing, so it is necessary to select certain shock points such as the railroads and

locomotive factories and concentrate our best workers there and send shock production groups to them.[18]

To be placed on a war footing essentially meant a *privileged* position, with the result that workers actually petitioned for this status to be conferred on their factory. Indeed, although the Bolshevik leaders could hardly have realized it, this 'shock' priority policy was a step in the direction of NEP. To guarantee the rations of some workers was to tell other workers to fend for themselves – and ultimately this fending could no longer be done in the semi-legal fashion tolerated in 1920.

A special mention should be made of the 'labour armies', if only to stress that they played a relatively unimportant part in the complex of labour militarization policies. The labour army concept was specifically tied to the existence of army units in an awkward transitional stage between combat readiness and demobilization. Some historians – fascinated, one suspects, by the scandalous term 'labour army' – have made these the centerpiece of Bolshevik economic legislation in 1920, asserting that Trotsky and co wanted to transform all of Russia into labour armies. In reality, Trotsky put least ideological weight on these policies and gave them the most cautious and empirical defence.[19]

Another feature of the labour militarization policies was that all of them assumed a readiness to apply compulsion to any extent necessary. This aspect hardly needs emphasis. What does need emphasis is the equally central role of material incentives, because historians have consistently ignored or even denied the existence of *any* role for material incentives. Trotsky argued at some length that lack of consumer goods meant that otherwise desirable policies of material incentive were not applicable. The same dire shortage meant that differential 'bonus' systems had to be applied despite their manifest unfairness ('the state should – this is of course obvious – put the best workers in the best conditions of existence by means of the bonus system'). We have seen this assumption at work in the increased ration given to 'militarized' factories.[20]

'Militarization' thus did not mean 'a transfer of a military model of ignoring material incentive over to the civilian economy'. On the contrary, Trotsky makes it quite clear that the labour armies themselves were using bonus systems that improved their productivity.[21] If anything, this kind of policy represents the 'civilianization' of the army rather than the reverse.

Many readers have gained the impression that Trotsky was calling for the maintenance of 1920 levels of compulsion into the indefinite future. Actually, Trotsky explicitly says that compulsion would steadily decrease as the economic crisis receded into the past, the material situation improved and people better understood the benefits of the new system.[22] The contrary impression is partly an artifact of the way the key term *trudovaia povinnost'* is translated in the English edition of *Terrorism and Communism*. I have translated this as 'labour duty', that is, something that is both a moral obligation and enforced by the state. One support for this translation is the equivalent German term *Arbeitspflicht*. Other possible translations are 'labour service' and 'labour obligation', 'Labour conscription' is sometimes seen and even 'forced labour', both of which I regard as tendentious. In the English edition of Trotsky's book, however, the term is translated as 'compulsory labour service' (compare the German term *Zwangsarbeit*). This translation is perhaps defensible, given the realities of the situation. Nevertheless it thoroughly obscures Trotsky's views on the *relation* between 'compulsion' (*prinuzhdenie*) and labour duty. Trotsky argued that *labour duty* was a basic socialist principle that would always be valid, while the *compulsion* needed to back it up during the revolutionary crisis would steadily decrease until it disappeared. This may or may not be an acceptable position, but it becomes opaque when the English translation has Trotsky asserting that 'the very principle of compulsory labour service is for the Communist quite unquestionable' (p. 135).

Another misunderstanding arises from the use of the word 'transition' in the rhetoric of this period. 'Transition' could refer to the whole era between the workers' revolution and the final construction of socialism. But it could also refer to the short-term transition from a capitalist regime to a socialist regime – that is, as Marxists understood it, from a regime of bourgeois class sovereignty to a regime of proletarian class sovereignty.

It is this second short-term revolutionary transition that understandably preoccupied the Bolshevik leaders in 1920. Bukharin and Trotsky both wanted to get across the same basic thesis about *this* transition; just as the advent of a proletarian regime required the political upheaval of revolution and civil war, so it required an economic upheaval that manifested itself by what Bukharin rather pompously called 'negative expanded reproduction' on a gigantic scale. Compulsion was an essential aspect of the transition period not only because of the quasi-inevitable political crisis but also because of the quasi-inevitable economic crisis.

Thus Trotsky scoffed at Jean Jaurès's idea that the transition to socialism could be accomplished by means of gradual democratization. 'In this connection he was deeply mistaken. History shows humanity another path – the path of the cruellest bloody clashes, of world imperialist butchery with civil wars to follow.'[23] It followed that a fall in productivity and in quantity of products was natural, 'given the transition of the national economy onto new rails'.[24] 'We know from experience and should have predicted from Marxist theory the inevitability of the deepest crises during the epoch of revolutions. [Society's development] is not a straight one but a zigzag one.'[25]

Looking back in 1922, Trotsky summed it up: 'Revolution opens the door to a new political system, but it achieves this by means of a destructive catastrophe.'[26] It is this understanding of the 'transition period' that informed Trotsky's polemic against Menshevik criticism. Trotsky pounced on a phrase in the Menshevik statement to the effect that compulsory labour was *always* unproductive under *all* circumstances. If this was the case, Trotsky retorted, then you could forget about socialism – because a worker conquest of power leads to a profound economic crisis that cannot be resolved without compulsion (among other things).[27] 'Over and over it becomes evident that for [the Menshevik orator] the tasks of the transition period – that is, the proletarian revolution – do not exist. This is the source of the utter irrelevance of his criticism, his advice, plans and recipes. We're not talking about how it will be twenty or thirty years from now – then, of course, things will be much better – but how we can climb out of economic breakdown *today*.'[28] In other words: don't talk about the socialist utopia, talk about the national emergency!

Trotsky also reasoned as follows: a *socialist* regime has a particular right to apply compulsion for the public interest. Socialism means a universal obligation to work. No idle parasites! He who does not work, neither shall he eat! Furthermore, socialism implies the regulated distribution of labour according to plan – it stands for the right of the collectivity as against the rights of the individual. If, at any time, circumstances are such that labour is absolutely necessary and it cannot be attained in any other way, then, undoubtedly, a socialist government has the right to use physical compulsion. In making this argument, Trotsky was not admitting that physical compulsion was or ever could be used against the labour force as a whole. He maintained that labour militarization would not be successful unless the large majority of the working class supported it. Physical compulsion was applied only to slackers. Nevertheless, the government should have no compunction about applying it.

Some people, including many socialists, find this argument shocking. Speaking as a historian, I will only say that Trotsky is not distorting the hostility of pre-war socialism toward non-working 'parasites'. Certainly this type of argument is not a product of 1920. Anyone who thinks otherwise should look at Bukharin's pronouncements on labour duty and labour discipline in early 1918, when he was in his Left Communist and allegedly 'libertarian' stage.[29]

The right to apply physical compulsion and the expediency of using it in any particular case are two different things:

The element of material, physical compulsion can be greater or smaller – that depends on many things, including the degree of wealth or poverty of a country, the heritage from the past, the level of culture, the condition of the transport system and of administrative mechanisms – but obligation, and consequently compulsion as well, is a necessary condition of taming bourgeois anarchy, of the socialisation of the means of production and labour and the reconstruction of the economy on the basis of a single plan.[30]

This passage certainly implies that, say, as the transport crisis eases up, the need for out-and-out compulsion will correspondingly decrease. This implication is further strengthened by the one passage in *Terrorism and Communism* where Trotsky does take a long-term perspective. According to Trotsky, the crucial long-term task for the regime is to raise productivity. If socialism turns out to be less productive than capitalism, it is doomed, but the productivity of labour under capitalism was 'the result of a long and stubborn policy of repression, education, organisation and incentives applied by the bourgeoisie in relation to the working class'.[31] Despite fundamental differences, socialist labour productivity would share one basic feature with its predecessor; it would be the result of a long process (especially in Russia where capitalism hardly accomplished its own historic mission) that used a variety of means. Repression is one of these means, but a minor one compared to moral influences and material incentive.[32]

This discussion more than any other in *Terrorism and Communism* does give a flavour of the Stalin era and its 'politics of productivity', to use Lewis Siegelbaum's phrase. 'A good engineer, a good mechanic, and a good carpenter must have in the Soviet Republic the same fame and glory as was enjoyed hitherto by outstanding agitators, revolutionary fighters and, in the period just passed, the most courageous and capable commanders and commissars' – such a sentence does have a 1930s feel about it. But historians have been so obsessed with saddling Trotsky with the cranky thesis that physical compulsion was the *only* short- and long-term method of socialist construction that they have entirely overlooked these genuine links.

To conclude, Trotsky's justification of the use of compulsion may be paraphrased as follows:

The economic ruin that threatens Russia and our limited resources means that compulsion is written into the situation. If backward elements of the working class do not understand the full gravity of the situation, we shall nevertheless ensure by whatever means necessary that they do their job. Of course this compulsion could only work because the bulk of the working class does understand the gravity of the situation – in fact, the continuing heroism of the Russian working class is a standing rebuke to the slander of such as Karl Kautsky. Of course this compulsion only works as one element in a broad array of measures based primarily on differential material rewards and campaigns to explain the nature of the national emergency. Of course the element of compulsion will steadily decrease as we pull out of the present crisis situation, until it finally disappears in full socialism.

This is all true, but none of it should obscure the fact that we as socialists have the right and the duty to use compulsory methods in order to defend the proletarian vlast' *(regime) and to get the economy on its feet again. The transition to socialism will always start off with the economic chaos and breakdown caused by revolution. If compulsory methods are always unproductive, as our critics claim, we will never get past this starting point.*

Not only the Mensheviks but critics within our own party compare our use of compulsion – undertaken in order to prevent the collapse of the economy and the ruin of the country – with the use of compulsion to build Egyptian pyramids or to conduct Arakcheev's nutty 'labour colony' experiments under Tsar Alexander. Are these critics liberals, are they pacifists, that they don't see the difference between compulsory labour used to satisfy elite whims and compulsory labour used to keep the masses from dying of cold and hunger? Harsh times require harsh measures, and we Bolsheviks are not the ones to flinch when the fate of the revolution and the country hang in the balance.

THE ROAD TO SOCIALISM DURING A 'CARICATURE PERIOD'

Marx wrote that the proletarian revolution does not unfold with such dazzling fireworks or so brilliantly as the bourgeois revolution. Kerensky's historical story was over in nine months, but we attack, retreat and again attack, and we always say that we have not traversed even a small portion of the road. The slowness of the unfolding of the proletarian revolution is explained by the colossal nature of the task and the profound approach of the working class to this task.[33]

Thus did Trotsky assess the situation in December 1920 (a period when the hallucinations of war communism were supposed to be at their height). The metaphor of a journey along the road to socialism was fundamental to Marxism since it differed from other varieties of socialism, primarily in its vision of how and by whom socialism would be achieved. The better we grasp the implication of this and related metaphors, the better we can understand the Bolshevik rhetoric of 1920 (or any other time).

Even granting that they had travelled only a short distance of the journey, the Bolsheviks felt that they had much to brag about. The very possibility of travelling down the road was due to the daring conquest of political power in 1917. Despite adverse conditions, they had managed to travel some part of the journey. They were definitely headed in the right direction and progress would be quite rapid once the war was over and the country was united.

Nevertheless, in another rhetorical context, a speaker who earlier had quite sincerely made all these positive points could put the emphasis on other aspects of the same situation: we are not yet a socialist society, we still have a long and difficult way to go, and at present we suffer from a combination of the breakdown of the old and the embryonic nature of the new.

The road metaphor can also help us grasp what the advent of NEP changed and what it did not change in the Bolshevik outlook. In a 1922 speech to the Comintern that defended the New Economic Policy, Trotsky claimed that 'none of us thought that having taken over the *vlast'*, it was possible to remake society overnight'. On the contrary, war communism was 'the regime of a blockaded fortress with a disorganised economy and exhausted resources' – methods that could not fail to damage the economy severely. War communism inevitably created a 'bureaucratic surrogate of socialist [economic] unification', since 'old methods of economic verification were removed by the civil war before we succeeded in creating new ones'. Obviously, 'there was no communism in Russia. There was no socialism here and there could not have been.'

Trotsky nevertheless admitted that the Bolsheviks prior to NEP had been over-optimistic on one point. They believed they could move forward out of the post-civil-war crisis of 1920 towards socialism 'without large economic shifts, shake-ups and retreats, that is, by a more or less straight ascending line'. Progress toward socialism would take place 'by means of corrections and changes in the methods of our war communism' (for example, an adequate exchange equivalent would be given to the peasants for their grain). This optimism was partly based on the hope that a European revolution would bail the Bolsheviks out, after which Russia would thankfully switch from the role of the locomotive engine of socialism to its caboose.[34]

The knee-jerk reaction of historians when confronted with passages of this sort is to say something along the following lines: 'Well, sure, Trotsky and other Bolshevik leaders claimed afterwards that they did not have utopian expectations of remaking society overnight, but this was just a cover-up. The Bolsheviks sang quite a different tune during war communism itself!' In point of fact, Trotsky has here described quite accurately both the sober and the uplifting aspect of what he and others were saying in 1920. This can be illustrated by Trotsky's thoughts on planning and the coordination of industrial enterprises.

The evidence is confusing at first because the 1920 slogan 'single economic plan' had two quite distinct meanings. In speeches in the spring of that year, and in *Terrorism and Communism*, 'single economic plan' referred to a basic strategy for overcoming the crisis: first solve the transport crisis, then go on to machine-building and so forth.[35] This was a plan for recovery rather than for coordinating ongoing economic activity. This 'single economic plan' properly belongs in our earlier discussion of the national emergency. Trotsky took the basic idea from a pamphlet by S.I. Gusev published at the beginning of the year. The brunt of Gusev's argument is: let's not get fancy here with high-faluting socialist projects, but focus our attention exclusively on the most elementary and pressing tasks.[36]

There was nothing particularly socialist about the actual set of stages advocated by Gusev and Trotsky. At the Ninth Party Congress, Gusev's 'plan' was both attacked (by Rykov) and defended (by Bukharin) as a strategy appropriate to *any* devastated economy. Trotsky strongly defended Gusev's plan, but he was mainly interested in it as an agitational device for focusing energy and explaining to the workers why they needed to make sacrifices.[37]

When Trotsky resumed his speech on economic matters at the end of the year, 'single economic plan' had taken on the socialist connotation of centralized coordination of economic activity in lieu of the market. Trotsky had discussed aspects of this issue throughout the year. What particularly exercised him was *glavkokratiia*, a term he invented that rapidly became a byword in 1920. Each nationalized and amalgamated industry was headed up by a 'head committee' or *glavny komitet* or, in common parlance, a *glavk*. *Glavkokratiia*, or rule by the Moscow 'head committees', was highly resented by just about everybody else in the Bolshevik establishment.

The essence of *glavkokratiia* was the absence of meaningful coordination, since each *glavk* controlled its own industry with only tenuous links to anyone else. The problem was most intense in the localities, where competing representatives from the central *glavki* almost literally fought it out. Trotsky recited horror stories of how the localities were prevented from effective use of their own locally available resources while they waited months for some non-forthcoming permission from Moscow. Trotsky summed up a basic structural reason for the prevailing economic chaos: 'The centre doesn't know and the locals don't dare.'[38]

This inevitable combination of a broken-down old system and an embryonic new system meant that Soviet Russia was now in a 'caricature period' of transition.[39] One solution might have been to charge ahead to full centralized coordination. But Trotsky scotched that idea. An 'immediate leap' into full centralization was impossible and any such hope was a 'bureaucratic utopia'.[40] The difficulty was that 'our economy is oriented toward a single plan, but this single plan does not exist – in fact, there does not yet exist any apparatus for either working out or implementing such a plan'.[41] Some Bolshevik supporters may have a naive expectation of the existence of a plan 'as something complete and whole. We haven't got that far yet and won't for a long time.' The task of national electrification alone would require ten, maybe thirty years, and this electrification was an essential prerequisite for bringing technical progress and culture to the peasantry. How can there be a single centralized plan as long as this great task remains unaccomplished – as long as 'the socialist economy is a series of isolated islands in the agricultural ocean?'[42]

Given the inadequacies of *glavkokratiia*, it was wrong to blame the locals when they responded to urgent needs any way they could. Trotsky made all these points in a speech of January 1920 to a party audience that was not published until the mid–1920s – understandably, in view of its stunning frankness. The two greatest symbols of outlaw economic activity in 1920 were home-brewing (*samogonka*) and 'sackmanism' (*meshoshchnichestvo*). Home-brewing used precious grain to make vodka for local consumption while sackmanism channelled grain into the black market. Yet Trotsky was prepared to shock his audience by announcing that

> *samogonka* is the protest of local needs against the centralism that does not satisfy them . . . I am speaking about the semi-contraband or completely contraband production that occurs in the localities and plays an enormous economic role, because otherwise the country will be ruined. How can one live without horseshoes, without nails? Either you steal them from the warehouses or you make them yourself with primitive methods.[43]

Another obstacle to rational economic coordination was the collapse of the money system. Looking ahead, Trotsky assumed that in the not-too-distant future some sort of measure of labour would play the coordinating role that money had played under capitalism. But what was on his mind in 1920 were the difficulties created by the absence of either capitalist or socialist value measures. Back in the old days, he told his listeners, market competition had coordinated economic activity – in a primitive and barbaric way, true, but nevertheless it had ensured some sort of equilibrium. But money prices were incapable of playing that role now:

> In our work we have bumped up against the important question of how to compare the work of production in comparison with the results that we get. The old accounts are conducted in rubles – and everybody well knows how much our Soviet ruble is worth . . . If I told you that transport absorbed 3 billion or 15 billion rubles, you would greet both the one and the other figure with the same lack of surprise. We have to find a value instrument that answers to the needs of socialist society.[44]

The result, *hic et nunc*? 'The old significance of money is destroyed and a new apparatus of distribution is still not functioning. And, comrades, this helps to explain all our troubles, including the fuel crisis.'[45] Why, then, had the Bolsheviks destroyed the money system before they were able to replace it? Because revolutionary necessity demanded that they smash not only the state but the economy: 'There is no way of building [the new] without destroying the old, because you have to take power out of the hands of the bourgeoisie.'[46] These outbursts show why Trotsky was able to accept so easily – one feels, with relief – the return of a functioning money system under NEP.

Trotsky's sarcastic sallies against *glavkokratiia* and its manifold defects struck such a chord that by the end of the year he became frightened at his own success and tried to cool things down (possibly at the invitation of the Politburo):

> Much more serious [than opposition within party circles] is what's happening in the more profound strata, among the workers male and female and the peasants male and female. And there's no doubt about it – here there is dissatisfaction, completely natural and lawful dissatisfaction with the economic position, that is, with overwhelming poverty. This dissatisfaction can take sharp forms among the dark masses, it can express itself in elemental and stormy protests of indignation, strikes in factories by the more backward elements of the working class. And when we blame everything on the bureaucracy, then all we're doing is planting prejudices in the heads of the most backward, hungry and freezing labouring masses. They're going to start thinking that there is some sort of central monster called 'the bureaucracy' that holds material goods in its hands and doesn't give them to the masses. People will start relating to it as a class enemy, just as earlier the worker did to the capitalist.[47]

One can easily see from these speeches that the Bolshevik leaders were themselves weary of continually issuing calls for further sacrifice:

> War is a cruel trade and the organs of war are cruel ones; their work consists in the merciless impoverishment of all the living forces and means of the country. When the war approaches its end, then those elements of exhaustion and dissatisfaction that accumulated during the war make themselves known. And this is a good thing, because it testifies to the vitality of the organism itself.

Russian workers are understandably disillusioned after the collapse of their 'unrealistic expectations'. As a result, 'the wide mass still to this day does not feel in appropriate fashion what the soviet regime really is'.[48]

Maybe next spring, Trotsky mused at the end of the year, we could tear down some of Moscow's rotten, filthy, disease-ridden apartment buildings and replace them with ones like those in New York City – buildings that included a bath, that provided gas and electricity and where the trash was collected every day. If we could build just one building like this, the response would be colossal. Because up to now the workers see the wheels turning but they don't see the economic machinery working.[49]

Such were the dreams of 'war communism' – whether modest or grandiose, the reader must judge.

ENTER THE HISTORIANS

We find in Trotsky's speeches of 1920 innumerable variations on two overriding themes. One is the austere 'blood, sweat and tears' evocation of the economic ruin facing the country unless extraordinary efforts were made. The other is an insistence on the manifold difficulties created by the breakdown of the capitalist system combined with the primitive, incomplete 'caricature' version of socialist institutions set up during the war.

When we turn to the historians, we find a near-unanimous portrayal of the Bolshevik outlook in 1920. We learn that the Bolsheviks ignored the national crisis in favour of ideological experiments. We further learn that the Bolsheviks viewed the institutions of 1920 as an embodiment of full socialism and as an admirable and workable long-term system. The principal body of evidence adduced for these assertions are the speeches of Trotsky.

What is the origin of the framework that dominates the interpretation of these particular texts? Why is it not only dominant but also unchallenged? One fact answers both questions. Historians on the left created the framework. Historians in the Trotskyist tradition – starting with Trotsky himself – played the major role in this process. Paradoxically – given the charge that Trotsky ignored the national emergency – the key theme of the framework developed by these historians is that there was no serious national crisis. An obvious and painless solution existed, namely, the early introduction of NEP and the legalization of the free grain market. Only ideological blinders kept the Bolsheviks from realizing this.

One of the earliest and most influential statements of this argument is Trotsky's memoir, *My Life*, published in 1930. The four or five pages devoted to economic policies in 1920 in these memoirs are a disappointment for the historian. Trotsky does not even mention labour militarization, labour duty, labour armies, exactness, *glavkokratiia* or the other issues discussed in this essay. His entire aim is a polemical one, to explain away his conflict with Lenin during the 'trade union discussion' of late 1920 and early 1921 and to show that he was actually much closer to Lenin than the 'epigones' (aka all the other leaders of the Bolshevik party).

As often with Trotsky, he tells a story to show that he was right all along. In March 1920 he proposed replacing grain requisitioning with a food-supply tax. If this proposal had been accepted, much suffering would have been avoided. Nevertheless, Lenin and the politburo turned it down. 'Once the transition to market methods was rejected, I demanded a correct and systematic implementation of "war" methods in order to attain real results in the economy.' His views on the trade unions grew out of the logic of these war methods. When Lenin finally caught up with Trotsky and advocated NEP, Trotsky instantly supported him – but he did not correspondingly change his views on the unions quickly enough. Only on this last point does Trotsky actually admit error.[50]

This little parable has had an immense influence on later views of 'war communism' as a set of unnecessary and destructive measures motivated by ideological blindness. Nevertheless, it is full of holes. It is not important for our purposes that Trotsky has strongly misrepresented his proposal of March 1920.[51] What concerns us here is Trotsky's suggestion that he adopted his labour policies only because his March proposal was turned down. However, these policies were all in place and elaborately defended by Trotsky some time *before* he made his quasi-proto-NEP proposal.

Trotsky does not explain how his March proposal would have addressed the pressing problems that gave rise to the various militarization policies. The only concrete policy he does describe in his memoirs is the effort to revive the transport system from its near-death experience. And here, oddly enough, Trotsky stresses how vital this work was and how necessary were the methods adopted. He sums up: 'These results were attained by emergency methods of administrative pressure that inevitably arose from the grave position of transport.' (True, he then adds 'as well as the system of war communism itself' – but this tacked-on reference to 'war communism' seems supererogatory.)[52]

In any event, we know for a fact that Trotsky did *not* repudiate the labour militarization policies of 1920. Twice after the publication of *My Life*, Trotsky authorized foreign reprints of *Terrorism and Communism*. He warned the workers that this is what real revolutions look like and asserted:

At the time of the civil war, when this book was written, the Soviets were still under the flag of 'war communism.' This system was not an 'illusion' – as the Philistines often maintained afterwards – but an iron necessity. The question was how the wretched resources were to be applied, mainly for the needs of the war, and how production, on however small a scale, was to be

kept alive for these same ends and without any possibility of the work being
paid for. War communism fulfilled its mission in so far as it made victory a
possibility in the civil war.[53]

The influence of Trotsky's parable can be seen in the changing assessment of
'war communism' by Trotsky loyalist Victor Serge. Writing in 1922, Serge
condemns the Kronstadt rising and defends Bolshevik policy.[54] In his book-
length study from the late 1920s, *Year One of the Russian Revolution*, Serge
considers war communism at greater length and justifies it in terms that go
well beyond the chronological framework of the book. Defining war
communism as 'an ambitious attempt to organise socialist production', he
argues that it was responsible for victory in the civil war and *not* responsible
for the decline in production. He also asserts that if international circumstances had been more favourable the same methods might have achieved
great success. In all this, he follows Trotsky's *Terrorism and Communism* and his
1922 speech to the Comintern.[55]

In 1937, the tone is strikingly different. In *Destiny of a Revolution*, Serge
cites Trotsky's memoirs to show that in 1920, 'by misfortune Lenin's clear-
sightedness is defective this time, he doesn't see the possibility of quitting the
road of war communism without surrendering to the rural counter-revolution'.[56] The bitterness of Serge's attack on war communism becomes more
intense in his memoirs written in the mid–1940s. Here the definition of 'war
communism' is expanded to include everything he disliked about the regime,
including the party monopoly, the terror and requisitioning (that is, taking
grain without compensation). Bolshevik policy suggestions arose solely out
of a stunning ignorance of what was really going on (Serge seriously suggests,
for example, that the head of the food-supply ministry thought the black
market was completely unimportant). But now Serge adds an element that is
not in Trotsky's memoirs – the claim that in 1920 the Bolshevik leaders
thought that their policies were not transitory measures but communism *tout
court*.[57]

This claim became the keystone of Isaac Deutscher's immensely influential
chapter on war communism in the first volume of his biography of Trotsky.
This chapter – 'Defeat in Victory' – is the foundation text for all further
academic discourse on war communism. Deutscher very explicitly argues
that the crisis could have been solved without any unpleasantness:

> To cope with [the crisis] one of two courses of action had to be taken. The
> government could stop the requisitioning of food from the peasant and
> introduce an agricultural tax, in kind or money. Having paid his taxes, the
> peasant could then be permitted to dispose of his crop as he pleased, to

consume it, sell it, or barter it. This would have induced him to grow the surpluses for urban consumption. With the flow of food from country to town restored, the activity of the state-owned industries could be expected to revive. This indeed would have been the only real solution. But a reform of this kind implied the revival of private trade; and it could not but explode the whole edifice of war communism, in the erection of which the Bolsheviks took so much pride.[58]

It all seems so simple. Money was notoriously valueless, but a money tax would have provided the government with necessary resources. There were no industrial consumer items then available, but the peasants would have undertaken backbreaking labour in order to get them. The workers had no food, but they would have gladly waited many long months until the extra grain presumably sown in spring 1920 became available for exchange. The transport system was on the point of collapse, but massive new demands on the system created by a private market in grain would have repaired the locomotives and gotten snow off the tracks without harsh labour discipline and compulsory labour duties. Soviet Russia was still completely isolated and threatened with invasion, but the inability to feed a large army would not have created any security threat.

At the end of the passage, Deutscher suggests the motive for refusing such an obvious solution – the Bolsheviks' pride in the edifice of war communism. They *liked* taking grain without compensation. 'The Bolshevik was . . . inclined to see the essential features of fully fledged communism embodied in the war economy of 1919–20.'[59] Having identified the Bolshevik view of socialism with the war economy, Deutscher proceeds to identify the war economy with Stalin's concentration camps. Trotsky argued that 'the work-ers' state had the right to use forced labour; and he was sincerely disappointed that they did not rush to enrol in the labour camps . . . What was only one of many facets in Trotsky's experimental thinking was to become Stalin's alpha and omega.'[60]

The Deutscher scenario became even more usable for the right when Moshe Lewin and others decided to use war communism as a polemical weapon in their advocacy of 'market socialism'. Lewin puts the blame for the economic crisis of 1920 squarely on Marxist hostility to the market. War communism started when the Bolsheviks

> began to speed up the dismantling of [capitalist] mechanisms and to replace them with more direct controls and distributive administrative techniques, apparently as a deliberate implementation of a suddenly rediscovered theory. This conception of a socialist economy explains why the illusion could

spread, why with undue obstinacy it was adhered to for far longer than the economy could bear, and why it was disastrous.[61]

In turn, the failure of war communism explains why Lenin, Bukharin and Trotsky began to rethink and redefine socialism as compatible with markets. Unfortunately there was a 'swing of the pendulum' under Stalin back to war communism and the original Marxist anti-market definition of socialism. Thus we see that the aim of Lewin's narrative is to draw the tightest possible link between the Marxist conception of socialism, the illusions of war communism, the disastrous state of the Russian economy in 1920, and the tyrannical Stalin era.

Lewin and other were so engaged in their fight for reform of the Soviet system that they did not notice how effective their own narrative was in the hands of the right. The right did understand these implications – that is why writers such as Martin Malia and Robert Conquest willingly cite Lewin as an authority on war communism, even though his account is utterly undocumented.[62]

The consensus on war communism created by Deutscher and Lewin is still unchallenged today. The chapter on war communism in Orlando Figes' *A People's Tragedy* is so strongly derivative of Deutscher that Figes even uses the same chapter title, 'Defeat in Victory'. Figes uses Deutscher's imagery to make Deutscher's points. Trotsky was not particularly concerned with the national emergency, but only with 'the bureaucratic fantasy of imposing Communism by decree.' This shows his affinity with Stalin: 'Both were driven by the notion that in a backward peasant country such as Russia state coercion could be used to provide a short-cut to Communism'. The main difference with Deutscher is that Figes adds a new – although, if we accept their shared view of the situation, more plausible – moral: 'The perversion was implicit in the system from the start.'[63]

In essential agreement with Figes about Trotsky in 1920 is a recent book by S.A. Smith. Smith is a representative of the left as that term is understood in academic Soviet studies, that is, someone who is not organically incapable of mentioning that the Bolsheviks were sometimes hemmed in by objective constraints. In his *The Russian Revolution: A Very Short Introduction*, for example, we find an innovative discussion of the real dilemmas driving food-supply policy. Yet when it comes to 1920, Smith reverts to form. We are again introduced to Trotsky, 'the most enthusiastic exponent of the idea that "obligation and compulsion" could be used to reconstruct economic life on the basis of a single plan'. True, 'not all Bolsheviks were enamoured of the idea of the labour army as a microcosm of socialist society'. (Although Smith notes that 'not all Bolsheviks' had these crazy ideas, he is uninterested in what these presumably more sane Bolsheviks thought, probably because Trotsky's nuttiness makes better copy.) After a mention of illusions about money, Smith concludes: 'Over the winter of 1920–21 such euphoria was rapidly dispelled.'[64]

This description is, as advertised, very short and yet it packs in a great many misconceptions. As we have seen, Trotsky tied the use of compulsion strongly to the economic crisis and had no intention of relying on it exclusively even under those circumstances. The 'plan' mentioned here is a broad set of priorities for getting out of the pit of economic breakdown and not a socialist plan that replaced the market – Trotsky insisted that a plan in this sense was many years away. Trotsky described the labour army as a microcosm of contemporaneous Soviet (not 'socialist') society in the same sense that any army reflects the society that produced it, and the specific point Trotsky wanted to make with the comparison was the possibility of class collaboration.

The corpus of Trotsky's pronouncements in 1920 is a crucial source for any engagement with the big questions of the Russian Revolution. The aims of the Revolution, their relation to pre-war revolutionary and socialist traditions, their role in determining the outcome of the Revolution, the role of the Bolshevik party in leading and/or repressing popular revolt – none of these issues can be seriously debated without a firm grasp of Trotsky's reaction to a crisis that he regarded as an inevitable companion to revolution. And Trotsky is only one of the voices of 1920, albeit among the more voluble and authoritative of them. This essay has not aimed at tackling the big questions themselves but rather at making such a discussion possible. We have to know that we do not know the basic elements of the Bolshevik outlook during these years. This salutary realization will not occur as long as historians who disagree on so much else join hands in affirming the reality of the will-o'-the-wisp that is Bolshevik 'euphoria' in 1920.

6

The New Anti-Communism: Rereading the Twentieth Century

Enzo Traverso

As many analysts have observed with great astonishment, the fall of the Soviet Union and the end of the Cold War did not usher in a more 'objective', less passionately and ideologically oriented approach to the history of the twentieth century, but rather a new wave of anti-communism: a 'militant', fighting anti-communism, all the more paradoxical inasmuch as its enemy had ceased to exist. In some ways, Paris is its capital. It reached its zenith in 1995 with the publication of *The Passing of an Illusion* by François Furet.[1] Two years later came *The Black Book of Communism*, an anthology edited by Stéphane Courtois, whose aim was to show that communism was much more murderous than Nazism.[2] On the other side of the Atlantic Ocean, the old school of Cold War historians seems to have rediscovered its youth, as *The Russian Revolution* by Richard Pipes (1990) and *The Soviet Tragedy* by Martin Malia (1994) show.[3] In this context Ernst Nolte, a conservative historian who had been isolated since the *Historikerstreit* of the mid-1980s, when Jürgen Habermas and many German historians accused him of rehabilitating the Nazi past, suddenly achieved a new legitimacy.[4] The old revisionism became acceptable, and even fashionable. Praised by Furet in a long footnote to *The Passing of an Illusion*, the once unpopular scholar is now highly regarded in France, where several of his books have been published (most recently his highly controversial *Der europäische Bürgerkrieg, The European Civil War*).[5]

These historians cannot be lumped together without an explanation. In fact, they belong neither to the same national context nor to the same intellectual generation; furthermore, the quality of their works is very uneven. Nevertheless, the exchange of letters between Nolte and Furet[6] on the one hand and Courtois' preface to the French edition of Nolte's *The European Civil War* on the other hand reveals a host of 'elective affinities' and forges a sort of united front in the present historical and political debate. Beyond their methodological divergences, their battles as 'engaged' historians converge on an essential point: anti-communism raised to the status of an historical paradigm, a hermeneutic key to the twentieth century. In the dock is the Russian Revolution, approached in different ways but always interpreted as the first step towards modern totalitarianism.

Within this anti-communist wave, Nolte appears as a forerunner. Perceived as a left historian by many observers at the beginning of the 1960s, when he published *Three Faces of Fascism*,[7] he has taken the lead among German conservative historians since the mid-1980s, with the outbreak of the *Historikerstreit*. A former student of Martin Heidegger, he belongs to an intellectual tradition of nationalism and conservatism that unquestionably possesses, from Treitschke to Meinecke and from Heidegger to Schmitt, its *titres de noblesse*. But his place within this current is that of an epigone, in a time in which it has lost any greatness or power to fascinate and its apocalyptic appeal rings like a distant echo of the past. Today, this culture has abandoned its radical tendencies and adapted itself to a more conventional conservatism. After the Second World War, the 'conservative revolution' ceased to exist. All that remains is a wounded national pride, sometimes a nationalist *ressentiment*, and more often an apologetic vision of the German past.[8] All those features pervade Ernst Nolte's work.

Many writers before him interpreted the twentieth century as a time of civil war, first European and then international. The concept of 'world civil war' *(Weltbürgerkrieg)* already appears in the writings of Ernst Jünger and Carl Schmitt.[9] Jünger used it in his war journal in 1942, namely in a passage devoted to his visit to the Eastern front. Schmitt used it in *Der Nomos der Erde*, his first work published after the war, in which he analysed the crisis of the *Jus Publicum Europeum*, i.e. the international order created with the Reformation and effectively destroyed in the spasms of the twentieth century's total wars.[10] In this perspective, the civil war was the apogee of the 'Political' conceived as the site of an 'existential' conflict between 'friend' and 'enemy'. This concept would later be used by several historians, often on the other side of the political spectrum, such as Arno J. Mayer and Dan Diner. In different ways, they analysed the period 1914–45 as the culmination of a modern 'Thirty Years War', emphasizing that the Second World War was at one and the same time a military, a geo-political, and an ideological conflict in which not only great powers but also antithetical global visions clashed (in a kind of *Weltanschauungskrieg*).[11]

Nolte suggests a different interpretation. In his opinion, the 'European civil war' did not begin in 1914 with the fall of the ancient imperial and dynastic order, the outbreak of a world war, the brutalization of political life in the old continent and the opening of a new cycle of revolutions and counter-revolutions that finally led to the modern totalitarianism. According to Nolte, the 'European civil war' started in 1917 with the Russian Revolution, which was followed two years later by the birth of the Communist International, a 'party of the world civil war'.[12] This is the well-known thesis that provoked a violent controversy among German historians in 1986: Auschwitz as a 'copy', of course extreme but nevertheless derivative, of an 'Asiatic' barbarism originally introduced to Europe by the Bolsheviks. How can we explain Nazi crimes, which were perpetrated by a regime born in a European, modern and civilized nation? According to Nolte, the answer lies in the trauma provoked in Germany by the October Revolution. As the first totalitarian regime to adopt a politics of terror and of 'class extermination' from the onset of the Russian civil war, Bolshevism acted on the German mind as both a 'frightful image' (*Schreckbild*) and a 'model' (*Vorbild*).[13] Thus, Nazi genocide and criminal practices could be explained as an 'exacerbated' reaction to a threat of annihilation embodied by Russian Bolshevism. In others words, Nolte regards Nazi anti-Semitism as a 'particular kind of anti-Bolshevism' and the genocide of the Jews as 'the inverted image of another extermination, that of a world *class*, by the Bolsheviks'.[14] In order to defend his thesis, Nolte underlines the exceptional scale of Jewish involvement in the Russian and Central European communist movement. Since the Jews were considered responsible for the massacres perpetrated by the Bolshevik regime (the destruction of the bourgeoisie), the Nazis concluded that they had to 'exterminate them, as both a retaliation and a preventive measure'. Auschwitz is thus explained by the gulag, 'the logical and factual forerunner' of Nazi crimes, as Nolte wrote in his notorious article in 1986.[15]

It is interesting to observe that in this reconstruction of the origins of totalitarianism, the collectivization of Soviet agriculture at the beginning of the 1930s is practically ignored. The death of several million Russian and Ukrainian peasants from starvation and mass deportations appears much less important, in Nolte's approach, than the violence of the civil war after the Revolution. At the same time, his reconstruction of the history of the Russian civil war is very superficial (on this point, his book is incomparably less well documented than the works of Edward H. Carr, Orlando Figes or Nicolas Werth).[16] For example, he gives no estimate of the number of victims. His attention is focused less on the real horrors of this conflict than on its portrayal and distortions in the German collective consciousness. His thesis on the founding character of Bolshevik violence and on the derivative, 'reactive' origins of Nazism rests on an extremely weak and controversial foundation. In fact, his key primary source is counter-revolutionary propaganda. Thus, he accepts as ready money the various (never verified) accounts diffused by tsarist and nationalist émigrés about the tortures practised by an imaginary 'Chinese Cheka'. In particular, he resurrects the frightening legend of the 'cage of rats' (*Rattenkäfig*), which has been narrated in different versions from Octave Mirbeau to George Orwell.[17] Nolte's key source is a second-hand quotation. In 1924, Serguei Melgunov, a Russian Social-Revolutionary émigré, published *Red Terror in Russia* in Berlin. After warning against several evident 'exaggerations', Melgunov spent many pages quoting another exile, namely R. Nilostonsky's accounts of the Russian civil war.[18] Examining Nolte's different sources, German historian Hans-Ulrich Wehler placed these quotations in their original context; a White propaganda pamphlet published in Berlin in 1920, *Der Blutrausch des Bolschewismus* (*The Blood Lust of Bolshevism*), essentially devoted to describing the Cheka's atrocities. Wehler gives a sample of the booklet's prose: 'Behind the communist imposture of Moscow, there is the triumph of Jewish world imperialism which, according to the thesis of the Zionist congress, must be realised through the pitiless extermination of the whole Christian population.'[19] Of course, this legend of the Chinese Cheka was afterwards diffused first by the Nazi newspaper the *Völkischer Beobachter* and then in another pamphlet by Alfred Rosenberg, *Pest in Russland*. Together with many other statements on the violence of Bolshevik propaganda at the time of the Russian civil war, this legend constitutes the essential 'documentary' basis on which Nolte builds his interpretation of Nazism, of Hitler's anti-Semitism and of the 'preventive' nature of the German war against the Soviet Union.

Nolte's collection of quotations does not prove a thesis, but rather summons up a certain atmosphere. Because of its abundant documentation, his book is not uninteresting as a study of the perception of Bolshevism in Nazi Germany. At the same time, his complete lack of critical distance from his sources and his adherence to an 'image of the enemy' of this type are astonishing. After presenting Nazism as a form of inverted Bolshevism, he relates the history of the latter by borrowing many stereotypes from the German conservative literature of the 1930s, reproducing all its fears and irrational phobias.[20] Nolte does genuinely grasp an essential feature of Nazism; its counter-revolutionary nature, that of a movement born as a reaction against the Russian Revolution and German Spartacism, as a militant anti-Marxist and anti-communist force. That is true of fascism – Mussolini's as well as Hitler's – and of the counter-revolution more generally, which is always inextricably, 'symbiotically' linked to revolution. October 1917 provoked a frightening trauma among the European bourgeoisie, comparable in many respects to the shock experienced by the aristocracy after 1789. The Soviet dictatorship, as well as the ephemeral

Soviet republics that appeared in Bavaria and Hungary in 1919–20, spread fear and even panic among the ruling classes. Nevertheless, that is only one aspect of the problem and it would be very simplistic to reduce the origins of Nazism to this reactive dimension. Certainly, the post-war political crisis created the conditions for its birth – contrary to Sternhell's thesis, which dates the beginning of fascism to the end of nineteenth century, in the France of the Dreyfus Affair[21] – but many components of its ideology, and in particular its anti-Semitism, were older than the Russian Revolution. Doubtless, the revolutions accentuated an already widespread hatred of Jews, but Nazi anti-Semitism was very strongly rooted in the tradition of *völkisch* nationalism, which had impregnated the different tendencies of German conservative culture for several decades. Hitler's anti-Semitism was formed in Vienna at the beginning of the twentieth century, when it could be neither contaminated by anti-communism nor fuelled by the role of Jews in the Russian Revolution and the political upheavals in Central Europe.[22]

Following a tendency that first appeared after 1789, counter-revolution does not limit itself simply to 'restoring' the old regime; it 'transcends' the past, taking on a modern dimension, trying to build a new social and political order, acting as a 'revolution against the revolution' (which explains the strong 'revolutionary' rhetoric and style of both Italian and German fascism).[23] But the content of the fascist counter-revolution is older; it elaborates and mobilizes a whole number of pre-existing cultural and ideological elements in a new synthesis. Nationalism and imperialism, Pan-Germanism and the idea of 'living space', 'redemptive' anti-Semitism and racism, eugenics and extermination of the 'lower races', hatred of the left and charismatic dictatorship are tendencies that had appeared, in more or less developed forms, from the end of the nineteenth century on. Nazism did not create them, it simply radicalized them.

Unlike the French Revolution, which, propagated by Napoleon's armies, was actually at the origin of a European civil war, the Russian Revolution entered a phase of 'internalization' after the defeat of the various insurrectionary attempts in Central Europe. Born during a world war, it led first to a domestic civil war and then to Stalinism. After the troubles of the 1920s and the stabilization of its frontiers, the Soviet regime did not attack international capitalism – with which it tried to establish a *modus vivendi* – but rather launched a domestic war against the peasantry and traditional Russian society. For his part, Hitler probably considered the Soviet Union a class dictatorship, but his image of the enemy was filtered through the categories of eugenics and racial biology. In his eyes, the USSR represented the threat of a destructive revolution, not as the leading force of the international proletariat, but essentially as the result of a diabolical alliance between the

Jewish intelligentsia and 'Slavic subhumanity (*Untermenschentum*)'.[24] Nazism perceived communism as a mortal enemy embodying an anti-national force; the proletariat was only its social body, not its real subject. The genocide of the Jews was not conceived as a response to a supposed class extermination but much more, in Social Darwinist terms, as a necessary step in a process of natural selection, as the conquest of the 'living space' for the superior race.

If Nazism achieved a fusion of three different struggles – a colonial assault on the Slavic world, a political struggle against communism and the Soviet Union, and a racial fight against the Jews – into a unique war of conquest and extermination,[25] this means that its model could not be Bolshevism. It would be more relevant and coherent to find its 'model' in the colonial wars of the nineteenth century, which were actually conceived by the European imperialist powers as the appropriation of 'living space', a colossal plundering of the conquered territories, a process of enslavement of the indigenous peoples and, according to a Social Darwinist model, the destruction of 'inferior races'. Such colonial wars have often taken the form of extermination campaigns by European armies that were convinced they were carrying out a 'civilizing mission'. In a completely different historical context, they were inspired by the same fanaticism and crusading spirit that characterized the Nazi war against the USSR. 'Exterminate all the brutes!': this slogan, evoked by Joseph Conrad in *Heart of Darkness*, was applied by Europeans in Africa in the second half of the nineteenth century before being adopted by the Nazis in Poland, Ukraine and Russia during the Second World War. In contradiction to his own thesis, Nolte himself recalls this essential aspect of the German war, emphasizing Hitler's aim of transforming the Slavic world into a kind of 'German India'. He quotes Reich Commissar Erich Koch, who claimed to be carrying out a colonial war in Ukraine, 'as among niggers'.[26] During the first period of the war on the Eastern front in 1941–42, Hitler's 'table talks' with Martin Bormann were riddled with references to Eastern Europe's future, as an empire for the Germans comparable with what Asia, Africa and the Far West had been for the British, French and US.[27] The historical laboratory for Nazi crimes was not Bolshevik Russia but the colonial past of Western civilization, in the classical era of industrial capitalism, imperialist colonialism and political liberalism. Formulating it in Nolte's own words, we could appropriately describe this historical background as the 'causal nexus' and the 'logical and factual precedent' for Nazi violence. But it is not at all surprising that the new anti-communist paradigm completely ignores this historical genealogy.

We can recognize an element of truth in Nolte's remark that Nazi Germany appeared almost as a *Rechtsstaat* in comparison with Stalin's USSR.[28] Of course, this means considering the Third Reich a state based on a legal order, not a liberal state. The Hobbesian image of Behemoth, the biblical monster evoked by Franz Neumann in order to describe Nazi Germany as 'a non-state, a chaos, a rule of lawlessness and anarchy',[29] could probably be applied more accurately to Stalin's USSR than to the Nazi regime. The Soviet Union was created by a revolution that had profoundly modified the class structure of society. Unlike Germany, where the traditional economic, bureaucratic and military elites had kept their power, this revolution had 'levelled' the structure of society and created new political hierarchies. Insofar as the political regime was based on a new social structure in which all traditional privileges were abolished, nobody could avoid the threat of repression and deportation. At the apogee of the great Terror, any kulak could become an enemy of socialism, any party member could be a secret spy, any technician could be a saboteur, any former Menshevik could be a counter-revolutionary, any long-time party member could be suspected of Trotskyism and condemned as a traitor, etc. In Nazi Germany, on the contrary, violence was strictly codified. With the obvious exception of political anti-fascists (especially social-democrats and communists), its targets were different minorities classified as not belonging to the German *Volk* and as enemies of the 'Aryan race': Jews, Gypsies, the congenitally ill, homosexuals, 'asocial' people, etc. Unlike anti-fascists, who were persecuted because of their political activities, these minorities' 'crime' was simply to be alive. The political order that corresponded to this racial-biological hierarchy of society was obviously inhuman and deeply undemocratic, but not necessarily 'irrational' or chaotic. In other words, Nazi terror did not threaten society as a whole.

Prisoner of the contradictions of the Nazi 'polycracy', the German totalitarian system was no more finished or effective than Stalin's was. The fact is that Stalinism bore no relation to the racist and biological *Weltanschauung* that inspired Nazi crimes.[30] Stalinism, on the one hand, was characterized by a police state, blind repression, a totalitarian organization of society, 'feudal–military exploitation' of the peasantry (in Bukharin's words), deportation of peoples judged as 'non-reliable' or suspected, according to paranoid criteria, of collaboration with the enemy. Nazism, on the other hand, was characterized first by a 'synchronized' (*gleischhaltet*) society that was organized along ethnic and racial lines, then by a colonial war for conquest of German 'living space' in the Slavic world and a war of extermination against the Jews, both converging in the destruction of the USSR and 'Judaeo-Bolshevism'. These completely different patterns exclude the hypothesis of a 'causal nexus' between Nazism and Stalinism's crimes. They also considerably limit the value of the concept of totalitarianism, which is based on their formal similarities. The interpretation of totalitarianism's origins proposed by Nolte conceals an essential source of Nazism: eugenics, with its projects of racial purification (to the point of euthanasia). Developed in Western Europe beginning at the end of nineteenth century, in the epoch of classical liberalism, this ideology became the central axis of the Nazi political project.[31]

Forgetting such fundamental aspects, Nolte's analogy inevitably takes on an apologetic flavour. In his book, he uses the concept of genocide in a very broad and not very rigorous way. On the one hand he recognizes the peculiar character of Nazi genocidal policies, but on the other hand he applies this word to all violence occurring during the Second World War. For example, he imputes an 'openly genocidal intention' to Churchill, quoting several passages of a letter to Lord Beaverbrook in June 1940 in which the British prime minister mentioned the means to be used in the war against Germany. Nolte defines the deportation of 'punished peoples' in the USSR as 'ethnic massacres practiced in a repressive and a preventive way'. Finally, he qualifies the Anglo-American war against Nazi Germany as 'almost exclusively a war of extermination', adding that the expulsion of German populations living beyond the Oder-Neisse line was an 'ethnic murder'.[32] Of course such comparisons are highly questionable: they erase any distinction between genocide – the planned extermination of a human group – and forced displacement of a population, however authoritarian, inhuman and reprehensible it may be, as well as between genocide and war crimes (a category to which we could consign the bombing of German civilians between 1942 and 1945). But the main problem raised by all these comparisons lies in their hermeneutic framework: the explanation of Auschwitz and of the Nazi war more generally as a preventive genocide and a preventive war, both generated by a regime facing the threat of a terrible destruction and acting from an elemental instinct of self-defence.

During the *Historikerstreit*, Habermas described Nolte's thesis as 'a kind of damage limitation' (*ein Art Schadensabwicklung*)[33] that enabled Nolte to obfuscate all the German roots of Nazism and attribute its crimes, albeit indirectly, to Bolshevism. According to Saul Friedländer, Nolte's approach tends to radically modify the historical picture, displacing Germany as a whole on to the side of the victims.[34] In Nolte's view, Germany does not appear as a society divided between a hard core of perpetrators, a more or less broad layer of accomplices and, with the exception of a minority of anti-fascist opponents, a great majority of passive bystanders, but as a single bloc of victims, as a menaced nation that naturally identified with the regime that tried to organize its defence (and lost its way in criminal excess). In this way, Nolte simply evacuates the question of 'German guilt' (*deutsche Schuldfrage*) – a question that Karl Jaspers raised in 1945 and that could easily be extended to the whole of Europe occupied by the Third Reich. Jaspers distinguished four different forms of guilt: the criminal guilt of the direct perpetrators, the political guilt of the institutions and organized forces that supported Hitler's power, the individual guilt of the accomplices, and the 'metaphysical' guilt of all citizens who recognized the criminal character of the Nazi regime but accepted it without protesting. Defined in this way, guilt was the source of a historical responsibility that the German nation was obliged to assume in order to regain its place within the international community.[35] By contrast, Nolte's interpretation of the 'European civil war' puts Germany as a whole on the side of the victims including the Nazi regime, which was threatened first by a Bolshevik uprising directed from Moscow and then by a war of extermination waged by both Soviet and Allied military forces. The persecutor transformed into a victim: Nolte's revisionism lies in this reversal of the historical perspective. Much more than a canon of historiography, which is very difficult to define, this revisionism concerns a widespread historical consciousness.

A corollary of these premises is Nolte's inclination to legitimate – without agreeing with – Holocaust denial, attributing to its supporters a set of 'often honourable' motivations.[36] For instance, in his correspondence with Furet, he writes that denial 'should be accepted as a phenomenon internal to the scientific development'.[37] Although he expressed sceptical reservations about this position, the French historian was not scandalized by such a complacent attitude. Despite their sometimes considerable historical disagreements, Furet accorded his German colleague his regard and admiration. In the last analysis, they found common ground – we could say a common 'passion' – in anti-communism, to which they added an important corollary: *anti*-anti-fascism. That was enough to transform all their disagreements into a normal 'exchange of ideas'. According to Nolte, anti-fascism was only the mask of a totalitarian regime. With the exception of a few details, Furet shared this point of view. In *The Passing of an Illusion*, anti-fascism is reduced to a facet of Stalinist ideology, as a kind of democratic camouflage, or a stratagem allowing Bolshevism 'at the moment of the great Terror to present itself as liberty by virtue of a negation'.[38] Reading Furet, one could easily conclude that neither democratic anti-fascism nor anti-Stalinist communism ever existed.

In 1947, Herbert Marcuse broke off a correspondence he had just begun with Martin Heidegger, his former mentor, because of Heidegger's apologetic attitude towards Nazism, which made all dialogue impossible. Heidegger refused to distinguish between the extermination of the Jews by Nazism and the expulsion of the Germans living outside of new German frontiers.[39] In 1986, Habermas showed the same indignation towards Nolte.

With the composure of his blasé liberalism, Furet reserved his contempt for other adversaries. When Nolte suggests giving scientific credibility to Holocaust denial, Furet expresses only polite scepticism, a mere shadow of the sarcasm and polemical fury he deployed some years earlier in trying to demolish the 'populist–Leninist vulgate' of Claude Mazuric and Albert Soboul concerning the interpretation of the French Revolution.[40] Perhaps Furet had tried to imitate his great model, Alexis de Tocqueville, who described socialists in his *Souvenirs* as 'rabble' (*canailles*) but remained a loyal friend and intellectual accomplice of Gobineau, the founder of modern racism, throughout his life.[41]

In the foreword to the French edition of his book on the 'European civil war', Nolte qualifies Marxism as an 'ideology of extermination', and Bolshevism, 'its practical application', as a 'reality of extermination'.[42] We can hardly find similar formulations in Furet's writings. Following Raymond Aron, he was still capable of distinguishing between concentration camps like Buchenwald and Dachau, the goal of which was forced labour and where death was a result of the conditions imposed on the inmates, and extermination camps like Treblinka and Auschwitz-Birkenau, which actually functioned as killing factories.[43] This difference is implicitly erased in Courtois' introduction to *The Black Book of Communism*, where he asserts a structural homology between communist 'class genocide' and Nazi 'race genocide'.[44] In a more recent essay Courtois goes even further. Now he presents the Lubianka, the GPU building in Moscow, as a 'killing centre' entirely comparable to Auschwitz, whose only difference lay in the means of destruction utilized: on the one hand traditional executions by shooting, on the other hand the gas chambers. (A very similar position was taken earlier, during the *Historikerstreit*, by Hitler's biographer, Joachim Fest.)[45]

Basically, our three scholars share a common vision of communism as an 'ideocracy', a political system generated by an ideological essence. Its historical antecedent is inevitably perceived to be the Terror of the French Revolution. 'As in 1793', writes Furet in *The Passing of an Illusion*, 'Revolution as a whole derives from the revolutionary idea'.[46] According to Nolte, the French Revolution was the first historical attempt to 'realise the idea of exterminating a class or a group'. Thereafter, the Bolsheviks were inspired by an 'extermination therapy' first developed by the French revolutionists.[47] Finally, Courtois considers the 'extermination of the people' (*populicide*)[48] perpetrated by the Jacobins in the Vendée as a massacre prefiguring Bolshevik and Nazi violence, all three being the expression of an 'ideocracy'.

In fact, the violence of the Jacobin Terror came from below. Marat, Danton and Robespierre sought to organize and contain it within a legal framework. It was an expression of an emergency dictatorship – Lazare

Carnot called it a *dictature de la détresse* – which led first to the *levée en masse* when the Revolution was threatened by a foreign military coalition, then to the Committee of Public Safety, when reaction organized itself inside the country. According to Robespierre and Danton, it was a question of replacing popular vengeance, dangerously blind and raging, with 'the sword of the law'. Following Edgar Quinet, Arno J. Mayer analyses the Vendée as a classical civil war marked by excess and fanaticism on both sides. Expressing Catholic, royalist and peasant resistance to revolutionary transformations, the Vendée war took the form of a military reaction that was repressed by force. Today's comparison with a genocide,[49] Mayer underlines, is not at all appropriate, because the victims of the Vendée were essentially soldiers. The target of Jacobin 'fury' was not a people but the counter-revolution, in a region where 90 per cent of the priests refused to swear an oath of loyalty to the nation, law and constitution and finally organized a royalist army.[50] But the 'ideocratical' explanation allows our conservative historians to avoid all historical analysis.

The concept of 'ideocracy' was first formulated at the end of the 1930s by a German émigré, Waldemar Gurian, a former student of Carl Schmitt who became a theoretician of totalitarianism.[51] The golden age of this concept was the Cold War in the early 1950s, when Israeli historian Jacob L. Talmon situated the roots of modern totalitarian ideologies in the radical democratic utopias of Rousseau and Marx.[52] Adopting this perspective, many scholars have presented the tradition of counter-revolutionary thought as the first embryonic expression of a critique of totalitarianism. Unlike Hannah Arendt, who presented Edmund Burke's rejection of the Rights of Man as one of the ideological matrices of modern racism and notably of Nazism, Robert Nisbet celebrated the author of the *Reflections on the Revolution in France* as a forerunner of twentieth-century anti-totalitarian crusaders.[53] Among the most recent historians to stigmatize the communist 'ideocracy', the most prolific are probably the Americans Richard Pipes and Martin Malia. Inspired – like Furet – by the reactionary historian Augustin Cochin, Pipes compares the '*sociétés de pensée*' of the French Enlightenment to the circles of the Russian intelligentsia of the end of the nineteenth century. After stressing their deep affinities, he concludes that the 'dry terror' of such intellectual movements laid the foundations for the 'blood terror' of the revolutionary dictatorships, both Jacobin and Bolshevik. In other words, the Committee of Public Safety derived from the *Encyclopédie* just as the Cheka was an outcome of the Populist circles of the tsarist epoch. Concerning the White Terror, whose victims numbered several hundred thousand people between 1918 and 1922, Pipes has nothing to say. It simply did not exist. 'Terror is rooted in the Jacobin ideas of Lenin', he writes, adding that its main goal was 'the physical extermination of the "bourgeoisie" '. We can observe that the quotation marks are not put around the verb, exterminate, but the object, the bourgeoisie, a very loose concept including, in his interpretation, not only a social class but, more generally, 'all those who, independently of their economic and social status, opposed Bolshevik policies'.[54] Although a bit less radical, Malia subscribes to the same logic. He describes communism as the realization of an unnatural 'utopia' and presents Soviet history as the manifestation of a harmful ideology: 'In the world created by the October Revolution, we are never facing a *society*, but only a *regime*, an "ideocratic" regime.'[55] All these approaches reduce the core of revolutionary experience to the terror – the Jacobin republic of 1793–94 and the Bolshevik dictatorship of 1918–22 – which can be essentially, if not exclusively, explained by such categories as psychosis, passion, ideology and fanaticism. Evoking Tocqueville, Pipes compares the revolution to a 'virus'.[56] For his part, Furet describes it as the triumph of 'the illusion of politics'.[57] Following this hypothesis, he has studied the history of communism as the trajectory of an autarchic concept, devoid of any social dimension. Thus, the communist experience was the rise and fall of an 'illusion'. In his first book on the French Revolution written with Denis Richet in 1965, Furet opposed 1789 to 1793, distinguishing between the liberal revolution and its *dérapage* ('going off the rails').[58] But now, revolution itself is seen as 'going off the rails'. The Bolshevik revolution was intrinsically bad from its inception. From this point of view, communism appears basically as a messianic-political experience, a kind of 'secular religion' practised by its adepts as a faith and a passion.

Nolte is perhaps the only conservative historian today concerned with suggesting an interpretation of the origins of totalitarianism. According to him, an essential thread in the first half of twentieth-century history lies in the fundamental opposition between Bolshevism and Nazism, the former introducing the spiral of violence and cumulative radicalization that led to a war of extermination. Unconcerned with its origins, Courtois reduces communism to a simply criminal phenomenon. His reading of the past erases all historical ruptures, its social and political dimensions, and the sometime tragic dilemmas of its actors, and compresses it into the linear continuity of a totalitarian system. The Russian civil war, famine, the collectivization of agriculture, the gulag and deportation did not flow from a plurality of causes, and their explanation may even escape their historical context to a very great degree; they simply become the different external manifestations of a unique, intrinsically criminal ideology – communism. Its birth goes back to the *putsch* of October 1917. With Courtois, the ideological determinism of the relation between Revolution and Terror needs no explanation; it is simply postulated *a priori*. Stalin becomes the administrator of Lenin and Trotsky's projects, and his crimes lose the 'erratic' and 'improvized' character detected by historians like Nicolas Werth and Arch Getty.[59] On the one hand, they appear as massacres that were rigorously planned – a diagnosis that is acceptable for the great purges and the gulag, but highly debatable for the collectivization, the most extensive of its crimes – and, on the other hand, they are presented as products of their malignant ideological roots. A criminal ideology, communism, took millions of victims: Lenin was its architect, Stalin its most important executor. These men play the role of authentic demiurgic heroes reminiscent, though in an upside-down way, of the myths propagated in the old days by the Stalinist vulgate. In this way, anti-communist historiography simply proposes, as Claudio Sergio Ingerflom rightly observed, 'an anti-Bolshevik version of a "Bol-shevized" history'.[60]

Pushed onwards by the impetus of his relentless crusade against the great evil of the twentieth century, Courtois forgets some basic rules of historical comparison: putting events in context, recognizing their international or national character, keeping in mind the duration of a political regime, etc. For instance, he forgets that unlike Nazism, which existed only twelve years and underwent a continous radicalization until its implosion during the war, the USSR existed for seventy-four years and went through a revolutionary, a 'Thermidorian', a totalitarian and a long post-totalitarian phase. In Courtois' eyes, it is simply meaningless to consider communism as a plural and contradictory phenomenon, distinguishing between Trotsky and Stalin, Bela Kun and Enrico Berlinguer, Robert Hue and Pol Pot. It is also superfluous to separate Stalinism from its communist victims or to make distinctions between the movements and the regimes, between a revolutionary utopia and a ruling bureaucracy, between patterns of liberation and oppression, or between an anti-fascist resister and a KGB agent.[61] Of course, the frontiers that separate the different forms of communism are not always perfectly clear – at times they may even be very ambiguous – but they exist, and should prevent us from reducing this open 'field of experience' to a monolithic phenomenon. In fact, Courtois scrupulously avoids considering such 'com-plications'. In his eyes, communism is criminal as both ideology and reality, and always identical at all times and in all places.

Courtois' simplifications have obliged some historians, including those very close to him like Marc Lazar, to take their distance. According to Lazar, Courtois' 'fundamental fault' lies in his attempt to 'privilege homologies, very rare in [historical] reality, instead of making analogies', that is, discerning the common elements that may exist between two such globally distinct realities as Nazism and communism.[62] This is the difference, in Lazar's opinion, between a critical and a merely ideological use of the concept of totalitarianism. But this critique does not convince Courtois, who incessantly repeats his certitudes. He demands a 'Nuremberg of communism' (like the French fascist leader Jean-Marie Le Pen) and points an accusing finger at the 'fundamentalism' of both Jewish and communist accounts of the past. This is the main cause, in his opinion, of scholars' reluctance to apply his own historical comparison (Nazism and communism as the twin faces of the same totalitarian genus). If his interpretation has been widely criticized, he suggests, this is due to the hateful influence on French university and research institutions until 1989 of 'the formidable ideological power' of communism, a 'propaganda machine perfectly organised from the end of the twenties and pervasive in public opinion, including the universities'.[63]

Basically, Courtois has invented nothing. He simply proposes a new version of the old McCarthyist theory of the communist conspiracy. In a 1950 essay, Isaac Deutscher painted a fine and acute portrait of the ex-communist who transformed himself during the Cold War into a visceral anti-communist, disposed to fight Soviet totalitarianism with totalitarian methods. The ex-Maoist Stéphane Courtois fits this ideal–typical portrait very well. Often, writes Deutscher, the ex-communist brings with him

> the lack of scruple, the narrow-mindedness, the disregard for truth, and the intense hatred with which Stalinism has imbued him. He remains a sectarian. He is an inverted Stalinist. He continues to see the world in white and black, but now the colours are differently distributed. As a communist he saw no difference between Nazism and communism. Once, he accepted the party's claim to infallibility; now he believes himself to be infallible. Having once been caught by the "greatest illusion", he is now obsessed by the greatest disillusionment of our time.[64]

Reviewing *The Passing of an Illusion*, Eric J. Hobsbawm has written that it was not the first book of the post-communist era, but the latest product of the Cold War.[65] Such an appraisal seems even more appropriate to Stéphane Courtois. He inherited from his mentor neither the sense of proportion, nor the erudition, nor even the pleasure in narration that marked the style of the historian of the French Revolution. The only legacy he received from Furet is anti-communism.

However, criticizing anti-communist clichés does not solve the problem of the historical comparison between National Socialism and Stalinism. Of course, that requires a reappraisal of the Russian Revolution, the civil war and their relationship to Stalinism. Such questions are not at all closed and continue to invite new and controversial interpretations. Indubitably, we cannot refuse the ideological schemes of anti-communist historiography by means of another brand of apologetic historicism. Some Marxist scholars were tempted to reverse Nolte or Courtois' scheme and to present Stalinism as the response to a colossal threat to the existence of the USSR itself. Nazism, whose 1941 *Blitzkrieg* proved its project of extermination, embodied this menace; Stalinism, with its regrettable crimes, was the inevitable consequence.[66] Of course, the Stalinist response was disproportionate and criminal in its extreme consequences, but finally it was a derivative and exogenous politics. This approach is the symmetrical, Marxist version of Nolte's historical revisionism.

Unquestionably, the isolation of the Russian Revolution – encircled by a hostile capitalist world – in the years between the wars was a historical fact. We can keep this reality in mind in order to explain the dictatorship, but not to legitimate the Cheka's repression, the Moscow trials, the Ukrainian famine or the gulag. If the concept of European civil war is not enough to justify a mono-causal explanation of Nazism, neither does it allow a similar analysis of Stalinism. We can certainly distinguish between revolutionary terror, born in the midst of civil war and fuelled by the violence of the counter-revolution, and Stalinist terror, launched as a 'revolution from above' within a country at peace, menaced neither by domestic social reaction nor by foreign military intervention.[67] Nevertheless, this difference does not eliminate the problem of Bolshevik policies at the inception of the Soviet experience.

Before the First World War, Marxism was the cultural background shared by both Russian Bolshevism and German social democracy, by Lenin and Kautsky. Until 1914, Lenin considered himself a disciple of Kautsky, whose theories he tried to apply to the analysis of the Russian society.[68] If the same ideology inspired both the actors and the sharpest critics of the Revolution, it is difficult to conclude, with Nolte and Courtois, that Bolshevik ideology produced the Russian civil war. Several choices and measures, like the dissolution of the Constituent Assembly, censorship, suppression of all political opposition, the Cheka's executions, the creation of the first labour camps in 1919, and the repression of the Kronstadt uprising two years later, cannot be derived from Marxism in the same way that the Nuremberg laws and Auschwitz can be coherently derived from the racist and biological *Weltanschauung* of National Socialism. But if the Red Terror was not an automatic byproduct of an ideology, it certainly resulted from political choices. The rapidity with which a military and political dictatorship, a single-party regime theorizing and practising violence as a means of building a new society, took shape in Russia needs to be explained. The extent of repression and the stifling of all criticism – including criticism coming from within the revolutionary camp (Martov is an example) – cannot be explained exclusively as a result of the historical context, the White Terror or the threat constituted by the anti-Soviet military coalition. Inevitably, such measures raise the question of the role played by Bolshevik ideology in the formation of Soviet totalitarianism.

Doubtless, the Soviet regime's choices were made in a context of civil war, whose violence was terribly great and murderous. The magnitude of this violence was a legacy of the First World War – the 'brutalization' of social and political life (in George Mosse's words) – in a backward country without a democratic tradition; and the sharpness of the conflict between the social and political forces involved in the revolutionary process inevitably accentuated this tendency to resort to violence when the Bolsheviks took power. The old institutions had lost their legitimacy, Lenin's government was supported by the soviets but challenged outside them, the state monopoly of violence had been broken, peasant rebellion had broken out in the countryside and soldiers wished to leave the front. In other words, it was a classical civil war, with all its 'furies'. As with the *levée en masse* and the Vendée repression in France, the Cheka and war communism were, according to Arno Mayer, the result of a context where 'panic, fear and pragmatism mixed with hubris, ideology and iron will'.[69] Red Terror was a response to White Terror, in a situation of endemic violence, with its spiral of radicalization and excess, that the Bolshevik government tried to control and channel. Once we recognize this historical context, it is possible to debate the role played by ideology in the Bolshevik policy. It did not produce the civil war, but it intensified the conflicts and accentuated the resort to violence, thus contributing to the erection of an authoritarian, undemocratic regime, which finally destroyed all the emancipatory hopes of 1917.

The cult of violence understood as a 'midwife' of history, the complete underestimation of the role of law in the new revolutionary state, and a normative vision of dictatorship as an instrument of social transformation; these elements did not derive from the circumstances, but rather helped shape the Bolshevik response to it. Ideology and fanaticism played a role in the Red Terror – a work like Trotsky's *Terrorism and Communism* (1920)[70] was its most coherent theoretical systematization – just as they had played a role in the Jacobin Terror (later lucidly criticized by Marx).[71] When Lenin presented the suspension of law as a way to overcome 'bourgeois democracy' and Trotsky identified proletarian dictatorship with forced labour and state control of trade unions, violence had lost its objectively imposed and spontaneous character and become a government system justified in the name of *Raison d'État*.[72] The cold terror of Stalinism, deployed through the deportation of the kulaks and the political purges of the 1930s, does not change the fact that the foundations of Soviet totalitarianism were laid by Lenin and Trotsky's dictatorship during the civil war. The result of their policies was probably in many respects the opposite of their intentions (as Lenin recognized in his testament), but this does not change the objective impact of their acts. Victor Serge, a strange combination of Bolshevik and libertarian who participated in the October Revolution, was among the first to draw this balance sheet, in the early 1930s.[73] If we do not recognize these evident dynamics, our critique of twentieth-century revisionist reinterpretations by anti-communist scholars like Nolte or Furet will appear weak and not very credible, to say the least.

It is time to sum up the different forms of the new anti-communist paradigm. For Nolte, it is the key to interpreting the last century, completely subsumed under the sign of civil war (first European, then international). In spite of its limits and its apologetic aims, his vision is not uninteresting, insomuch as he puts the conflict between fascism and communism at the heart of the century. Furet's anti-communism is more in keeping with the ruling *Zeitgeist*. After postulating a philosophically and historically debatable equation between capitalism and democracy, he tends to reduce both fascism and communism to a tragic parenthesis on the inescapable path to liberalism. 'The greatest secret of the complicity between Bolshevism and fascism', he wrote in *The Passing of an Illusion*, 'remains their common enemy, which they reduce or exorcise, thinking it as in its death-throes, but which nevertheless constitutes their soil: simple democracy.'[74] Courtois, the least interesting of our three scholars, does not go beyond the old assimilation of communism to Nazism, two totalitarian regimes based on the same project of exterminating an enemy class (the bourgeoisie) or an enemy race (the Jews). He thus proposes a liberal democracy freed from the legacy of anti-fascism – one of its constitutive elements in continental Europe – and directly based on anti-communism. National-conservative resentment (Nolte), the spirit of revenge of a late Cold-War crusader (Courtois), an apology of liberalism and a historical farewell to revolution by an intellectual who has accepted capitalism as the impassable horizon of our time (Furet): these are the three variants of the new anti-communist historical paradigm.

None of these three approaches can grasp the fundamental difference that separates communism from fascism, in spite of their criminal outcomes and of the formal affinities of their ruling systems. The Stalinist legacy, made up of a mountain of ruins and dead, did not erase the origins of communism in the tradition of the Enlightenment and eighteenth-century rationalist humanism. Marxism descended from this cultural tradition and was one of its main currents until the First World War and the Russian Revolution. This relationship explains the fact that many critics (and victims) of Stalinism combated it in the name of Marxism, communist ideas, democratic principles and humanist values. By contrast, fascism and Nazism, in spite of their racist scientism and their cult of modern technology, were extreme outcomes of the Counter-Enlightenment. 'The year 1789 will be expelled from history', declared Josef Goebbels in 1933, when Nazism came to power in Germany. Unlike communism, fascism did not wish to destroy capitalist society but opposed the figure of the leader and the principle of authority to democracy and popular sovereignty, order and hierarchy to freedom and law, race and nation to individuality and humanity. The instrumental rationality at the heart of the modern world's violence – total wars and atomic bombs, concentration camps and industrial killing – does not change this fundamental difference. Any theory of totalitarianism that shows itself indifferent to this difference is condemned to understand nothing of the history of the last century.

Communism, Nazism, Colonialism:
What Value has the Analogy?

Marc Ferro

Since the collapse of communism in the USSR, the comparison between this form of rule and Nazism has inspired numerous studies. In fact, insofar as their method is concerned, Jan Valtin (*Out of the Night*, 1941) and Vasily Grossman (*Life and Fate*, written during the 1950s) as well as Margarete Buber-Neumann (*Under Two Dictators*, 1949) had already established the parallel. The comparison between the Nazi camps and the gulag was also an old one, and David Rousset was the first, at the time of the Kravchenko trial in 1947, to pronounce the word gulag, before Solzhenitsyn popularized it around 1964.[1]

These comparisons had been previously theorized by the German anti-fascists, who in Bonn after 1945 had again taken up the concept of totalitarianism, applied before the war to fascist Italy and to Nazi Germany, and to them alone, by the leaders of those very countries. At the time they had the task of drafting the Basic Law of the future Federal Republic: 'it must not be totalitarian as had been the Nazi regime and as was the Soviet regime'. Associated with this draft were the Social Democrat Kurt Schumacher and Hannah Arendt, who was at the time in exile in the US.

Since then the analyses have merely confirmed the conformity of these regimes to the model, the concept of totalitarianism becoming a clone by a sort of tautological equivalence.[2]

Starting from this model which defines the essential features – single party, terror, cult of the leader, mystique of power and, for Nazism, racism – it was possible to establish which regimes corresponded more or less to it, whether they used the term or not and whatever may have been the degree of terror, so that Pol Pot's regime in Cambodia and Kadar's Hungary are put into the same sack.

It is quite curious to note that the enthusiasts for this comparison are happy to refer to the works of Hannah Arendt, without observing that she confined this comparison to the Stalinist period, and above all that she associated totalitarianism with imperialism. As for Ernst Nolte, who compares the fascist regimes with each other, he limits Nazi totalitarianism to the years 1933–45, in order to make it into a sort of historical accident, a phenomenon without roots, as it were.[3] In fact there was scarcely any colonial rule more racist than that of the Germans in Tanganyika and South West Africa. Is it necessary to recall that by adding a swastika to the flag of Karl Peters, General von Epp intended to glorify this precursor in the field of collective crimes in Tanganyika before 1914? The latter was in fact recalled on the basis of complaints from socialist and Catholic circles, and under these pressures Wilhelm II before 1914 even had to cancel the decree for the extermination of the Hereros (*Vernichtungsbefehl*).[4]

Between colonialism and the Nazi regime at least, there exists in fact a kinship well identified by the West Indian poet Aimé Césaire, who pointed out that what 'the very Christian bourgeois of the twentieth century . . . cannot forgive Hitler for is not *crime* in itself . . . it is not *the humiliation of man as such*, it is the crime against the white man . . . and the fact that he applied to Europe colonialist procedures which until then had been reserved exclusively for the Arabs of Algeria, the coolies of India and the blacks of Africa'.[5] Now this parallel is valid on other levels. Thus we can note that in British 'imperial' films, whether made in England or the US, we find the same alternative that Nazi anti-Semitism presented. In *The Charge of the Light Brigade* (Tony Richardson, 1968) the native who preserves his customs is a barbarian while the educated native, here a Hindu, is almost always a villain; it is the same in *Jud Süss* (Veit Harlan, 1940), either he remains a Jew and is contemptible, or else he modernizes and must be distrusted.

As for the communist regimes, the colonial subject sees them from the standpoint of repression certainly, rather than in the context of the question of the single party. In Soviet Islamic countries, they see in them first of all regimes which, through their secular character, have destroyed and devastated their freedom, in this case their relation to Sharia law. What Islamic law had regulated was replaced by the secular regime in favour of laws made to give a juridical framework to its domination. Hence they have in view regimes as dissimilar as those of the Soviets and that of the secular democratic French republic, which for the colonized Muslims are only variants of the same model.[6] This time it is Lenin and Clemenceau who are the two enemies put in the same sack.

This detour enables us to show that the concepts of totalitarianism, democracy, colonialism, etc., certainly express the essence of certain regimes, yet obscure the way in which societies have experienced them, whether or not they were on the receiving end. With conceptual history, the history of ideas, everything happens as though once the regimes were established and their functioning had been described, their social anchorage had disappeared. In the extreme case the colonizer can ignore the very existence of the populations that existed prior to his installation – without mentioning those he had previously massacred in the Caribbean, in North America, in Australia and in Central Africa. Thus during the 1950s in Algeria, considering themselves at the bottom of the social scale in view of the pre-eminence exercised by the large settlers, a great many French workers and minor state employees voted Communist: they simply forgot that below them there were the Arabs, for the Arabs didn't count. They hardly counted in Palestine either, when the state of Israel was created. The Jews in Israel and the French in Algeria saw themselves as being simultaneously victims and on the left. The Jews because of the Holocaust and because, at that time, they were secular and members of the Labour Party; the French because they were the descendants of those exiled by Louis Napoleon, or because they were supporters of the 1871 Commune or the Spanish Republic.[7]

To consider ideas, opinions and theories independently of their manifestation in social life is thus reductive and impoverishing. All the more so because such ideas do not necessarily form coherent wholes: one can call oneself a democrat and not question the existence of a vanguard or of a charismatic leader, one can speak in the name of a class while proposing measures that concern society as a totality, etc. But above all, if it is true that people can act on the basis of their convictions, the events that shatter their lives also destroy their points of reference. On the eve of the 1914 war, for example, the fragility of ideological positions was obvious. At the Congress of the Socialist International, delegates formed groups not by tendency (revisionist, radical) but by nations, thus reproducing the very order they claimed to be opposing: French Socialists showed themselves to be seeking revenge against the Germans, and were cordially condescending towards the Russians. Or else the divergences between Socialists reproduced an inverted model of alliances between states, the Russian Bolsheviks being allied to the German left-wingers, so that all were subject to the disposition of relations between states and according to their national allegiance.[8] It is this national feeling which, in 1914, swept everything aside, this 'instinct', as Croce said, 'which is deeper than all argument'. Thus at the first sound of the bugle, neither the sovereign people which charged the enemy after having shouted 'war on war', nor those who spoke in its name and found reasons for their about-face, adopted the behaviour which would confirm the ideas they were supposed to hold.

Everything was turned upside down, and the war confused the traditional divisions. On to the divisions situated on one axis – conservatism, reform, revolution – new ones were superimposed: 'warmongering, neutralism, pacifism'. On the eve of the Second World War, in the French Parliament a new line-up was superimposed, which was different but recalled the previous one, when, threatened by the joint attraction of communism and fascism, the parliamentary world shifted from the left–right division to one between warmongering and pacifism: Reynaud stood alongside Blum, and Déat alongside Laval.

Above all, cataclysms reveal the fragility of abstract positions: 'what seemed important becomes insignificant'.[9] New scales appear, noted Henri Bergson. For example, in France, the pre-1914 divisions disappeared, such as that of the Church against the Republic. A new hierarchy of values replaced the old one; the primary school teacher, the miner and the railway worker gave way to disabled ex-servicemen, the soldiers from the trenches, the nurses.

In Algeria during the 1950s a reversal of attitudes could be observed. Before 1956–58, the Arabs were overpoliticized, aware of the slightest tremblings of the planet; the Europeans wanted to ignore the rising danger, they repressed it, 'went to the beach'. After 1958 it was the reverse. Muzzled by the growth of terror exercised by the FLN, the Muslims no longer dared express their ideas or their feelings, on the contrary, the Europeans stood in the breach, for or against de Gaulle; only a few of them were heard of until a good number went over to the OAS – former Socialist or Communist voters for the most part.[10]

Thus in analysing the nature of totalitarian or colonial or other regimes, the study of ideas and of their history is much too limited unless it is linked to the study of mentalities and of the actions of the groups which make up society.

Tsarist Russia in 1917 represents the sole historical case where the fall of the monarch was accompanied by a total collapse of the state and of the social bodies that, traditionally, ensured the continuity of institutions, the permanence of societies and the domination of a small minority. So that from the summer of 1917, the weakening of the Provisional Government left only one choice: support either the project of soviet power or that of a return to order. The latter programme is defined as follows: defence against social revolution, reactivation of the role of the army and the church, the appearance of new men (often former revolutionaries who had gone over to national defence), cult of the leader, recourse to violence against democratic leaders, and anti-Semitism. In each of its elements, or almost, this model proposed by General Kornilov and by Savinkov prefigured the structures of Nazism or fascism, but to imagine that the Italians or the Germans were inspired by it makes no more sense than to claim, as Nolte does, that the Nazi terror was inspired by that of the Bolsheviks and was only a response to it.

Reaction failed – for example the White rising after October – and these attempts added to the exasperation of those who had greeted February as the dawn of a great hope. It added a new fury to the violence which had come from below before the war, and which was reawakening; besides the great landowners, it struck officers. Originally this violence owed nothing to the Bolsheviks, but subsequently it was the Bolshevized soldiers who inhabited the lower stories of the Soviet state apparatus and perpetuated it. Only Lenin and a few others were pleased by this, but no sooner had the Bolsheviks taken power than they associated this violence from below with a violence from above directed against all their political rivals.

In her study of totalitarianism, Hannah Arendt claims that she does not understand why, once victory had been won, the violence continued. This is because her analysis starts from the point of view of the leaders and, as far as this violence was concerned, the political victory of the Bolsheviks was not sufficient to appease those who, in the cities or in the countryside, still had reserves of resentment.

As for the terror of specifically Bolshevik origin, it responded, after victory, to a different logic.

The Revolution had broken out in the name of justice, to put an end to inequity; now, those who triumphed in October, feeling confident on the basis of the correctness of their analyses, judged that they had been able to succeed because of their sense of history. Certainly, the absolute power which the Bolsheviks established responded to the human appetite for power, but this power also wished to be undivided because the science which had led to its triumph could not be shared; its exercise was incompatible with that of democracy. The elimination of political opponents did not always respond to a will for violence, such as the resentment of the humiliated; it belonged to historical necessity. The party did not consider its violence to be criminal; it wanted it to be effective. After October, when Lenin asked for capitalists to be arrested, it was not in the name of equity, to punish them for having exploited the workers, but inasmuch as they constituted an obstacle to the building of socialism.[11]

Subsequently, it was a case of 'cleansing' the social body by suppressing elements, which, even innocently, might slow down the progress of the regime, and the accomplishment of its programmes. At the Kravchenko trial in 1949, the French public could not understand that those who had survived the camps did not know what they had been accused of; it was presumed that those condemned must necessarily be guilty of something. In fact it was the omniscient party-state that took on the task of defining their offences as it defined those of the leaders condemned in the show trials. Later, and following the same logic, those who denied the scientific status of the party's analyses were defined as sick and sent to psychiatric hospitals.[12] But after Khrushchev's bluster about how the USSR 'would soon overtake America' (in a speech of 1957) the leaden case that enclosed society began to melt under the force of anecdotes and bursts of laughter.

But the questioning had deeper roots. As early as 1918, numerous Bolsheviks had been concerned by the party's absolutism, and if its violence was at this time considered inevitable, like that of 1793 in France, it caused the militants distress, as Victor Serge had testified in the 1920s. But this terror was not perceived as emanating from a twin source; the other revolutionaries saw in it simply the hand of the Bolsheviks, and these Bolsheviks adopted this violence from below to legitimate their right to govern.

Independently of the criticism of opponents, émigrés and former foreign sympathizers, which continued to grow but which was obscured by the achievements of a successful revolution and was later stifled abroad by the urgency of the fight against fascism, a questioning of the regime began to spring from society itself, and indeed from the authorities controlled by the party-state, as early as the 1950s. Whether published or not, writers set the pace – from Grossman to all the *samizdat* authors, Solzhenitsyn first of all, who was allowed to publish, notably in *Novy Mir*, by the first 'thaw' initiated by Khrushchev. Film directors such as Tarkovsky in *Ivan's Childhood* (1962) accompanied them, as did Klimov (*We Welcome You*, 1964) before the subterranean explosion that paved the way for *perestroïka*.

During these three decades – 1956–89 – the regime had rejected the violence of the Stalin era due, it was claimed, to the personality cult – an explanation that cleared the Communist party of responsibility and, abroad, helped to confirm Trotskyist positions. But in 1989 the party fell and by laying all the responsibility for the country's ills on Lenin, the former leaders were immediately cleared of guilt and, recycled, they set out to create a new society.[13] In this society, which was ever more informed and lucid about the defects and blockages of the economic and political system, faith in the infallibility of the party had long ago disappeared.

Thus the regime collapsed from within, contrary to all those who asserted that the system was immutable because it was 'totalitarian'.

There is nothing of all this in the relations between German society and the Nazi regime. It collapsed from outside, from defeat, and the Germans said: 'We did not deserve that, we did not deserve to be led to such a catastrophe.'[14] Of course, as in Russia in the early years of the regime, there were oppositionists. But the success and victories of the leaders produced a consensus much broader than in the USSR. Not one Nazi, before or after 1945 – unlike the communists – ever criticized the regime.

Whereas in Russia, by a spectacular reversal, as early as 1989, a whole part of society rejected communism and went so far as to deny the existence of a rising against Nicholas II – reviving the myth of a reforming tsar, then an October Revolution which was a mere *coup d'état* – in Germany, two decades passed before questions were asked about the nature and origins of a regime with an adored *Führer*.

The restriction of this research to the period 1933–45 – except in the work of Hannah Arendt and of Fritz Fischer in 1961[15] – made it possible, first of all, to dissociate anti-Semitism from the racism which prevailed earlier, not only in the colonies but also with respect to the Slavs: 'this inferior race in relation to Germans pure of any admixture', as Bismarck said. By neglecting to recall this inheritance, it is easy to make the Soviet regime the standard for the crimes of the twentieth century, and Nazism merely into a form of defensive response to the onslaught of communism, even going so far as to see the Nazi extermination camps as a mere response to the Soviet camps (previously, in 1941, in *Ohm Kruger*, Hans Steinhoff had made the British concentration camps during the Boer War the ancestors of the Nazi camps).

This chronological restriction had the effect of whitewashing the Germans, something that had already been assisted by the Nuremberg war crimes trial where the top leaders, heads of the Wehrmacht as well as Nazis, had been considered as solely responsible for the war and its atrocities. The subsequent measures of denazification and other action against doctors, killers from the camps, etc., scarcely grazed the surface of German society. At Nuremberg, moreover, the German victims of Nazism – resisters, church members, Social Democrats – were not even allowed to testify, which would have extended the range of responsibility, whereas the German lawyers of the Nazi leaders could, for example, accuse the Soviets of the Katyn massacres.[16]

In 1968, Leiser's *Mein Kampf* did indeed question young Germans about their parents' conduct. During the 1980s, the 'historians' controversy' (*Historikerstreit*) did raise the question of genocide under the guise of revitalizing the problem of the nature of Nazism. However, by lining up 'intentionalists' for whom genocide was inherent in Hitler's project against 'functionalists' who considered that that circumstances of the war had been decisive, they ended up forgetting the share of responsibility falling on individual Germans, which explains the response produced by Daniel Goldhagen's book in 1997, which confronted it head on.[17]

Meanwhile, the presumed innocence of the German people had the corollary of establishing communism as the sole model of totalitarianism.

The denunciation by communists themselves of the crimes committed in the USSR – Khrushchev's 1956 speech – contributed to the process of making Nazism commonplace. To identify terror in the USSR with Nazi terror, inasmuch as a victim at Magadan or in Ukraine deserves as much compassion as a victim of Auschwitz, comes down to making a clean sweep of 'biological racism', even if Lenino-Stalinist scientism also predetermined crimes. Now from the moment when Nazism defined itself as the 'party of applied biology' (Goebbels), it is possible to understand by what route the gas chambers became a decisive historical issue. Unless one denies their existence (the negationists), they appear as an excess, or the product of circumstances (revisionists and functionalists), and the making commonplace of this extermination will have achieved its aim. First the responsibility for massacres linked to the nature of communism is laid on the USSR, not merely on circumstances. The freeing of Nazism from guilt can go even further: in *Hitler, a Film from Germany* (1977), Syberberg gives us to understand that in the colonies it was the democracies which provided the prototype for collective massacres with the aim, there too, of creating a 'new man'. Moreover, the Vietnam War, with its bombing, was nowhere condemned so much as in Germany. And the Australian example was also able to testify that a democracy could be guilty of crimes. When in 1993 the prime minister in Canberra proposed to submit to a popular referendum the decision by the High Court to restore certain lands to Aboriginals who had been robbed of them in the previous century, the Anglican archbishop of Perth declared: 'The state government is using Nazi methods.'[18] Is not this resort to the 'democratic' will instead of an appeal to legitimacy and equity also one of the practices of totalitarianism?

Thus, by confining German guilt to a few leaders, by not analysing the deep roots of Nazism, by centring the study of communist rule on the Stalinist period, we end up with a confused situation that allows us to drift in any direction. The principle feature is to marginalize the question of the participation of society in the functioning of regimes: did not Bolsheviks and Nazis use and manipulate the vote of the majority against justice and right?

The cinema has faced up to these problems. In Germany before Fassbinder, Fleischmann had approached the practices of everyday fascism in *Hunting Scenes from Lower Bavaria* (1968) and likewise Schlöndorff in *Young Torless*, the action of which is set at the beginning of the century and which thus shows that certain forms of cruelty existed prior to Nazism. In the USSR, *Repentance* by Abuladze (1987) shows just how far a society can become allied with cowardice, and *Burnt by the Sun* by Mikhalkov shows how the need to act, ambition, self-interest and lust for power transform 'decent people' into rogues and criminals – in other words how society is responsible.

Without a study of the part played by society in the establishment and functioning of regimes, how can we understand their mechanisms?

One of the essential differences between colonial regimes and Nazism is that, although the latter incorporated society within itself, excluding and exterminating hostile or racially different elements, in the overseas territories the dominated populations were in a substantial majority (unless they had been exterminated) and there was no question of incorporating them into the dominant society. On the other hand there certainly was incorporation in Russia as soon as the tsarist Empire gave way to the Soviet regime. One proof of this is that after the disappearance of the Soviet Union, the former apparatchik and Gorbachev's one-time foreign minister, Shevardnadze, was elected president of the independent Republic of Georgia, and former Soviet leaders rule in Tashkent and Ashkhabad. It is hard to imagine, fifty years ago, Harold Macmillan being chosen to rule in Rangoon, and Guy Mollet presiding over the destiny of an independent Algeria alongside Ben Bella.

It is true that for a time the so-called *pieds-rouges* (French who settled in Algeria after independence) took part in the birth of the new Algeria, but that didn't last, just as there had been priests and citizens of metropolitan France alongside the victims of repression, and also *pieds-noirs* (settlers of European origin) like Camus. In black Africa, however, this incorporation of the native society into the church was taken further than elsewhere.

While colonization was imposed by force or by trickery, it was through democratic means that the Bolsheviks came to power, as did the Nazis. Subsequently the former perverted the representative process, while the latter did not feel the same need to do so. Examining those who went over to National Socialism, a study in 1934 distinguished between those 'who honestly, but without clarity of thought, quite consciously sacrificed in-tellect', others 'who, in spring 1932, still considered Hitler to be the devil himself', but now claimed 'they had really always been national socialist but had just failed to recognise the movement', and others still who 'had seen in Hitler the leader of a plebeian, semi-Bolshevik revolution, which they feared would be the ruin of bourgeois society'. 'There are the bourgeois types who were particularly enthusiastic . . . More common, however, are the silent opponents . . . Amongst them are many German Nationalists and conser-vatives.'[19]

Certainly, in societies in crisis, electoral behaviour offers only a very feeble snapshot of behaviour, which historically is not very reliable. Moreover, this comparison between Russia in 1917–20 and Germany in 1933–35 is scarcely relevant. We have mentioned the main features, however, because they form a sort of necessary transition, inasmuch as people want to see in the dissolution of the Constituent Assembly in 1918 or in the German elections of 1932–33 the starting-points for the rule of a single party; in fact in Germany only the headquarters of the political parties protested and in

Russia the people remained indifferent to this anti-democratic measure. Subsequently, in Germany as in Russia, the oppositionists were soon in the camps while the others went over to the regime.

Among the features that define totalitarian regimes, one specific characteristic in Russia is said to be the destruction of civil society. It is true that the domestication of social and political institutions (trade unions, soviets, cooperatives etc.) or their destruction (neighbourhood committees, factory committees, factory committee soviets, feminist leagues, doctors' organizations, etc.) sterilized the relations between the new state and society. However, the incorporation into the party-state of a popular and plebeian apparatus coming from below created a new type of 'bureaucracy'. From 1917 to 1940 there was a 'plebeianization' of the state apparatus and the slow evaporation of the old Bolsheviks of bourgeois origin, the purges taking care of this renewal from below.[20] On the other hand, apart from Goering, the Nazi leaders did not belong to the upper administration or to the nobility, as did Lenin, Kollontai, Chicherin or Smilga. Their workplace or meeting-place was not the library but the café. Once in power, they certainly destroyed the trade unions and banned parties, but they did not destroy the other institutions of civil society; they purged them and became part of them. W.S. Allen has shown how they proceeded in one small town and Ian Kershaw has described the efforts of the state employees, whom the Nazis did not like, to make themselves accepted.[21] On the other hand, in the USSR the former servants of the state were pushed out by the rise of apparatchiks of popular origin who had come from below. In a 1928 report on the *Solovki*, 'special destination camps', we can see what fate was reserved for these bourgeois who were deported to northern Russia.

Unlike the communists, the Nazis did not seek to destroy the structures of the former state, but simply to domesticate them. These institutions came to them. From this point of view, the comparison of the fate and behaviour of the medical profession and the army in the two countries is characteristic. In the USSR the authorities laid hands on the scientific community, and by a sort of 'socialist racism' (Michel Foucault) eliminated those of its members who did not come up to requirements.[22] The latter ended up by challenging the way in which their opposition was described as mental illness. Nothing of the sort happened in Germany where, in order to preserve their privileged status, the doctors enthusiastically applied the party's directives. The establishment of eugenicist ideas, which they had held before 1933, was well worth 'a bit of anti-Semitism' and a few other experiments. Some doctors were investigated by the American authorities in 1945 but most of them got chairs in genetics at Münster or Göttingen. Germany's defeat did not entail theirs.[23]

The same contrast is found in the case of the army. In the USSR the body of officers and NCOs was smashed and it was no longer an institution within society; in Germany, however, the Nazis safeguarded the structures of the military order – something that, originally, was one of the factors causing conflict between Roehm and Hitler. But the specificity of the army as a social institution remained intact, and leaders like Rommel were determined not to belong to the party, whereas in the USSR the comings and goings of the same men between the party and the army increased, even if the army reacquired its traditional values. The army genuinely associated the old and the new while the Cheka, later the GPU, then the NKVD and the KGB, were pure products of the regime.

Today the accent is put on crimes committed by Russian soldiers in Chechnya, while in the Soviet period such crimes were not attributed to the army but to the NKVD. But the inventory of crimes committed by the German army, especially against resisters and partisans, has put an end to the myth of a regime in which the only criminals were the Nazis. These crimes were not only committed against the Jews, but also in Serbia, in Poland and in Russia, which gives Goldhagen's argument about the 'anti-Semitic heritage' of the Germans a more relative significance. This in no way reduces the horrible nature of these offences.[24]

What the Nazis were responsible for was the destruction of the civilized nature of society. A doctor who practised euthanasia wrote to his wife in 1942: 'the job is going like clockwork', and he enumerated the victims he was despatching each day; the confessions collected recently by the Mis-cherlishes bear witness to the cruelty of 'everyday executioners', of which Bartov has collected other examples. Common soldiers were themselves victims of Nazification and they knew that they would be executed if they did not obey orders; the officially appointed extermination groups (*Einsatz-gruppen*) also contained civil servants, legal experts and teachers, nearly all of whom had had higher education. Their methods recall those of the Cheka. Thus in one case totalitarianism was wholly established, while in the other it was not.

Through these two examples, it seems that the destruction of civil society defined as a determining factor in the transition to repression and terror is not the phenomenon which really explains it, since in Germany at least the coherence of social institutions was actually reinforced, with insubordination by the army only appearing at the moment of defeat, and not as a result of the criminal practices of the regime. The contribution of the cultural or political heritage also fails to explain the violence committed, since one society, Russia, was regarded as backward, while Germany was seen as advanced.

Do we find any of these features in the practice of colonialism? At the time of conquest or of struggles for independence certainly. As far as the latter are concerned, it is well known that in the case of Algeria the agents of repression would not have believed themselves capable of the acts they committed. But the same was true of the agents of terrorism, who were as violent and criminal towards their own side as towards the colonizers.

As for the rest, we can already observe that in some respects the study of colonialism may borrow its tools or observations from the analysis of such totalitarian regimes. In the latter cases, alongside a *Black Book* a *Rose-Coloured Book* had appeared. All these regimes were the victims simultaneously of similar opprobrium and of similar eulogy. In the case of the USSR we do not need to be reminded what stories those from our own country returning from Moscow were able to tell about the 'Soviet paradise', this magic land from which pilgrims brought back an unwavering commitment.[25] Meanwhile other pilgrims were fascinated by the achievements of fascism and Nazism, regimes which had cut unemployment, undertaken major public works and 'where the trains ran on time'.

At the very same time these different regimes were the object of violent criticisms, based on facts, bloody facts: but who wanted to listen?

Now in the case of colonization, we can observe that the *Black Book* came before the *Rose-Coloured Book*. Las Casas' first report dates from 1540, but gradually the *Rose-Coloured Book* came out on top, in the name of Christ, of the struggle against the slave trade, in the name of civilization. It is true that the arguments in its defence were nourished by those who benefited from the exploitation of the colonies, in Bristol as in Nantes or in Lisbon, unless the colonists themselves intervened to justify their presence overseas.

Simultaneously the questioning took numerous forms. Among others in the twentieth century, socialist ideology has not failed to evoke the negative aspects of colonization, and even to criticize the very principle. Its line of argument was part of the very substance of Marxist discourse. For history teachers to be well aware of it and to spread their knowledge, 'they must be constrained by clearly defined syllabuses', wrote Lenin to the historian Pokrovsky.

> In these syllabuses, we must establish themes that will objectively require them to adopt our point of view; for instance, put on the syllabus the history of colonisation. This theme will lead them to expound their bourgeois point of view, namely what the French think of the behaviour of the British in the world; what the British think of the French; what the Germans think of both of them. The literature on the subject will thus oblige them to speak of the atrocities of the capitalists in general. (Letter to Pokrovsky, published in 1929 in *Pravda*.)

In the same spirit, after the Second World War, Jacques Arnault wrote *Procès du colonialisme (Colonialism on Trial)* for the Nouvelle Critique publishing house (1958).

As we enter a new millennium, by a reversal of mentalities linked to the dramas of the preceding century, to the awareness of violence committed here and elsewhere, part of the opinion of the old nations of Europe has adopted an ideology of human rights which has in its sights the whole set of crimes committed in the name of the red state, the brown state, the nation state and the 'victories of civilization'.

Generous in their denunciation of the crimes of communism or Nazism, these Western societies are happy today to pretend to believe that those of colonialism were hidden from them.

Now this belief is a myth, even if some of the excesses committed have indeed been cleansed from common memory.

Thus, in France, school textbooks of the first two-thirds of the twentieth century told of the enthusiasm with which Bugeaud and Saint-Arnaud burned the Arab encampments during the conquest of Algeria; how in India, at the time of the Indian Mutiny in 1857, British officers placed Hindus and Muslims at the mouths of cannons; how Pizarro executed Atahuallpa, Emperor of the Incas; how Galliéni put the Madagascans to the sword. These acts of violence were known, in the case of Algeria, from the time of Tocqueville. In Tonkin, witnesses saw a hundred times 'stakes with human heads on them, constantly replaced', pictures of which appeared in magazines back in France. General Lapasset, quoted by C.R. Ageron in 1972, considered as early as 1879 that 'the gulf between settlers and natives will one day be filled with corpses'.[26]

All these facts were well-known, public. But if it was asserted that to denounce them had the motive of challenging 'the task of France' their existence was denied; the government may be wrong, but my country is always right . . . This conviction is internalized and is preserved, nourished as much by the self-censorship of citizens as by the censorship of the authorities, even today. For example, in France none of the films or television programmes which 'denounce' abuses committed in the colonies is in the top hundred of the television ratings or of box-office successes.[27]

Across the Atlantic, a shift concerning the extermination of the Indians has taken place, with one sort of Western giving way to another, with Delmer Daves' *Broken Arrow* (1950), a pro-Indian and anti-racist film, produced before the crimes committed by the US Air Force during the Vietnam War which contributed to perpetuating the shift; but in reality this new awareness has scarcely modified Washington's policy towards Indian 'reservations'. In Australia the awareness is even more recent, thanks to the action by

Aboriginals and lawyers, but as we have seen the white 'democratic majority' is opposed to it having any real effects.

These observations oblige us to give a new perspective to the role of the main actors in history, whether in the metropolis or in the colonies, and also of the traditional division into historical periods.

Thus in France, for example, around 2000, following testimonies from Algerians who had been torture victims, high-ranking soldiers such as Generals Massu and Aussaresses have recognized the facts, but explained them by the struggle against terrorism. These facts, moreover, were no more unknown than others, and during the Algerian War many voices were raised in *Esprit* – as today in Russia against the violence committed in Chechnya – to stigmatize actions that the military authorities denied or continue to deny. And, in the case of the Algerian *départements*, there was brutality against nationalists long before the war broke out, essentially by the police.[28]

According to the Algerians, terrorism was a response to this violence by the colonizers. The colonized thus replace the binary relation terrorism/torture with the triad repression/terrorism/torture.

Of course colonization consisted of more than these excesses of colonialism. But it should not be forgotten what preceded them – the violence of conquest, 'pacification' – by relegating them to a past that is over and done with, as though it were a question of a chapter of history which had no relation to repression and the terrorism of liberation struggles in the 1950s. Nor should we forget, notably in Algeria, the violence which the colonized committed among themselves, the heritage of which is still with them today.

To this observation should be added an established conclusion: overseas, as well as the state authorities and the colonized, we should not forget to add other actors of history – the settlers and the lobbies they formed in the metropolis; and among the colonized, proselytizing Islam.

Just as we should not forget that the history of communism and Nazism has not always been that of ideology or of the functioning of these regimes, of their politics, but also the history of the more or less conscious and active participation of the citizens in their action, in their successes and their failures.[29]

In another of its aspects, the analysis of colonialism can be referred to that of totalitarianism: the examination of the intentions of the promoters. We know that prior to the excesses committed by Nazism and communism the respective programmes of their leaders were not just different but diametrically opposed. How can we 'dare' to compare the racist project of the Nazis with that of the socialists, however corrupted it may have been? So what is the position with the projects of colonization and the results of its practice? On the one side getting wealthy, Christianizing, civilizing . . . On the other, forced labour, modernized development, the decline of the subsistence economy . . . To make this confrontation it is necessary, in the first place, just as it is necessary to draw up the balance sheets, to check what was accomplished knowingly and what was only half accomplished, or not at all. How many schools, hospitals and dams were built, and for which beneficiaries? But to the conscious balance sheet of this colonization, or to its black and rose-coloured aspects, must be added the identification of situations and balance sheets which were neither desired nor expected.

Here are two examples of these 'perverse' results.

First of all the effects of French educational policy in Algeria. Fanny Colonna has shown very well that, as it developed, secular education nourished the ideas of the elite, forming emancipated citizens who became emancipators and who inspired insurrection – which, to be honest, was never the intention; but it did not allow the humble to rise, whereas on the other hand in the republican project, the school was supposed to work to reduce inequalities; in fact these inequalities were even reinforced. And often it was the least educated who, in order to survive, joined the French army.

Another example: the medical balance sheet of British policy in India. The metropolis did not attempt to care for three hundred million natives, reserving its care for the British and those of the Indians who were in contact with the Empire's agents and settlers in order the better to protect them: soldiers, tax-collectors, etc. To try to respond to the needs of the situation in the country, the metropolis considered it was necessary to create a body of native doctors. The result? Fifty years later, an influx of Indian doctors are staffing the metropolitan hospitals, replacing the British practitioners who have gone to the private sector to flee the effects of the Welfare State.[30]

This double lesson shows there can be a large gap between the intentions of a policy and its results, which does not mean that the former should be ignored in favour of studying only the latter.

We could carry on drawing parallels, which admittedly is a bit sterile. For such comparisons take no account of the specific echoes produced by each of these factors which are not situated on the same level. However, in the case of individuals they are compressed in the space of an existence, whether it be a peasant, an official or a soldier, for whom everything is turned upside down in the space of a few days or a few hours, something which they are unable either to initiate or to control. The resentment which they inherited might have the weight of several centuries, and their own anger that of a few months: the orders they give or receive are conceived in a few seconds. In this way impulses contract, when their beats have neither the same extent nor the same frequency.

A compression of history, such is the effect of situations and circumstances which transform individuals and mark them for life – though this in no way diminishes the need to judge their responsibility and the part they have played. It has made them into wild animals.

What Produces Democracy? Revolutionary Crises, Popular Politics and Democratic Gains in Twentieth-Century Europe

Geoff Eley

CONCEPTUALIZING DEMOCRACY AFTER COMMUNISM

At the end of the twentieth century, talk of democracy was inevitably dominated by the dramatic and universalizing consequences of the ending of the Cold War. Those consequences were both structural, because they seemed lasting, pervasive and limiting for the future, and dynamic, because they appeared to encounter ever-diminishing resistance. The revolutions of 1989 in Eastern Europe, the dissolution of the Soviet Union in 1991 and the generalized collapse of communism understandably encouraged perceptions of a momentous and irreversible forward movement, even of an 'end to history' or a 'world-historical' transition. Yet in most commentaries the primary meanings of those great events have been decisively located not in any enrichment of democratic political capacities or the empowerment of popular participation, but in the economy. The new 'freedoms' deemed to have been established were inspired far more by commitment to property, trade, contract and enterprise than by political ideals based on sovereignty, constitutional liberties and expanding citizenship. The market, rather than democracy, supplied the main measure of this contemporary transition.

In the wake of 1989, in fact, the public languages of politics became tightly drawn around a bluntly limiting range of permissible argument and belief. The debacle of Soviet-type planned economies dramatically reinforced the headlong retreat from Keynesianism, the drive for deregulation, and the growing disregard for public goods. The unfolding of a profound transformation in the acceptable roles of government and the common sense of 'the economy' left smaller and smaller space for anything resembling socialist advocacy, let alone the imagining of practicable alternatives to capitalism. Even as socialism revealed its exhaustion as a viable economic programme with credible purchase on either policy-making or popular belief, capitalist models of the economy based on the free market exercised an apparently unstoppable ascendancy. On the largest front, supra-national, national and regional economic and political arrangements were being relentlessly re-configured into what we now call globalization.

In contemporary parlance – among political scientists, in the talk of journalists and other media pundits, in the rhetoric of public figures, and in the broadest popular understandings – the question of democracy has become inseparably sucked back into these surrounding contexts. Market forces and their triumph, rather than democratization as such, are considered the prime movers of the present. *They* – and not the collective agency of human actors – are deemed the instigators of change and therefore the source of any legitimizing arguments. The strength and integrity of 'the market' provide the dynamism necessary for progress – either negatively, by sweeping away democracy's impediments (as in the collapse of communism, or the ending of apartheid, or the dismantling of various types of military and authoritarian dictatorship), or positively, by releasing the energies of private accumulation and the correlative desires for individualized advancement. But at the same time this power of the market is accepted as limiting – as imposing default restrictions on what national governments can any longer hope to pursue, particularly in the Keynesian and welfare-statist directions that earlier connoted the democratic project.

In this new cultural climate Marxist ideas found it uncommonly hard to obtain a hearing. But if Marxist critiques were more or less driven from the public field, the celebratory tones of pro-market advocacy ironically con-firmed one set of Marxist claims. The well-nigh universal triumph of market principles – not just as a system of ideas for describing an untrammelled capitalist economy, but also as a set of precepts for all areas of public policy and social life – became the fundament for a brutally frank materialist theory of politics based on the movement of the economy. Indeed, our remarkable contemporary conjuncture – in which the public values, dominant ideas, and range of realistic politics are all thought to be tied so consistently to an overriding logic of capital accumulation and the ruling dictates of the economy – seems eerily reminiscent of the triumph of capitalism on a world scale imagined by Karl Marx and Friedrich Engels in *The Communist Manifesto*, first published in 1848.

As it happens, in its 1996 *World Development Report*, entitled *From Plan to Market*, the World Bank summarized the transition of the former socialist countries to a 'market orientation' in precisely these terms, describing the momentousness of the changes of the 1990s by invoking the *Manifesto*'s famous phrase 'all that is solid melts into air'.[1] Indeed, this image of the victorious free-market order establishing itself on a genuinely global scale, dissolving all the forms of anti-capitalist recalcitrance and sweeping away the impediments to expansion, has become an extraordinarily apposite one for the early twenty-first century. As Eric Hobsbawm observed in his 'Modern Edition' of the *Manifesto* for its 150th anniversary, Marx and Engels offered insights of 'startling contemporary relevance', including:

> the recognition of capitalism as a world system capable of marshaling production on a global scale; its devastating impact on all aspects of human existence, work, the family, and the distribution of wealth; and the understanding that, far from being a stable, immutable system, it is, on the contrary, susceptible to enormous convulsions and crisis . . .[2]

Marxist thought is widely consigned to the scrapheap, in other words, just as the forms of capitalist power in the world come closer than ever to vindicating a powerful aspect of the Marxist critique. Events that at one level are taken to have refuted Marxism's validity as a theory of the direction of history – communism's ending, the collapse of viable alternatives to capitalism, the obstacles to a politics centred around class – at another level precisely instantiate Marxism's analysis of the dynamism of capitalism. Similarly, neo-liberal thinking has now made the possibilities for democracy so strictly dependent on a particular conception of the economy as to put any vulgar Marxist to shame. The space for any realistic politics – meaningful actions of government in society – is strictly demarcated in this way of thinking by the needs of the economy conceived in market terms.

In these contemporary discussions, 'democracy' *per se* has acquired a peculiarly epiphenomenal place. 'Democratization' figures in post–1989 discourse certainly as an abstract ideal, but understood mainly as an effect, or as an extrapolation from larger processes, rather than as a priority attracting resources in its own right.[3] Thus one set of approaches stresses the role of elites in managing the democratic transition, defining the passage to democratic governing relationships as a top-down process of rearrangement and reform, as opposed to a process of pressure and mobilization from below. Commenting on an earlier cycle of 'transitions from authoritarian rule' in southern Europe and Latin America during the later 1970s, for example, Adam Przeworski argued that: 'It seems as if an almost complete docility and patience on the part of organised workers are needed for a democratic transformation to succeed', because the key breakthroughs occur only when parts of the elites move into action.[4] In that sense, negotiated transitions to post-communism through the round tables in Poland and Hungary become the paradigmatic cases for characterizing the changes of 1989. In contrast, the wider popular mobilizations in the GDR and Czechoslovakia fade out of significance, while the Bulgarian and Romanian transitions also become narrated as a top-down process of manoeuvring from above. In an earlier example of the same type, the managerial aspects of the Spanish transition during 1977–78 become emphasized to the detriment of the crescendo of popular militancy preceding them in 1974–76; and the Portuguese Revolution of 1974–75 becomes recoded as the 'breakdown', which the negotiated normalizing of the later 1970s then made good.

In that sense, the prospects for successful democratization in post-communist societies are seen to be lodged elsewhere, in two types of restructuring – one occurring in the economy, the other in civil society. On the one hand, the viability of democratic initiatives is tied to the ability of national elites to follow through on a market-centred process of economic reform. 'Freeing the economy' in that powerful neo-liberal sense becomes the essential prerequisite for any successful democratic political transition to occur. But on the other hand, creating a strong 'moral consensus', grounded by a dense and resilient infrastructure of social institutions – civil society – is seen to be equally crucial. Without either of these twin foundations, democracy will fail. It remains a weak and artificial implantation, according to this view, intruded into societies lacking the civic competence and political culture that could allow it to flourish. Democracy here presupposes deep-historical, underlying processes of societal growth and cultural sedimentation, which alone produce the default behaviours necessary before democratic political arrangements can work – that is, the *habitus* of competent citizenship which (it is argued) communist societies, frozen into postures of administered conformity, never had the chance to acquire.[5]

Within these perspectives, the success of the newly established democracies becomes a secondary effect of histories preceding elsewhere, whether via the progress of neo-liberal economic reform or via the growth of a complex and variegated civil society. Political culture (or the effective exercise of democratic citizenship) is made primarily dependent on economics (a capitalist market order) and social history (the growth of civil society). This also presumes a particular reading of the history of 'the West' (usually meaning Britain, France and the United States), where the deep-historical model of long-run socio-economic development and democratic acculturation is taken to reside. But in this case, too, the more complex histories of popular militancy, societal conflict and bitterly conducted political struggles that were actually constitutive for the establishing of democracy in those countries – through which democratic competence and the capacity for citizenship had to be produced – are flatly effaced.[6]

In my view, these contemporary approaches to democratic transition are shockingly ahistorical, showing astonishing disregard for the actual guidance several hundred years of Western European history might provide. The power of our contemporary conjuncture is being allowed to erase a vital set of available knowledges and understandings in this way. It impedes our access to the earlier histories of democratization in the twentieth century, which might otherwise provide some important cautionary reminders, as well as a far more critical perspective on the quality of the present democratic gains. In order to make the case for a particular paradigm of post-communist transition, one in which neo-liberal celebrations of the 'market' have ruthlessly monopolized the languages of 'reform', other ways of thinking about democracy's conditions of possibility – democracy's other genealogies – are necessarily suppressed.[7] To adapt Ernest Renan's famous adage, contemporary democratic advocacy registers the necessity of getting one's history wrong, of selectively appropriating some experiences and forgetting others, of ensuring that the past will be misremembered and misread.[8]

HISTORIANS, REVISIONISM AND REVOLUTION

As the editors of this volume point out, a vital dimension of current treatments of democracy has been the reinterpreting and diminishment of the decisive popular democratic breakthroughs of the past, from the English Revolution of the seventeenth century, through the great French Revolution and associated popular revolts of the first two-thirds of the nineteenth century, to the Russian Revolution of 1917 and the forms of twentieth-century popular militancy based on labour movements. Thus an early casualty of the collapse of the Soviet Union, to take the most obvious example, was the impressively accumulating scholarship on the social history of the Bolshevik Revolution, which since the later 1970s had been carefully establishing the patterns of working-class mobilization and popular hopes that endowed Bolshevik actions during 1917 with a vital source of legitimacy. During the 1980s, this mainly North American and British historiography moved rapidly through a succession of periods, from the revolutionary years themselves to the civil war and the complexities of the New Economic Policy and thence to the coercive rigours of the industrialization drive and the big violence of Stalinism. In so doing, the scholars concerned assembled an exciting new basis for judging the relationship of the forms of Bolshevik politics in these different periods to the associated logics of state formation, to the complex pressures and constraints imposed by the emerging Soviet society, and – last but not least – to the agency exercised by different categories of social actors.[9]

For opponents of that new scholarship, in contrast, the ignominious ending of Soviet history in 1991 cast a blinding light across those earlier Bolshevik decades, exposing the Revolution's essential lack of legitimacy and abruptly cancelling the claims of the new socially oriented historiography.[10] In the triumphalist neo-liberal climate of the early 1990s, a recharged anti-Bolshevism then easily gained momentum, rapidly reinforced by the ill-digested revelations tumbling from the freshly opened Moscow archives. A strictly political reading of 1917 became reinstated: the mass disorder of the First World War may have produced Bolshevism's historic opening, this asserted, but the later violence of Soviet history came only from the dictatorial utopianism of Bolshevik ideology, always already inscribed in the very idea of trying to make a revolution in the first place – that is, in the illusory belief of revolutionaries that society was available for the remaking.[11]

For those of us who first learned our Bolshevik history in the 1960s from the likes of Leonard Schapiro, Richard Pipes, George Katkov and Sergej Utechin, before any of the new social histories of the Revolution had started to appear, these resulting terms of discussion ring depressingly familiar.[12] The effectiveness of Lenin and his party in 1917 is now again being attributed to the ruthlessness of their drive for power: centralist organization, authoritarian leadership, conspiratorial methods, absolute conviction, belief in the direction of history – all these qualities sufficiently defined Bolshevik success, according to this view. In other words, after two decades of emphasizing Bolshevik responsiveness to popular aspirations and the degree to which broad social movements were driving the political process in 1917, social historians now find themselves confronted by a resurgent conspiratorial interpretation pugnaciously reviving the autonomy of politics.[13] Lenin's 'Jacobinism' has returned to the centre of the agenda, signifying lack of pluralism, propensity for dictatorship, and the sacrifice of people to a cause.

This revisionism is self-consciously harnessed, often aggressively, to a congratulatory validation of post-communist socio-political arrangements and the normative liberal democracy of the West. Moreover, communist conceptions of political order are not the only ones this new anti-Bolshevik historiography seeks to read 'out' of history as unworkable and ethically impermissible alternatives. Deep suspicion of direct democracy and partici-patory forms is also at work, because these anti-Bolshevik critiques cleave to the narrowest of parliamentary-democratic and legalistic institutional ground. Their reversion to a restrictive liberal idea of democracy, as opposed to the more expansive populist or socialist affinities displayed by the social historians, also revives another canonical text of Cold War liberalism, Jacob Talmon's *Origins of Totalitarian Democracy*, which couched its anti-commun-ism in the most right-wing reading of the French Revolution's Jacobin phase.[14] In this intended de-legitimizing of radicalism, 'revolution' becomes democracy's mortal foe. The current rewriting of Russian history thus bespeaks a more general view of political progress that endorses only gradualism, evolution, and peaceful paths of development, while treating mass actions and direct challenges to authority as always destructively counter-productive. Abandoning legal channels, it insists, can only ever lead to disaster. In William G. Rosenberg's words: 'The tropes of criminality, betrayal, catastrophe, and tragedy [are] refashioned from their familiar anti-Jacobin and anti-Bolshevik uses into elements of an older conservative narrative about revolution itself.'[15]

In other words, the wholesale de-legitimizing of the Russian Revolution is linked to larger assumptions about the past sources and trajectories of progressive political change – about how, historically, the key gains for democracy could occur. Through that resurgent conservative vision of the past, the great revolutionary crises of modern European history are threatened with relegation to the place previously reserved for them by the self-satisfied consensus historiography dominating the scene before the turn to social history in the 1960s. As in the heyday of the Cold War, revolutions are nowadays being treated once again as exclusively destructive and damaging events – as dysfunctions, as breakdowns, as outbreaks of irrationality, as misguided popular explosions, as disastrous detours, as mendacious conspiracies of the power-hungry, as the regrettable consequences of backwardness and the irredeemable incompetence of *ancien régimes*, as disruptions of otherwise healthily proceeding development. Revolutions in this view have nothing positive to offer. Coercion, intolerance and authoritarianism are inscribed at their very core. Terror unfolds naturally from the ideological zeal of the revolutionaries, who seek to inflict abstract and impossible dreams of an ideal socio-political order on to the messy and resistant realities of the actually existing world.

But this view of revolutions – as primarily political events intelligible through the ideas motivating or situating their actors and produced by the discursive environments making them possible – can only be sustained by isolating the language of the revolution from the dense and sophisticated social histories accumulating since the 1970s, against whose findings histories of ideas surely demand to be contextualized. The contemporary animus against revolutions is actually a reversion to much older traditions of thought, whose successive questioning and revival during the broad historiographical conflicts of the past fifty years compose a vital part of the setting for my own discussion. To make sense of this current thinking, accordingly, we need to remind ourselves of these earlier interpretive battles. Between the late 1950s and the start of the 1970s, in fact, the established ways of regarding

revolutionary violence – as an expression of the ruthlessness of the revolutionaries in a wider narrative of irrationalism and excess, which belittled
and effaced the motives and agency of the ordinary participants – had been
decisively challenged by an imaginative new historiography of social protest
and collective action emerging from the English-speaking world, much of it
focused around the French Revolution.

In pioneering studies concentrated in the late eighteenth and early
nineteenth centuries, George Rudé, Eric Hobsbawm, Charles Tilly and
Edward Thompson transformed perceptions of food riots, machine-break-
ing, urban crowds, popular uprisings, and all manner of collective actions, so
that it became possible to see the popular violence accompanying or
precipitating revolutionary crises as rationally based, socially explicable
and morally legitimate.[16] Under this inspiration, a rapidly growing army
of researchers then claimed European history's great insurrections for social
analysis, beginning with the storming of the Bastille and the popular *journées*
of the 1790s, continuing through 1830 and 1848, gathering up countless
more isolated local and national examples along the way, and culminating in
1871.[17] Converging with classic accounts of popular history by Georges
Lefebvre, Albert Soboul and Richard Cobb in France itself, this body of
work did much to establish the standing of the most radical phase of the
French Revolution as a legitimate popular democratic event.[18]

Measured against that earlier impact, the present sidelining of this impressive social history corpus and the effacing of its challenge is one of the
most remarkable effects of the new ascendancy asserted in the meantime by
revisionists over the French Revolution. Ironically, the 1989 revolutions
coincided with the bicentenary of that earlier event, which revisionists
successfully co-opted in order to declare that two centuries of continuing
public divisiveness about the meanings of the French Revolution were finally
over. Orchestrator-in-chief of this revisionist normalizing was François
Furet, who relentlessly reiterated his litany of world-historical correlations:
the collapse of communism confirmed the bankruptcy and final defeat of the
radical democratic fantasies first unleashed by the Jacobins; Eastern European
changes completed the legacies of the healthy ideas of the summer of 1789;
any more radical hopes, from the Jacobins themselves to the socialist and
communist movements of the twentieth century, were merely violent and
irrationalist detours from an authentically democratic route. Amidst the
embittered polemics accompanying the 1989 commemorations, Furet re-
curred consistently to this line: 1917 (read Stalinism and the gulag) was the
future of 1793 (the Jacobin Terror), and the logic of 1793 began from 1789.
The 'fanaticism' of the Terror was authorized by the 'unlimited competence
attributed to political action' by the revolutionaries, by a 'political over-

investment' in the project of remaking society, and by 'the belief in extreme political wilfulness, the regeneration of man by the state'. Possessed by that ideology, 'the Revolution found itself set on a course toward disaster from the start'.[19]

For Furet and his fellow revisionists, this primacy of the political had to be tackled undeviatingly as such, without reference to either the findings of social history, structural factors of any kind, or circumstances 'external' to the history of the Revolution's ideas. Thus Furet's own 'political turn' was also a turning *against* social history, through an intellectual about-face even sharper than his earlier transmutation in the late 1950s from Stalinist *enragé* into the hammer of the 'Jacobino-Marxist' Left.[20] Moving beyond the justified critique of the 'social interpretation' of the Revolution, which had built steadily during the 1960s and 1970s from Alfred Cobban's early intervention, Furet based his new stance on a dogmatic refusal of *any* form of non-ideational contextualizing.[21] Philosophy, language and the history of concepts now exercised rigidly unambiguous precedence. Furet absolved ideas from *any* accountability to social context. Any desire to read political standpoints for their social meanings, or to explore the possible articulations between professions of belief and the construction of material interests, was now dismissed as vulgar-Marxist or tendentiously and simplistically reductive.

Indeed, Furet and his supporters vacated the territory of the social entirely, insisting simultaneously on the terroristic consequences of the revolution-aries' overestimation of politics, and on the need for historians to interpret the Revolution strictly within that very same framework of the political. It is hard to see how such rigid separation of ideas from circumstances could be at all defensible, although of course the nervousness surrounding any referen-cing of 'material' or 'extra-discursive' factors became a far more pervasive feature of historical discussion more generally during the 1990s. Unless we are prepared for an entirely 'textualized' understanding of social complexity, however, in which the permissible methods are reduced to the procedures of intellectual history and the techniques of literary criticism, or at best the ethnographic readings associated with the new cultural history, then the case for a critical and non-aggrandizing social history remains very strong. Neither the choices exercised by individual revolutionaries, from Saint-Just and Robespierre to the ordinary militants of the Paris sections, nor the con-stellations of exigencies, constraints and probabilities that structured how those choices actually became available, can be properly investigated without taking social context into account.[22] For all his haughty sophistication with 'ideas' and undoubted philosophical erudition, Furet's grasp of the relation-ship between ideas and society remained primitive in that sense. As Roger Chartier observed during the 1989 polemics:

> To desire to give the event a strictly philosophical and political reading is thus to subordinate . . . historical intelligibility to the conscience of contemporaries. That the revolutionaries believed in the absolute efficacy of the political – capable, according to them, of reforging the social body even as it regenerated the individual – does not imply that the historian must adopt their illusion.[23]

Thus the contraction of democratic advocacy during the 1990s around cramped and reduced conceptions of market relations and civic virtue, where I began this essay, together with the associated recession of class-based social analysis, mirrors a comparable revisionist trend among historians of the French and Russian Revolutions as well. Grandiosely conceived general accounts of those momentous turning-points now see their main meanings as disconnected from the broadly based societal crises, material conflicts and popular movements in which social historians had previously sought to ground their interpretations.[24] In particular, instead of legitimizing fundamental democratic breakthroughs, popular militancy now bears the odium of the Terror. The ideas and institutions of 'modern political culture' were already being created under the *ancien régime*, French revisionists now argue, only to be hijacked and derailed by the arrival and radicalizing of the Revolution.[25] Through the resulting experience, in this view, an enduring polarity of political allegiances was produced, thereby stunting and confining French political development for the next two centuries. Analogous consequences attended the history of the Bolshevik victory in the Russian Revolution, both reinforced by the French precedents and helping to further entrench their discursive power.

In the rest of this essay, I want to reaffirm the importance of revolutions to the most decisive democratic advances of the past two centuries. Contrary to recent revisionisms, the most meaningful and lasting gains for democracy have only ever been achieved via turbulence and disorder – as a result of the broadest popular mobilizations and organized collective action, often amidst violent public confrontations of escalating severity, usually accompanying a generalized societal crisis and breakdown of governmental order, and in the name of justified resistance against coercive forms of injustice, authority and oppression. Many different things will always be happening during such crises – other conflicts and dramas, other rhythms and temporalities of change, other meanings and motivations. As well as the pursuit of virtue, they entail much baseness, violence, cruelty and loss of life. But they nonetheless open an essential space for progress, meaning the enlargement of the political conditions and capacities enabling human well-being to be secured.

Confining our judgment of revolutions to the philosophical meanings and discursive architecture of their primary events – essentially the prescription of Furet – involves an extraordinary misperception of their generative conditions, lasting effects, experiential dynamism and general power. Deciding to limit our vision in that way, in common with any approach to the big challenges and conundrums of the past, requires the exercise of a political, ethical and intellectual choice. In my own view, therefore, revolutions are uniquely inspiring spectacles of popular democratic aspiration. They are constructive vehicles of necessary and desirable changes, despite all the attendant wreckage. And historically speaking, they are unavoidable. Moreover, to have clarified the relationship of revolutionary crises to the lives of ordinary people – particularly in the breadth and pervasiveness of the events concerned, their forms of cultural expression, and their internal dynamics – remains the lasting achievement of the social histories produced between the 1960s and 1980s. In the spirit of that democratic historiography, in what follows I want to re-complicate the discussion of democracy by offering some reflections on its twentieth-century dynamics of emergence.

DEFINING DEMOCRACY

Definitions of democracy begin with the constitutional question in the strict sense, with the juridically formalized conditions for democracy in the state. In that strict sense, full-scale democratization entails the following: popular sovereignty and accountable rule based on free, universal, secret, adult and equal suffrage, complemented by legal freedoms of speech, conscience, assembly, association and the press, backed by rights under the law and freedom from arrest without trial. By this standard, only the mildest degrees of democracy were attained in political systems anywhere before 1914. Full democracy was established only in four peripheral societies of the world – New Zealand (1893), Australia (1903), Finland (1906), and Norway (1913) – plus certain states and provinces of the western United States and Canada.[26] If we relax the definition's stringency along one major dimension and remove the requirement for women's suffrage, then France and Switzerland can also qualify as male democracies. In this full sense, it was only after 1918 that democracy acquired any general currency in Europe as a normal type of polity, and then only very uncertainly and provisionally, as the 1920s and 1930s abundantly confirmed. Democracy then received a further vital and more lasting increment in its international diffusion after 1945. These two dates – 1918 and 1945 – immediately establish the importance of a particular kind of societal context for the growth of democracy in European states, namely, the political dynamics of large-scale social and political mobilization associated with the two world wars.[27]

Moving beyond this more strictly juridical definition, though, we need ways of theorizing the circumstances under which democratic gains can realistically occur. That is, we have to encompass the dynamics of democracy's actual emergence and the messier contingencies of democracy's recorded eventuations, the complex histories producing its actually existing forms. And this requires focusing not only on the obvious political arenas of struggle in relation to parliaments and other representative institutions, and citizenship rights guaranteed by law, but also on a much wider series of contexts, which during the twentieth century have included at least the following:

1. The ambitious conceptions of social rights implied by the rise of the welfare state.
2. The enlargement of citizenship capacities in ways that might not receive explicit ratification on the national stage of politics or become institutionalized into law. This category includes both new claims for recognition *before* they attain juridical standing and the persisting unevenness in the law's ability to resolve discrepancies and imperfections.
3. The mobile boundary of distinctions between the public and the private in fields of regulation and intervention oriented around issues of personhood, intimate relations, and the social body, particularly those concerning family, sexualities and moral order.
4. The variegated political space of an increasingly mass-mediated public sphere.

These are all areas of social practice and social relations dramatically called into question during revolutionary crises. Moreover, here I am taking the gendered character of these questions as understood, meaning both their necessarily gendered dimensions in the fundamental sense pioneered by contemporary feminist theory and the explicitly gendered distinctions between women and men in the details of the democratic changes *per se*.[28] In assessing the extent and efficacy of a particular democratic advance, accordingly, we need to consider not only the degree to which women were included in the gains, but also the relationship of the changes concerned to the ordering of sexual differences.

Finally, it is worth noting the huge discrepancy here between the expanded definition of democracy I am offering and the highly formalistic understandings that mainly dominate the contemporary discourses of post-communist transition. My own argument is that democracy eventuates not only from the achievement of specific institutional changes, juridical rights and formal constitutional procedures, but also from social and political conflicts across a much wider variety of fronts. That is, constitutional definitions have to be complemented by historical approaches focusing on the expansion of democratic capacities in other than juridical ways. In other words, democratization requires not only formal or juridical conditions of possibility, but has complicated dynamic dimensions as well. Yet for contemporary Eastern Europe and the former Soviet Union, the only broader context of this kind that tends to be conceded is the one defined by the market in economistic or philosophical ways.

Decisive enlargements of democracy, I want to argue in contrast, have occurred only rarely in very exceptional conjunctures, when extremes of socio-political crisis invite popular mobilizations of imposing scale, whose consequences break the mould of politics and open the door for change. In viewing the record of the twentieth century, it hardly requires historical intelligence of startling originality to notice that the key advances have accompanied periods of generalized societal upheaval, breakdowns of established authority, spiralling confrontations between polarized camps of political opponents, inflamed passions, regrettable excesses and extremes, and the collapse of preceding normality. Indeed, the most substantial and lasting gains for democracy have usually been enabled by precisely revolutionary crises of such a kind. Such crises compose an essential condition of possibility.

The clearest example can be found in the revolutionary conjuncture of 1917–23 accompanying the final stage of the First World War. Without exception, the newly instituted democratic polities of that time were fashioned from the opportunities yielded by popular movements mobilizing amidst the wreckage of *ancien régimes*.[29] The next wave of successful democratization in 1945–49 lacked the same kind of insurrectionary challenges, with some notable exceptions, but in continental Europe the wartime conditions of repressive endangerment and effective civil war created a similar opening, while the salience of popular Resistance struggles against Nazism substituted comparable dynamics of democratic insurgency. In each case, the momentum for breaking through to a more democratic future was generated by the intolerable violence of what came before.

Refusing to acknowledge those generative circumstances of unbearable and unprecedented state-originated violence, while indicting so forthrightly the violence of the revolutions themselves, produces the deafening silence of only one hand clapping. In each case, 1917–18 and the 1940s, the continuity of existing political arrangements had become irreparably sundered. Any return to an earlier status quo became out of the question, whether to the 'before' of the unreformed *ancien régimes* of pre-1914 Europe and the militarized mass death of the First World War, or to the 'before' of the narrowly based authoritarian polities of the 1930s and the radicalized monstrosity of Nazi-occupied Europe. To bracket those histories from consideration while singling out the violence of the succeeding revolutionary conjuncture seems speciously selective. The political turbulence encompassed by the one was inseparable from the earlier extremes of the other. Socio-political collapse of these magnitudes entailed political challenges that almost inevitably elicited coercive measures, angry demarcations, and violent clashes in response to any movement aiming for decisive reform, not least because the established powers were only too ready with their own iron fist. Ruling elites have only ever relinquished their privileges in response to overpowering popular pressures as their means of coercion crumbled away. In that sense, large and lasting democratic changes have only ever been fashioned from the dangerous opportunities revolutionary crises can help to create.

DIALECTICS OF CITIZENSHIP AND STATE, 1914–23

Once we approach democracy historically in this way – once we start historicizing the circumstances under which democratic forms can be proposed and secured – the insufficiencies of purely formal or juridical definitions become rapidly clear. In particular, it makes no sense to base our understanding of democracy on the limited parliamentary constitutions of the classic pre-1914 type, which had become characteristic for most of Europe since the 1860s, because the conflicts now enabling the new constitution-making breakthroughs of 1918 released aspirations which the old parliamentarian precepts could no longer contain. As my previous section has already alluded to, those conflicts issued from general societal crisis and political breakdown via conditions of mass insurrectionary turbulence. In their region of greatest extent in Central and Eastern Europe, they culminated in republican settlements going far beyond the modest constitutionalisms of the years before 1914. Moreover, the new changes of 1918–19 contained all the elements of the expanded definition of democracy suggested above.

Of course, struggles around parliamentary sovereignty and the integrity of the electoral process were still at the practical core of juridical democracy, and such struggles remained central to the new mobilizations after 1914. Where the revolutionary left neglected or dismissed their value, despising rather than acknowledging their insufficiencies, as in much of the early communist militancy and ultra-left traditions, democracy tended to suffer disastrously as a result. But during 1914–23 there were other dimensions of democratization that dramatically exceeded this moderate parliamentary and rights-based frame:

a) The impact of extra-parliamentary social movements on the terms of the democratic settlements in 1918–23 provides the first of these dimensions. Examples ranged from trade unions to women's movements and an often-bewildering array of single-issue and locally based campaigns, comprising the full panoply of collective action and organization in the wider societal field. Accordingly, a developed conception of civil society forms the necessary counterpart to definitions of a democratic polity based on constitutional law. During the immediate revolutionary crisis, and usually for long periods beyond it, such extra-parliamentary movements outgrew the ability of the parliamentary organs to represent them. The resulting gap became not only the trigger for serious tensions, presenting the provisional governments with serious problems of 'order' (perhaps the most familiar historiographical description), but also the source of the revolutions' greatest democratic energy.

b) The formation of welfare states supplies a second major instance. This was 'the making social of democracy', as one might call it, whose contradictory terms were pioneered in a wide variety of labour-movement, progressivist, managerial – technocratic, and moralizing contexts of reform activity in industrializing Europe beginning in the 1880s. The wartime circumstances of unparalleled societal mobilization then became crucial to the coalescence of a strong readiness for reform in government, in response both to the dictates of harnessing such enormous resources for the war effort and to all the calamitous human consequences of the conflict, from the horrendous scale of the military casualties to people's widespread hopes of post-war social improvements.

c) Yet a third dimension of extra-parliamentary dynamics involved the popular mobilizations of the early twentieth-century radical right. These movements were explicitly anti-democratic in conscious or formal orientations. Nonetheless, they practically expanded the bounds of participation within the public sphere, in ways symbiotically related to the production of new democratic capacities, which became extremely relevant for democracy's future prospects.

d) Finally, the direct democratic and community-based forms of participatory politics also need to be considered. These were most commonly associated with the soviets and workers' councils during 1917–21, but assumed a wide variety of additional forms crucial to the specificities of the popular democratic upsurge in Europe during this period.

To appreciate the indebtedness of democratization to the revolutionary dimensions of the conjuncture, we need to hold the overall configuration of political forces and possibilities in view rather than concentrating on the conscious agency of the revolutionaries alone. Thus in shaping the democratic contents of the political settlements after 1918, the insurrectionary maximalism of the Bolsheviks and the extreme lefts of the time mattered far less in itself than in the variety of reformist initiatives its challenge helped to precipitate. That is to say, even where the revolutionary left was at its weakest and Socialist parties made only small or modest gains in post-war elections, major reforms still ensued. Thus in France these included a law on collective agreements, the eight-hour day, and electoral reform between March and July 1919. In Belgium between 1918 and 1921, they comprised the eight-hour day, progressive taxation, social insurance laws and electoral reform. A similar Dutch package brought the eight-hour day, forty-hour week, social insurance legislation, public housing, the corporative involvement of trade unions in a new Ministry of Social Affairs, and votes for women. Comparable effects could be seen in Britain and Scandinavia. In Germany, Austria and the East-Central European successor states, new republican sovereignties became established via processes of national-democratic revolution, accompanied by varying degrees of social reform. Finally, in most of the successor states and some others there were major land reforms.[30]

This was a huge increment of reform. In a large part of Europe, democracy emerged from this post-war settlement far stronger than ever before. That zone encompassed the earlier Central and Northern European 'social democratic core', where Socialist parties surpassed twenty per cent of the popular vote in parliamentary elections before 1914 (Austria, Germany, Switzerland, Czechoslovakia, Scandinavia), together with France, the Low Countries and Britain.[31] Moreover, this impressive growth of the left took a very particular form – namely, less any specifically socialist advance than a further strengthening of parliamentary democracy, the expansion of workers' rights under the law, further recognition of trade unions, growth of civil liberties, and substantial social legislation, in some cases amounting to the beginnings of a welfare state. In particular, the enhancement of the public sphere – in parliamentary, publicistic and general cultural terms – was a vital strategic gain, especially in countries where public freedoms of expression had remained highly restricted before 1914. This toughening of civil society through the enhancement of the public sphere provided key supports for democratization, and in the newly created sovereignties of East-Central Europe (including the new republican sovereignty of Weimar Germany) the legal constitution of the public sphere was essential to the overall project of nation-forming too.

For example, the forms of liberal legality and strong formal constitutions were indispensable for the popular democratic potentials organized by Austrian and German social democrats during the 1920s. Without protection of the law, the achievements of Red Vienna and its counterparts in Germany were simply not imaginable. This was apparent not only from the demise of the two republics in 1933–34, which spelled the destruction of the Socialist movements and their legality, but also from the republics' original creation in 1918–19, which had first brought Austrian and German socialists to plausible national leadership. In this respect, the failure of those two parties to pursue more radical socialist policies during the revolutions of 1918–19 – the usual basis of left-wing critiques – mattered far less for democracy's future prospects than the new political capacities and legal resources that the liberalized constitutional frameworks now made available.

Two further points arise. First, both major increments of general European democracy in the first half of the twentieth century were made possible by prior circumstances of societal breakdown or transformation produced by war. Moreover, those transformations came from war of a special kind, notably, total war, or warfare requiring general societal mobilization over several years, bringing major expansions of the state's demands on society's resources and population. Earlier generalized moments of pan-European constitution-making during 1776–1815 and 1859–71, though not the abortive ones of 1830–31 and 1848–51, had also involved crises related to warfare, if not in quite the comprehensive manner of 1917–23 and 1945–49. On the other hand, the most recent of these constitution-making conjunctures, our own contemporary one of 1989–92, was not produced by the same kind of war-generated societal crisis, unless we posit a model of societal peacetime militarization, for which a strong case might certainly be made.[32]

Secondly, this relationship of democratic opportunity to war produced a central paradox, namely, the dependence of large-scale democratic breakthroughs on processes and conjunctures that massively strengthened state power. In other words, in the major twentieth-century explosions of democratic innovation we find a strikingly contradictory simultaneity – between processes that *qualify* state power and processes that *enhance* it. On the one hand, both world wars saw the production of new democratic capacities, which each time became organized into an impressive post-war settlement of legal, institutional and political reforms, codified into mainly republican constitutions, and grounded in the negotiation of a large-scale social compromise. This was a system of fundamental reforms linked to popular agency, which qualified and limited public authority, rendering it formally and practically accountable. On the other hand, however, both wars also fostered the emergence of an immeasurably more demanding state, partly improvised, partly elaborated through strategic designs, and generally borne by logics of unprecedented societal mobilization. This state's centralized claims, insidiousness and forms of distributed power seemed ever less susceptible to effective accountability and control.

One way of resolving this paradox is to remember a key precept, namely, that war is essentially destructive in its immediate material effects. For as well as strengthening the state, both during wartime conditions and in the process of building and securing the post-war settlements, war also led to the destabilizing and weakening, even the entire dissolution, of existing state forms. The vital difference here was between winners and losers: the First World War may have effected a general strengthening of the state in most cases during the war itself, but by 1917–18 it had also brought a catastrophic weakening of those states that turned out to be losers, notably the Russian, Ottoman, Austro-Hungarian, and eventually German multi-national empires. To them may also be added Italy, which was technically on the winning side, but experienced its victory largely as defeat. In contrast, the victor societies – Britain, France, but also Belgium, and by extension the Netherlands – were able to enjoy a powerful increment of democracy after 1918 without having to suffer this vacuum of the East-Central European political collapse.

The paradox may best be handled, perhaps, by some notion of social contract or historic compromise. Thinking about post-war reconstruction became centred around the promise of large-scale social improvements in most of the combatant societies during the high tide of wartime mobilization, but the specific terms of negotiation then varied with the political conditions accompanying the war's end. At its heart was the cashing of the patriotic cheque: the respective national citizenries expected substantial social and political reform in return for the sacrifices required by the wartime mobilization, whether generalized in relation to food shortages and other privations and forms of social discipline, including of course the appalling dimensions of the carnage and maiming at the front, or more specifically in relation to trade union incorporation, the modification of labour practices, and the reordering of the economy. Where political authorities collapsed in the midst of military defeat as in Germany and the Austro-Hungarian Empire, the way was open for linking the resultant settlement to more radical measures of political democratization and a stronger version of the welfare state. Where existing political arrangements remained intact, enhanced by the prestige of military victory as in Britain and France, the settlement was more modest on both counts, namely, a less complete extension of the franchise and a heavily compromised social deal.

The longer-term record was in any case mixed. On the one hand, the European-wide process of democratic constitution-making produced a dramatically transformed set of polities and international system. The new successor states in particular were all equipped with constitutions that were originally strongly democratic, linked to impressive projects of social reform, and further challenged and incited by the direct democracy of the soviets and workers' councils. On the other hand, by the end of the 1920s, in European terms very little of this settlement remained, and few of the new democratic capacities proved capable of outlasting the first post-war decade.

POPULAR CULTURES OF DEMOCRACY, 1945–68

There are many explanations for those instabilities of the democratic settlements after 1918, but one key lay in the distinctions between *constitution-making* and *culture-building*. For at one level, the political breakdowns of the 1920s and 1930s reflected the relative thinness of the emergent societal consensus and the fragility of its democratic values. To make sense of this fragility – and conversely to conceptualize the basis on which more stable democratic cultures might have been formed – we need to consider the role of the public sphere. As already intimated above, the toughening of civil society through the enhancement of the public sphere was a vital part of the democratic quality of the post-war political settlements in both 1918 and 1945, and in making this argument I am using the idea of the public sphere to encompass all the ways in which society's self-organization acquired legitimacy and legally protected public space – through collective organization of all kinds, through the formation of political identities, through the expression of opinion, through the circulation of ideas, and so forth.[33]

The strengthening of the public sphere may certainly be approached constitutionally as a matter of legal innovation and institutional change, and for this purpose both world wars revealed the same contradictory dualism already mentioned above, between the 'state-enhancing' and 'state-qualifying' logics of the war. In one way, those wartime conditions severely cramped and damaged public freedoms. The militarizing of public life and its heavy limitation via censorship, suspension of debate, surveillance, emergency laws and states of siege hardly promoted the opening up of the public sphere for democratic purposes, but rather hampered it. Yet conditions of patriotic mobilization also legitimized the voice of all those groups placing themselves inside the wartime consensus, in a process that certainly helped bring new groups into the recognized political nation – most obviously the organized working class, but also groups with far less of an established collective history such as women, and other social categories now available for political address, such as youth and the ordinary soldier.[34] The real question concerned how and whether these wartime shifts could become durably institutionalized through the renormalizing of political life in the return to peace, and in that respect the crucial variable became the weakness of the democratic consensus in the new states produced by the Central European military collapse. In those cases, the post–1918 leaderships proved incapable of organizing the emergent democratic consensus into a sufficiently broad and resilient political culture.

The field of interaction between reforms under the law, institutional developments and changing political culture was extremely important here. In aggregate, the various measures of democratization accompanying the end of the war in 1918–19 definitely translated into a new kind of public sphere, particularly where public freedoms had been imperfectly established and governmentally harassed before 1914, as in the German and Austro-Hungarian Empires. This enhancement of the public sphere proceeded from all the aspects of the new breakthrough to democracy – thus from the newly created republican sovereignties and associated discourse of citizenship, from the strengthening of parliamentary government, from protections for the press, from expansion of workers' rights under the law, from corporative recognition of trade unions, from the growth of civil liberties, from the graduation of social legislation into the welfare state, and so on.

Without benefit of this expanded and legally protected public sphere, whose rules and opportunities could be enjoyed on a national or society-wide scale, social movements would remain confined to their own defensive and self-referential, largely ghettoized, sub-cultural space. For popular democratic purposes, such a strengthening of the public sphere was a *sine qua non*, and at all events a huge strategic gain. Under the most repressive situations, after all, self-organization at a sub-cultural level is still possible in a defensive and inward-looking sense. But without secure or predictable access to any wider public domain, sub-cultures remain chronically weak. They become deprived of access to possible coalitions and therefore to the supports of a broad enough societal consensus. They lack either the national-popular credibility of a plausible counter-hegemonic claim – the necessary moral-political capital for governing – or the resources for resisting anti-democratic or counter-revolutionary repression, if that should come.

Where a robust societal consensus could be constructed, on the other hand, enjoying simultaneous legitimacy at the level of the state and breadth in popular culture, the grounding and resilience of popular democracy could be very strong. In contrast to the fragilities of the post-1918 settlements, in fact, a consensus of that kind *was* elaborated after the Second World War, drawing upon the democratic patriotisms of the war years, fusing the aspirations for a new beginning with the logics of economic reconstruction, and organizing itself within the anti-fascist integument of the post-war settlements. Between the late 1940s and the next breaking point of 1968, a democratically centred or inflected societal consensus was produced, providing a kind of template for the popular political imagination. That consensus was organized around a strongly liberal public sphere, with all the concomitant legal protections. It was fashioned from the popular democratic momentum of a wartime mobilization, which became linked to the social contract of a post-war settlement. The reformist strengths of that settlement made it possible for popular consciousness to identify with the state, which thereby acquired a new and lasting reservoir of moral capital.

In making this case, I want to use the example of post-war Britain. The institutional features of the British version of the Keynesian welfare-state synthesis are well-known. They included social security 'from the cradle to the grave', the National Health Service, the Butler Education Act, progressive taxation, strong public-sector policies, corporative economic management, strong ideals of trade union recognition and an integrative discourse of social citizenship.[35] But the persuasiveness and democratic breadth of this post-war settlement also had a vital cultural source.

In this context, patriotism – British national feeling – had acquired powerful inflections to the left. Pride in being British implied the egalitarianism of the Second World War, the achievement of the welfare state, and a complex of democratic traditions stressing decency, tolerance and the importance of everyone pulling together, in a way that honoured the value and values of ordinary working people. In the legitimizing narratives of popular memory surrounding this patriotism, both the founding rigours of the post-war Labour government and the normalizing complacencies of the succeeding Conservative administrations of the 1950s were important in their differing ways. But the lasting stability of this consensus, which endured into the 1970s, also depended on a larger cultural script binding the experiences of the 1930s and 1940s together. The post-war consensus also evoked images of the Depression, and by these means the patriotic comradeship of the war became reworked into a social democratic narrative of suffering and social redress.

In that narrative, the poverty of the 1930s became a sign for the difference and desirability of the new post-war present.[36] From the vantage point of the 1950s, the 1930s signified a massive failure of the system – the 'wasted years', the 'devil's decade', the 'low, dishonest decade', in the familiar parlance of the day. The imagery of dismal hardship, mass unemployment and hunger marches described an unacceptable past that could never be repeated, a societal misery requiring collective action and public responsibility. The

Second World War, accordingly, was a 'good war', not just because of its anti-fascist character (the quality usually adduced), but because the egalitarianism and social solidarities needed for victory also made an irrefutable case for equitable social policies in the peacetime to come. The breadth of the resulting post-1945 consensus behind the welfare state rested rhetorically on this suturing of the Depression and the War together, of *patriotism* and *social need, national interest* and *common good*. In popular memory this rendition of the 1930s and 1940s became an especially effective and resonant narrative holding intact a coherent sense of Britishness after the war. Here, for instance, is the playwright Dennis Potter, in other respects the least sentimental of cultural critics:

> . . . we were, at that time, both a brave and a steadfast people, and we shared an aim, a condition, a political aspiration if you like, which was shown immediately in the 1945 General Election, and then [in] one of the great governments of British history – those five, six years of creating what is now being so brutally and wantonly and callously dismantled was actually a period to be proud of, and I'm proud of it.[37]

The key here is far less any historical accuracy of Potter's description – the forms national history may actually have assumed during the 1940s or the actual record of the post-war Labour government – than its plausibility for the post-war generations, for we can only fully engage the question of democratization by also exploring its cultural dimension. In the case of post-war Britain, that means exploring the fields of popular identification the wartime experience brought into being, the complicated ways in which these became articulated to a post-war system of politics, the forms of legitimation they provided for the post-war state, and the supports they delivered for one kind of politics as against another.

The forms of cohesion and stability in a society – and the conditions under which these may be effectively renewed – depend crucially on the forms of identification forged in popular memory and popular culture with that society's political institutions and even with its state. In the twentieth century, in this respect, the European transnational constitution-making conjunctures associated with the aftermath of the two world wars were undoubtedly the key moments. In each case, the scale of societal mobilization, the radicalism of the institutional changes, and the turbulence of popular hopes all fractured the stability of existing allegiances and ripped the fabric of social conformity wide enough for big democratic changes to break through. But in the case of 1918, the forging of a new societal consensus around sufficiently strong popular identifications with the democratic state proved uneven and highly contested, as the political polarizations of the inter-war years and the rise of fascism only too tragically confirmed. After 1945, in contrast, the Western European consensus proved both broad and deep, engendering remarkably dense and resilient popular identifications with the post-war social and political order.

This Western European post-war consensus lasted for two decades, subsisting on the doubled memories of war and Depression. Its boundaries were only reached generationally, as capitalist reconstruction, the long boom, and consumer prosperity gradually changed the political landscape. By the 1960s, amidst the resulting cultural tensions, the reflex of continuing to invoke the benefits of the post-war reforms seemed to a younger generation too much like complacency. Moreover, the new clash of generations became all the more painful when parents themselves happened to be left-wing and absolutized their own experience, wielding 'the blackmail of past hardships' in order to silence critiques of the present. As Alessandro Portelli remarks of the Italian context of this transition: 'Older generations, those that went through Fascism, war, Resistance, hard times in the factories, poverty, and the Depression, often think they have a monopoly on history and blackmail the younger generation with it.'[38] Thus for Gaetano Bordoni, a communist barber in San Lorenzo in Rome, his daughter's political complaining and dismissiveness toward hard-won material comforts dishonoured his own generation's earlier anti-fascist sacrifices. As he put it: '. . . when I was ten years old, I carried a machine gun in the hills of Frosinone, along with my father, shooting it out . . . I mean, now at age ten you have a toy; I had a machine gun.' By leaving her steak uneaten on the dinner plate, Bordoni's daughter demeaned her father's life's meaning, Portelli argues, because material improvements were coupled in his mind with the winning of democracy. By dismissing material gains as nothing to do with 'freedom' and 'calling for more radical forms of struggle, the younger generation questions both the achievements of the anti-Fascist struggle and the current politics of the working-class Left'.[39]

For the older generation, the Second World War was the defining experience. In countries occupied by the Nazis (especially Italy and France), the anti-fascist legacies of the Resistance combined very powerfully with the reformist languages of reconstruction to make the prosperity of the 1960s feel like a final realization of the promise of Liberation. In Italy, where workers had barely escaped from the extreme bleakness of the 1950s, the improving standards acquired extra emotional power. 'What was the image of socialism then [in the 1950s]? It was, Everybody eats. Food for all. At the time, that was the most urgent problem, rather than alienation, say, or man-machine relationships [the big issues of 1968].'[40] In Britain, which was spared Nazi rule, the post–1945 welfare state and the wartime collectivism had analogous effects.

ENGENDERING DEMOCRACY

For any serious discussion of the expansion or contraction of democracy's boundaries, particularly with respect to the regulating of access and the question of who exactly acquires a voice, the gendering of citizenship becomes a vital concern. By now, in this respect, feminist critiques have shown just how pervasively the terms of modern social and political under-standing since the Enlightenment and French Revolution have relied on binary distinctions between what it means to be a woman or a man. Such gendered thinking has been constitutive for conceptions of citizenship and the associated inventories of rights and obligations. It has also organized our languages of political subjectivity and collective identification, from class and nationhood to religion and race, right down to the very concepts of personhood and the self.

The basic category of civil society presumed women's exclusion via the construction and naturalizing of claims about sexual difference, feminists have persuasively shown. Such claims mapped on to other distinctions of public and private, so that women became gendered primarily as mothers and managers of households, as opposed to social leaders and political agents. That being the case, women could not simply be added to the circle of citizenship in an egalitarian manner without profoundly disrupting the meanings of citizenship as such. On the contrary, demanding the inclusion of women entailed a more general willingness to 'deconstruct and reassemble our understanding of the body politic', because the question of women's access to the franchise was always over-determined by wider discourses of disablement and exclusion.[41] As we explore the limits and potential en-largement of democratic life in the twentieth century, therefore, the gendering of political capacities needs to be a crucial part of the approach.

The start of the twentieth century in Europe saw the first concerted challenge to the masculinity of the franchise by both mass socialist and specifically feminist movements. The years 1914–23 then brought an un-precedented destabilizing of gender regimes through both the politicizing of domestic life during the First World War and women's wartime recruitment into the economy, followed then by a re-normalizing of gender relations once the war had ended. Of course, that re-normalizing remained uneven, contested and incomplete. The early twentieth century also witnessed the rise of increasingly visible and extensive cultures of consumption and commercialized entertainment, epitomized by the department store and the cinema, where women acquired disproportionate visibility and presence. Concomitant changes in the public sphere – coming not only from the Northern and Central European enfranchisement of women in 1918–19, but also from the gendering of the new physical spaces of the city – decisively disrupted how women's political identities were coming to be understood.[42] There were two countervailing logics in that respect.

One logic sought to contain women's citizenship via languages of motherhood. Social ideals of motherhood were certainly not absent from discourses of women's rights before 1914, but suffrage movements had nonetheless been the main form of organized political campaigning. Pre-war advocates of women's emancipation stressed the priorities of political enfranchisement and the enlargement of constitutional rights. But under the impact of the First World War, female citizenship became conceptualized increasingly by foregrounding women's patriotic contributions as mothers. If the war economy depended on the large-scale recruitment of women into the workplace, their public recognition occurred mainly through their validation as mothers. Citizenship claims during the constitution-making of 1918–19 were made overwhelmingly on this basis. Moreover, given the powerful dominance of the male breadwinner ideology, which became built into the expanded post-1918 social policies, this maternalist discourse left no room for the viable defence of women's rights as workers. Public policies of the inter-war years – from the most generous Scandinavian versions, through the welfare state initiatives of Weimar Germany and Red Vienna, to the conservative models in Britain and fascism in Italy – addressed women aggressively in maternalist terms, recognising them inside the family and the domestic sphere. These popular terms of address became the sole legitimate and widely accepted ground for admitting women to citizenship.[43]

Moreover, as women became more publicly visible, with the limited economic independence provided by employment and the new modest degree of spending power, they became the objects of much social fear. The counter-discourse to the talk of freedom and emancipation was the discourse of endangerment and disorder. By the 1920s, the new entertainment media of radio, gramophone and film, the new physical spaces of the picture palaces and dance halls, the mass circulation newspapers and magazines, the machineries of fashion and style, the new markets for clothing and cosmetics, the appeals of advertising and the relative freeing of the body for display, were all giving younger women access to a new grammar of public expression:

> They took for granted the rights and freedoms won for them by [earlier] generations. They were the first modern generation of women who did not expect to spend their entire adult lives either in motherhood and exclusion

from the public world or in rebellion against that exclusion. They were women who could be defined neither in terms of the family, as were their mothers, nor in terms of work, as were their fathers and brothers. They were the women of the Machine Age, for whom the machine meant employment, consumer goods, modernity, individuality, pleasure.[44]

Unfortunately, the formal advocates of women's rights missed the point. Feminists were dismayed: 'Can [young women] really follow a difficult scientific demonstration or a complex piece of music, can they really feel the intensities of admiration or love when a good part of their thoughts is concerned with the question "Is it time to powder my nose again"?'[45] Socialist men complained about the frivolity and tawdriness of women's pleasures. Travelling through northern England, George Orwell saw only 'the same sheeplike crowd – gaping girls and shapeless middle-aged women dozing over their knitting'.[46] Female consumers were traitors to their class, a fifth column for bourgeois materialist values. To Orwell's mind, the new 'cheap luxuries' like 'fish and chips, silk stockings, tinned salmon, cut-price chocolate . . . the movies, radio, strong tea, and the football pools', were a boon to 'our rulers' and probably 'averted revolution'.[47] Inter-war socialists spoke contemptuously of 'the young prettily dressed girls' and their 'destructive' pleasures.[48] They found small political sympathy for the new generations of young working women – for the shop girls, hairdressers, typists, assembly-line workers and cleaners, who poured from the shops and offices at the end of the working day.

Thus the counter-logic to the recognition of women via maternalism was a misogynist logic of female degeneracy. In both cases, the main ground of contention around gender relations shifted away from questions of political rights and towards ideas of moral order, with profound consequences for the political imaginary of citizenship. Women entered political discourse between the wars in ways not easily assimilable to the accepted thinking about democracy. On the one hand, a general area of 'body politics', or perhaps biological politics, crystallized around the moral and reproductive domains of social policy innovation, including maternal and child welfare, reproductive technologies and regulation (contraception, abortion, sterilization), eugenicist social engineering, public health and social hygiene, policies for the control of youth, and the general regulation of morality and sexuality. On the other hand, the emergent culture of mass consumption placed the new identities on display. These were the twin domains – the politics of the body, the politics of consumption – which the inter-war right often brought ambitiously and successfully together, sometimes conservatively, as in Baldwin's Britain, but sometimes with activist aggression, as in fascist Italy and the Third Reich.

After the Second World War, this pattern was repeated. As in the 1920s, when the first wave of female enfranchisement did disappointingly little to dislodge the given political structures, women's recognition as voting citizens after 1945 failed to unlock an established gender regime. Once again, the dialectic of difference and equality supervened: even as women exercised their new political rights, the post-war social legislation tracked them out of the public domain. The main logics of post-war social reform fixed women firmly in the familial sphere of the home. 'During marriage most women will not be gainfully employed', William Beveridge had flatly declared, and European welfare legislation constitutively privileged the male 'breadwinner' in his delivery of the 'family wage'.[49]

In those mainly Catholic countries where women were finally admitted to full political citizenship in 1945–46, namely Belgium, Italy and France, the duality of spheres remained strikingly intact. Thus whereas the Algiers Assembly of April 1944 ensured that French women won the vote, in the wider field of public policy their place had barely changed. French socialists and communists mouthed the old nostrums about productive employment as the precondition of emancipation, while their trade unions perpetuated the gendered repertoire of female exclusion, family wages and unequal pay. At one level, women were recognized as citizen participants in the democratic nation. But at the more basic level, women's recognition was almost wholly subsumed by the family form, whether through the breadwinner rhetorics and the family wage, the restrictive trade union practices for married women, or the prevailing welfare-state paradigm.[50]

For women, therefore, the twentieth-century processes of democratization contained an extremely powerful contradiction. During the two world wars, women were wrenched out of domesticity by the wartime mobilizations, were brought into employment and other public roles, and were called upon for a commitment to the collective good. This process was motivated implicitly by promises of citizenship, an invitation to equality in the nation at the war's end. Yet beyond the novelty of juridical citizenship, in 1918 and 1945, women were re-normalized into subordinated forms of domesticity, in a gender regime of public and private, which brought women the opposite of emancipated personhood. Even the positive values of the welfare state brought their disabling reminders. The maternalist framing for so much of the welfare-state legislation fixed women in the home, especially in the strongest pro-natalist variants, which vested such central value in the welfare of the working-class child. Even the most radical approaches distinguished between housewife-mothers (the 'real' mothers working-class women should be given the right to become) and women who worked (younger women, childless women, professional women able to purchase childcare).

In this way and many others, the social democratic achievement of the welfare state constructed a domesticated and dependent place for women. Women were advantaged, but not emancipated, by the languages of social citizenship in the welfare state.

When the main organ of Labour Party support in 1945, the *Daily Mirror*, urged British women to 'Vote for Him', meaning their soldier husbands, it not only sold the promise of equal citizenship blatantly short, but also bespoke an entire universe of gendered social and political assumptions. During the Cold War, the mobilizing of patriotic sentiments against communism also found the rhetorics of family and home attractive, suturing an idealized domesticity to the threatened security of the nation and its way of life. If women were positioned mainly as mothers in this discursive economy, men were not only constructed as fathers, but still more powerfully as the bearers of public responsibility, in rigid systems of gender demarcation. In post-war democratic culture, the domestic regime of the full-time housewife-mother, supplied with social services, free milk and orange juice, and educated into technical competence, dividing responsibilities with the husband-breadwinner delivering the wage, carried the day.[51]

CONCLUSION

I end my discussion with the gendered aspects of democratization for several reasons. First, they highlight the limitations of democracy's earlier twentieth-century expansions. These not only halted at the threshold of the household, leaving patriarchal regimes of privacy broadly intact, they also brought women into public citizenship in skewed and partial ways. Yet second, gains for women nonetheless occurred only in the course of such broader revolutionary conjunctures. Women achieved access to a democratic voice when revolutionary crises opened a way. Third, the gendered foreshortening of any resulting advance points to the *unfinishedness* of democratic change. That also suggests key elements of the next period of radicalism, which opened with the generalized pan-European crisis of 1968. Gender transformations were certainly not the only ones prefigured in the explosions of that dramatic year. But the arrival of a new women's movement, the questioning of the family, the new politics of sexuality, the politicizing of personal life, and related features of the emergent politics of the later twentieth century were all given decisive impetus by the larger critiques which 1968 set into motion, from the discourse of alienation and the restructuring of labour markets to the renewed interest in community-based politics, direct action and small-scale participatory forms.

Since that time, certainly in theory and to a great extent in politics, feminists have turned the relationship of the personal and the political completely inside out, making it possible to remake entirely the connections between everydayness and public life. Contemporary feminists have extended the reach of 'the political' across the family and the workplace, sexuality and personal relations, health and education, and the ever-burgeoning demands and pleasures of consumption. Increasingly during the late twentieth century, democratic precepts compelled application to these domains too, bridging from the previously recalcitrant settings of everyday life to those of political agency and action. Democracy's expanding relevance in these directions makes it even harder than before to subsume its meanings into a narrowly institutional understanding of how and where politics takes place. That kind of narrowness certainly dominated most traditional forms of political history, but since the 1960s and 1970s politics has been spilling uncontainably beyond those older institutional limits. This breaching of the boundaries of politics remains the true cutting edge of radicalism since 1968, whether in the politics of knowledge or in political life itself. It casts the contemporary contraction of the democratic imagination around the dogma of the market in an appropriately conservative light.

As this essay began by arguing, since the fall of communism prevailing definitions of democracy cleave consistently to ideas of the free market and individual rights, confining legitimate political action to circumscribed spheres of social administration, the proceduralism of parliaments and the rule of law. Expecting anything more from politics, contemporary advocates insist, exceeds the realistic and permissible limits of the political domain. In a parallel historiographical development, leading specialists on the Russian and French Revolutions have sought to concentrate the meanings of those great events in similar fashion, postulating a necessary logic of violence, radicalism and terror once politics abandoned its self-limiting charge. Not accidentally, those revisionist critics began developing these stringently 'political' readings of revolutionary history during the 1970s and 1980s, just as the autonomies of politics in their own times were seriously breaking down.[52]

In treating the two post-war settlements of 1917–23 and 1945–49 as comparable revolutionary conjunctures, I tell a more complicated story. In these operative contexts of democratic innovation – democracy's *actuality* – the decisive gains came precisely from excess. Democratization entailed popular mobilizations of unusual intensity and scale. These became possible only in the midst of severe socio-economic conflicts, breakdowns of government, and crises of the whole society. Democratization was also violent, meaning not just the forms of direct action, polarization and coercive technique, but also a logic of confrontation. The old political mechanisms –

parliamentary process, the associated proceduralism, consensus building and the rules of civility – had all broken down. Any subsequent gains for democracy, potential or realized, always presupposed such crises, whether in 1989 or 1968 or in a variety of more restricted national examples, such as Hungary and Poland in 1956, Portugal in 1975, Spain in the mid 1970s, or Poland in 1980–81. In crises such as these – the great democracy-enhancing moments of the second half of the century – parliaments and committee rooms were always superseded by the streets.

9

Revolutions: Great and Still and Silent

Daniel Bensaïd

The party of flowers and nightingales is closely connected with the revolution.
Heinrich Heine, *History of Religion and Philosophy in Germany*[1]

We think a revolution is a straightforward answer, and we know that that too is not correct. These are vulgar simplifications of things.
Paul Valéry

It is the desirability of the revolution which causes a problem today.
Michel Foucault, 1977

I

A few years ago, the journal *Lignes*[2] published a survey about the 'desire for revolution'. Desire or need for revolution? This deceitfully juvenile desire, with vague suggestions of 1968, gives off the bitter scent of a faded flower left on a grave. Desire and longing, these are what are left over when the initial impetus and the original enthusiasm are definitively exhausted: a vague wish without force, covetousness without appetite, a death wish, a ghost of freedom, an erotic whim! A subjectivity enslaved to the impracticable feeling of the possible.

This desire which we believe to be liberated from needs is, ultimately, only the consumerist version of it: the desiring mechanism is, first of all, a consuming mechanism. It is the inverted reflection of the commodity on display, which makes eyes in order to tout for customers who are enticed by the luminous charms of the shop window.

The substitution of desire for need has a theoretical history, namely the replacement of labour-value by want-value by Leon Walras in his *Elements of*

Pure Economics in 1874. As marginalism makes value subjective, 'the object springs from desire'. To measure value, the economist Charles Gide thus replaced the excessively objective term 'utility' by that of 'desirability'. Consciously or not, Foucault drew on this tradition when he enquired, in the late 1970s, whether revolution was still desirable.[3]

II

As for revolution, that is a long story.

Jan Patočka sees in the very idea of revolution 'a fundamental feature of modernity'. Between Chateaubriand's essay on 'revolutions' and that of Hannah Arendt on 'Revolution', the idea lines up, through this process of being put in the singular, behind History, Progress, Science or Art. It is inscribed into the new semantic of times, where the past no longer illuminates the future, but where the future illuminates the present. After the French Revolution, revolution becomes the name given to the expectations and hopes of emancipation. Raised to the status of 'locomotive of history', it rushes on towards the future, with all its metallic power, until its mechanical dream is swallowed up in the derailment of cattle wagons.

Set up as a dim object of fetishistic desire, this revolution keeps one foot in the sacred. It still suffuses the event with a thirst for miracles. To come down from the transcendence of desire (with its cohort of temptations and sins) to the immanence of needs, a long slow labour of secularization was required, repeatedly thwarted, and always renewed. Through experiences and ordeals, revolution has little by little come down from heaven to earth, from divine revelation to profane history. The myth has become obliterated in favour of the project.

'The emancipation of the proletariat', wrote Marx in 1848, is the 'secret of the revolution of the nineteenth century'. The disclosure of this secret breaks the history of the world in two, divides the people against itself – class against class – and undoes the unitary myth of the Revolution and the Republic. It sows discord between the former and the latter. It draws out from the original simplicity the plural complexities of bourgeois or proletarian, conservative or social revolutions. In short, this disclosed secret causes revolution within revolution: 'February 25, 1848, had granted the *republic* to France, June 25 thrust the *revolution* upon her. And revolution, after June, meant: *overthrow of bourgeois society*, whereas before February it had meant: *overthrow of the system of government.*'[4]

To this social determination of revolutionary contents, the experiences of the Paris Commune or of October 1917 added the strategic determination of the struggle for power: mass strike and armed insurrection.

Today, on the contrary, everything goes on as if this profound movement of secularization had become exhausted, and as if, by going back through the revolutionary ages towards their mythical source, we were abandoning as we go the experiences and the contents. In the 1980s the strategic debate reached its degree zero. While actual revolutions bore the names of places and dates, the places seemed doomed to disappear in unlimited space. The dates were lost in a time stretched out in weariness, where we commemorated without inventing. The temporal perspective contracted into an eternal managerial present.

We do not yet know what, in this anaemia of the social imaginary, was a result of the conjuncture, of an ephemeral weariness produced by the heavy defeats of the past century, or of a new upheaval of historical times. But the result is that the revolutionary idea tends to lose its political substance and to be reduced to a stance of desire, aesthetic or ethical, to a judgment of taste or an act of faith. It seems torn between a will to resist without any perspective of counter-attack, and the expectation of an improbably redemptive miracle; between a pilgrimage to the purifying sources of an original revolution, and a waning desire for a conservative revolution, whose consensual velvet would cover the exact opposite of a revolution. This melancholy re-enchantment is thus a re-deception, which must be urgently countered by a new effort of historicization and an outburst of politicization.

Inasmuch as it is 'the non-inevitable part of becoming', profane revolution does not spring from a compulsive dynamic of desires, but from a dialectic of needs. It does not obey the whims of desire, but the reasoned imperative to change the world – to revolutionize it – before it disintegrates amid the din of ashen idols. This need is not a sad passion, determined to fill an irreducible gap, but the joyful passion of permanent revolution, in which are brought together duration and event, the determinate conditions of the historical situation and the uncertainties of political action which strives to transform the range of possibilities.

III

The problem with the term revolution is that it is akin to myth (in the Sorelian sense) as much as to concept. We must therefore begin by disentangling the meanings (or trying to). We may say, broadly, that revolution (since the French Revolution) has become the algebraic formula for social and political change in contemporary societies. From this point of view, it constitutes, in Kant's pre-Revolutionary terminology, 'a political prophecy', 'a considered expectation of the future', which organizes wills and structures their horizons of expectation. Inasmuch as it opens the way to another possible world, this idea is always just as necessary against ordinary resignedness, tactical accommodations, and against the dissolution of politics into channel-hopping.

As it becomes defined with the French Revolution, this notion of revolution is also linked to the elaboration of a modern temporality, to the 'semantics of historical times' studied by Kosseleck or Goulemot.[5] It is then associated with sentiments of acceleration, improvement, or progress. It is this representation of the world which has become problematic under the impact of the catastrophes of the last century. Consequently, we can grasp that the idea of revolution no longer fulfils in the same way its 'mythical' function (of an indeterminate image of the future, in the way that the general strike in Sorel represents an indeterminate image of the strategic event).

Finally, in the course of experience, the notion of revolution has taken on an efficacious strategic content. There was a time when we discussed these contents in practical terms: armed insurrection, insurrectional general strike, protracted people's warfare, dual power . . . Today these debates seem very far away, though they tend to re-emerge as a result of social crises and imperial wars.[6] There are numerous reasons for this. One, and not the least important, is expressed indirectly in certain texts by the Zapatista Subcomandante Marcos. If strategy (at least since Bonaparte) was the art of concentrating one's forces at one point at a given time, what then, in the dissolution of space and the dissemination of powers, becomes of this concentration in the age of networks? There is much to be discussed here. The military are always said to be fighting the last war, just as revolutionaries are always making the last revolution (or the last but one).

IV

The mole is single-minded. It moves quietly along: 'Great revolutions which strike the eye at a glance must have been preceded by a still and secret revolution in the spirit of the age, a revolution not visible to every eye . . .'[7] Out of the range of appearances and of what is apparent, it digs silently, secretly, when the world is asleep. If it is short-sighted, the age for its part is blind to 'its thrust, when it continues to burrow from within'.[8]

From Blanqui to Benjamin, via Joyce's Stephen, the infernal repetition of defeats is more like a nightmare from which we must awake than a peaceful dream. History, it is well-known, stammers and stutters. From tragedies to farces, from uncle to nephew, from Napoleon the Great to Napoleon the Little. From tragedies to tragedies: from the massacres of June 1848 to the Bloody Week that ended the Paris Commune.

Marx also recommences and repeats. From one allusion to another, the past is summoned to appear. The old mole of the *Eighteenth Brumaire* thus revives the ghost of the murdered king wandering beneath the stage in *Hamlet*. It is always a story of 'invisible burrowing', of the 'underground' and of ghosts, of pathways and passages: 'But the revolution is thorough. It is still journeying through purgatory.'[9] It scratches and undermines '*gründlich*', deeply, to the root.

'*Brav gewühlt, alter Maulwurf!*'
'Well burrowed, old mole!'

From translation to transposition, from slip of the tongue to shift in meaning, from Shakespeare to Schlegel, from Hegel to Marx, the old friend is transformed, until it feels strong enough to deal with the surface: 'The spirit often seems to have forgotten itself and to be lost, but internally divided against itself, it continues to work from within but forwards, as Hamlet says of his father's ghost: well said, old mole! canst work i' the earth so fast? – until it is strong enough to break through the crust of earth which hid it from the sun.'[10] Between the basement and the surface, between the stage and the wings, it is the unheroic image of preparatory abnegation, of the indispensable preliminaries, of the task before the threshold. An agent of depth and latency. A sort of invisible text which always runs beneath the visible text, which frequently corrects it and sometimes contradicts it.

V

The revolution interrupts the ordinary course of things. It is an event that causes a stir. 'Suppose that what the twenty-first century was incapable of saving from the twentieth were – that there are still events?' wonders Michel Surya. Might the disillusions of the age of extremes have destroyed the possibility of any event at all?

Since our resounding fall into modernity, 'revolution was the name of the event which did not occur, from which the whole name of the event derived; or which occurred, which is worse, in the form of its absolute denial. If there is no event to save, it is because the only one which we could have wished to be able to save was this horrible metamorphosis.'[11]

This injury to hope will weigh for a long time yet on the shoulders of coming generations. For a long time to come, it will darken the future. Rather than resigning ourselves to this disappearance without trace, there is perhaps still time to change a loss into a gain.

On condition that we desacralize and secularize the event itself.

That we snatch it from theology to restore it to profane history and politics.

Until the First World War, all politics was based on this possibility of an event which would resist 'the insidious notion of a historical law' which threatened to swallow it up. Just after that ordeal, Paul Valéry was already wondering whether the political spirit was not going to stop 'thinking by means of events', and whether we had not failed to rethink 'as appropriate' this fundamental notion: 'Henceforth any action makes a quantity of unforeseen interests echo in all directions, it engenders its sequence of immediate events.' Its effects 'make themselves felt almost instantaneously at any distance, return immediately to their causes, and are deadened only in the unexpected.' That is why 'the old historical geometry and the old political mechanics are not at all befitting'.[12]

Today post-modern rhetoric threatens the event in a quite different fashion. From the exhausted stuttering of the grand narratives emerges the deafening chorus of ventriloquial commodities. History recants around an eternal present. The spectre of Capital haunts the ruins of broken hopes. Tired of watching the horizon for an event which is not coming, watchers and numbed sentries let themselves drift into sleep.

Rejecting the inevitability of a history reduced to a commercial eternity, the philosophical discourses of the event respond to its political eclipse by its mystical celebration. 'Having emerged from nothing', it then presents itself as an absolute beginning, a 'pure prelude to itself', without antecedents or conditions.

Like the often dreamt-of first meeting of an amorous encounter, it seems simultaneously improbable and 'eternally self-evident'.

VI

What would an encounter be worth, if it did not shake certainties and destroy the insidious temptation of getting used to the order of things? For it still to be an event, it must be capable of letting itself be surprised and of risking itself wholly in the uncertainty of what arises.

But a sudden revelation or illumination would not make an event either. They would lack any historical logic, and we should quickly be reduced to banking on Providence or fate so that, occasionally, 'the impossible miracle of the event might come forth'. A profane politics would then become both unthinkable and impracticable.

That which marks a historical epoch 'lies not in the inherent qualities of the Event itself, but in its place – in the way it relates to the situation out of which it emerged'.[13]

In the condition of modern man, Péguy comments, the 'expectation of nothing' is not, for all that, 'just a worthless bit of expectation'. And the project without guaranteed result 'is not for all that a non-existent project'. It commits a responsibility towards the possible. Pure initiation into itself, the event is then 'a flowering of the possible in the instant', 'a broaching of the subject of time': 'Nothing is so mysterious as these upheavals, these renewals, these profound new beginnings. It is the secret of the event.'[14] As in revolution, however, these fresh beginnings and renewals imply that the slate is never blank, and that we never start from nothing, 'We always start again in the middle', Deleuze liked to say.

Inasmuch as 'it always happens to someone' and we cannot be that someone, we can hope to succeed in penetrating this secret and its mystery. Instead of celebrating it as 'the pure possibility of the possible', we must then ascribe the event to the historical conditions which determine its location. While a miracle is of the order of faith, the event determines the conditions of a politics in the form of a reasoned wager. The politics of the event breaks both with the routine of a 'socialism outside time' and with the reassuring 'laws' of a determinist history. The storming of the Bastille is only capable of being thought rationally through the crisis of the *ancien régime*. The October Revolution can only be thought through the upheaval of the war and the specificities of the 'development of capitalism in Russia', which make the country into the weakest link of the imperial order. The landing of the *Granma*, through the subordinate dictatorship of a corrupt dependent bourgeoisie. The commands of will may then correspond to the circumstances of the decision.

VII

There are therefore no authentic events except at the critical point where memory clings on to expectation, where experience goes out to meet forthcoming facts. Being expected, it nonetheless arises against all expectation. Thus it always appears as premature, untimely, inopportune. That is what gives it its strength. It gains meaning 'from its future' and from the new possibilities it inaugurates. It bears within it the 'conditions of its own comprehension'. Only its posterity will take the measure of this novelty. For it goes back to the root of the possibilities. It alters their horizon and proclaims 'a revolution of times'.[15]

Journalistic time, on the other hand, has no tomorrow. As mass producers of current events and news items, the media confuse ephemeral novelty with what will mark a historical epoch. Its present, ever begun afresh, is no longer situated in a perspective of duration which would reveal its meaning. Much reinforced by headlines, scoops and revelations, it offers cheaply the semblance of events. 'Once again, the instrument has got the better of us', observed Karl Kraus. The epoch 'is so prone to regard the special edition as the event'[16] that, despite the din they make, the trumpets of media reputation no longer make any walls tumble down.

A politics of the event is a strategic art of the inopportune. Necessarily untimely, it inevitably comes always too soon and always too late. The favourable moment is always premature. The modern idea of revolution appears as the stitch which joins historical necessity to the contingency of the event. For not only does political action expose itself to the uncertainty of its results, but it produces its own contingencies for itself. How can we account for this? By the Hegelian ruse of reason? Contingency then indicates the tenuous relation between the fragility of the possible and the consistency of the effective. It cannot be reduced either to pure chance or to the lacunae of an incomplete knowledge, it is inscribed in the very heart of history conceived as 'the act by which the spirit fashions itself in the form of the event'.[17]

'The test of this contingency' is a frequently painful experience of historical irrationalities: how can we reconcile the uncertainty of the event and the rationality supposed by the very concept of history? A history without events would be as unthinkable as an event without history. It becomes intelligible only through the 'changing texture' of what happens, but which might not have happened. The mere accomplishment of a predicted end would however suppress 'the test of contingency'.[18]

VIII

Of what 'historical necessity' is then the event the random part? Of the necessity of struggle and conflict, for only the struggle is predictable, not its outcome. The capitalist mode of production, Althusser insists, is not generated by the feudal mode of production 'according to the principles of genesis or descent'. It springs from the encounter – as strange as that of the umbrella and the sewing-machine on the operating table – between capitalized money, formally free labour power, and technical innovation. The event is the form taken by this combination which is not necessary.

The decisive instant 'when everything seems to be called into question again' thus defines politics as the 'collusion in the heart of history' of the virtual, which is multiple, and the actual, which is unique.

'There is the unforeseeable. That is the tragedy', observed Merleau-Ponty.

Moreover, it is necessary that this tragic freedom, at the risk of turning into the pure whim of desire, should know the limits assigned to it by conjuncture and circumstances. Unlike the saint or the classical hero, acting all in one go, the profane militant faces the uncertainty of a decision, of which the result always runs the risk of going against his intentions. The fragility of political and historical judgments is thus imposed as a necessary antidote both to dogmatic and doctrinaire temptations and to those of cynical indifference.

To change the world means interpreting it in order to change it. It also means changing it in the process of interpreting it.

IX

Strategic history and its memoirs of possibilities are thus distinguished from the platitudes of the accomplished fact. The same historians for whom the event is self-evident when it fits the presumed 'meaning' of history, quibble about mistakes in policies when it is a matter of going against the stream. That gives them 'the possibility of displaying their retrospective wisdom by enumerating and cataloguing mistakes, omissions and blunders'. Unfortunately, 'these historians do not indicate what path would have enabled a moderate to triumph in a revolutionary period, or, on the other hand, indicate a reasonable and successful revolutionary policy in a Thermidorian period'.[19] Registrar of the accomplished fact, this history of historians sacrifices the contingent to the necessary, and the possible to the real.

Critical history on the other hand deciphers the event from the point of view of the intervention of its actors. It releases the captive possibilities from the accomplished fact. Against the implacable force of circumstances, the test of contingency and the uncertainty of struggle thus open a breach in the bleak sequence of labours and days.

Marx thought politics 'in a horizon torn between the chance of encounter and the necessity of revolution':[20]

> World history would indeed be very easy to make if the struggle were taken up only on condition of infallibly favourable chances. It would, on the other hand, be of a very mystical nature, if "accidents" played no part. These accidents themselves fall naturally into the general course of development and are compensated again by other accidents. But acceleration and delay are very dependent on such "accidents", which include the "accident" of the character of those who first stand at the head of the movement.[21]

Having abandoned the speculative philosophy of history in favour of the critique of political economy, Marx inscribes his acute sense of the event – wars and revolutions – in the systemic logic and laws which 'act as tendencies' of *Capital*. Against the providential mysticism of universal history, he takes uncertainty into consideration. But its role has scarcely been recognized when it seems to be immediately neutralized by a mechanism of counterweights and compensations. The 'chances' cancel each other out in their outcome which is foreseeable 'in the framework of the march of evolution'. The 'dark crossroads' are erased in an alternation of accelerations and decelerations. The singularity of events is lost again in the grand narrative of progress, and political contingency melts into historical necessity.

This return of 'reason in history' hardly enables us to grasp the enigma of Thermidor and its recurrence. The enigmatic intertwining between revolution and counter-revolution is reduced to a comforting difference between bourgeois revolutions and proletarian revolutions, of which the outcome remains, in short, guaranteed:

> Bourgeois revolutions, like those of the eighteenth century, storm swiftly from success to success, their dramatic effects outdo each other, men and things seem set in sparkling brilliants, ecstasy is the everyday spirit, but they are short-lived, soon they have attained their zenith, and a long crapulent depression seizes society before it learns soberly to assimilate the results of its storm-and-stress period. On the other hand, proletarian revolutions, like those of the nineteenth century, criticize themselves constantly, interrupt themselves continually in their own course, come back to the apparently accomplished in order to begin it afresh, deride with unmerciful thoroughness the inadequacies, weaknesses and paltrinesses of their first attempts, seem to throw down their adversary only in order that he may draw new strength from the earth and rise again, more gigantic, before them, and recoil again and again from the indefinite prodigiousness of their own aims, until a situation has been created which makes all turning back impossible, and the conditions themselves cry out:
>
> *Hic Rhodus, hic salta!* Here is the rose, here dance!'[22]

So social revolutions only retreat in order to advance better.

If the inaugural revolution shines like a magnificent sunrise, counter-revolution is crooked and dim. It is revealed after the event. Too late. When it is already accomplished. For revolution and counter-revolution are not a simple process of advance and retreat on the same temporal axis. They are not symmetrical. An expert in reaction, Joseph de Maistre, has given the game away: counter-revolution is not a revolution in the opposite direction, an inverted, backward revolution, but the 'opposite of a revolution'.

X

According to Merleau-Ponty, revolutions are 'true as movements' and 'false as regimes'. According to Mannheim, the institutional order is never anything but the 'baleful residue' of Utopian hope. For Badiou, Thermidor indicates the end of the event, as sudden and miraculous as its inrush, a 'betrayal of fidelity' rather than a social and historical reaction. The recurrent alternation of the openness of events and its bureaucratic closure thus confirms the intermittence of a politics reduced to a few rare moments of epiphany.

From Marx to Trotsky, the paradoxical formula of 'revolution in perma-nence' indicates the problematic knot between event and history, between rupture and continuity, between the moment of action and the duration of the process. Merleau-Ponty stresses that, in Trotsky, historical reason is no longer a secularized divinity driving the train of the world. Although history is thus emancipated from both teleology and economic determinism, he nevertheless suspects the remnant of a belief in a predicted end.

In fact everything depends on the way the concept of revolution is articulated with historicity. In a genetic perspective, 'permanent revolution' may very well be merely the false nose of a secular faith in guaranteed progress. The ambiguous notions of 'transcendence' or 'growing over' thus illustrate the evolutionist interpretation 'of a revolution in which each stage is contained in embryo in the preceding stage'.[23]

But 'permanent revolution' may also assume a meaning contrary to the mechanical stageism (illustrated in sinister fashion in the Stalinist scriptures by the dreary chronology of modes of production): a performative and strategic meaning. It thus expresses the hypothetical and conditional link between a revolution circumscribed within a determinate space-time, and its spatial ('world revolution') and temporal (it 'necessarily develops over decades') extension. The revolutionary transformation of the world then assumes the dimension of a 'continual internal struggle' of the constituent power against its Thermidorian petrifaction.

XI

The relationship between resistance, event and history is achieved in the strategic notion of crisis, where the faults of normality and the miscarriages of routine take on their full force. Etymologically, crisis is a moment of decision and truth, when history hesitates in face of a point of bifurcation where the bushy paths of 'lateral possibilities' open up.

A characteristic theme of modernity, crisis represents the dark side of progress. It has acquired its current meaning by passing from medical vocabulary to economic and then political vocabulary. The economic 'great crisis' of 1929 coincides strangely with Freud's *Civilization and its Discontents* (1929) or Husserl's *The Crisis of European Sciences* (1935). For Husserl, 'the crisis of European sciences' means that their scientific status has become dubious. In the social and political crisis, the legitimacy of institutions and the power of the established order are in turn shaken. It is as if the discontent were foretelling the crisis, and as if the crisis were affecting the different spheres of social and intellectual life.

The discontent is the critical moment of repressive disillusion. Symptom of a new discontent in civilization, the disenchanted discourse of post-modernity today becomes favourable to the 'melancholy cruelty' of aimless action. The crisis, on the other hand, is the active part of the discontent. In a flickering of eyelids, the mole then glimpses the light.

From Marx to Lenin, the crisis has taken on a clearly strategic sense. Henceforth it indicates the 'factual node' which upsets the field of possibilities. It clarifies antagonisms. It imposes a hierarchy on contradictions. It combines social rhythms and disentangles multiple attachments.[24]

Since the beginning of the seventeenth century, Marx states, Europe has not seen any radical revolution 'not preceded by a commercial and financial crisis'. 'It is enough to mention the commercial crises that by their periodical return put on trial, each time more threateningly, the existence of the entire bourgeois society. In these crises there breaks out an epidemic . . . Society suddenly finds itself put back into a state of momentary barbarism.'[25] The crisis may still be delayed by a few weeks, but it must break out. It is thus presented as the way in which 'the conflict must be continually overcome' and as the form in which the broken equilibrium is violently re-established. This diagnosis does not escape what Michel Dobry describes as an 'illusion of causation'. The fact that the commercial crisis precedes the revolutionary crisis seems to establish a direct link between them, confirmed by the medical metaphor of the 'epidemic'.

But Marx does not merely interpret the chronological succession as a causal relation. He penetrates the internal logic of economic and financial crises. But the economic crisis is still only light without heat, the form of the possible which is 'most abstract' and 'lacking in content'. It is not the mechanical cause of political crises, but merely the condition that makes them possible. The transformation of a crisis into a revolutionary crisis depends on the capacity of the actors to grasp the strategic opportunity of the conjuncture. The action of a coherent force endowed with a clear project then becomes a decisive condition for the outcome:

> it is not every revolutionary situation that gives rise to a revolution; revolution arises only out of a situation in which the above-mentioned objective changes are accompanied by a subjective change, namely, the ability of the revolutionary *class* to take revolutionary mass action *strong*

enough to break (or dislocate) the old government, which never, not even in a period of crisis, "falls", if it is not toppled over.[26]

Lenin thus stresses an essential feature of crisis: the 'deobjectification' of social relations and the insistence that 'laws of history' are not inevitable.[27] The outcome of the crisis is played out with two or more protagonists, and the actors become stabilized as characters through 'the exchange of blows'.

XII

Since the middle of the 1970s, the world has become settled in an atmosphere of crisis which short-lived economic upturns have not managed to dissipate. The social, ecological and technological future remains darkened by anxieties and dangers. The indefinable crisis lingers. The fear of a terrible end is prolonged eternally in the stretching out of an endless dread.

This is something quite different from an industrial or financial crisis: a new discontent in civilization. It is a global crisis of social relations and relations between humanity and its natural environment, a general disordering of spaces and rhythms. The crisis in civilization is a crisis of disproportion and of mismeasurement. This goes on and extends itself in a decay that leads nowhere. Negri deduces the hypothesis that large-scale crisis would disappear with modernity in favour of a post-modern proliferation of 'small crises' branching out like a rhizome. If it transpires that state sovereignties are being undone in the mesh of an imperial network, it is not surprising that rapid and violent crises about identifiable questions of power are giving way to slow crises of 'corruption'.

The notion of crisis would then change meaning and function. It would no longer be a hole in the structure, a break in the continuity. Henceforth it would be an integral part of history. It would coincide with 'the general tendency of history'. It would be the very modality of it.[28] Here we rediscover the catastrophist tones which Negri claimed to be avoiding. Marx considered more soberly that capital was becoming the obstacle to its own development.

Today this contradiction has reached a critical point. But how do we get out of it?

We have seen many decadent empires and many civilizations in ruins. History is not a long peaceful river. It has no guaranteed happy ending. If the crisis is not yet the event, it shows the concrete possibility of it. Its outcome is not settled in advance. The alternative, liberation or barbarism, posed at the beginning of the last century, is more urgent than ever. From world wars to nuclear bombing, from genocides to ecological disasters, barbarism has subsequently taken a lead of several lengths The crisis appears as something quite different from a mere 'historical turning point': as a great transition, a crucial junction, at the meeting-point between the constraints of the situation and the contingency of action.

Catastrophe can still be averted. If . . .

There is no other choice than to apply ourselves to it.

And this, precisely, is the mole's job.

XIII

Hegel described the 'still and secret' revolution which preceded the appearance of a new spirit. Through the irrationalities of history, the crafty burrowing of the mole traced, in his view, the path of Reason. The mole is in no hurry. It 'does not have to hurry'. It needs 'length of time' and 'has plenty of time'. It does not withdraw to hibernate, but in order to drill a tunnel. Its deviations and retrogressions lead it where it wants to emerge. It does not disappear, it merely becomes invisible.

This metaphor of the mole is, according to Toni Negri, condemned by post-modernity: 'We suspect that Marx's old mole has finally died.'[29] Its digging gives way to the 'infinite undulations of the snake' and to reptilian struggles. This verdict is still based on the chronological illusion according to which post-modernity is succeeding a modernity relegated to the museum of antiquities. But the mole is ambivalent. Modern and post-modern at the same time. Discreetly busy in its 'subterranean rhizomes' and suddenly, thundering in revolt.

Under the pretext of abandoning grand historical narratives, the philosophical discourses of post-modernity favour mystics and mystagogues: a society which no longer has prophets has fortune-tellers, said Chateaubriand. They are appropriate to periods of reaction and restoration. After the massacres of June 1848 and the Eighteenth Brumaire of Napoleon the Little, the socialist movement was thus gripped with 'christolatry'.[30]

To mystical and sooth-saying affirmation, Pierre Bourdieu contrasted the conditional, preventive and performative language of the prophet: 'Just as the priest is in league with the ordinary order, likewise the prophet is the man of situations of crisis, where the established order topples and where the whole future is suspended.'[31]

The prophet is not a priest. Nor a saint.

Even less a fortune-teller. But rather a strategist.

To ward off the crisis, unplanned resistances and wagers on a hypothetical salvation by events cannot suffice. We must stand fast both on the logic of history and the unpremeditated nature of the event. We must remain available for the contingency of the latter, without losing the thread of the former. This is the very challenge of political action. For the spirit does not progress in empty time, 'but in a time that is infinitely full, filled with struggle'.[32]

And of events whose advent the mole is preparing.

With slow impatience. And with hasty patience.

The mole is a prophetic animal.

Notes

Introduction

1 Anthony Giddens, *Beyond Left and Right: The Future of Radical Politics*, London, 1994, p. 51.

2 Donald Sassoon, *One Hundred Years of Socialism: The West European Left in the Twentieth Century*, London, 1997, p. 777.

3 Richard Bellamy, *Liberalism and Modern Society: A Historical Argument*, Pennsylvania, 1992, p. 310.

4 Quoted *ibid*.

5 Quoted in Anthony Arblaster, *The Rise and Decline of Western Liberalism*, Oxford, 1984, p. 347.

6 Joseph Schumpeter, *Capitalism, Socialism and Democracy*, London, 1987, p. 269; Alasdair Macintyre, 'Recent Political Thought' in David Thomson, ed., *Political Ideas*, Harmondsworth 1990, pp. 180–90; Richard Bellamy, 'Schumpeter and the transformation of capitalism, liberalism and democracy', *Government and Opposition*, 1991, vol. 26, pp. 500–519.

7 Heinz Lubasz, 'Introduction', in Heinz Lubasz, ed., *Revolutions in Modern European History*, New York, 1966, p. 7.

8 Quoted Bellamy, *op cit.*, pp. 129–30.

9 *Ibid*, p. 156–7.

10 Michael Bentley, *The Climax of Liberal Politics: British Liberalism in Theory and Practice 1868–1918*, London, 1987, p. 126.

11 Perez Zagorin, 'The English Revolution 1640–1660', *Journal of World History*, vol. 2, no. 4, 1955, pp. 895–914.

12 C.B. Macpherson, *The Real World of Democracy*, Oxford, 1966, pp. 2–3.

13 Macintyre, 'Recent Political Thought', p. 185.

14 As Ran Halévi put it in his obituary of Furet, his work was not on the Revolution as such, but on 'the fate of revolutionary passion', *Le Monde*, 16 July 1997.

15 Michel Rocard, *Journal inattendu du RTL*, cited in *Le Monde*, 2 November 1988. Rocard, a former member with Furet of the right-wing Socialist

Party faction, the PSU, proposed on his election in 1988 to embark on 'the reform of the infinitely small'.

16 Furet interviewed in 1995, cited in *Le Monde*, 7 May 1999.

17 Mona Ozouf, cited in Isser Woloch, 'On the Latent Illiberalism of the French Revolution', *American Historical Review*, 95(5), December 1990, p. 1465.

18 Florence Gauthier, 'Critique du concept de "révolution bourgeoise", appliqué aux Révolutions des droits de l'homme et du citoyen du XVIIIe siècle', *Actuel Marx*, 20, 1996.

19 David Blackburn and Geoff Eley, *The Peculiarities of German History: Bourgeois Society and Bourgeois Politics in Nineteenth-Century Germany*, Oxford, 1984, pp. 88–9.

20 Daniel Bensaïd, *Moi, La Révolution*, Paris, 1989, p. 131.

21 Bernard-Henri Lévy, *Barbarism with a Human Face*, New York, 1979, pp. 193–4.

22 *Le Monde*, 17 June 2000, carries an account of the conference.

23 Nolte was the subject of a note in Furet's *The Passing of an Illusion*. The two men subsequently engaged in correspondence, which was published in François Furet and Ernst Nolte, *Fascism and Communism*, Lincoln, 2001.

24 Furet, *Le Monde*, 23 September 1997.

25 *Wirtschaftswoche*, 30 March 1997. Cited in Alex Callinicos, 'Reformism and Class Polarisation in Europe', *International Socialism*, 85, winter 1999.

26 Ricardo Carcova, 20 December 2001. Cited in Chris Harman, 'Argentina: Rebellion at the Sharp End of the World Crisis', *International Socialism*, 94, Spring 2002, pp. 3–48.

27 Edgar Morin, *Le Monde*, 9 June 1989.

28 Russell Jacoby, *The End of Utopia: Politics and Culture in an Age of Apathy*, New York, 1999.

29 See, for example, Michael Hardt and Antonio Negri, *Empire*, Cambridge MA 2001; George Monbiot, *The Age of Consent: A manifesto for a new world order*, London, 2003; Hilary Wainwright, *Reclaim the State. Experiments in Popular Democracy*, London, 2003; John Holloway, *Change the World Without Taking Power*, London, 2002; Alex Callinicos, *An Anti-Capitalist Manifesto*, Cambridge, 2003.

Chapter 1

1 Lawrence Stone, *Causes of the English Civil War, 1529–1642*, London, 1972, p. 31.

2 Most notably Macaulay and S.R. Gardiner, *History of the Great Civil War*, London, 1893.

3 R.H. Tawney, 'The Rise of the Gentry: 1558–1640', *Economic History Review*, 11:1, 1941; Christopher Hill, *The English Revolution, 1640*, London, 1940; Christopher Hill, 'A Bourgeois Revolution?' in J.G.A. Pocock, ed., *Three British Revolutions*, Princeton NJ, 1980; Lawrence Stone, *The Crisis of the Aristocracy, 1558–1641*, Oxford, 1965; Lawrence Stone, *Social Change and Revolution in England, 1540–1640*, London, 1965; and Lawr-

ence Stone, *The Causes of the English Revolution, 1529–1642*, London and New York, 1972.

4 Christopher Hill, *The English Revolution 1640*. It needs to be pointed out that Hill's characterization of the Civil War and Revolution changed over time. In the 1960s, Hill abandoned his earlier bourgeois revolution paradigm and accepted the court and country interpretation put forward by Perez Zagorin. By the 1980s, however, Hill had reworked the bourgeois revolution paradigm in order to emphasize the significance of the unintended bourgeois consequences of the Revolution. In light of the empirical problems that the traditional social interpretation was faced with – and which will be discussed below – Hill argued that a revolution could still be bourgeois even if it was not led by the bourgeoisie. The unintended consequences of the English Revolution, he argued, laid the groundwork for the further development of capitalism in England. For this revamped statement of the bourgeois revolution, see Christopher Hill, 'A Bourgeois Revolution?', in Pocock, ed., *England's Three Revolutions*, 1980. For brief overviews of Hill's various positions on the Civil War and Revolution, see R.C. Richardson, *The Debate on the English Revolution*, London, 1977, and Norah Carlin, *The Causes of the English Civil War*, Oxford, 1999. For an insightful, yet critical, look at the whole corpus of Christopher Hill's work, see Alastair Maclachlan, *Inventing Revolutionary England*, New York, 1996.

5 'To speak of a transition from a feudal to a bourgeois society is to decline upon a *cliché*. But a process difficult to epitomize in less hackneyed terms has left deep marks on the social systems of most parts of Europe.' R.H. Tawney, 'Rise of the Gentry: 1558–1640', *The Economic History Review*, 11:1, 1941, p. 6.

6 This is not to say, of course, that Tawney was a Marxist. It is well known that he wasn't. Indeed, when asked whether or not the English Revolution was a bourgeois revolution, Tawney responded in the affirmative, but then qualified his answer by stating that the bourgeoisie was on both sides. This is a significant insight, but insofar as Tawney replaces the bourgeoisie with a rural bourgeoisie that confronts, as a class, a feudal nobility, his interpretation can still be said to adhere to the problems of the bourgeois revolution paradigm.

7 The legacy of the bourgeois revolution loomed large in England. See Perry Anderson, 'Origins of the Present Crisis', in *English Questions*, London, 1992. For a rebuttal of his explanation, from a Marxist perspective, see E.P. Thompson, 'The Peculiarities of the English', *Socialist Register*, London, 1965. For a critical discussion on the Marxist conception of the bourgeois revolution, see George C. Comninel, *Rethinking the French Revolution*, London, 1988. See also Robert Brenner, 'Bourgeois Revolution and the Transition to Capitalism', in A.L. Beier and David Cannadine, eds, *The First Modern Society*, Cambridge, 1989.

8 Lawrence Stone, 'The Anatomy of the Elizabethan Aristocracy', *Economic History Review*, vol. 18, no. 1/2, 1948, pp. 1–53.

9 Stone, *Causes*, p. 27.

10 Trevor-Roper's interpretation, however, was itself quite fragile, for he was never able to explain how agrarian incomes suffered under a period of

inflationary prices (which would suggest the opposite – that agrarian based incomes would rise), nor was he able to adequately demonstrate that court fortunes could be built up to the extent that he claimed. In the end, while Trevor-Roper successfully undermined the statistical basis of Stone's early work, he was unable to establish his own interpretation on any solid empirical ground.

11 C.B. Macpherson, *The Political Theory of Possessive Individualism*, Oxford, 1962. For a critical response to Macpherson, which takes him to task for failure to consider alternative conceptions of propriety, see Iain Hampsher-Monk, 'The Political Theory of the Levellers: Putney, Property and Professor Macpherson', *Political Studies, 14:4*, 1976. See also J.C. Davis, 'The Levellers and Democracy', *Past and Present*, 40, 1968. Christopher Hill eventually accepted Macpherson's interpretation of the Levellers – at least in terms of their position on the franchise – while Davis would later become enamoured with the revisionist history of the 1970s and move away from relating political thought to its specific social context.

12 J. Frank, *The Levellers: a History of the Writings of Three Seventeenth-Century Social Democrats*, Cambridge MA., 1955.

13 G.E. Aylmer, *The Levellers in the English Revolution*, London, 1975; A.L.S. Morton, *The World of the Ranters*, London, 1970.

14 'The immediate needs of the soldiers (arrears and indemnity) are still emphasised, but the minds of the Agitators run on to the settlement of the kingdom upon principles of justice and common right.' A.S.P. Woodhouse, *Puritanism and Liberty*, second edition, London, 1974, p. 22.

15 D.W. Petegorsky, *Left-Wing Democracy in the English Civil War*, London, 1947.

16 Christopher Hill, *The World Turned Upside Down*, Harmondsworth, 1972.

17 For the Diggers in the context of European Reformation, see L.H. Berens, *The Digger Movement in the Days of the Commonwealth: as revealed in the writings of Gerrard Winstanley, the Digger, mystic, and rationalist, communist and social reformer*, London, 1906. For the Diggers within an indigenous context of lower-class radicalism, see Christopher Hill, 'From Lollards to Levellers', in A.L. Morton, and M.C. Cornforth, *Rebels and their Causes: essays in honour of A.L. Morton*, New Jersey, 1979.

18 George Juretic, 'Digger No Millenarian: The Revolutionizing of Gerrard Winstanley', *Journal of the History of Ideas*, 36:2 (April–June 1975). For the Diggers as utopian socialists, see George Sabine, 'Radicals and Communists', in George Sabine, *A History of Political Theory*, New York, 1953.

19 As to an extent Perez Zagorin had done, arguing that the significance of the Revolution lay in its development of a liberal political order – complete with the development of parliamentary sovereignty. Perez Zagorin, 'The Social Interpretation of the English Revolution', *Journal of Economic History*, 19:3 (September 1959), pp. 376–401.

20 G.R. Elton, 'A High Road to Civil War?', in Charles H. Carter, ed., *Essays in Honour of Garret Mattingley*, New York, 1966; Herbert Butterfield, *The Whig Interpretation of History*, London, 1931; Conrad Russell, 'Introduction', *The Origins of the English Civil War*, Oxford, 1973.

21 What is interesting here is that, at this point in time at least, Russell is not opposed to the principles of the social interpretation – situating the causes of the conflict within a context of social change – rather, he is opposed to what was, at the time, the current exposition of the social interpretation. But a new social interpretation will need to be based upon the political activity of the 'industrious sort of people', the tradesmen, artisans and other entrepreneurial urban men. These are the men who formed the backbone of the New Model Army and the Levellers, organizations that Russell considers to be revolutionary. Russell, *Origins*, p. 9.

22 The content of this paragraph is taken from Russell, *Origins*.

23 Whigs emphasize the existence of political tensions between Crown and Parliament beginning with James' first Parliament in 1604.

24 Revisionists either downplay or reject the divisions of royalist and parliamentarian up until *after* the outbreak of war. Norah Carlin, *The Causes*, p. 74.

25 Conrad Russell, 'Parliamentary History in Perspective, 1604–1629', in Richard Cust and Ann Hughes, eds, *The English Civil War*, London, 1997.

26 Russell argues that Parliament's control over the legislative process was the result, not of parliamentary strength but, rather, the lack of political will or desire on behalf of the Crown to legislate. As evidence of this, he points to the lack of substantive legislation passed by Parliament in the early Stuart period. One significant legislative success by Parliament, however, was the blocking of James's attempt to unite the parliaments of England and Scotland. Russell, however, downplays the constitutional significance of this event, claiming that in the aftermath of this defeat, James showed 'little desire to legislate' (Conrad Russell, *Parliaments and English Politics, 1621–1629*, Oxford, 1979, p. 46). Hirst, however, interprets this event differently: 'The debates on the entirely non-fiscal problems of union with Scotland early in James's reign showed that contemporaries saw Scots law as a major threat to English law and English ways.' Derek Hirst, 'The Place of Principle', *Past and Present*, 92, 1981, p. 86.

27 Russell, 'Parliamentary History', p. 48.

28 Russell, *Parliaments and English Politics*.

29 Mark Kishlansky, 'The Emergence of Adversary Politics in the Long Parliament', *Journal of Modern History*, 49:4, December 1977, pp. 617–40.

30 John Morrill, 'The Religious Context of the English Civil War,' in Cust and Hughes, eds, *The English Civil War*.

31 Morrill, 'The Religious Context', pp. 164, 165, 167.

32 John Morrill, 'The Army Revolt of 1647', in J. Morrill, ed., *The Nature of the English Revolution*, London, 1993.

33 J.C. Davis, 'Radicalism in a Traditional Society: The Evaluation of Radical Thought in the English Commonwealth 1649–1660', *History of Political Thought*, 3:2, Summer 1982.

34 Davis, 'Radicalism', pp. 197–201.

35 Davis, 'Radicalism', p. 199.

36 'Radicalism can only have some connection with reality if society has a radical potential within it; if it is, in some sense, a society in transition. But what if it is not – what if we are looking at radicals in a traditional society,

one where continuity prevails over change, where inertia shapes the future and the past legitimates the present?' Davis, 'Radicalism', p. 199. Davis' rejection of the social transformation argument rests on three propositions. First, England remained an agrarian-based society at the end of the seventeenth century; second, monarchy was restored in 1660; third, England remained a Christian society in the sense that a state Church was not abolished. Davis' contention that the agrarian basis of English society is a sufficient characteristic of its 'traditionalism' will be addressed in the next section.

37 Davis, 'Radicalism', p. 213.
38 Conal Condren, *The Language of Politics in Seventeenth-Century England*, New York, 1994.
39 Condren, *Language*, p. 149.
40 Condren, *Language*, p. 155.
41 Condren, *Language*, p. 155.
42 Condren, *Language*, p. 158.
43 J.C. Davis, 'Religion and the Struggle for Freedom in the English Revolution', *The Historical Journal*, 35, 1992, p. 508.
44 Lotte Mulligan and Judith Richards, 'A "Radical" Problem: The Poor and the English Reformers in the Mid-Seventeenth Century', *Journal of British Studies*, 29:2, April 1990, pp. 118–46.
45 Janet Coleman rejects this historicist notion of 'caging' a political thinker within his or context to the extent that 'they perish with the leaving behind of the historical time in which they came to light'. Janet Colemen, 'The Voice of the "Greeks" in the Conversation of Mankind', in Dario Castiglione and Iain Hampsher-Monk, *The History of Political Thought in National Context*, Cambridge, 2001.
46 J.C. Davis, *Utopia and the Ideal Society: A Study of English Utopian Writings, 1516–1700*, Cambridge, 1981.
47 This raises another serious problem with the revisionist reliance on 'tradition', 'shared assumptions' and 'common beliefs': the notion itself is vague and elastic enough to preclude any kind of antagonism ortension. Where do we draw the line between the 'manifold diversity of meaning between and within discourse' and outright contradiction and antagonism? See Mulligan and Richards, 'A "Radical" Problem', p. 122.
48 R.B. Seaberg, 'The Norman Conquest and the Common Law: The Levellers and the Argument from Continuity', *The Historical Journal*, 24:4, November 1981, pp. 791–86.
49 Seaberg, 'The Norman Conquest', p. 608.
50 Glenn Burgess, 'On Revisionism: An Analysis of Early Stuart Historiography in the 1970s and 1980s', *The Historical Journal*, 33:3, 1990, p. 609.
51 Burgess, 'On Revisionism', Davis, 'Radicalism'.
52 Burgess admits that despite their battle against social reductionism, 'some individual revisionists may have been guilty of a sort of vulgar Namierism'. Burgess, 'On Revisionism', p. 614.
53 See Kishlansky, 'The Emergence of Adversary Politics'.
54 John Morrill, 'The Religious Context of the English Civil War', in John Morrill, *The Nature of the English Civil War*.

55 As Burgess triumphantly states, 'revisionists have recently shown a greater unwillingness to see religious ideology as reducible to social and political purposes, and to stress the importance of religion as a motivating force, than their predecessors'. Burgess, 'On Revisionism', p. 614. Interestingly, the revisionist Burgess cites as a leading proponent of this renewed emphasis on religion, Kevin Sharpe, has since referred to himself as a 'post-revisionist', implying that his position has now moved beyond revisionism. See Kevin Sharpe, *Remapping Early Modern England*, Cambridge, 1999.

56 In 1981, Christopher Hill rearticulated his conception of the bourgeois revolution to emphasize the belief that a revolution can still be bourgeois in the absence of a consciously revolutionary bourgeoisie. Colin Mooers makes the argument, also building on Perry Anderson, that Europe was made into a bourgeois society through a series of revolutions that, despite the absence of revolutionary bourgeoisie, were bourgeois nonetheless. Colin Mooers, *The Making of Bourgeois Europe*, London, 1991. Lawrence Stone, while criticizing Hill's characterization that the Revolution was indeed bourgeois, agrees with Hill on many of the consequences of the Revolution. Lawrence Stone, 'The Bourgeois Revolution of Seventeenth Century England Revisited', *Past and Present*, 109, November 1985, pp. 53–4.

57 This characterization of the transition from feudalism to capitalism is based upon the interpretation put forth by Robert Brenner, in his various articles on the subject. There is a long, contentious and rich literature within the Marxist historical tradition regarding the nature of the transition from feudalism to capitalism. For the initial 'transition debate', see Maurice Dobb, *Studies in the Development of Capitalism*, New York, 1947; Rodney Hilton, ed., *The Transition from Feudalism to Capitalism*, London, 1978. For the following 'Brenner Debate' see T.H. Aston and C.H.E. Philpin, eds, *The Brenner Debate: Agrarian Class Structure and Economic Development in Pre-Industrial Europe*, Cambridge, 1985. For a good overview of both debates and its overall significance for an understanding of capitalism, see Ellen Meiksins Wood, *The Origin of Capitalism: A Longer View*, London, 2002.

58 George C. Comninel, 'English Feudalism and the Origins of Capitalism', *Journal of Peasant Studies*, 27:4, 2000, pp. 23–4.

59 Rodney Hilton, 'Feudalism or *Feodalité* and *Seigneurie* in France and England', in Rodney Hilton, *Class Conflict and the Crisis of Feudalism*, revised edition, London, 1990, p. 159. However, as Duby points out, attempts were made by the lords to appropriate the powers of royal jurisdiction in the twelfth century. But apart from some remote areas in Wales and Scotland, these attempts failed and by the mid-twelfth century, the king had effectively consolidated the powers of *haute justice* in his own hands. Georges Duby, *Rural Economy and Country Life in the Medieval West*, Columbia SC, 1968, pp. 194–5.

60 On the crisis of feudalism, see Rodney Hilton, 'Was there a General Crisis of Feudalism?' in *Class Conflict and the Crisis of Feudalism: Essays in Medieval Social History*, London, 1990.

61 Rodney Hilton, *Bond Men Made Free*, London, 1973.

62 Robert Brenner, 'The Agrarian Roots of European Capitalism', in Aston and Philpin, *The Brenner Debate*, p. 293.

63 For a discussion of the periodization of the enclosure movement, see R.H. Tawney, *The Agrarian Crisis of the 16th Century*, London 1912. Tawney distinguishes between three periods of enclosure: the first beginning in the medieval era and representing merely the conversion of arable to pasturage; the second in the fifteenth and sixteenth centuries representing the expropriation of the peasantry; and the third beginning in the early eighteenth century and proceeding through parliamentary sanction.

64 Comninel, 'English Feudalism'.

65 Comninel, 'English Feudalism', p. 36.

66 E.P. Thompson, *Customs in Common*, New York, 1994, p. 137.

67 James Holstun, *Ehud's Dagger: Class Struggle in the English Revolution*, London, 2000, p. 378.

68 Thompson, *Customs*, p. 175–6.

69 Ellen Meiksins Wood, 'From Opportunity to Imperative', *Monthly Review*, July–August 1994, pp. 14–40.

70 Wood, 'From Opportunity', p. 36.

71 Ellen Meiksins Wood, *The Origin of Capitalism*, New York, 1999, p. 71.

72 The term improvement itself comes from the middle English work *improwen* which means to enclose land for cultivation. *Emprouwer* is the Anglo-Norman term meaning to turn a profit. This word itself stems from a combination of the Old French *prou*, meaning profit. Thus, in the early modern period, 'productivity and profit were inextricably connected in the concept of improvement'. Wood, *Origin*, p. 81.

73 For a discussion on the historically specific form of English Lordship and its relationship to both the Norman Conquest and the rise of agrarian capitalism, see Comninel, 'English Feudalism'.

74 This puts a serious damper on the revisionist emphasis on patronage as a motivational factor for the 'great rebellion'. Rather than political conflict taking the form of competition for access to a patrimonial state, political conflict took the form of changing the nature and role of the state itself. It is this that makes the political conflicts of the Stuart era different from the baronial revolts of the medieval and Renaissance era.

75 Robert Brenner, *Merchants and Revolution: Commercial Change, Political Conflict, and London's Overseas Traders, 1550–1653*, London, 2003, pp. 651–2.

76 Perry Anderson, *Passages from Antiquity to Feudalism*, London, 1996, p. 160.

77 Brenner, *Merchants*, p. 655.

78 The bulk of this paragraph is based on Brenner's analysis of the divisions within the English merchant community. See Brenner, *Merchants*.

79 Brian Manning, *The English People and the English Revolution, 1640–1649*, New York, 1976. For a more detailed account of the alliance between improving landlords and merchant-interlopers, see Brenner, *Merchants*.

80 For an examination of the comparative differences between English and French theories of resistance, see George Sabine, *History of Political Thought*, New York, 1937; and Ellen Meiksins Wood, *The Pristine Culture of Capitalism*, London, 1991.

81 Ellen Meiksins Wood and Neal Wood in their *A Trumpet of Sedition: Political Theory and the Rise of Capitalism, 1509–1688*, London, 1997, argue

that this position can be seen as early as 1645 in the pamphlet *England's Miserie and Remedie*.

82 'The Putney Debates', in David Wootton, ed., *Divine Right and Democracy*, Harmondsworth, 1986, p. 286.

83 Wood, *The Pristine Culture of Capitalism*, p. 68.

84 David McNally, 'Locke, Levellers and Liberty: Property and Democracy in the Thought of the First Whigs', *History of Political Thought*, 10:1, Spring 1989.

85 Gerrard Winstanley, *A Declaration from the poor oppressed people of England, directed to all that call themselves Lords of Manors, . . . that have begun to . . . cut, or . . . do intend to cut down the woods and trees that grow upon the Commons and Waste land*, London, 1649, p. 79.

86 Winstanley, p. 86.

87 Winstanley, p. 85.

88 Winstanley, p. 86.

89 For an insightful discussion relating Winstanley to traditional paternalist critics of enclosures as well as their improving apologists, see J. Holstun, *Ehud's Dagger: Class Struggle in the English Revolution*, London, 2000.

90 J.M. Nesson, 'The Opponents of Enclosure in Eighteenth-Century Northamptonshire', *Past and Present*, no. 105, November 1984, pp. 114–39.

91 F.D. Dow, *Radicalism in the English Revolution, 1640–1660*, Oxford, 1985, p. 77.

92 Winstanley, p. 90.

93 Neal Wood, *Reflections on Political Theory: A Voice of Reason from the Past*, London, 2002, pp. 124–5.

Chapter 2

1 Walter Benjamin, cited in Françoise Proust, *L'histoire à contretemps. Le temps historique chez Walter Benjamin*, Paris, 1994, pp. 53–4, 30. See also Daniel Bensaïd, *Marx for Our Times: Adventures and Misadventures of a Critique*, London, 2002.

2 Cornelius Castoriadis, 'Les divertisseurs', *Le Nouvel Observateur*, 20 June 1977. Reprinted in Syvlie Bouscasse and Denis Bourgeois, *Faut-il brûler les nouveaux philosophes?*, Paris, 1978, p. 198.

3 Bernard-Henri Lévy, *Barbarism with a Human Face*, London, 1979, p. 154.

4 André Glucksmann, *La cuisinière et le mangeur d'hommes. Essai sur l'Etat, le marxisme, les camps de concentration*, Paris, 1975.

5 Bernard-Henri Lévy, cited in Castoriadis, 'Les divertisseurs', p. 200.

6 Christian Jambet and Guy Lardreau, *L'Ange*, cited in François Aubral and Xavier Delcourt, *Contre la Nouvelle Philosophie*, Paris, 1977, pp. 26–7.

7 Dominique Lecourt, *The Mediocracy: French Philosophy Since the mid-1970s*, London, 2001, p. 151.

8 Bernard-Henri Lévy, *Barbarism with a Human Face*, p. 191.

9 Pierre Nora, cited in Lecourt, *The Mediocracy*, p. 74.

10 Lévy, *Barbarism with a Human Face*, p. 195.

11 Maurice Clavel, cited in *Magazine littéraire,* 'Les dieux dans la cuisine', Paris, 1978.
12 Perry Anderson, *In the Tracks of Historical Materialism,* London, 1983, p. 32.
13 See, for example, Luc Ferry and Alain Renaut, *La pensée 68. Essai sur l'anti-humanisme contemporain,* Paris, 1988 and François Furet, Jacques Julliard, Pierre Rosanvallon, *La République du centre. La fin de l'exception française,* Paris, 1988.
14 Luc Boltanski and Eve Chiapello, *Le nouvel esprit du capitalisme,* Paris, 1999.
15 Alain Badiou, *Ethics: An Essay on the Understanding of Evil,* London, 2001, p. 16.
16 Lecourt, *The Mediocracy,* p. 114.
17 Badiou, *Ethics,* p. 9.
18 Michael Löwy, 'La "poésie du passé": Marx et la Révolution Française', in Collectif, *Permanences de la Révolution. Pour un autre bicentenaire,* Paris, 1989, pp. 248–50.
19 George V. Taylor, 'Non-capitalist Wealth and the Origins of the French Revolution', *Annales Historiques de la Révolution,* lxxii, 1967, Guy Chaussinand-Nogaret, *La noblesse au XVIIIe siècle,* Paris, 1974.
20 On this see François Dosse, '1789–1989 – Sous le linceul: la Révolution', in Collectif, *Permanences de la Révolution. Pour un autre bicentenaire.*
21 George Rudé, *Interpretations of the French Revolution,* London, 1972.
22 François Furet, *Penser la Révolution Française,* Paris, 1978, p. 29–32.
23 Furet, *Penser la Révolution Française,* p. 205.
24 Furet, *Penser la Révolution Française,* pp. 105, 107.
25 Furet, *Penser la Révolution Française,* p. 105.
26 Furet, *Penser la Révolution Française,* p. 129.
27 Furet, *Penser la Révolution Française,* p. 189.
28 François Furet, *Le passé d'une illusion,* Paris, 1994.
29 Furet, *Penser la Révolution Française,* p. 189.
30 Furet, *Penser la Révolution Française,* p. 47.
31 Bill Edmonds, 'Revisionists and the French Revolution', *European History Quarterly,* 17, 1987, p. 200.
32 Alfred Cobban, *Aspects of the French Revolution,* New York, 1968. Cited in Rudé, *Interpretations of the French Revolution,* p. 25.
33 Gwynne Lewis, *The French Revolution: Rethinking the Debate,* London, 1993, p. 70.
34 J.H. Clapham, *The Economic Development of France and Germany 1815–1914,* Cambridge, 1961, p. 6.
35 Alfred Cobban, *A History of Modern France,* volume 2, Harmondsworth, 1961, pp. 226.
36 William Doyle, *The Origins of the French Revolution,* Oxford, 1999, p. 25.
37 William Doyle, *The Origins of the French Revolution,* pp. 2, 40.
38 Henri Maler and Denis Berger, *Une certaine idée du communisme: Repliques à François Furet,* Paris, 1996, p. 52.
39 Alfred Cobban, *The Social Interpretation of the French Revolution,* p. 67.
40 Furet, *Penser la Révolution Française,* p. 193.
41 Edmonds, 'Revisionists and the French Revolution', p. 209.
42 Edmonds, 'Revisionists and the French Revolution', p. 203.

43 Edmonds, 'Revisionists and the French Revolution', p. 202.

44 George C. Comninel, *Rethinking the French Revolution: Marxism and the Revisionist Challenge*, London, 1987.

45 Doyle, *The Origins of the French Revolution*, p. 5.

46 Lefebvre, cited in Rudé, *Interpretations of the French Revolution*, p. 25.

47 Stedman Jones, cited in David Blackbourn and Geoff Eley, *The Peculiarities of German History: Bourgeois Society and Politics in Nineteenth-Century Germany*, Oxford, 1984, p. 83.

48 Blackbourn and Eley, *The Peculiarities of German History*, p. 82.

49 Régis Debray, 'Diviser pour rassembler', *Espaces Temps*, nos. 38–39, 1988. Cited in Steven Laurence Kaplan, *Farewell, Revolution: The Historians' Feud, France, 1789/1989*, Ithaca and London, 1995, p. 89.

50 Daniel Guérin, *Class Struggle in the First French Republic: Bourgeois and Bras Nus 1793–1795*, London, 1977, p. 72.

51 Georges Lefebvre, *The French Revolution: From its Origins to 1793*, London, 2001, p. 169.

52 Alex Callinicos, 'Bourgeois Revolutions and Historical Materialism', *International Socialism*, 43, Summer 1989, p. 145.

53 Lewis, *The French Revolution*, p. 27.

54 Lefebvre, *The French Revolution*, pp. 88–9.

55 Guérin, *Class Struggle in the First French Republic*, p. 3.

56 Lewis, *The French Revolution*, pp. 76, 112.

57 Guérin, *Class Struggle in the First French Republic*, pp. 26–7.

58 Colin Lucas, cited in Lewis, *The French Revolution*, p. 110.

59 Comninel, *Rethinking the French Revolution*, p. 200.

60 Claude Langlois, 'François Furet: L'Atelier de la révolution,' *Esprit*, 162 (June 1990), pp. 12–21.

61 Callinicos, 'Bourgeois Revolutions and Historical Materialism', p. 141.

62 Alan S. Milward and S.B. Saul, *The Economic Development of Continental Europe 1780–1870*, London, 1973.

63 William Reddy, *The Rise of Market Culture: The Textile Trade and French Society, 1750–1900*, Cambridge, 1984, p. 137.

64 Tessie P. Liu, *The Weaver's Knot: The Contradictions of Class Struggle and Family Solidarity in Western France, 1750–1914*, Ithaca, 1994, p. 117.

65 Liu, *The Weaver's Knot*, pp. 97–127.

66 Douglass C. North and Robert Paul Thomas, *The Rise of the Western World: A New Economic History*, Cambridge, 1973, p. 3.

67 Liu, *The Weaver's Knot*, pp. 128–58.

68 Peter McPhee, 'The French Revolution, Peasants, and Capitalism', *American Historical Review*, 94, 1989, and *A Social History of France 1780–1880*, London, 1992.

69 Jean-Laurent Rosenthal, *The Fruits of Revolution: Property Rights, Litigation, and French Agriculture, 1700–1860*, Cambridge, 1992, p. 35.

70 McPhee, *A Social History of France*, p. 222.

71 Richard Roehl, 'French Industrialization: A Reconsideration', *Explorations in Economic History*, 13, 1976, pp. 263–4.

72 R.J. Holton, *The Transition from Feudalism to Capitalism*, Basingstoke, 1985, p. 191.

73 Pierre Léon, 'La conquête de l'espace national', in F. Braudel, and E. Labrousse, *Histoire économique et sociale de la France*, volume 3, Paris, 1993, p. 273. See also Sanford Elwitt, *The Making of the Third Republic: Class and Politics in France, 1868–1884*, Baton Rouge, 1975.

74 Denis Berger, 'La Révolution plurielle, pour Daniel Guérin', in Collectif, *Permanences de la Révolution. Pour un autre bicentennaire*, p. 202.

75 Edmonds, 'Revisionists and the French Revolution', p. 197.

76 Keith Michael Baker, *Inventing the French Revolution: Essays on French Political Culture in the Eighteenth Century*, Cambridge, 1990, p. 6.

77 Furet, cited in Maler and Berger, *Une certaine idée du communisme*, p. 62.

78 Furet, *Penser la Révolution Française*, p. 88.

79 Furet, *Penser la Révolution Française*, p. 121.

80 Lefebvre, *The French Revolution*, p. 116.

81 Maler and Berger, *Une certaine idée du communisme*, p. 160.

82 Doyle, cited in Edmonds, 'Revisionists and the French Revolution', p. 197.

83 François Furet, 'The French Revolution Revisited', in Gary Kates, ed., *The French Revolution: Recent Debates and New Controversies*, London, 1998, p. 85.

84 William H. Sewell, Jr., 'Historical Events as Transformations of Structures: Inventing Revolution at the Bastille', *Theory and Society*, 25, 1996, pp. 841–81.

85 Furet, *Penser la Révolution Française*, p. 201.

86 Lefebvre, *The French Revolution*, p. 117.

87 Löwy, 'La "poésie du passé"', pp. 239–41.

88 Löwy, 'La "poésie du passé"', p. 241.

89 Karl Marx, *The Eighteenth Brumaire of Louis Bonaparte*, Peking, 1978, pp. 10–13.

90 Marx, *The Eighteenth Brumaire of Louis Bonaparte*, p. 9.

91 Trotsky, *The History of the Russian Revolution*, cited in John Molyneux, 'Is Marxism Deterministic?', *International Socialism*, 68, Autumn 1995, p. 54.

92 Marx, *The Eighteenth Brumaire of Louis Bonaparte*, p. 10. See also Bensaïd, *Marx for Our Times*, p. 22.

93 Marx, *The Eighteenth Brumaire of Louis Bonaparte*. p. 13.

94 Trotsky, *The History of the Russian Revolution*, New York, 1980, p. 160.

95 Trotsky, *My Life: An Attempt at an Autobiography*, New York, 1970, pp. 368, 538.

96 William H. Sewell Jr, 'A Rhetoric of Bourgeois Revolution,' in Kates, ed., *The French Revolution*, pp. 151–3.

97 Trotsky, *My Life*, p. 539.

98 Trotsky, *The History of the Russian Revolution*, p. 111.

99 Baker, *Inventing the French Revolution*, p. 6.

100 Sewell, 'A Rhetoric of Bourgeois Revolution', pp. 147–8.

101 Plekhanov, *The Role of the Individual in History*, cited in Molyneux, 'Is Marxism Deterministic?' p. 66.

102 Paul Ginsborg, 'Gramsci and the Era of Bourgeois Revolution', in John A. Davis, ed., *Gramsci and Italy's Passive Revolution*, London, 1979, pp. 31–66.

103 Georg Lukács, *A Defence of* History and Class Consciousness: *Tailism and the Dialectic*, London, 1999, p. 50.

104 Georg Lukács, *History and Class Consciousness*, London, 1983, p. 185.
105 Bensaïd, *Marx for Our Times*, pp. 21–2.
106 Trotsky, *The History of the Russian Revolution*, pp. 321, 435.
107 Bensaïd, *Marx for Our Times*, p. 22.
108 Proust, *L'histoire à contretemps* p. 53.
109 Furet *Le passé d'une illusion*, p. 201. Cited in Maler and Berger, *Une certaine idée du communisme*, p. 155.
110 Furet, *Le passé d'une illusion*, p. 18. Cited in Maler and Berger, *Une certaine idée du communisme*, p. 167.
111 Maler and Berger, *Une certaine idée du communisme*, pp. 167–70.
112 Trotsky, *The History of the Russian Revolution*, p. 51.
113 Maler and Berger, *Une certaine idée du communisme*.
114 Guérin, *Class Struggle in the First French Republic*, p. 86.
115 Furet, *Le passé d'une illusion*, pp. 25–6.
116 Maler and Berger, *Une certaine idée du communisme*, p. 31.
117 Furet, *Le passé d'une illusion*, pp. 34, 35.
118 Furet, *Le passé d'une illusion*, p. 33.
119 Marx, *The Eighteenth Brumaire of Louis Bonaparte*, p. 14.
120 Maler and Berger, *Une certaine idée du communisme*, p. 186.
121 See Maler and Berger, *Une certaine idée du communisme*, p. 187.
122 Furet, cited in Maler and Berger, *Une certaine idée du communisme*, p. 198.
123 Walter Benjamin, cited in Proust, *L'histoire à contretemps*, p. 85.

Chapter 3

1 Artificial shortages, or sudden price rises, made food supplies unavailable for those on low wages.
2 Georges Lefebvre, *The Great Fear of 1789*, London, 1973, Part I, chapter 5, Part II, chapter 3.
3 See the fine works by Marc Bloch, *French Rural History*, London, 1966 and *Feudal Society*, London, 1961.
4 For a long time historians have misinterpreted the project of the Society of the Friends of the Blacks, seeing it as a proposal to *abolish slavery*, when it was for the *abolition of the slave trade* and its replacement by the breeding of slaves on the spot. See for example the works of Gabriel Debien, *Les colons de Saint-Domingue et la révolution. Essai sur le club Massiac*, Paris, 1953.
5 These pioneers are C.L.R. James, *Black Jacobins*, London, 1938, revised edition London, 1980, and Aimé Césaire, *Toussaint L'Ouverture. La révolution française et le problème colonial*, Paris, 1961. For my part I have attempted to explore these trails more deeply in Florence Gauthier, *Triomphe et mort du droit naturel en révolution, 1789–1795–1802*, Paris, 1992.
6 *Correspondance secrète des colons*, Paris, 1790, letter of 11 January 1790.
7 Jean Pierre Faye, *Dictionnaire politique portatif en cinq mots*, Paris, 1982, entry on 'terreur', pp. 101–50.
8 The decree of 13 May 1791 maintained slavery in the colonies and that of 24 September excluded free people of colour from civil and political rights

in the colonies. The decree of 13 May has long been concealed in historical writing; see Césaire, *Toussaint L'Ouverture* and Gauthier, *Triomphe et mort*.

9 Robespierre, 'On the need to revoke the decrees which attach the exercise of the rights of the citizen to those who pay the silver *marc* in tax.'

10 The secret correspondence of the royal family, discovered in the iron cupboard following their arrest on 10 August, provides ample proof of their treachery.

11 Thus it is surprising that nowadays the term 'Jacobin centralism' is apparently used to indicate a form of government with a strong executive and state apparatuses responsible only to this single executive, something that was not the case! Without being able to develop this point here, we consider it is a diversion which – at a time when Europe is being constructed precisely in the direction of the forfeiture of popular sovereignty – seeks to conceal the original experience of social democracy based on the rights of man which restored sovereignty to the people.

12 At the Jacobin Club on 2 January 1792, Robespierre had analysed the dangerous consequences of the proposal for a war of conquest presented by Brissot and his supporters: 'The most absurd idea which can be engendered in a politician's head is that it is sufficient for one people to enter arms in hand into the territory of another people in order to make the latter adopt the former's laws and constitution. No one likes armed missionaries and the first advice given by nature and by prudence is to repel them as enemies'. *Oeuvres*, Paris, 1954, volume VIII, p. 81.

13 See the account left by one of the Equals, Buonarroti's *History of Babeuf's Conspiracy for Equality*, London, 1836.

14 The colonial problem has been remarkably obscured since the late nineteenth century in historical writing on the revolutions of the late eighteenth century, even in the works of Marxists. It is undoubtedly one of the most significant fields of research which has been rediscovered in the last fifteen or so years.

15 Alphonse Aulard, one of the first historians of the revolutionary government, had well understood that there was no dictatorial form, but he believed that the 1793 Constitution, as soon as it was voted, was not applied in any respect. This is both strange and erroneous. Historical writing has been happy to repeat this error of Aulard's on the non-application of the Constitution. It is curious that it has not noticed that the selfsame Aulard saw nothing dictatorial in this government! See his *The French Revolution: A Political History*, London, 1910, vol. IV, pp. 281–82. Karl Marx's viewpoint is also of interest. He saw no dictatorship and wrote on this point what different currents of Marxism have unfortunately omitted or left in obscurity: 'The legislature made the French Revolution; in general, wherever it has emerged in its particularity as the dominant element, it has made the great, organic, general revolutions. It has not fought the constitution, but a particular, antiquated constitution, precisely because the legislature was the representative of the people, of the will of the species. The executive, on the other hand, has produced the small revolutions, the retrograde revolutions, the reactions. It has made revolutions not for a new constitution against an old one, but against the constitution, precisely because the

executive was the representative of the particular will, of subjective arbitrariness, of the magical part of the will.' (*Contribution to the Critique of Hegel's Philosophy of Law*, in Marx and Engels, *Collected Works*, London, 1975ff, vol. III, p. 57.)

16 And not on 9 Thermidor Year II (27 July 1794). This political court was replaced on 31 May 1795 by a military commission.

17 See Emile Campardon, *Le tribunal révolutionnaire*, Paris, 1866, vol. II, p. 224.

18 Jean-Pierre Faye, *Dictionnaire politique portatif en cinq mots*, p. 62.

Chapter 4

1 Morgan Philips Price, *Dispatches from the Revolution: Russia 1916–1918*, Tania Rose, ed., London, 1997, pp. 108, 110.

2 In this they shared some of Trotsky's ambiguity, for although he too declared that Stalin had betrayed the Revolution and sought to uphold a vision of it as a libertarian event, he still saw in Stalin's Russia, even if only at the level of state ownership of the means of production, the basis of an alternative society.

3 There are several historiographical discussions from 'revisionists' in retreat, for example, Steve A. Smith, 'Writing the History of the Russian Revolution After the Fall of Communism', *Europe-Asia Studies*, 46:4, 1994, pp. 563–78; Ronald Grigor Suny, 'Revision and Retreat in the Historiography of 1917', in David Holloway and Norman Naimark, eds, *Reexamining the Soviet Experience: Essays in Honor of Alexander Dallin*, Boulder, CO, 1996, pp. 25–50.

4 Orlando Figes, *A People's Tragedy: The Russian Revolution 1891–1924*, London, 1996.

5 Tamara Kondratieva and Dmitry Shlapentokh focus explicitly on this Jacobin–Bolshevik link and take a position close to Furet's. See Tamara Kondratieva, *Bolcheviks et jacobins. Itinéraire des analogies*, Paris, 1989; Dmitry Shlapentokh, *The French Revolution in Russian Intellectual Life: 1865–1905*, Westport, C, 1996; *The French Revolution and the Russian Anti-Democratic Tradition: a Case of False Consciousness*, New Brunswick, 1997; *The Counter-revolution in Revolution: Images of Thermidor and Napoleon at the time of Russian Revolution and Civil War*, New York, 1999.

6 Thus Stephen Kotkin, who established his reputation after the main revisionist wave but shared many of its belated concerns, wrote in 1998 of the killing of the tsar and his family that 'the ragtag squad's drunken sadism will inevitably become a metaphor for the Bolshevik regime and an enduring source of sympathy for Nicholas II, formerly Nicholas the Bloody'. See his '1991 and the Russian Revolution: Sources, Conceptual Categories, Analytical Framework', *Journal of Modern History*, 70:2, June 1998, pp. 384–425; and subsequent responses from Abbot Gleason and Robert V. Daniels.

7 For a short discussion of some of the issues see J. Frankel, '1917: The Problem of Alternatives', in Edith Rogovin Frankel, Jonathan Frankel, Baruch Knei-Paz, eds, *Revolution in Russia: Reassessments of 1917*, Cambridge, 1992, pp. 3–13

8 Such examples of history as legitimation would be Paul Gregory's *Before Command*, Princeton NJ, 1994, which paints a rosy view of the economic prospects of tsarist Russia, and Mary Schaeffer Conroy, ed., *Emerging Democracy in Late Imperial Russia*, Niwot CO, 1998 – especially the editor's introduction, which attempts a similar beautification of the political system. It is interesting that Gregory in a later Russian work based on his earlier book makes a more limited case. See his *Ekonomicheskii rost rossiiskoi imperii (konets XIX – nacholo XX v). Novye podschety i otsenki*, Moscow, 2000.

9 Quoted in Charles Timberlake, 'The Concept of Liberalism in Russia' in C.E. Timberlake, ed., *Essays on Russian Liberalism*, Columbia, 1972, p. 7.

10 Neil Harding, ed., *Marxism in Russia: Key Documents 1879–1906*, Cambridge, 1983, p. 24.

11 See Richard Pipes, *Struve, Liberal on the Left 1870–1905*, Cambridge MA, 1970, *passim*; Leonard Schapiro, *Russian Studies*, London, 1988, pp. 21–127.

12 The fullest discussion of Trotsky's analysis is Baruch Knei-Paz's, *The Social and Political Thought of Leon Trotsky*, Oxford, 1978. Much of the original argument can be found in Leon Trotsky, *Our Political Tasks*, London, n.d.; L. Trotsky, *1905*, Harmondsworth, 1972.

13 One example of this was the way that ministers of finance came from non-traditional sections of the bureaucracy. See M. Prokovsky, 'Bourgeoisie', in M.N. Pokrovskii, *Russia in World History: Selected Essays*, Ann Arbor, 1970, pp. 69–88. Another example could be the development of company law, see Thomas C. Owen, *The Corporation under Russian Law, 1800–1917: A Study in Tsarist Economic Policy*, New York, 1991. In these terms *some* of the arguments in David Blackbourn and Geoff Eley, *The Peculiarities of German History: Bourgeois Society and Politics in Nineteenth-Century Germany*, Oxford, 1984 also have relevance to Russia.

14 Paul Miliukov, *Constitutional Government for Russia: An Address Delivered before the Civic Forum in Carnegie Hall, New York City, 14 January 1906*, New York, 1908, p. 24. For a convenient summary of the key issues relating to the changing and the resulting election results see I.D. Thatcher, 'Elections in Russian and early Soviet History', in Ian D. Thatcher, ed., *Regime and Society in Twentieth-Century Russia*, Basingstoke, 1999, pp. 27–43.

15 Paul Miliukov, *Constitutional Government for Russia*, p. 22.

16 This opposition of most liberals to the Stolypin reforms cannot be stressed too strongly since it rarely figures in discussion of late tsarist Russia. They saw them as illegitimate, constitutionally derived as they were from exceptional legislation rather than through the Duma; they saw them as a concession to the nobility and something that would stimulate conflict between peasants without bringing any automatic improvement in their economic lot. This was also the position of Peter Struve but interestingly this is only dealt with briefly in Pipes' biography. Richard Pipes, *Struve, Liberal on the Right, 1905–1944*, Cambridge MA, 1980.

17 William Rosenberg, 'Kadets and the Politics of Ambivalence, 1905–1917,' in C. Timberlake, ed., *Essays on Russian Liberalism*, Columbia, 1972, pp. 139–163; William Rosenberg, *Liberals in the Russian Revolution: The Constitutional Democratic Party, 1917–1921*, Princeton, 1974.

18 Quoted in Pipes, *Struve*, p. 177.

19 Haimson first argued in 1964 that pre-war Russia was in a potentially revolutionary crisis because of a dual polarization of urban society against the tsar and the bureaucracy and within urban society between the upper and lower 'strata' (sic). He now argues that at the top this was a 'suspended crisis' on both sides because of the fear of unleashing conflict from below. He also now stresses that the social process of class formation in St Petersburg, and especially the metalworking factories of the Vyborg area, was more advanced that he first suggested. This takes his argument even closer to that made by the left about the character of the crisis leading to revolution. See Leopold Haimson, ' "The problem of political and social stability in urban Russia on the eve of War and Revolution" Revisited', *Slavic Review*, vol. 59, no. 4, 2000, pp. 848–75.

20 Pipes, *Struve*, p. 209, 216. It is interesting to consider how Pipes, in his positive evaluation of Struve's 'liberal conservatism', deals with his 'liberal imperialism'. He suggests that Struve's fault was that he did not recognize that Russia 'lacked the overflow of national energies' which explained colonialism and imperialism elsewhere. Not only is this a vacuous explanation of imperialism it avoids dealing with the way that the merging of liberalism, nationalism and imperialism across the advanced world fed the mutual competition that led to war. *Ibid.*, p. 92.

21 M.N. Pokrovskii, 'Russian Imperialism in the Past and Present', *Prosvechenie*, 1914, no. 1, translated, in M.N. Pokrovskii, *Russia in World History*, p. 123.

22 Peter Gatrell, *Government, Industry and Rearmament in Russia, 1900–1914: The Last Argument of Tsarism*, Cambridge, 1994

23 Hans Rogger made the argument that the speedy conclusion of the *union sacrée* in Russia on the part of the liberals showed that the 'political crisis' at the top before July was less serious and more bridgeable than the social crisis below'. See Hans Rogger, 'Russia in 1914', *Journal of Contemporary History*, 1:4, December 1966, pp. 95–120.

24 Paul Miliukov, *Political Memoirs, 1905–1917*, Ann Arbor, 1967, pp. 305–6.

25 Paul Miliukov, *Political Memoirs*.

26 Morgan Philips Price, *Dispatches from the Revolution*, pp. 18–19.

27 Alexander Shlyapnikov, *On the Eve of 1917*, London, 1982, p. 19. Gurko made a similar point in his memoirs: 'the war excited neither patriotism nor indignation among the peasants and factory workers [but] it deeply stirred the patriotic sentiments of the educated classes'. Quoted in Raymond Pearson, *The Russian Moderates and the Crisis of Tsarism 1914–1917*, Basingstoke 1977, p. 20.

28 Paul Miliukov, *The Russian Revolution, Vol. 1, The Revolution Divided: Spring 1917*, R. Stites, ed., Gulf Breeze FL, 1978, p.

29 Raymond Pearson, *The Russian Moderates and the Crisis of Tsarism*, p. 111.

30 Raymond Pearson, *The Russian Moderates and the Crisis of Tsarism*. See also Leopold Haimson, ' "The Problem of Political and Social Stability in Urban Russia on the Eve of War and Revolution" Revisited', pp. 860–3 for the debates on the Cadets and Progressives.

31 This sleight of hand is not, of course, unique to liberals but they are our focus here. We might note, however, the way that the Orthodox Church

saw its role as one of both spiritually invigorating the bloodshed at the front and using that bloodshed as a means of invigorating itself at home. Archbishop Arsenii told the Council of State in July 1914 that, 'the Lord is and will be with us. This war must be looked upon as a holy crusade.' In the first years of the war the assumption was that this blood sacrifice was achieving its effect; 'from the court to the peasant a spiritual movement is in progress' said one member of the Holy Synod. The internal effect of the killing at the front said another commentator, 'is nothing less than the Spirit of God moving amongst the people'. Moreover, despite the fact that this was largely a war fought between Christians, it was easy to extend the rhetoric of the crusade, 'Submit, Ye Heathen, for God is with Us' said Father Mankovskii in the Duma in 1916. See John Curtiss, *Church and State in Russia: The Last Years of the Empire, 1900–1917*, New York, 1940; J. Curtiss, *The Russian Church and the Soviet State, 1917–1950*, Boston MA, 1953.

32 *The National Question in the Russian Duma: Speeches by Professor Miliukov, Dzubinsky, Tchkeidze, Freedman, Djafaroff, Kerensky etc.*, translated and arranged E.L. Minsky, London, 1915.

33 Stanislav Kohn, 'The Vital Statistics of European Russia during the World War 1914–1917', in S. Kohn and A. Meyendorff, *The Cost of the War to Russia*, New Haven, 1932, pp. 13–41.

34 For a fuller discussion of this data see Michael Haynes and Rumy Husan, *A Century of State Murder: Death and Policy in Twentieth-Century Russia*, London, 2003, pp. 43–5. Most of the difference between the upper and lower bounds arises from uncertainty over the numbers missing and the numbers dying of wounds.

35 S.A. Novosel'skii, 'Materialui po statistike traumatizma, blezennosti i invalidnosti v voinu 1914–1917gg', in *Trudui Kommissii po obstedovaniou santitarnuikh polsledstvii voinu 1914–1920gg*, Moscow, 1923, pp. 181–201.

36 C. Merridale, *Night of Stone: Death and Memory in Modern Russia*, London 2000, p. 126.

37 Novosel'skii, 'Materialui po statisitke traumatizma, boleznennosti i invalidnosti v voinu 1914–1917gg', pp. 181–201.

38 See Merridale, *Night of Stone*, pp. 148–51; Catherine Merridale, 'The Collective Mind: Trauma and Shell-Shock in Twentieth-Century Russia', *Journal of Contemporary History*, 35:1 January 2000, pp. 39–56.

39 See Peter Gatrell, *A Whole Empire Walking: Refugees in Russia during World War I*, Bloomington, 1999.

40 For Volkov's figure see *Naselenie Rossii v XX veke. Istoricheskie ocherki tom 1: 1900–1939*, Moscow, 2000, p. 78. This source also draws attention to an uncorroborated figure of 100,000 for victims of war 'terror' between 1914–1917.

41 Alexander Blok, 'The Intelligentsia and the Revolution', *Znamia truda*, no. 122, January 19 1918, translated in M. Raeff, ed., *Russian Intellectual History: An Anthology*, New York, 1966, p. 365.

42 See Maxim Gorky, *Untimely Thoughts: Essays on Revolution, Culture and the Bolsheviks, 1917–1918*, New York, 1968. I have discussed Gorky's attitude to popular habits and violence in an unpublished paper 'Maxim Gorky and

the "Zoological Anarchism" of the Russian Working Class', Study Group on the Russian Revolution, University of Leeds, January 1997.

43 *Rabochaia zhizn'*, no. 14, 1917, pp. 3–4 as quoted in Merridale, *Night of Stone*, p. 140.

44 Merridale, *Night of Stone*, pp. 119–21.

45 Rosenberg, *Liberals in the Russian Revolution*, pp. 90, 190.

46 Rosenberg, *Liberals in the Russian Revolution*, pp. 55, 188.

47 Struve tried to use the Marxist past to lecture socialists on socialism. See P. Struve, 'Illuzii russkikh sotsialistov', *Russkaia svobda*, no. 7, 7 June 1917, pp. 3–6.

48 Abraham Ascher, ed., *The Mensheviks and the Russian Revolution*, London, 1976, pp. 95–7.

49 Miliukov, *The Russian Revolution*, pp. 464–74; Rosenberg, *Liberals in the Russian Revolution* p. 198.

50 Pipes, *Struve*, p. 241. Geoffrey Swain has argued that there is little evidence that a second coup from the right was being actively *planned*. But the key question is what possibilities are inherent in the crisis and the capacity to mobilize quickly to seize the opportunity. See Geoffrey Swain, 'Before the Fighting Started: A Discussion on the Theme of "the Third Way" ', *Revolutionary Russia*, 4:2, December 1991, pp. 210–34.

51 Theory and practice moved so quickly in 1917 that there was no opportunity for an agreed statement of shared theories. Trotsky always insisted that his ideas and Lenin's converged theoretically as well as practically in 1917. This linkage is also argued by B. Knei-Paz, 'Russian Marxism: Theory, Action and Outcome', in E. Rogovin Frankel, J. Frankel, B. Knei-Paz, eds, *Revolution in Russia: Reassessments of 1917*, Cambridge, 1992, pp. 406–20.

52 Knei-Paz, *The Social and Political Thought of Leon Trotsky*, p. 176.

53 In Petrograd at this time the very young Leonard Schapiro reportedly modelled a plaster bust of Marat showing it off to his equally young friend Isaiah Berlin, who was presumably impressed. Michael Ignatieff, *Isaiah Berlin: A Life*, London, 1998, p. 25.

54 Neil Harding, *Lenin's Political Thought*, Vol. 2, London, 1981, p. 150.

55 Ascher, *The Mensheviks*, pp. 97–101.

56 Leon Trotsky, 'What Next? After the July Days', in Louis C. Fraina, ed., *The Proletarian Revolution in Russia*, New York, 1918. Available at: http://www.marxists.org/archive/trotsky/works/1917/julydays.html

57 Ascher, *The Mensheviks*, pp. 101–3; L. Lande, 'The Mensheviks in 1917', in L. Haimson, ed., *The Mensheviks from the Revolution of 1917 to the Second World War*, Chicago, 1976, p. 29.

58 Quoted in V.I. Lenin, 'Can the Bolsheviks Retain State Power?', in *Collected Works*, vol. 26, London, 1964, p. 128.

59 See Michael Melancon, *The Socialist Revolutionaries and the Russian Anti-War Movement, 1914–1917*, Columbus, 1990.

60 R.F. Byrnes, 'Russian Conservative Thought before the Revolution', in T. Stavrou, ed., *Russia Under the Last Tsar*, Minneapolis, 1969.

61 A. Blok, 'The People in the Intelligentsia', *Zolotoe runo*, no. 1, 1909, trans. in Marc Raeff, *Russian Intellectual History An Anthology*, New York, 1966, p. 359.

62 Knei-Paz, *The Social and Political Thought of Leon Trotsky*, p. 50; Pipes, *Struve*, p. 10.
63 V.V. Rozanov, *Solitaria*, London, 1927, p. 148, 180.
64 Miliukov, *Constitutional Government*, loc. cit.
65 Marshall S. Shatz and Judith E. Zimmerman, trans. and eds, *Vekhi: Landmarks*, Armonk NY, 1994, pp. 80–1. In the first edition of the book Gershenzon actually wrote 'we must bless' which led his critics to argue that he welcomed repression. What he actually meant, he said, was 'the horror' that because of the people's hatred intellectuals were condemned to see the authority they despised as their defenders.
66 A large number of contributions from the debate were collected together in *Vekhi – pro et contra: antologiya*, St Petersburg, 1998.
67 See Joan Neuberger, *Hooliganism: Crime, Culture and Power in St. Petersburg, 1900–1914*, Berkeley CA, 1993.
68 Miliukov, *Political Memoirs*, pp. 300–18, 402–04.
69 Quoted in Pearson, *The Russian Moderates*, p. 105, 179.
70 Michael Cherniavsky, ed., *Prologue to Revolution: Notes of A.N. Iakontov on the Secret Meetings of the Council of Ministers, 1915*, Englewood Cliffs NJ, 1967, p. 199.
71 Quoted in Pearson, *The Russian Moderates*, p. 83.
72 I have discussed some of the issues relating to actual violence in M. Haynes, 'The Debate on Popular Violence and the Popular Movement in the Russian Revolution', *Historical Materialism*, no. 2, Summer 1998, pp. 185–214.
73 Rosenberg, *Liberals in the Russian Revolution*, p. 190.
74 See Adriana Tyrkóva-Williams, *From Liberty to Brest-Litovsk. The First Year of the Russian Revolution*, London, 1919.
75 Pitrim Sorokin, *Leaves for A Russian Diary – and Thirty Years After*, Boston MA, 1950, pp. 19, 22, 26, 33, 49, 47. Sorokin's account was first published in 1924 and is written in diary form but it is not clear how much was written as a diary.
76 Sergii Bulgakov, 'Heroism and the Spiritual Struggle', translated in Sergii Bulgakov, *Towards a Russian Political Theology*, R. Williams, ed., Edinburgh, 1999, p. 103.
77 Sergii Bulgakov, *Russkaia mysl'*, 1918, translated as 'At the Feast of the Gods: Contemporary Dialogues', *Slavonic and East European Review*, vols. 1–3, 1922–23, pp. 172–83; 391–400, 604–22. A more recent translation is in Bernice Glatzer Rosenthal, trans. William Woehrlin, *From the Depths*, Irvine CA, 1986, pp. 65–118.
78 Ascher, *The Mensheviks*, p. 101.
79 E.P. Thompson, *The Making of the English Working Class*, Harmondsworth, 1968, pp. 9–10.
80 Morgan Philips Price, *Dispatches from the Revolution*, p. 85.
81 Nikolai Sukhanov, *The Russian Revolution 1917: A Personal Record by N.N. Sukhanov*, Princeton, 1984, pp. 631–2.

Chapter 5

1 Lev Trotsky, *Sochineniia*, Moscow, 1925–27, vol. 15, p. 1, appeal written in April 1920.
2 Trotsky, *Sochineniia*, 15, pp. 27–52, speech of 12 January 1920, and 15, p. 102, speech of 6 January 1920.
3 E. H. Carr, *The Bolshevik Revolution, 1917–23*, New York, 1951–3, vol. 2, p. 196.
4 A word that occurs surprisingly often; for a recent example, see S.A. Smith, *The Russian Revolution: A Very Short Introduction*, Oxford, 2002, p. 82.
5 Vladimir N. Brovkin, *Behind the Front Lines of the Civil War: Political Parties and Social Movements in Russia, 1918–1922*, Princeton, 1994, p. 270.
6 Martin Malia, *The Soviet Tragedy: A History of Socialism in Russia, 1917–1991*, New York, 1994, p. 130.
7 Sheila Fitzpatrick, *The Russian Revolution, 1917–1932*, Oxford, 1982, p. 76.
8 Moshe Lewin, *Political Undercurrents in Soviet Economic Debates*, Princeton, 1974, p. 33.
9 Robert Conquest, *Harvest of Sorrow: Soviet Collectivization and the Terror-Famine*, New York, 1986, p. 48; Bertrand Patenaude, 'Peasants into Russians,' *Russian Review*, 54:4, October 1995, pp. 552–70.
10 Leszek Kolakowski, *Main Currents in Marxism*, Oxford, 1981, vol. 3, pp. 28–9.
11 Kolakowski, *Main Currents in Marxism*, vol. 3, p. 29.
12 Trotsky, *Terrorism and Communism*, 12, p. 135. The English translation made in the early 1920s has been reprinted as Leon Trotsky, *Terrorism and Communism*, Ann Arbor, 1961. All citations to *Terrorism and Communism* are newly translated from the Russian, but references to the Ann Arbor edition are provided as a convenience.
13 Trotsky, *Sochineniia*, 15, pp. 86–7, 6 January 1920.
14 Trotsky, *Sochineniia*, 12, pp. 188–9, 9 April 1920; this revealing passage was dropped from the version of this speech in *Terrorism and Communism*.
15 Trotsky, *Sochineniia*, 15, p. 423, 2 December 1920.
16 'Ekh, nam ne khvataet tochnosti!', Trotsky, *Sochineniia*, 21, pp. 359–62; see also 21, p. 5, *Pravda* article of 10 July 1923.
17 Trotsky, *Sochineniia*, 17/2, p. 353–5, December 1919.
18 Trotsky, *Sochineniia*, 15, p. 46, 12 January 1920.
19 'Naturally, the army apparatus as such is not adapted to the leadership of the labor process. But we didn't try to interfere in this.' Trotsky, *Terrorism and Communism*, 12, p. 145, English edition, p. 152.
20 Trotsky, *Terrorism and Communism*, 12, p. 160, English edition, p. 168. I discussed this issue at greater length in '*Vlast*' from the Past: Stories told by Bolsheviks', *Left History*, 6:2, Fall 1999, pp. 40–1.
21 Trotsky, *Terrorism and Communism*, 12, p. 149, English edition, p. 156; see also 15, p. 259.
22 Trotsky, *Sochineniia*, 15, p. 88–91, 6 January 1920; 15, pp. 107–14, Theses for Ninth Party Congress.
23 Trotsky, *Sochineniia*, 17/2, p. 338, December 1919. Trotsky went on to praise Jaurès' ideas about a militia system.

24 Trotsky, *Sochineniia*, 15, p. 103–6, 25 March 1920.
25 Trotsky, *Sochineniia*, 17/2, p. 368, 25 March 1920. The first sentence seems to be an allusion to Bukharin's *Economy of the Transition Period* that had just appeared and whose main claim to originality was its demonstration that deep economic crises were inevitable in revolutions.
26 Trotsky, *Sochineniia*, 12, pp. 327–31. On 'transition', see also 15, pp. 52–7 and 15, p. 413 as well as many passages in *Terrorism and Communism*, including 12, pp. 133–6 and 12, pp. 161–6.
27 The rewording in *Terrorism and Communism* of the relevant passage in the original speech in April brings out the train of thought. Compare 15, pp. 179–80, original speech with 12, p. 133, *Terrorism and Communism*, English edition, pp. 138–9.
28 Trotsky, *Terrorism and Communism*, 12, pp. 161–2, English edition, pp. 170–1.
29 Nikolai Bukharin, *Programma kommunistov, bol'shevikov*, Moscow, 1918. The chapters on labour duty and labour discipline reprinted in Bukharin, *Izbrannye proizvedeniia*, Moscow, 1990.
30 Trotsky, *Terrorism and Communism*, 12, p. 134, English edition, p. 140. The meaning of 'single plan' in this passage is discussed the next section.
31 Trotsky, *Terrorism and Communism*, 12, p. 140, English edition, p. 146.
32 Trotsky, *Terrorism and Communism*, 12, p. 138–144, English edition, p. 144–50
33 Trotsky, *Sochineniia*, 15, p. 428, 2 December 1920.
34 Trotsky, *Sochineniia*, 12, p. 301–56, November 1922. Trotsky recommended this 1922 report as an appendix to *Terrorism and Communism*, 12, p. 1.
35 This plan was the opposite of any 'leap' mentality: 'There is no point in trying to predict whether the first or the following periods will be measured by months or by years.' *Terrorism and Communism*, 12, p. 150, English edition, p. 158.
36 Gusev's pamphlet *Edinyi khoziaiivstennyi plan i edinyi khoziaistvennyi apparat* is reprinted in *Ob edinom khoziaistvennom plane*, Moscow, 1989. It is indicative that Gusev has disappeared in the secondary literature.
37 *Deviatyi s'ezd RKP(b)*, Moscow, 1960, pp. 127–32, 135–9. There is a direct connection between Trotsky's remarks and his thoughts on 'primitive socialist accumulation' a couple of years later.
38 Trotsky, *Sochineniia*, 15, pp. 146–52, Ninth Party Congress, March 1920.
39 Trotsky, *Sochineniia*, 15, pp. 94–7, 6 January 1920, see also 15, pp. 146–52, Ninth Party Congress, March 1920.
40 Trotsky, *Sochineniia*, 15, pp. 10–14, December 1919; 15, pp. 94–7, 6 January 1920.
41 Trotsky, *Sochineniia*, 15, pp. 218–21, December 1920.
42 Trotsky, *Sochineniia*, 15, pp. 233–7, 4 January 1921.
43 Trotsky, *Sochineniia*, 15, p. 95, 6 January 1920. The same passage contains similar remarks on sackmanism.
44 Trotsky, *Sochineniia*, 15, pp. 434–5, 2 December 1920.
45 Trotsky, *Sochineniia*, 17/2, p. 369, 3 March 1920.
46 Trotsky, *Sochineniia*, 17/2, p. 369, 3 March 1920, see also 15, pp. 221–5.
47 Trotsky, *Sochineniia*, 17/2, pp. 502–3, December 1920. Note that this speech was published in *Pravda* at the time.

48 Trotsky, *Sochineniia*, 15, p. 401, 2 December 1920; 17/2, p. 371, 25 March 1920; 15, p. 437, 2 December 1920. For another eloquent Trotsky statement on mass disillusionment, see Lih, '*Vlast*' From the Past', pp. 41–2.

49 Trotsky, *Sochineniia*, 15, pp. 437–8, 2 December 1920. Trotsky was living in New York when the Russian Revolution broke out.

50 *Moia zhizn*', Moscow, 1991, pp. 437–46. Trotsky writes that he made his proposal in February and this is the date given in the historical literature. According to the editors of the 1991 Russian edition, however, the proposal was submitted to the politburo on 20 March 1920 (p. 581).

51 Compare the text in *Novy kurs* of 1924 with the full text in Trotsky, *Sochineniia*, 17/2, pp. 543–4. It is indicative that, as far as I know, the full text of this historic proposal is not available in English.

52 Trotsky, *Moia zhizn*', pp. 437–46.

53 From the introduction to the 1935 English edition, see p. xliii of the Ann Arbor edition of *Terrorism and Communism*, which also contains the introduction to the 1936 French edition.

54 D.J. Cotterill, ed., *The Serge–Trotsky Papers*, London, 1994, pp. 15–20.

55 Victor Serge, *Year One of the Russian Revolution*, Peter Sedgwick, ed., London, 1972, first published 1930, pp. 350–72.

56 Serge, *Destiny of a Revolution*, London, 1937, pp. 140–1.

57 Serge, *Memoirs of a Revolutionary 1901–1941*, Oxford, 1963, pp. 117, 113, written in the mid–1940s and first published in French in 1951.

58 Isaac Deutscher, *The Prophet Armed: Trotsky, 1879–1921*, New York, 1965, p. 490, first published 1954. For a more detailed analysis of this chapter, see Lih, "*Vlast*" From the Past'.

59 Deutscher, *The Prophet Armed*, p. 489.

60 Deutscher, *The Prophet Armed*, p. 516, order of passages rearranged.

61 Moshe Lewin, *Political Undercurrents*, pp. 81–3, republished under the title *Stalinism and the Seeds of Soviet Reform* in 1991.

62 Conquest, *Harvest of Sorrow*, p. 48; Malia, *The Soviet Tragedy*, p. 175.

63 Orlando Figes, *A People's Tragedy: The Russian Revolution 1891–1924*, London, 1996, pp. 722–3.

64 S.A. Smith, *The Russian Revolution: A Very Short Introduction*, Oxford, 2002, p. 82.

Chapter 6

1 François Furet, *Le passé d'une illusion. Essai sur l'idée communiste au XXe siècle*, 1995; English translation: *The Passing of an Illusion: The Idea of Communism in the Twentieth Century*, Chicago, 2000.

2 Stéphane Courtois, ed., *Le livre noir du communisme. Crimes, terreur, répression*, Paris, 1997; English translation. *The Black Book of Communism: Crimes, Terror, Repression*, Cambridge MA, 1999.

3 Richard Pipes, *The Russian Revolution 1899–1919*, London, 1992; Martin Malia, *The Soviet Tragedy*, New York, 1992.

4 *Historikerstreit. Die Dokumentation der Kontroverse um die Einzigartigkeit der nationalsozialistische Judenvernichtung*, Munich, 1987.

5 Ernst Nolte, *Der europäische Bürgerkrieg 1917–1945. National-Sozialismus und Bolchewismus*, Ullstein, Berlin, 1987, hereafter quoted in the French translation: Ernst Nolte, *La guerre civile européenne 1917–1945. National-socialisme et bolchévisme*, préface de S. Courtois, Paris, 2000.

6 François Furet and Ernst Nolte, *Fascisme et communisme*, Paris, 1998, English translation: *Fascism and Communism*, Lincoln, 2002.

7 Ernst Nolte, *Three Faces of Fascism*, New York, 1998 (first published in 1966).

8 On German conservative historiography, see Karl-Heinz Roth, 'Revisionist Tendencies in Historical Research into German Fascism', *International Review of Social History*, vol. 30:3, 1994, pp. 429–55.

9 Ernst Jünger, *Tagebücher*, vol. 2, Stuttgart, 1963, p. 433.

10 Carl Schmitt, *Der Nomos der Erde im Völkerrecht des Jus Publicum Europaeum* (1950), Berlin, 1974.

11 See the introduction to Arno J. Mayer, *The Persistence of the Old Regime*, New York, 1981, and Dan Diner, *Das Jahrhundert verstehen. Eine universalhistorische Deutung*, Munich, 1999, pp. 21–25.

12 Ernst Nolte, *La guerre civile européenne*, pp. 27, 583, 594.

13 Ernst Nolte, 'Vergangenheit, die nicht vergehen will. Eine Rede, die geschrieben, aber nicht gehalten werden konnte', *Historikerstreit*, pp. 39. See also Nolte, *La guerre civile européenne*, p. 45.

14 Nolte, *La guerre civile européenne*, pp. 555–6.

15 Nolte, 'Vergangenheit, die nicht vergehen will', *Historikerstreit*, p. 45.

16 Orlando Figes, *A People's Tragedy: The Russian Revolution, 1891–1924*, London, 1996; Nicolas Werth, 'Un état contre son peuple', *Le livre noir du communisme*, pp. 49–295.

17 Nolte, 'Vergangenheit, die nicht vergehen will', *Historikerstreit*, p. 44, and Nolte, *La guerre civile européenne*, pp. 142–3.

18 Serguëi P Melgunov, *La terreur rouge en Russie 1918–1924*, Paris, 1927, p. 144.

19 R. Nilostonski, *Der Blutenrausch des Bolschewismus. Berichte eines Augenzeugen*, Berlin, 1920, p. 48, quoted in Hans-Ulrich Wehler, *Entsorgung der deutschen Vergangenheit? Ein polemischer Essay zum Historikerstreit*, Munich, 1988, chapter 4. The first version of the story of the 'cage of rats' belongs to Octave Mirbeau (*Le jardin des supplices*, Paris, 1986, pp. 216–18), as indicated by Alain Brossat, *L'épreuve du désastre. Le XXe siècle et les camps*, Paris, 1995, pp. 357–72.

20 See Pier Paolo Poggio, *Nazismo e revisionismo storico*, Rome, 1997, p. 135.

21 Zeev Sternhell, *The Birth of Fascist Ideology*, Princeton NJ, 1994.

22 See Ian Kershaw, *Hitler 1889–1936: Hubris*, London, 1998, p. 152.

23 George L. Mosse, *The Fascist Revolution*, New York, 1999. On fascism as a 'revolution against the revolution', see Mark Neocleous, *Fascism*, Buckingham, 1997, chapters 3 and 4.

24 Dan Diner, *Das Jahrhundert verstehen*, pp. 53, 219.

25 Arno J. Mayer, *Why Did the Heavens Not Darken? The 'Final Solution' in History*, New York, 1988.

26 Nolte, *La guerre civile européenne*, p. 545.

27 Adolf Hitler, *Libres propos sur la guerre et la paix*, Paris, 1952.

28 Nolte, *La guerre civile européenne*, pp. 453–63.
29 Franz Neumann, *Behemoth: Theory and Practice of National Socialism*, New York, 1942.
30 Dan Diner, 'Nazism and Stalinism: On Memory, Arbitrariness, Labor, and Death', *Beyond the Conceivable: Studies on Germany, Nazism, and the Holocaust*, Berkeley CA, 2000, pp. 195–7.
31 Stefan Kühl, *The Nazi Connection: Eugenics, American Racism, and German National Socialism*, New York, 1994, and Peter Weindling, *Health, Race and German Politics between National Unification and Nazism, 1870–1945*, Cambridge, 1989.
32 Nolte, *La guerre civile européenne*, pp. 542–3.
33 Jürgen Habermas, 'Eine Art Schadensabwicklung. Die apologetische Tendenzen in der deutschen Zeitgeschichtsschreibung', *Historikerstreit*, pp. 62–76.
34 Saul Friedländer, 'A Conflict of Memories? The New German Debates about the "Final Solution"', *Memory, History, and the Extermination of the Jews of Europe*, Bloomington, 1993, pp. 4–35.
35 Karl Jaspers, *The Question of German Guilt*, New York, 1947.
36 Nolte, *La guerre civile européenne*, pp. 552–3.
37 Furet, Nolte, *Fascisme et communisme*, p. 93.
38 Furet, *Le passé d'une illusion*, p. 266.
39 See this exchange of letters in Herbert Marcuse, *Technology, War and Fascism*, London, 1998, pp. 261–8.
40 François Furet, 'Le catéchisme révolutionnaire', *Penser la révolution française*, Paris, 1978, pp. 133–207.
41 Alexis de Tocqueville, *Œuvres complètes*, vol. IX (*Correspondance d'Alexis de Tocqueville et d'Arthur de Gobineau*), Paris, 1959.
42 Nolte, *La guerre civile européenne*, p. 20.
43 Raymond Aron, *Démocratie et totalitarisme*, Paris, 1965, pp. 298–9.
44 Stéphane Courtois, 'Les crimes du communisme', *Le livre noir du communisme*, p. 19.
45 Stéphane Courtois, 'Le *Livre noir* et le travail historien sur le communisme', *Communisme*, 2000, no. 59–60, p. 109. Joachim Fest, 'Die geschuldete Erinnerung', *Historikerstreit*, pp. 100–112.
46 Furet, *Le passé d'une illusion*, p. 84.
47 Ernst Nolte, 'Zwischen Geschichtslegende und Revisionismus?', *Historikerstreit*, p. 29.
48 Courtois, 'Les crimes du communisme', *Le livre noir*, p. 18.
49 See for example two books by Reynald Secher, *La Vendée vengée*, Paris, 1985, and *Juifs et Vendéens. D'un génocide à l'autre*, Paris, 1991; Patrice Guenniffey, *La politique de la Terreur. Essai sur la violence révolutionnaire 1789–1794*, Paris, 2000; Alain Gérard, *'Par principe d'humanité'. La Terreur et la Vendée*, Paris, 2000.
50 Arno J. Mayer, *The Furies: Violence and Terror in the French and Russian Revolutions*, Princeton NJ, 2000, chapter 9, pp. 323–70.
51 Waldemar Gurian, 'Totalitarianism as Political Religion', in Carl J. Friedrich, ed., *Totalitarianism*, Cambridge MA, 1953, p. 123.
52 Jacob L. Talmon, *The Origins of Totalitarian Democracy*, London, 1952.

53 Hannah Arendt, *The Origins of Totalitarianism*, New York, 1976, pp. 299–302; Robert Nisbet, '*1984* and the Conservative Imagination', in Irving Howe, ed., *1984 Revisited*, New York, 1983, pp. 180–206.
54 Pipes, *The Russian Revolution*, pp. 789–94.
55 Martin Malia, *The Soviet Tragedy*, introduction.
56 Pipes, *The Russian Revolution*, p. 122.
57 Furet, *Penser la Révolution française*, p. 98.
58 François Furet and Denis Richet, *The French Revolution*, London, 1970.
59 See J. Arch Getty and Roberta Manning, eds, *Stalinist Terror: New Perspectives*, New York, 1993.
60 Claudio Sergio Ingerflom, 'De la Russie à l'URSS', in Michel Dreyfus, ed., *Le siècle des communismes*, Paris, 2000, p. 121.
61 Marcello Flores, *In terra non c'è il paradiso. Il racconto del comunismo*, Milan, 1998, p. 10.
62 Marc Lazar, '*Le livre noir du communisme* en débat', *Communisme*, 2000, no. 59–60, pp. 21–2.
63 Courtois, '*Le livre noir* et le travail historien sur le communisme', p. 95
64 Isaac Deutscher, 'The Ex-Communists' Conscience' (1950), *Marxism, Wars and Revolutions. Essays from Four Decades*, London, 1984, pp. 53–4.
65 Eric J. Hobsbawm, 'Histoire et illusion', *Le Débat*, 1996, no. 89, p. 138.
66 See for example the book (otherwise very interesting) by Domenico Losurdo, *Il revisionismo storico. Problemi e miti*, Bari-Rome, 1996.
67 On 'Stalin's Revolution' see Sheila Fitzpatrick, *The Russian Revolution*, New York, 1994, chapter 5, pp. 120–47.
68 Claude Lefort, *La complication. Retour sur le communisme*, Paris, 1999, pp. 59–64.
69 Mayer, *The Furies*, p. 234.
70 Trotsky, *Terrorism and Communism*, Ann Arbor, 1972.
71 François Furet, *Marx and the French Revolution*, Chicago, 1988.
72 Elfriede Müller, 'Die Bolschewiki und die Gewalt', *Archiv für die Geschichte des Widerstandes und der Arbeit*, 1998, no. 15, pp. 157–8, 183.
73 Victor Serge, *Memoirs of a Revolutionary*, Iowa City, 2002.
74 Furet, *Le passé d'une illusion*, p. 39. Furet's thesis was criticized by Denis Berger and Henri Maler, *Une certaine idée du communisme. Répliques à François Furet*, Paris, 1996, chapter I, pp. 17–57, as well by Daniel Bensaïd, *Qui est le juge? Pour en finir avec le tribunal de l'Histoire*, Paris, 1999, p. 166.

Chapter 7

1 Jan Valtin, *Out of the Night*, London, 1941, 1946; Vasily Grossman, *Life and Fate*, London, 1985 (written during the 1950s and confiscated by the KGB); Margarete Buber-Neumann, *Under Two Dictators*, London, 1949; David Rousset, *A World Apart*, London, 1951. On the fascism/communism parallel see François Furet, *The Passing of an Illusion*, Chicago, 1999, chapter VI, pp. 156–208, and also Arendt.
2 Hannah Arendt, *The Origins of Totalitarianism*, London, 1958 (first published as *The Burden of our Time*, London, 1951).

3 Ernst Nolte, *Les mouvements fascistes*, Paris, 1969; Ernst Nolte, *Der Europäische Bürgerkrieg: 1917–1945, Nationalsozialismus und Bolschewismus*, Frankfurt am Main, 1987.

4 Maurice Baumont, in Charles-André Julien, *Les techniciens de la colonisation*, Paris, 1947; see also M. Korinman, *Deutschland über Alles*, Paris 1999, essential on the link between Pangermanism and Nazism; Joël Kotek and Pierre Rigoulot, *Le siècle des camps*, Paris, 2000.

5 Aimé Césaire, *Discourse on Colonialism*, London and New York, 1972, p. 14.

6 Abdelassane Yassine, *Islamiser la modernité*, Paris, 1998.

7 Marc Ferro, ed., *Le livre noir du colonialisme XVIe–XXIe. De l'extermination à la repentance*, Paris, 2003, pp. 9–38.

8 Georges Haupt, *Le congrès manqué*, Paris, 1965.

9 Cited by Philippe Soulez, *Les philosophes et la guerre de 1914*, Saint Denis, 1988, p. 21.

10 Based on the author's own observations.

11 Marc Ferro, *October 1917: A Social History of the Russian Revolution*, London, 1980.

12 Victor Kravchenko, *I Chose Freedom*, New York, 1946; also M. Malaurie, *L'affaire Kravtchenko*, Paris, n.d., and the testimony of G. Martinet in *Histoire Parallèle*, 16 January 1989, no. 493, la Sept-Arte.

13 Maria Ferretti, 'La mémoire refoulée. La Russie devant le passé stalinien', *Annales*, no. 6, 1995, pp. 1237–57.

14 Norbert Frei, *National Socialist Rule in Germany*, Oxford, 1993.

15 Fritz Fischer, *Germany's Aims in the First World War*, London, 1967.

16 Telford Taylor, *The Anatomy of the Nuremberg Trials*, New York, 1992.

17 Tim Mason, 'Intention and Explanation: A Current Controversy about the Interpretation of National Socialism', in Mason, *Nazism, Fascism and the Working Class*, Cambridge, 1995, pp. 212–30.

18 Rowan Callick, *Financial Times*, 11 March 1993.

19 Frei, *National Socialist Rule in Germany*, pp. 156–57.

20 Ferro, *October 1917*.

21 W.S. Allen, *The Nazi Seizure of Power: The Experience of a Single German Town 1930–1935*, Chicago, 1965; I. Kershaw, *Popular Opinion and Political Dissent in the Third Reich, Bavaria 1933–1945*, Oxford, 1983.

22 M. Foucault, *Il faut défendre la societe, Cours au Collège de France de 1976*, Paris, 1997.

23 Paul Weindling, 'Weimar Eugenics: The Kaiser Wilhlem Institute for Anthropology, Human Heredity and Eugenics in Special Context' *Annals of Science*, no. 42, 1985, pp. 303–18.

24 Daniel J. Goldhagen, *Hitler's Willing Executioners*, London, 1996, reviewed by Jean Solchany, *Revue d'histoire moderne et contemporaine*, 44:3, July–September 1997, pp. 514–30. Mention should also be made of P. Sorlin, *L'antisémitisme allemand*, Paris, 1969, which is not considered by Goldhagen.

25 Rachel Mazuy, *Croire plutôt que voir? Voyages en Russie soviétique 1919–1939*, Paris, 2002.

26 Charles-Robert Ageron, *Politiques coloniales au Maghreb*, Paris, 1973, p. 229.

27 Béatrice Fleury-Vilatte, *La mémoire télévisuelle de la guerre d'Algérie*, Paris, 1992.

28 General Aussaresses, *Services spéciaux, Algérie 1955–57*, Paris, 2001; Pierre Vidal-Naquet, *Torture, Cancer of Democracy: France and Algeria 1954–62*, Harmondsworth, 1963.
29 See the various works on the USSR by Moshe Lewin and Nicholas Werth, and on Germany by Ian Kershaw.
30 Fanny Colonna, *Instituteurs algériens, 1833–1939*, Paris, 1975; Radhika Ramasubban, 'Imperial Health in British India', in Roy MacLeod and Milton Lewis, eds, *Disease, Medicine and Empire*, London, 1988.

Chapter 8

1 The Report's blurb expressed this: 'Between 1917 and 1950, countries with one-third of the world's population seceded from the market economy and launched an experiment in constructing alternative systems of centrally planned economies. This transformed the political and the economic map of the world. *World Development Report 1996*, the nineteenth in this annual series, is devoted to the transition of these countries – in particular, those in Central and Eastern Europe, the newly independent states of the former Soviet Union, China, and Vietnam – back to a market orientation.' See World Bank, *World Development Report: From Plan to Market*, Oxford, 1996. For the original reference, see Sheila Rowbotham, 'The Tale That Never Ends', in Leo Panitch and Colin Leys, eds, *The Socialist Register 1999: Global Capitalism Versus Democracy*, New York, 1999, p. 354.
2 Jacket description to Karl Marx and Friedrich Engels, *The Communist Manifesto: A Modern Edition*, with an introduction by Eric Hobsbawm, London, 1998. The 150th anniversary attracted widespread attention in the daily and periodical press. New editions were also introduced by John Toews, Boston, 1999, Martin Malia, New York, 1998, and Mark Cowling, New York, 1998.
3 For an interesting argument to this effect, see George Soros, 'Who Lost Russia?', *New York Review of Books*, 13 April 2000, pp. 10–16.
4 Adam Przeworski, 'Some Problems in the Study of the Transition to Democracy', in Guillermo O'Donnell, Philippe C. Schmitter, and Laurence Whitehead, eds, *Transitions from Authoritarian Rule: Comparative Perspectives*, Baltimore, 1986, p.63.
5 For a critique of neo-liberal prioritizing of the market, which in the early 1990s programmatically subsumed all other social and political goals into strategies of radical privatization as a form of 'shock therapy,' see Peter Gowan, 'Neo-Liberal Theory and Practice for Eastern Europe', *New Left Review*, 213, September–October 1995, pp. 3–60.

See also the subsequent exchange between John Lloyd, 'Eastern Reformers and Neo-Marxist Reviewers', and Peter Gowan, 'Eastern Europe, Western Power and Neo-Liberalism', *New Left Review*, 216, March–April 1996, pp. 119–28, 129–40.

An emblematic text for the neo-liberal viewpoint was Francis Fukuyama, *The End of History and the Last Man*, New York, 1992, while an especially influential version of the argument from the standpoint of civil society can be found in Ernest Gellner, *Conditions of Liberty: Civil Society and its Rivals*, Harmondsworth, 1996. For typical renderings of the argument in the wider public sphere, see Michael Ignatieff, 'On Civil Society', *Foreign Affairs*, March–April 1995, pp. 135–6; George Soros, *Underwriting Democracy*, New York, 1991, and *Open Society: Reforming Global Capitalism*, New York, 2000. This perspective hinges on a classical distinction between constitutional definitions of citizenship and cultures of participation. For another contemporary version exercising pervasive ideological power, see Robert Putnam, *Making Democracy Work: Civic Traditions in Modern Italy*, Princeton, 1993. Putnam later applied his argument to the United States, first in a 1995 article and then in the hugely influential *Bowling Alone: The Collapse and Revival of American Community*, New York, 2000. The approach is applied on a country-by-country basis in Robert Putnam, ed., *Democracies in Flux: The Evolution of Social Capital in Contemporary Society*, New York, 2002. See also Francis Fukuyama's later work, *Trust: Social Virtues and the Creation of Prosperity*, New York, 1995.

6 For more subtle, historically sophisticated treatments of the transition, see Katherine Verdery, *What Was Socialism and What Comes Next?*, Princeton, 1996; and Michael Kennedy, *Cultural Formations of Postcommunism: Emancipation, Transition, Nation, and War*, Minneapolis, 2002.

7 For more critical approaches, see especially Gowan, 'Neo-Liberal Theory and Practice'; Alice Amsden, et al., *The Market Meets its Match: Restructuring the Economies of Eastern Europe*, Cambridge MA, 1994; Adam Przeworksi, *Democracy and the Market: Political and Economic Reforms in Eastern Europe and Latin America*, Cambridge, 1991. For a good general commentary with bibliography, see the final chapter, 'The World after the Cold War,' in James E. Cronin, *The World the Cold War Made: Order, Chaos, and the Return of History*, New York, 1996, pp. 237–81.

8 See Ernest Renan, 'What is a Nation?', in Geoff Eley and Ronald Grigor Suny, eds, *Becoming National: A Reader*, New York, 1996, pp. 42–55.

9 For an early report from the midst of that new historiography, see Ronald Grigor Suny, 'Toward a Social History of the October Revolution', *American Historical Review*, 88, 1983, pp. 31–52.

10 I am not suggesting that this vital social historiography has been wholly discarded. But during the 1990s a definite transition to 'cultural' approaches occurred, as a result of which the main lens for judging the Bolshevik Revolution ceased to be the primacy of popular agency foregrounded by the social historians, usually linked to some broadly structuralist notion of societal crisis, and became instead a new culturalist analytic emphasizing post-Foucauldian approaches to Bolshevik governmentality. A pivotal text here was Stephen Kotkin's study of the creation of the new industrial city of Magnitogorsk, *Magnetic Mountain: Stalinism as a Civilization*, Berkeley, 1995, in which both historiographical sensibilities simultaneously coexisted. Trained at Berkeley by Reginald Zelnick, one of the key social history pioneers, Kotkin was also inspired directly by Michel Foucault, who taught at Berkeley in 1982–83, the year before he died. In the meantime, influenced by Zygmunt Bauman and the revival of Hannah Arendt, a younger cohort of Soviet historians has been reworking this post-Foucauldian understanding of governmentality into a blunt and undifferen-

tiated conception of 'modernity'. That understanding of 'the modern' increasingly collapses Soviet specificities into a universalizing argument about the exigencies of state-driven social transformations, the associated 'disciplinary' practices, and their consequences for ordinary subjectivity. See especially Stephen Kotkin, '1991 and the Russian Revolution: Sources, Conceptual Categories, Analytical Frameworks', *Journal of Modern History*, 70, 1998, pp. 384–425; and for Foucault's influence, Kotkin, *Magnetic Mountain*, pp. 21–3, 392–3. Another key recent work is Amir Weiner, *Making Sense of War: The Second World War and the Fate of the Bolshevik Revolution*, Princeton, 2001. See also Zygmunt Bauman, *Modernity and the Holocaust*, Oxford, 1989 and Hannah Arendt, *The Origins of Totalitarianism*, New York, 1951.

11 The powerful senior exponents of this view are Richard Pipes, *The Russian Revolution*, New York, 1990, and Martin Malia, *The Soviet Tragedy*, New York, 1994. More generally see Vladimir N. Brovkin, ed., *The Bolsheviks in Russian Society: The Revolution and the Civil Wars*, New Haven, 1997, and Brovkin's own works, *The Mensheviks after October: Socialist Opposition and the Rise of the Bolshevik Dictatorship*, Ithaca, 1991; *Behind the Front Lines of the Civil War: Political Parties and Social Movements in Russia, 1918–1922*, Princeton, 1994; and *Russia after Lenin: Politics, Culture, and Society, 1921–1929*, London, 1998.

12 I'm invoking my own experience as an undergraduate between 1968–69. Only E.H. Carr's multi-volume history and a two-part article by Leopold Haimson provided any counterveiling help for a social historical understanding. See Leonard B. Schapiro, *Origins of the Communist Autocracy: Political Opposition in the Soviet State, First Phase, 1917–1922*, London, 1955, and *The Communist Party of the Soviet Union*, London, 1960; Richard Pipes, *The Formation of the Soviet Union: Communism and Nationalism, 1917–1923*, Cambridge MA, 1954, and *Social Democracy and the St. Petersburg Labor Movement, 1885–1897*, Cambridge MA, 1963; George Katkov, *Russia 1917: The February Revolution*, London, 1967; Vladimir Ilyich Lenin, *What is to be Done?*, Sergej V. Utechin, ed., Oxford, 1963; Sergej V. Utechin, *Russian Political Thought: A Concise History*, New York, 1964. The prevailing uniformity of interpretation was well indicated by the proceedings of a conference marking the fiftieth anniversary of the Revolution, where the only outliers were Marc Ferro and Oskar Anweiler, neither of whose works were available in English, and E.H. Carr. See Richard Pipes, ed., *Revolutionary Russia*, Cambridge MA, 1968. See also Edward Hallet Carr, *The Bolshevik Revolution, 1917–1923*, 3 vols, Harmondsworth, 1966; Leopold Haimson, 'The Problem of Social Stability in Urban Russia, 1905–1917,' *Slavic Review*, 23, 1964, pp. 619–42 and 24, 1965, pp.1–22.

13 The new social history of the 1970s and 1980s also stressed the basic continuities between Bolshevism and social democracy elsewhere in Europe, as against earlier interpretations which found essential affinities between Lenin's alleged 'Blanquism', conspiratorial proclivities, secrecy, insurrectionism, puritanical and centralist model of party discipline, preference for dictatorship and the authoritarianism of the Jacobin tradition.

Whereas the older Cold War histories treated *What is to be Done?* and the split between Bolsheviks and Mensheviks as a peculiar expression of these tendencies produced by the exceptional backwardness of Russian conditions, recent studies see Lenin's perspectives in 1902–03 as broadly continuous with the classical thinking of Karl Kautsky and the Second International mainstream. Compare Robert Service, *The Bolshevik Party in Revolution 1917–1923*, London, 1979, and Neil Harding, *Lenin's Political Thought: Theory and Practice in the Democratic and Socialist Revolutions*, London, 1983, with Pipes's account in *Social Democracy* and Utechin's edition of *What is to be Done?*

14 Jacob Talmon, *The Origins of Totalitarian Democracy*, Boston, 1952.

15 William G. Rosenberg, 'Beheading the Revolution: Arno Mayer's "Furies"', *Journal of Modern History*, 73, 2001, p. 909. Rosenberg's article is an extended review of Arno J. Mayer's *The Furies: Violence and Terror in the French and Russian Revolutions*, Princeton NJ, 2000, which grapples centrally with the question of violence and its place in the revisionist critiques of both revolutions.

16 For an indication of this path-breaking work, see especially the following: George Rudé, *The Crowd in the French Revolution*, Oxford, 1959, and *The Crowd in History: A Study of Popular Disturbances in France and England, 1730–1848*, New York, 1964; Eric Hobsbawm, *Labouring Men: Studies in the History of Labour*, London, 1964, and *Primitive Rebels: Studies in Archaic Forms of Social Movement in the Nineteenth and Twentieth Centuries*, Manchester, 1959; Charles Tilly, *The Vendée*, Cambridge MA, 1964; Eric Hobsbawm and George Rudé, *Captain Swing: A Social History of the Great English Agricultural Uprising of 1830*, London, 1968; Edward Thompson, *The Making of the English Working Class*, London, 1963, and 'The Moral Economy of the English Crowd in the Eighteenth Century', *Past and Present*, 50, 1971, pp. 76–131.

17 For the flavour of this vast scholarship, see Robert J. Holton, 'The Crowd in History: Some Problems of Theory and Method', *Social History*, 3, 1978, pp. 219–33; Charles Tilly, 'Getting It Together in Burgundy, 1675–1975', *Theory and Society*, 4, 1977, pp. 479–504; Tilly, *The Contentious French: Four Centuries of Popular Struggle*, Cambridge MA, 1986.

18 See Georges Lefebvre, *The Great Fear of 1789: Rural Panic in Revolutionary France*, New York, 1973; Albert Soboul, *The Parisian Sans-Culottes and the French Revolution, 1793–1794*, Oxford, 1964; Richard Cobb, *The People's Armies: The Armées Révolutionnaires, Instrument of Terror in the Departments, April 1793 to Floréal Year II*, New Haven, 1987; original French edition, Paris, 1961–63; Cobb, *The Police and the People: French Popular Protest, 1789–1820*, Oxford, 1970.

19 The quoted phrases are partly Furet's own, partly Kaplan's rendition. See Steven Laurence Kaplan, *Farewell, Revolution: The Historians' Feud, France, 1789/1989*, Ithaca, 1995, pp. 81, 105.

20 For Furet's intellectual and political trajectories, see Kaplan, *Farewell, Revolution*, pp. 50–143, esp. 63–6; Sunil Khilnani, *Arguing Revolution: The Intellectual Left in Post-War France*, New Haven, 1993, pp. 155–78;

François Dosse, *New History in France: The Triumph of the Annales*, Urbana, 1994, pp. 182–213.

21 See Alfred Cobban, *The Social Interpretation of the French Revolution*, Cambridge, 1964. The key work announcing the 1980s revisionism was François Furet, *Interpreting the French Revolution*, Cambridge, 1981.

22 For two demonstrations of how this social context might be addressed, one at the level of Jacobin discourse overall and one at the grass roots, see Jean-Pierre Gross, *Fair Shares for All: Jacobin Egalitarianism in Practice*, Cambridge, 1997; and Morris Slavin, *The French Revolution in Miniature: Section Droits-de-l'Homme, 1789–1795*, Princeton NJ, 1984. For an incisive critique of Furet in the context of his final book, *The Passing of an Illusion: The Idea of Communism in the Twentieth Century*, Chicago, 1999, see Eric Hobsbawm, 'History and Illusion', *New Left Review*, 220, November–December 1996, pp. 116–25.

23 Kaplan, *Farewell, Revolution*, p. 110. For discussion of Chartier's critique of Furet and his camp, and of Furet's arrogant response, see ibid., pp. 110–12, 210–11.

24 The best-known and most stylish of these general histories is Simon Schama, *Citizens: A Chronicle of the French Revolution*, New York, 1989. Furet's own general history is *The French Revolution, 1770–1814*, Oxford, 1996. See also François Furet, *Revolutionary France, 1770–1870*, Oxford, 1995.

25 See especially the four volumes edited by Keith M. Baker, François Furet, Colin Lucas and Mona Ozouf, *The French Revolution and the Creation of Modern Political Culture*, Oxford, 1987–94, and Baker's own *Inventing the French Revolution: Essays on French Political Culture in the Eighteenth Century*, Cambridge, 1990.

26 Interestingly, these were all 'frontier societies'. My statement stands only with another vital caveat: New Zealand and Australia count as 'full democracies' only if exclusions by race are disregarded, whether in relation to Maori and Aboriginal populations or in relation to non-white immigration.

27 For the dynamics of democracy's international diffusion, see Göran Therborn, 'The Rule of Capital and the Rise of Democracy', *New Left Review*, 103, May–June 1977, pp. 3–42; John Markoff, 'Really Existing Democracy: Learning from Latin America in the 1990s', *New Left Review*, 223, May–June 1997, pp. 48–68, and *Waves of Democracy: Social Movements and Political Change*, Newbury Park CA, 1996; Atilio Borón, 'Latin America: Between Hobbes and Friedman', *New Left Review*, 130, November–December 1981, pp. 45–66.

28 See especially Carole Pateman, *The Sexual Contract*, Cambridge, 1988, and 'The Fraternal Social Contract', in John Keane, ed., *Civil Society and the State: New European Perspectives*, London, 1988, pp. 101–28; Nancy Fraser, 'What's Critical about Critical Theory? The Case of Habermas and Gender', in Seyla Benhabib and Drucilla Cornell, eds, *Feminism as Critique*, Minneapolis, 1987, pp. 31–55; Joan W. Scott, *Gender and the Politics of History*, New York, 1988; Kathleen Canning, *Languages of Labor and Gender: Female Factory Work in Germany, 1850–1914*, Ithaca, 1996; Canning,

'Gender and the Politics of Class Formation: Rethinking German Labor History', in Geoff Eley, ed., *Society, Culture, and the State in Germany, 1870–1930*, Ann Arbor, 1996, pp. 105–41; Canning, 'Feminist Theory after the Linguistic Turn: Historicizing Discourse and Experience', *Signs*, 19, 1944, pp. 368–404; Canning, 'Social Body, Body Politics: Recasting the Social Question in Germany, 1875–1900', in Laura J. Frader and Sonya O. Rose, eds, *Gender and Class in Modern Europe*, Ithaca, 1996, pp. 211–37.

29 We need to distinguish here between those polities that were already relatively democratic, as in Scandinavia, the Low Countries, France and Britain, and the rest of Europe, including the territories covered by the Russian, Austro-Hungarian and German Empires, the Balkans, southern Europe and Ireland, where democratic polities were created only through the upheavals of 1917–1923. Even so, widespread turbulence occurred in the former category of societies. The relative stability of the latter's existing political arrangements was aided either by having stayed out of the war or from ending on the winning side. In other words, the degree of revolutionary instability and the strength of popular democratic momentum was indissolubly bound to the experience of military defeat and attendant political collapse.

30 Land reforms were passed in Romania, Yugoslavia, Bulgaria, Greece, Czechoslovakia, Poland, the Baltic states and Finland. For a full discussion of the 1917–23 conjuncture, see Geoff Eley, *Forging Democracy: The History of the Left in Europe, 1850–2000*, New York, 2002, pp. 152–64.

31 For this idea of a Central and Northern European social democratic core before 1914, see ibid. pp. 62–84.

32 For an argument of this kind, see Michael Geyer, 'The Militarization of Europe, 1914–1945', in John R. Gillis, ed., *The Militarization of the Western World*, New Brunswick, 1989, pp. 65–102. In conjunction with the depleting effects of the arms race and the associated economic pressures of the Cold War, the destabilizing consequences of Soviet military involvement in Afghanistan functioned analogously to the effects of the two world wars, helping generate the political urgencies of the Gorbachev era and feeding directly into the Eastern European crisis of 1989.

33 See Jürgen Habermas, *The Structural Transformation of the Public Sphere: An Inquiry into a Category of Bourgeois Society*, Cambridge MA, 1989; and Craig Calhoun, ed., *Habermas and the Public Sphere*, Cambridge, MA, 1992. For my own extensive reflections on the idea, see Geoff Eley, 'Nations, Publics, and Political Cultures: Placing Habermas in the Nineteenth Century', in Calhoun, ed., *Habermas*, pp. 289–339, and 'Politics, Culture, and the Public Sphere', *positions*, 10, Spring 2002, pp. 219–36.

34 For one original and imaginative attempt at exploring this process of absorption into the public sphere via changing codes of public address, see Belinda Davis, *Home Fires Burning: Food, Politics, and Everyday Life in World War I Berlin*, Chapel Hill, 2000. According to Davis, the different categories of war-related relief-entitlement devised by the state for the distribution of welfare provided women with a basis for declaring public identities and making citizenship claims. More generally, the pressure of food shortages during the war, and the complex reciprocities entailed in

government responsiveness to crowd actions and the restiveness of the streets, vitally redefined the nature of public space with profound consequences for the legitimacy of government and the making of public claims. For another study connecting the social dynamics of everyday life to an argument about politics and the public sphere, see Thomas Lindenberger, *Straßenpolitik: Zur Sozialgeschichte der öffentlichen Ordnung in Berlin, 1900 bis 1914*, Berlin, 1995. See also Belinda Davis, 'Reconsidering Habermas, Politics, and Gender: The Case of Wilhelmine Germany', in Eley, ed., *Society, Culture, and the State*, pp. 397–426.

35 For two decades now the character of the post-war settlement in Britain has been the subject of much continuing debate. The strongest restatement of an older consensus about the achievements of the post-war Labour government is Peter Hennessy, *Never Again: Britain, 1945–1951*, London, 1992, while Steven Fielding, Peter Thompson and Nick Tiratsoo, in *'England Arise!' The Labour Party and Popular Politics in 1940s Britain*, Manchester, 1995, question the existence of any further-reaching popular desires for radical change. For rejoinders to the latter, see the forum 'Labour and the Popular', *History Workshop Journal*, 43, Spring 1997, including Sarah Benton, 'The 1945 "Republic" ', pp. 249–57; John Marriott, 'Labour and the Popular', pp. 258–66; and James Hinton, '1945 and the Apathy School', pp. 266–73. For my own thoughts, see Geoff Eley, 'Legacies of Antifascism: Constructing Democracy in Post-War Europe', *New German Critique*, 67, Winter 1996, pp. 73–100, and 'Finding the People's War: Film, British Collective Memory, and World War II', *American Historical Review*, 105, 2001, pp. 818–38. For my purposes here, these disagreements over the extent of the 1945 changes are mainly irrelevant: my argument concerns the political culture of popular identification with '1945' that was nonetheless forged.

36 Since the later 1970s, the Depression's place in British collective memory has been radically reshaped. Under the impact of Thatcherism's retelling of the story, the new 'present' of the 1980s became itself fundamentally different from the older 'present' that had previously prevailed. The reworking of popular memory became a central feature of public rhetorics, pedagogy and popular culture during the 1980s. I have discussed aspects of this process in two other essays: *'Distant Voices, Still Lives*. The Family is a Dangerous Place: Memory, Gender, and the Image of the Working Class', in Robert Rosenstone, ed., *Revisioning History: Film and the Construction of the Past*, Princeton, 1995, pp. 17–43, and 'Finding the People's War: Film, British Collective Memory, and World War II'. See also Roger Bromley, *Lost Narratives: Popular Fictions, Politics and Recent History*, London, 1988; Patrick Wright, 'A Blue Plaque for the Labour Movement? Some Political Meanings of the National Past', in *On Living in an Old Country: The National Past in Contemporary Britain*, London, 1985, pp. 135–59; Kevin Poster, *Fighting Fictions: War, Narrative and National Identity*, London, 1999.

37 Dennis Potter, *Seeing the Blossom: Two Interviews and a Lecture*, London, 1994, p. 9.

38 Alessandro Portelli, 'Luigi's Socks and Rita's Makeup: Youth Culture, the Politics of Private Life, and the Culture of the Working Classes', in *The*

Battle of Valle Giulia: Oral History and the Art of Dialogue, Madison, 1997, p. 241.

39 Ibid., pp. 243–4.

40 Ibid., p. 240.

41 Pateman, 'Fraternal Social Contract', p. 123.

42 See the essays of Mica Nava, 'Modernity Tamed? Women Shoppers and the Rationalization of Consumption in the Interwar Period', *Australian Journal of Communication*, 22, 1995, pp. 1–19, 'Modernity's Disavowal: Women, the City and the Department Store', in Mica Nava and Alan O'Shea, eds, *Modern Times: Reflections on a Century of English Modernity*, London, 1996, pp. 38–76, and 'The Cosmopolitanism of Commerce and the Allure of Difference: Selfridges, the Russian Ballet and the Tango, 1911–1914', *International Journal of Cultural Studies*, 1, 1998, pp. 163–96. See also Lisa Tickner, *The Spectacle of Women: Imagery of the Suffrage Campaign 1907–1914*, Chicago, 1988; Sally Alexander, 'Becoming a Woman in London in the 1920s and 1930s', in *Becoming a Woman and Other Essays in 19th and 20th Century Feminist History*, London, 1995, pp. 203–24. For France, see Mary Louise Roberts, *Civilization without Sexes: Reconstructing Gender in Post-War France, 1917–1927*, Chicago, 1994, and *Disruptive Acts: The New Woman in Fin-de-Siècle France*, Chicago, 2002. For Germany, see Atina Grossmann's classic articles, '*Girlkultur* or a Thoroughly Rationalized Female: A New Woman in Weimar Germany?', in Judith Friedlander, Blanche W. Cook, Alice Kessler-Harris, and Carroll Smith-Rosenberg, eds, *Women in Culture and Politics: A Century of Change*, Bloomington, 1986, pp. 62–80, and 'The New Woman and the Rationalization of Sexuality in Weimar Germany', in Ann Snitow, Christine Stansell, and Sharon Thompson, eds, *Powers of Desire: The Politics of Sexuality*, New York, 1983.

43 See especially Susan Pedersen, 'The Failure of Feminism in the Making of the British Welfare State', *Radical History Review*, 43, 1989, pp. 86–110, and 'Gender, Welfare, and Citizenship in Britain during the Great War', *American Historical Review*, 95, 1990, pp. 983–1006; Geoff Eley and Atina Grossmann, 'Maternalism and Citizenship in Weimar Germany: The Gendered Politics of Welfare', *Central European History*, 30, 1997, pp. 67–75. For a general overview, see Eley, *Forging Democracy*, pp. 185–200.

44 Jill Julius Matthews, 'They Had Such a Lot of Fun: The Women's League of Health and Beauty between the Wars', *History Workshop Journal*, 30, Autumn 1990, p. 47.

45 Helena Stanwick, in the *Manchester Guardian*, 24 August 1932, quoted by Brian Harrison, *Prudent Revolutionaries: Portraits of British Feminists between the Wars*, Oxford, 1987, p. 320.

46 Sonya Orwell and I. Angus, eds, *The Collected Essays, Journalism and Letters of George Orwell*, vol. I, Harmondsworth, 1970, p. 207.

47 George Orwell, *The Road to Wigan Pier*, London, 1937, quoted by Beatrix Campbell, *Wigan Pier Revisited: Poverty and Politics in the Eighties*, London, 1984, pp. 217, 227.

48 Marie Juchasz, in a speech to the SPD's Kiel Congress in 1927, quoted by Heinrich August Winkler, *Der Schein der Normalität. Arbeiter und Arbeiterbewegung in der Weimarer Republik 1924 bis 1930*, Berlin, 1985, pp. 353–5.

49 See Lynne Segal, ' "The Most Important Thing of All" – Rethinking the Family: An Overview', in Segal, ed., *What Is To Be Done About the Family?*, Harmondsworth, 1983, p. 19.
50 For a general overview, see Eley, *Forging Democracy*, pp. 320–8.
51 For a fine study of how this process worked in the Federal Republic of Germany, see Robert G. Moeller, *Protecting Motherhood: Women and the Family in the Politics of Post-War West Germany*, Berkeley, 1993; also Robert G. Moeller, 'Reconstructing the Family in Reconstruction Germany: Women and Social Policy in the Federal Republic, 1949–1955', in Moeller, ed., *West Germany under Construction: Politics, Society, and Culture in the Adenauer Era*, Ann Arbor, 1997, pp. 109–33.
52 At one dinner party connected with the San Francisco meeting of the American Historical Association in December 1994, François Furet railed against contemporary feminism as 'the new Committee of Public Safety'.

Chapter 9

1 Heinrich Heine, *History of Religion and Philosophy in Germany*, North Queensland, 1982, p. 72.
2 *Lignes*, new series no. 04, February 2001.
3 On the 'marginalist innovation' and its philosophical, aesthetic and literary repercussions, see the fascinating book by Jean Joseph Goux, *Frivolité de la valeur*, Paris, 2002.
4 Marx, *The Class Struggles in France*, in Karl Marx and Friedrich Engels, *Collected Works*, London, 1975ff, vol. x, p. 71.
5 Reinhart Koselleck, *Le futur passé. Contribution à la sémantique des temps historiques*, Paris, 1990 and *L'expérience de l'histoire*, Paris, 1997. Jean-Marie Goulemot, *Le règne de l'histoire. Discours historiques et révolutions*, Paris, 1996.
6 The echo of the recent books by Toni Negri (*Empire*) or John Holloway (*Change the World without Taking Power*) is in a sense evidence of this renewal. On this see my book *Un monde à changer. Mouvements et stratégies*, Paris, 2003.
7 G.W.F. Hegel, *Early Theological Writings*, Chicago, 1948, p. 152.
8 G.W.F. Hegel, *Lectures on the History of Philosophy*, London, 1955.
9 K. Marx, *The Eighteenth Brumaire of Louis Bonaparte*, in Marx and Engels, *Collected Works*, vol. xi, p. 185.
10 Hegel, *Lectures on the History of Philosophy*. '*Well said, old mole*', said Hamlet. '*Brav alter Maulwurf! Wühlst so hurtig fort!*' translates Schlegel ('Dig well and promptly, worthy old mole!). '*Brav gearbeitet, wackerer Maulwurf*' ('Well worked, worthy mole!' interprets Hegel). '*Brav gewühlt, alter Maulwurf!*', sums up Marx, whose idea of digging (*gewühlt*) adds to the simple labour of Hegel a touch of subversion. On these transformations of the mole, see Martin Harries, 'Homo alludens. Marx's *Eighteenth Brumaire*', in *New German Critique*, autumn 1995, pp. 35–64.
11 Michel Surya, article in the *Quinzaine littéraire*, 1 August 2000.
12 Paul Valéry, *Regards sur le monde actuel*, Paris, 1996, p. 17.
13 Slavoj Žižek, *The Ticklish Subject*, London, 1999, p 140.

14 Charles Péguy, *Clio*, Paris, 1931, pp. 170 and 228.
15 See Claude Romano, *L'événement et le temps*, Paris, 1999.
16 Karl Kraus, *In These Great Times*, Manchester, 1984, pp. 76, 80.
17 See Hegel, 'Reason in History', introduction to *Lectures on the Philosophy of World History*, Cambridge, 1975.
18 Bernard Mabille, *Hegel. L'épreuve de la contingence*, Paris, 1999.
19 Pierre Naville, *Trotski vivant*, Paris, 1988, p. 85.
20 Louis Althusser, 'Le courant souterrain du matérialisme de la recontre,' in Ecrits philosophiques et politiques, vol. 1, Paris, 1994, p. 574.
21 Marx, Letter to L. Kugelmann, 17 April 1871, in Marx and Engels, *Collected Works*, vol. xliv, pp. 136-7.
22 K. Marx, *The Eighteenth Brumaire of Louis Bonaparte*, Marx and Engels, *Collected Works*, vol. xi, pp. 106-7.
23 Trotsky, *Permanent Revolution*, London, 1962.
24 While rejecting the idea of crisis as a moment of clarification and truth, Michel Dobry gives a subtle analysis of certain characteristic features of political crises such as the tendency to multisectoral unification of sectoral logics, the accentuation of the tactical interdependence of decisions, 'the conjunctural desectorisation of social space', the reduction of the autonomy of social sectors in conjunctures of high political fluidity, the 'simplification of social space', or again 'the unidimensionalisation of personal identity' beyond the multiplicity of roles. See Michel Dobry, *Sociologie des crises politiques*, Paris, 1992.
25 Marx and Engels, *Manifesto of the Communist Party*, in Marx and Engels, *Collected Works*, vol. vi, pp. 489-90.
26 V.I. Lenin, 'The Collapse of the Second International', in *Collected Works* Moscow, 1960ff, vol. xxi, p. 214. In *History and Class Consciousness*, Georg Lukács gave a more radical turn to this subjectivist tendency: 'When compared to earlier crises the qualitative difference in the decisive, the "last" crisis of capitalism . . . is, then, not merely that its extent and depth, its quantity, is simply transformed into a change in quality. Or more accurately: this transformation is distinguished by the fact that the proletariat ceases to be merely the object of a crisis; the internal antagonisms of capitalist production . . . now flourish openly.' (Georg Lukács, *History and Class Consciousness*, London, 1971, p. 244.)
27 On this point see Dobry, *Sociologie des crises politiques*, p. 154.
28 Michael Hardt and Toni Negri, *Empire*, Cambridge MA and London, 2000, pp. 385-400.
29 Hardt and Negri, *Empire*, p 57.
30 Gustave Lefrançais, *Souvenirs d'un révolutionnaire*, Paris, 1971, p. 191.
31 Pierre Bourdieu, 'Genèse et structure du champ religieux', *Revue française de sociologie*, 12, 1971, p. 331.
32 Hegel, *Lectures on the History of Philosophy*.

Contributors

Daniel Bensaïd is Professor of Philosophy at the University of Paris-VIII and author of over a dozen works on politics and philosophy, including *Moi, la révolution* (1989), *Marx for Our Times* (2002) and *Fragments mécréants* (2005).

Geoff Eley is Professor of History at the University of Michigan and the author of several books including *Forging Democracy: The History of the Left in Europe, 1850–2000* (2002) and *A Crooked Line. From Cultural History to the History of Society* (2005).

Marc Ferro is Director of Studies in Social Sciences at the Ecole des Hautes Etudes en Sciences Sociales in Paris. He is the author of many major works on modern history, including *October 1917: A Social History of the Russian Revolution* (1980) and *The Use and Abuse of History or How the Past Is Taught* (1984), and is editor of *Le livre noir du colonialisme* (2003).

Florence Gauthier lectures at the University of Paris-VII and is author of *Les caractères originaux de l'histoire rurale de la révolution française* (1999) and *Triomphe et mort du droit naturel en révolution* (1994).

Mike Haynes lectures at the University of Wolverhampton and is author, with Rumy Husan, of *A Century of State Murder? Death and Public Policy in Russia*, (2003).

Geoff Kennedy is based at York University, Ontario. His most recent work on seventeenth-century Britain has appeared in the journal *Historical Materialism*.

Lars T. Lih is an independent scholar of Russia whose most recent work is *Lenin Rediscovered: 'What is to be Done?' In Context* (2005).

Enzo Traverso is Professor of Political Science at the Jules Verne University of Picardy. His publications include *The Origins of Nazi Violence* (2003) and *Le totalitarisme* (2001).

Jim Wolfreys lectures at King's College London and is the author, with Peter Fysh, of *The Politics of Racism in France* (2003).

In addition the authors wish to thank Sebastian Budgen and Megan Trudell for their help with the creation of the manuscript and Ian Birchall for his translations.

Index

A People's Tragedy (Figes) 15, 94, 136
absolutism 7, 161
active citizens 77
Africa 78–9, 157, 164
Agreement of the People 44–5
Algeria 157, 158, 159, 164, 167, 169
Allen, W. S. 165
Althusser, Louis 209
American Civil War 61
American War of Independence 1, 2, 7
Anderson, Perry 23, 51
Anglas, Boissy d' 90, 91
anti-Bolshevik propaganda 141
anti-capitalism 19, 29
anti-communism 138, 143, 150–2, 154
anti-democratic movements 186
anti-fascism 146, 156, 194
anti-Semitism 22, 140, 141, 142, 143, 162, 165
Arabs 158, 159
Arendt, Hannah 22, 148, 156, 156–7, 160, 162, 203
Arnault, Jacques 168
Aron, Raymond 147
Australia 163, 168, 182
Austria 187, 188, 189

Babeuf, Gracchus 52, 88
Badiou, Alain 52, 212
Baker, Keith 54, 63, 67
barbarism 214–15
Bavaria 142
Belgium 187, 198
Bellamy, Richard 5, 6
Benjamin, Walter 50, 70
Bensaïd, Daniel 16, 23

Bentley, M. 9
Bergson, Henri 159
Berlin 14
Berlioz, Hector 8–9
Beveridge, William 198
biological politics 197, 200
Black Book of Communism, The (Courtois) 17, 138, 147
Blok, Alexander 103, 111
Bolivia 1
Bolsheviks
    absolutism 161
    assessment of 3, 132
    cause of success 177
    and the collapse of the money system 130
    de-legitimizing 177–8
    democratic organization 110
    destruction of civil society 165
    ideology 9, 152, 153
    Jacobinism 106–7, 108–9, 177
    legitimacy 55, 95
    militarization policies 120–7, 134, 135
    optimism 127, 137
    rejection of historical development 21
    rise to power 164–5
    situation, 1920 118–19, 127–8
    victory 109–10, 116–17
    violence 141, 160
Bordoni, Gaetano 194
Bosnian Crisis, 1908-9 99
Bourdieu, Pierre 215
bourgeoisie, the 16, 56–63
Broken Arrow (film) 168
Buber-Neumann, Margaret 156
Bucharest 14

Budapest 14
Bukharin, Nikolai 124, 125
Bulgakov, Sergii 114–15
Bulgaria, democratization 175
Burgess, Glenn 35–6
Burke, Edmund 7, 58–9, 148
Burnt by the Sun (film) 163
Butterfield, Herbert 29

Canada 182
Capital (Marx) 210
capitalism
  agrarian 26, 37, 38–40, 46, 47
  class power 40–1, 46–7
  coercion 39–40
  and democratization 175
  development of 2, 71
  free market 173
  labour value 126
  legitimacy 5
  mode of production 209
  origins 1–2, 53–4, 62
  Russian 96
  and the Russian Revolution 208
  transition from feudalism 37–44, 49, 55
  victory 18
Carnot, Lazare 147–8
Carr, Edward H. 140
Castoriadis, Cornelius 50
Césaire, Aimé 157
Charles I, King 2, 30, 31
Charles II, King 2
Chartier, Roger 180–1
Chateaubriand, René, Vicomte de 203
Chaussinand-Nogaret, Guy 52
Chechnya 166, 169
China 1, 10, 11
Chinese Cheka, the 141
Chkeidze, N. S. 102
Churchill, Winston 145
Citizens (Schama) 21
citizenship 72, 76, 77, 87, 175, 183, 195–9
civil society 165–6, 186, 187, 190, 191,
  195
Civilization and its Discontents (Freud) 212
class conflict 25–8, 29–30, 49, 203
class consciousness 111–16
class formation 37–8, 43, 49
Clavel, Maurice 51
Cobb, Richard 179
Cobban, Alfred 15, 55, 56, 68, 180
Cochin, Augustin 53, 148
Cohen, Stephen 12
Cold War 94, 138, 148, 172, 178, 199
colonialism 80, 80–2, 84–5, 88, 157–8,
  159, 164, 166–71

Colonialism on Trial (Arnault) 168
Colonna, Fanny 169
colour prejudice 79
common good 193
Communism 138–55
  attraction of 9–10
  collapse of 18
  colonialism 157
  comparison with Nazism 22, 138–55,
    156–71
  Courtois on 149–51, 154
  criticism of 11–12
  Furet on 14, 16–17, 147
  illusion of 149
Communist International, the 140
Communist Manifesto, The (Marx and
  Engels) 173–4
Comninel, George 57
concentration camps 16, 51, 140, 147, 156
conceptual structures 33–5
Condren, Conal 33–4
Congress of the Socialist International,
  1914 158
Conquest, Robert 136
Conrad, Joseph 143
consensus 30–1, 48
consent 45–6
constitution-making 188, 190, 196
contingency 209
coolie trade 78
counter-revolution 141–2, 211
Courtois, Stéphane 17, 22, 138, 138–9,
  147, 149–51, 154
crisis 212–16
Crisis of European Sciences, The (Husserl)
  212–13
Cromwell, Oliver 2
Cuba 10
culture-building 190
Czechoslovakia, democratization 175

Dahrendorf, Ralf 6
Daily Mirror (newspaper) 199
Danton, Georges 147–8
Davis, J. C. 32–3, 35
death penalty 90
Debray, Régis 57
Declaration of the Rights of Man
  and the 1791 Constitution 76
  and the 1792 Constitutional debate 83
  1793 version 85, 86, 89
  claim of universality 2–3
  illusion of 57–8
  proclaimed in St Domingue 85
  as terror 80–2
  violation of 16

decolonization 10, 88
Deleuze, Gilles 208
democracy
  communal 83
  conceptualising 172–6
  contexts 183
  definitions 6, 182–5, 185, 200
  dialectics of citizenship and state 185–90
  enlargements in 184–5
  and gender 195–9, 199–200
  judicial 182–3, 184, 185
  popular cultures of 190–5
  popular participation 23
  and reform 187, 188–9
  relationship to war 188–9
  revisionism and 176–82
  and social breakdown 188
  socialisation 186
  three worlds of 11–12
  transition to 174–6
democratization 173, 174–6, 182, 184,
   185–90, 190–5, 198–9, 200–1
Der Nomos der Erde (Schmitt) 139
desire 202–3
Destiny of a Revolution (Serge) 134
determinism 14, 55, 68
Deutscher, Isaac 11, 22, 134–5, 136,
   151
Dictionary of the Revolution (Furet and
   Ozouf) 21
Diggers, the 28, 29, 32, 35, 46–8
Diner, Dan 139
discontent 212–14
Dobry, Michel 213
Dow, F. D. 48
Doyle, William 55–6, 57, 64
Dylan, Bob 70

economic development 62
economic power 21
economic reconstruction 192
economic reductionism 36
economic transition 20–1
Edmonds, Bill 55, 63
Eighteenth Brumaire of Louis Napoleon (Marx)
   205–6
Eisenstein, Sergei 50
elections 164–5, 187
Elements of Pure Economics (Walrus) 202–3
Eley, Geoff 16, 23, 57
elites 18, 59, 175, 185
Elton, G. R. 29
empiricism 68
enclosure movement 39, 47
Engels, Friedrich 94, 173–4
English Civil War 2, 25, 26, 27, 29, 30–1

English Revolution 25–49
  background 1–2
  changing relations of power 41–2
  class conflict 25–8, 29–30
  and class formation 37–8, 43, 49
  leadership 26–7
  Marxist interpretation 26–7
  parliamentary politics 30–3
  radicalism 25–6, 30–6
  revisionist view of 20, 25–6, 29–30, 30–
   6, 48–9
  revolutionary ideas 28–9, 44–8
  social interpretations 26–30
  and social transformation 36–44
  the transition from feudalism to
   capitalism 37–44
  Zagorin on 10
English state, formation of 41–2
Enlightenment, the 6, 54, 66
equality 45–6, 58, 72, 81, 182
Equals, the 88
ethics 52
eugenics 145, 165
Europe, social democratic core 187
European civil war 139–40, 152
exclusion 51
extra-parliamentary social movements 186

fascism 141–2, 167 *see also* Nazism
fascist counter-revolution 142
Faye, Jean-Pierre 80, 90
feminist movements 195–9, 200
Ferro, Marc 22
Fest, Joachim 147
feudalism 1–2, 26, 37–44, 49, 55, 58, 62
Figes, Orlando 5, 15, 94, 136, 140
Finland 182
First World War 3, 9, 100–3, 105, 113,
   153, 158, 177, 185, 189, 195, 196,
   207
Fischer, Fritz 162
Fitzpatrick, Sheila 119
Fondation Saint-Simon 17–18
Foucault, Michel 50, 165, 203
France
  agriculture 61–2
  Algerian education policy 169
  constitution of 1795 15–16
  democratic institutions suppressed 15
  expansionism 82
  Furet on the state of the nation 18
  hierarchy of values 159
  modernization 59–62
  occupation 194
  pre-eminence 2
  reforms, 1914–23 187, 189

school textbooks 168
seigneurialism 73–5, 82
separation of powers 83
'stagnation without stability' 55
suffrage 182
textile industry 60–1
the Third Republic 62
women admitted to full citizenship 198
Fraternal Society of Both Sexes 87
freedom 46, 58, 71, 72, 81, 172, 182, 187, 194
French Revolution 52–66, 71–92
  active citizens 77
  agrarian legislation 82, 86
  aims and outcomes 119
  background 2–3
  Berlioz on 8–9
  as bourgeois revolution 56–63
  the 'citizens of 4 April 1792' 81–2
  and the colonial question 80, 80–2, 84–5, 88
  the Committee of Public Safety 16–17, 89, 148
  Constitution of 1789 81
  Constitution of 1791 76
  Constitution of 1793 89
  Constitution of 1795 90–1
  the Constituent Assembly 73, 76–7, 78, 80, 80–1, 85
  the Convention 82
  Corn War 71, 76, 82–3
  de-legitimizing 177–8
  and the definition of revolution 204–5
  dictatorship 88–9
  economic consequences 55, 62
  and economic transition 20
  end of 13–14, 52–6
  failure of 91–2
  food prices 87–8
  Furet's interpretation 13–19
  the Girondin government 82–5
  the Great Fear 73–5
  hunger 58
  importance of 7
  influence 106
  the Legislative Assembly 81–2
  link to totalitarianism 15
  martial law 76, 78, 81, 83, 86, 88
  Marxist accounts 57, 64–6
  monarchy abolished 82
  the Montagnard Convention 86–90
  the Mountain 83–4, 86
  mythical element 63–4
  the National Assembly 56–63, 64, 68, 72
  origins 53, 54
  parties 83

passive citizens 77, 81
peasant uprisings 73–5, 76–7
and political change 63–6
as popular democratic event 179
principle aspects 52
principles of the Declaration of Rights contradicted 80–2
the Prolegomena of Liberty, 1789 72
property qualifications 81
revisionist view of 14–16, 20, 52–66, 69–70, 179–81, 200
the revolutionary government 88–9
the Revolutionary Tribunal 89–90
the sans-culottes 15, 53
seigneurialism 73–5, 82
separation of powers established 83
slavery and 78–80, 84–5, 88
social contract 74–5
storming of the Bastille 64, 208
suffrage 77–8, 82, 86–7
the Terror 15, 17, 51, 54, 65, 90, 147–8, 149, 179–80, 181
the Thermidorian Convention 90, 92
war of conquest 82, 84, 85, 90, 91
French Revolution and the Creation of Modern Political Culture, The (Baker) 54
Freud, Sigmund 212
Friedländer, Saul 145
From Plan to Market (World Bank) 173–4
Fukuyama, Francis 4, 5, 12
Furet, François
  anti-communism 154
  and class 57, 58
  on Communism 14, 16–17, 147
  concentration on the event 63, 182
  and the end of the French Revolution 13–14, 52–5
  on the French Revolution 13–19
  on history 64
  and Holocaust denial 146–7
  and Nolte 16, 138–9
  rejection of necessity 68–70
  and the relationship between ideas and society 179–81
  on the Russian Revolution 16–17, 149
  and slavery 21
  status 5, 22, 138

G7 4
Gatrell, Peter 100
Gauthier, Florence 15, 20–1
gender, and democracy 195–9, 199–200
genocide 140, 145, 147, 162
gentry, rise of the 27–8
German Democratic Republic, democratization 175

'German guilt' 145–6, 162–3, 163
Germany 156, 187, 188, 189, 196 *see also*
    Nazism
Gershenzon, Mikhail 112–13
Getty, Arch 150
Giddens, Anthony 5
Gide, Charles 203
Ginsborg, Paul 67
globalization 173
Glucksmann, André 16, 51–2
Goldhagen, Daniel 162, 166
Gorbachev, Mikhail 12
Gorky, Maxim 103
Goulemot, Jean-Marie 205
Great Britain
    Butler Education Act 192
    the Commonwealth 2
    Indian policy 169
    National Health Service 192
    reforms, 1914–23 187, 189
    the Restoration 2
    societal consensus 192–3
    the 'wasted years' 192–3
    welfare state 192, 194–5
    women's status 196
Grossman, Vasily 156, 161
Guadeloupe 88
Guardian, the (newspaper) 93
Guérin, Daniel 58–9, 69
guilt 145–6
gulags, the 16–17, 51, 140, 150, 156
Gurian, Waldemar 148
Gusev, S. I. 129
Guyana 88, 91

Habermas, Jürgen 138, 145, 146–7
Haiti, Republic of 91
Harding, Neil 107
Haynes, Mike 21
Heart of Darkness (Conrad) 143
Hegel, Georg 51, 215
Heidegger, Martin 139, 146
Herzen, Alexander 95
Hill, Christopher 26, 33
Hilton, Rodney 38
historical comparison 150–2
historical debate 4
historical development 21
historical necessity 209, 209–10
historical perspective, reversal of 146
Historikerstreit (Historians' Debate), the 16,
    138, 139, 145–6, 147, 162
history
    critical 210
    conceptual 157–8
    definitions 67

direction of 14
end of 172
Marxist interpretation 53, 57, 68
narrative 15
new 5
revisionist 15
and revolutions 210–11, 212
strategic 210
teleological interpretations 64
Whig 25–6, 29, 30–1
Hitler, a Film from Germany (Syberberg) 163
Hitler, Adolf 141, 142, 142–3, 143, 164
Hobbes, Thomas 28, 144
Hobsbawm, Eric J. 151, 174, 179
Holocaust, the 17, 140, 145, 158
Holocaust denial 146–7
Hungary 142, 174–5, 201
Hunting Scenes from Lower Bavaria (film) 163
Husserl, Edmund 212–13

idealogic dynamic, the 14–15
ideologues 70
ideas, history of 22
ideocracy 147–9
ideology 20, 31, 36, 54, 56, 152
    Bolshevik 9, 152, 153
imperialism 99–100, 143
India 157, 169
individual, role of the 67, 68
Ingerflom, Claudio Sergio 150
interests 49, 56
International Monetary Fund 4
Interpreting the French Revolution (Furet) 17
Ireton, Henry 45, 46
Israel 158
Italy 194, 196, 198

Jacobinism 106–7, 108–9, 177
Jacobino-Marxist Left, the 180
Jacobins, the 54, 56, 63, 65, 66, 177–8,
    179
Jacoby, Russell 23
Jaspers, Karl 145–6
Jaurès, Jean 124
Jews 140, 143, 144, 158
Jünger, Ernst 139

Kant, Immanuel 204
Katkov, George 177
Kennedy, Geoff 20
Kerensky, Aleksandr 104, 107
Kershaw, Ian 165
Keynesianism 172, 173, 192–3
Khrushchev, Nikita 161, 162
Kishlansky, Mark 31, 32
Knei-Paz, Baruch 106

Koch, Erich 143
Kolakowski, Leszek 120
Konovalov, Alexander 99
Kornilov, General Lavr G. 105
Kosseleck, Reinhart 205
Kraus, Karl 209

labour-value 126, 202–3
Lacoste, Elie 57
Langlois, Claude 59
law 47
Lazar, Marc 150–1
Le Pen, Jean-Marie 151
Lecourt, Dominique 51
Lefebvre, Georges 52, 56, 57, 63, 64, 73–5, 179
Left Socialist Revolutionaries 3
Leiser, Erwin, 162
Lenin, V. I. 3, 55, 105, 106, 132–3, 150, 152, 153–4, 160, 167, 177, 213, 214
Levellers, the 28, 32, 35, 44–6
Lévy, Bernard-Henri 16–17, 51, 70
Lewin, Moshe 135–6
Lewis, Gwynne 58
liberal democracy, imposition of 23
liberal imperialism 99–100
liberalism
    and the bourgeoisie 16
    classical 7–9
    crisis 8–9
    emasculation of 5–6
    emergence of 4
    failure in Russia 95–105
    intensification of doubts about 12–13
    negativism 8
    origins 6–7
    and the Russian Revolution 9
    universal claims 7
Life and Fate (Grossman) 156
life, right to 75
Lignes (journal) 202
Lih, Lars 21–2
Liu 60–1, 62
Locke, John 28
Lollards, the 29
Löwy, Michael 52, 65
Lubasz, Heinz 7
Lukács, Georg 67

Macintyre, Alastair 6, 8, 12–13
McPhee, Peter 61
Macpherson, C. B. 11, 28
Mainz, Republic of 84
Maistre, Joseph de 211
Malia, Martin 136, 138, 148, 149
Mannheim, Karl 211–12

Maoism 50
Marat, Jean Paul 84, 147–8
Marcuse, Herbert 146
market dependence 40–1
market forces 172–4, 176
Martov, Julius 108, 110
Marx, Karl 65–6, 69, 70, 108, 173–4, 203, 205–6, 210–11, 212, 213–14
Marxists and Marxism
    and capitalism 173–4
    and colonialism 167–8
    conceptions of radicalism 25–6
    criticism of 51, 63
    and the Diggers 29
    and the French Revolution 57, 64–6
    and ideology 36
    interpretation of history 53, 57, 68
    interpretation of the English Revolution 26–7
    Nolte on 147
    and progress 53
    revisionism 152
    and social transformation 37
Mayer, Arno J. 139, 148, 153
Mazauric, Claude 147
media, the 208–9
Mein Kampf (Leiser) 162
Melgunov, Serguei 141
Mensheviks 21, 107, 109–10, 115, 125
mercantile trade 43
Méricourt, Théroigne de 52
Merleau-Ponty, Maurice 209, 211, 212
Merridale, Catherine 102–3
Miliukov, Paul 98, 99, 100–1, 103–4, 105, 112, 113
Mirabeau, Honoré, Comte de 3
Mitterrand, François 13
modernity 18, 19, 212
modernization 59–62
monarchy 1–2, 6–7, 41–2, 82
Morrill, John 5, 31, 32
Mosse, George 153
motherhood 196
motivations 56
Mulligan, Lotte 34–5, 35
My Life (Trotsky) 132–3

Napoleon I, Emperor of France 3, 66, 91
national interest 193
natural rights 45, 76, 78, 85, 92
Nazism
    anti-communism 143
    collapse of 161
    colonialism 157, 164
    comparison with Communism 22, 138–55, 156–71

and the Counter-Enlightenment 154–5
counter-revolutionary nature 141–2
Courtois on 149–51, 154
crimes 140, 143, 144, 162–3, 166
destruction of civil society 165
genocide 145, 147, 162
imperialism 143
and military order 166
Nolte's failure to grasp nature of 141–2
origins 140–2
racist policies 144, 152, 156, 163
rehabilitating 138
rise to power 164–5
totalitarianism 143–5, 157
violence 144
necessity 68–70
Negri, Toni 214, 215
Netherlands, the 187, 189
Neumann, Franz 144
New Left Review 23
new left, the 11
New Model Army Agitators 28, 32, 44–5
New Zealand 182
Nisbet, Robert 148
Nolte, Ernst
Communism and Nazism 22, 138–49,
154, 159
dating of Nazi totalitarianism 157
failure to grasp nature of Nazism 141–2
and Furet 16, 138–9
on genocide 145
and 'German guilt' 145–6
Holocaust denial 146–7
and Ideocratic regimes 147–9
status 16–17
Norman Conquest 38, 39
North, Douglas C. 61
northern man, rights to dominate the
world 91
Norway 182
Nuremberg war crimes trials 162

Ohm Kruger (Steinhoff) 162
Origins of Totalitarian Democracy (Talmon)
177–8
Orwell, George 197
Out of the Night (Valtin) 156
Ozouf, Mona 21

Paine, Thomas 6
Palestine 158
Papon, Maurice 17
Pareto, Vilfredo 8
Paris 8–9, 138
Paris Commune 66, 83, 90, 203, 205, 215
Paris riots, 1968 11

Passing of an Illusion, The (Furet) 14, 17, 68,
138, 146, 147–8, 151, 154
passions 56
passive citizens 77, 81
Patoèka, Jan 203
patriotism 191, 192, 193, 199
Pearson, Ronald 102
Péguy, Charles 207–8
permanent revolution 105–6, 211–12
Peshekhonov, A. V. 109
Physiocrats, the 72, 78
Pipes, Richard 15, 96, 105, 138, 148–9,
149, 177
Pokrovsky, M. N. 100
Poland 174–5, 201
policy results 168–9
political autonomy 69
political change 63–8
political consciousness 3
political economy 71
political participation 186
popular militancy, stigmatization 181
Portelli, Alessandro 194
Portugal 175, 201
post-modernity 207, 215
Potter, Dennis 193
popular mobilization 18, 19
power, relations of 41–2, 46–7, 49
Prague 11, 14
Preobrazhenskii, S. A. 103
Price, Morgan Philips 93, 101, 116
production, modes of, transition between 65
production, relations of 40–1, 46, 60–1
property 45, 58, 61, 73–5
property qualifications 77–8
Proust, Françoise 68
Przeworski, Adam 174
public life, militarization of 190–1

Quinet, Edgar 148

radicalism 8
definition 33–4
denial of existence 25–6, 30–6
realism 32–3
Raimond, Julien 79, 80
Rainsborough, Colonel 45
reaction, forces of 7
realism and realists 32–3
reason 6
reciprocal rights 78, 92
Red Terror in Russia (Melgunov) 141
Red Vienna 188, 196
reductionism 15–16, 25
Reflections on the Revolution in France
(Nisbet) 148

relativism 22
Renan, Ernest 176
Repentance (film) 163
Rethinking the French Revolution (Comninel)
    57
revisionism
    and democracy 176–82
    historiography 68
    problem of approach 48–9
    and revolutions 14–16, 68–70
    and social transformation 36–44
    tension within 35–6
    world view 18
Revolutionary France (Furet) 54
Revolutionary Republican Women 87
revolutions
    alternatives within 7
    bourgeois 27, 37, 53–5, 56, 56–63, 70
    and change 2
    and crisis 212–16
    de-legitimizing 176–8
    definitions 204–5
    degeneration 9
    desire for 202–5
    dynamics 63–8
    as dysfunctions 178
    as event 207–9
    and historical necessity 209, 209–10
    and history 210–11, 212
    impact 1, 4
    invisible aspects 205–6
    judgement of 182
    loss of substance 204
    new models develop 10–12
    permanent 105–6, 211–12
    revisionist view of 14–16, 68–70
    role 20–1
    secularization 203–4, 206–7
    social historiography 178–9
    Socialist 66
    status 203–4
    strategic debate 203–4, 205
    Trotsky on 125
Riabushinskii, Paul 99
Richards, Judith 34–5, 35
Richet, Denis 53, 149
rights 58–9, 78, 85, 90–1, 183
rights of man and the citizen 71, 72
Robespierre, Maximilien 15, 81, 84, 88,
    147–8
Rocard, Michel 13
Roman illusion, the 65–6
Romania, democratization 175
Rose-coloured Book 167
Rosenberg, Alfred 141
Rosenberg, William G. 104, 178

Rosenthal, Jean-Laurent 61
Rousset, David 156
Royal Navy 84–5
Rozanov, Vasilii 112
Rudé, George 179
Russell, Conrad 5, 29–30, 30–1, 32
Russia
    capitalism 96, 208
    the Constitutional Democrats or Cadets
        97–9, 100–2, 104, 107–8, 109, 113
    constitutional reform, 1905–8 97–9,
        111–12
    economic development 97, 99, 100, 101
    and the First World War 100–3, 105,
        113
    First World War casualties 102–3
    liberal failure 95–105
    liberal imperialism 99–100
    the October Manifesto 97, 112
    peasantry 111
    pogroms 112
    refugees 103
    strikes 112
    Tsarism 97
Russian Civil War 3, 122, 140, 142, 149–
    51, 152
Russian Revolution 93–117, 118–37 *see
    also* Bolsheviks; Russia; Soviet Union
    aims and outcomes 119–20, 137
    background 3–4
    Bolshevik victory 109–10, 116–17
    choices 21
    class consciousness and 111–16
    the Constituent Assembly 110
    counter-revolution 141–2
    de-legitimizing 176–8
    and the development of capitalism 208
    and the failure of liberalism 95–105
    the February Revolution 103–5
    Furet on 16–17, 149
    internalization 142–3
    isolation 152
    Jacobinism 106–7, 108–9
    the Kornilov coup 105, 108
    liberalism and 9
    mainstream historiography 93–4
    militarization 120–7
    New Economic Policy (NEP) 121, 123
    the October Revolution 94, 105–10,
        108, 140, 149, 154, 160, 162
    the Provisional Government 104, 107–8,
        159
    revisionist view of 15, 93–5, 139, 176–8,
        181, 200
    situation, 1920 118–20
    social continuity 94, 95

social history of 12
the Socialist Revolutionaries (SR) 105, 107, 109, 109–10
as start of European civil war 140
struggle 203
Trotsky on 3, 66, 108
violence 159–60
Russian Revolution, The (Pipes) 138
Russian Revolution, The (Smith) 136
Russo-Japanese War 99

sacred, the 203
Saint-André, Jeanbon 57
St Domingue 79–80, 81–2, 84–5, 88, 91
Saint Lucia 88
Sassoon, Donald 5
Scandinavia 187, 196
Schama, Simon 5, 15, 21, 68
Schapiro, Leonard 96, 177
Schmitt, Carl 139, 148
Schumacher, Kurt 156
Seaberg, R. B. 35
Second World War 139, 143, 145, 159, 191, 192, 193, 194
secularization 203–4, 206–7
Sedgwick, Peter 11
segregation 79, 81, 88
seigneurialism 73–5, 82
semantics of historical times 205
separation of powers 83
Serge, Victor 134, 154, 161
Sewell, William 64, 66, 67
Shlyapnikov, Alexander 101
Siegelbaum, Lewis 126
slavery 20–1, 71, 72, 78–80, 81, 84–5, 88, 91
Smith, S. A. 136–7
Soboul, Albert 52, 56, 57, 58, 147, 179
social cohesion 193–4
social conflict 15, 20
social context 49
social contract 73, 74–5, 189
Social Darwinism 143
social determination 203
social development 21
social historiography 55, 63, 178–9
social history 94, 175
social mobilization 189
social reductionism 35–6, 48–9
Social Revolutionaries 21
social rights 183
social stability 193–4
Socialism
emergence of 8
failure of 5
labour value 126

and markets 135–6
and parasites 125
societal consensus 191–5
Society of Citizens of Colour 79
Society of Friends of the Blacks 79
socio-economic development 175
socio-political collapse 185
Solzhenitsyn, Aleksandr 50–1, 53, 156, 161
Sorokin, Pitrim 114
sources 141
sovereignty 32, 44–5, 72, 73, 81, 83
Soviet Tragedy, The (Malia) 138
Soviet Union 118–37 *see also* Bolsheviks
army 166
class relations 121–2
collapse of 12–13, 18–19, 94, 138, 156, 161, 162, 172, 176, 177
collapse of money system 129–30
collectivisation 140
colonialism 164
compulsion 123–7, 136–7
Courtois on 149–51
crimes 50, 150, 162–3, 166
dissatisfaction 130
economic coordination 128–9
economic crisis 120–7, 134–7
genocide 145, 147
glavkokratiia 129–30, 132
Ideocracy 148–9
the Kravchenko trial 160
labour 122–4, 125, 129, 137
Macpherson on 11
material incentives 123
militarization 132–4
New Economic Policy (NEP) 128, 130, 132
parasites 125
Red Army 121–2
reform 12
repression 144
'single economic plan' 127–30
situation, 1920 118–20
'Soviet paradise' 167
torture 141
transition to socialism 124–5, 127–32
violence 149, 152–4, 160–1
war communism 21–2, 119–20, 127, 128, 130–1, 133–6
Spain 175, 201
Stalin, Josef 10, 93, 95, 149–50
Stalinism 12, 22, 92, 93–4, 94–5, 142, 144, 151–2, 153, 161
state power 188–9
Steinhoff, Hans 162
Sternhell, Zeev 142
Stolypin, Pytor 97–8

Stone, Lawrence 15, 25, 26, 27
struggle 209
Struve, Peter 95–6, 99–100, 105, 112
sub-culture 191
suffrage 28, 45–6, 77–8, 82, 86–7, 182,
    187, 195–9
sugar cultivation 71–2
Sukhanov, N. 116–17
Surya, Michael 206
Switzerland 2, 182
Syberberg, Hans Jürgen 163

Talmon, Jacob L. 148, 177–8
Tanganyika 157
Tawney, R. H. 26–7, 27
Taylor, George V. 52
Terrorism and Communism (Trotsky) 120,
    124, 126, 127, 133–4, 153
The European Civil War (Nolte) 138–9
third way, the 5
Third World 11–12, 12
Thomas, Robert Paul 61
Thompson, Edward 179
Three Faces of Fascism, The (Nolte) 16, 139
Tilly, Charles 179
time 50
Tocqueville, Alexis de 54, 69, 147
totalitarianism 15, 22, 51, 52, 88–9, 139,
    140, 143–5, 148–9, 156, 157, 159,
    160, 165–6
totalizing theories 50–1
transcendence 212
Traverso, Enzo 22
Trevelyan, G. M. 4
Trevor-Roper, H. R. 27
Trotsky, Lev 21–2, 118–37
    analysis of Russian development 96–7
    assessment of 132–7
    on class relations 121–2
    on the collapse of the money system
        129–30
    and compulsion 123–7, 136–7
    on dissatisfaction 130
    marginalized 9
    on material incentives 123
    on militarization 120–1, 132–4
    on the NEP 128
    permanent revolution 105–6, 212
    and the Red Terror 153
    on revolution 125
    on Russia, 1920 118
    on the Russian Revolution 3, 66, 108

and the 'single economic plan' 127–30
    and social change 65
    speeches 119
    and the transition to socialism 124–5,
        127
Turgot, Anne Robert Jacques 78
Tyrkóva-Williams, Ariadna 114

Under Two Dictators (Buber-Neumann) 156
United States of America 10–11, 168, 182
Utechin, Sergej 177

Valéry, Paul 207
Valtin, Jan 156
value 202–3
Vekhi (Landmarks) 112–13, 114–15
Vietnam War 11, 163
Volkov, M 103
Voltaire 6
Vovelle, Michel 52

wage-labour 47–8
Walras, Leon 202–3
want-value 202–4
war, and democracy 188–9
war communism 21–2, 119–20, 127, 128,
    130–1, 133–6
Warsaw 14
Webb, Sidney and Beatrice 10
Wehler, Hans-Ulrich 141
welfare state 173, 186, 189, 192, 194–5,
    196
Werth, Nicolas 140, 150
Whig interpretation of history 25–6, 29,
    30–1
William I, King 39
Winstanley, Gerrard 29, 35, 46–8
Wirtschaftwoche (journal) 18
Wolfreys, Jim 20
women 52, 78, 82, 87, 182, 183, 187,
    195–9, 199–200
women's rights 195–9
Wood, Ellen 41
World Bank 4, 173–4
world civil war 139
World Trade Organization 4

Year One of the Russian Revolution (Serge)
    134
Young Torless (film) 163

Zagorin, Perez 10

Printed in the United States
by Baker & Taylor Publisher Services